*The Palgrave Macmillan Transnational History Series*

Series Editors: **Akira Iriye**, Professor of History at Harvard University, and **Rana Mitter**, University Lecturer in Modern History and Chinese Politics at the University of Oxford

This distinguished series seeks to: develop scholarship on the transnational connections of societies and peoples in the nineteenth and twentieth centuries; provide a forum in which work on transnational history from different periods, subjects, and regions of the world can be brought together in fruitful connection; and explore the theoretical and methodological links between transnational and other related approaches such as comparative history and world history.

Editorial Board: **Thomas Bender**, University Professor of the Humanities, Professor of History, and Director of the International Center for Advanced Studies, New York University; **Jane Carruthers**, Professor of History, University of South Africa; **Mariano Plotkin**, Professor, Universidad Nacional de Tres de Febrero, Buenos Aires, and member of the National Council of Scientific and Technological Research, Argentina; **Pierre-Yves Saunier**, Researcher at the Centre National de la Recherche Scientifique, France and Visiting Professor at the University of Montreal; **Ian Tyrrell**, Professor of History, University of New South Wales

*Titles include*:

Desley Deacon, Penny Russell and Angela Woollacott (*editors*)
TRANSNATIONAL LIVES
Biographies of Global Modernity, 1700-present

Gregor Benton and Edmund Terence Gomez
THE CHINESE IN BRITAIN, 1800–PRESENT
Economy, Transnationalism and Identity

Sugata Bose and Kris Manjapra (*editors*)
COSMOPOLITAN THOUGHT ZONES
South Asia and the Global Circulation of Ideas

Martin Conway and Kiran Klaus Patel (*editors*)
EUROPEANIZATION IN THE TWENTIETH CENTURY
Historical Approaches

Joy Damousi, Mariano Ben Plotkin (*editors*)
THE TRANSNATIONAL UNCONSCIOUS
Essays in the History of Psychoanalysis and Transnationalism

Jonathan Gantt
IRISH TERRORISM IN THE ATLANTIC COMMUNITY, 1865–1922

Glenda Sluga
THE NATION, PSYCHOLOGY, AND INTERNATIONAL POLITICS, 1870–1919

*Forthcoming*:
Matthias Middell, Michael Geyer, and Michel Espagne
EUROPEAN HISTORY IN AN INTERCONNECTED WORLD

**The Palgrave Macmillan Transnational History Series**
**Series Standing Order ISBN 978–0–230–50746–3 Hardback**
**978–0–230–50747–0 Paperback**
(*outside North America only*)

You can receive future titles in this series as they are published by placing a standing order. Please contact your bookseller or, in case of difficulty, write to us at the address below with your name and address, the title of the series and the ISBN quoted above.

Customer Services Department, Macmillan Distribution Ltd, Houndmills, Basingstoke, Hampshire RG21 6XS, England

# Europeanization in the Twentieth Century

## Historical Approaches

Edited by

**Martin Conway**
*Fellow and Tutor in History, Balliol College, University of Oxford*

and

**Kiran Klaus Patel**
*Professor in Modern History, European University Institute, Florence*

First published 2010 by
PALGRAVE MACMILLAN

Palgrave Macmillan in the UK is an imprint of Macmillan Publishers Limited, registered in England, company number 785998, of Houndmills, Basingstoke, Hampshire RG21 6XS.

Palgrave Macmillan in the US is a division of St Martin's Press LLC, 175 Fifth Avenue, New York, NY 10010.

Palgrave Macmillan is the global academic imprint of the above companies and has companies and representatives throughout the world.

Palgrave® and Macmillan® are registered trademarks in the United States, the United Kingdom, Europe and other countries.

ISBN 978–0–230–23268–6     hardback

This book is printed on paper suitable for recycling and made from fully managed and sustained forest sources. Logging, pulping and manufacturing processes are expected to conform to the environmental regulations of the country of origin.

A catalogue record for this book is available from the British Library.

Library of Congress Cataloging-in-Publication Data
Europeanization in the twentieth century : historical approaches / [edited by] Martin Conway, Kiran Klaus Patel.
    p. cm. — (Palgrave macmillan transnational history)
    Summary: "This book presents a multi-authored study of Europeanisation across the twentieth century from the First World War to the present day"—Provided by publisher.
    ISBN 978–0–230–23268–6 (hardback)
    1. Europe—Civilization—20th century. 2. National characteristics, European.
3. Transnationalism—Social aspects—Europe—History—20th century.
4. Political culture—Europe—History—20th century. I. Conway, Martin, 1960–
II. Patel, Kiran Klaus.
    CB427. E87 2010
    940.5—dc22

2010012006

10  9  8  7  6  5  4  3  2  1
19  18  17  16  15  14  13  12  11  10
Printed and bound in Great Britain by
CPI Antony Rowe, Chippenham and Eastbourne

# Contents

# Preface

This volume is the product of a team of British and German historians who came together because of our shared interest in exploring whether the concept of Europeanization is a useful one when applied to the history of twentieth-century Europe. We are grateful to all those who enabled us to develop this project and to bring it to fruition. In particular, we are grateful to the German Research Council, the *Deutsche Forschungsgemeinschaft* (DFG) and the Arts and Humanities Research Council (the AHRC) for funding the three-year research programme that enabled us to hold the four workshops out of which this volume has emerged. In particular, we owe an especial debt to Marion Müller of the DFG, who initially encouraged us in preparing this funding application.

We are also very grateful to the *Fritz Thyssen Stiftung* which provided the funding for our initial workshop, out of which this project emerged, and to Humboldt University in Berlin, the Robert Schuman Centre for Advanced Studies and the Department of History and Civilisation, both at the European University Institute (EUI) in Fiesole and the Modern European History Research Centre (MEHRC) of the Faculty of History in the University of Oxford for their support and assistance with the project. In Fiesole, we are particularly grateful to Laura Burgassi and Mia Saugman, and in Oxford we are indebted to the administrators of the MEHRC, Teena Stabler and Jane Cunning, for their unfailing support with the detail generated by such a project.

We are also grateful to all those scholars who have encouraged our project, by participating in the workshops and offering academic advice. They include Stefano Bartolini, Jane Caplan, Chris Clark, Anne Deighton, Robert Evans, Martin van Gelderen, Diana Panke, Antonella Romano, Martina Steer, Philipp Ther and Kenneth Weisbrode. We owe a particular debt to Christoph Jahr, who was one of the founding members of the project, and who contributed so generously to all of the workshops of the project. We are also indebted to Dara Price for undertaking much of the editorial work on the volume and for compiling the index.

Above all, as editors, we are especially indebted to the other members of the project for their intellectual and personal investment in this volume. Collaborations between historians from different areas of Europe remain less common than one might expect, and we feel very fortunate to have been able to benefit from the sense of a shared academic culture which the project generated. If this book leads to other similar joint collaborations between British and German historians, or any other bi- or multinational groups, it will have served a very useful purpose in encouraging the very phenomenon which this book seeks to explore.

MARTIN CONWAY
KIRAN KLAUS PATEL

# Series Foreword: 'Europeanization'

For a small continent, Europe has wielded a great deal of historical heft. And the discourses spread by the best and the worst of that continent's experiences (from the Enlightenment to imperialism), including nationalism, communism, and fascism, have unarguably shaped the late modern era across the globe. No surprise, then, that so much brilliant historical work has gone into showing the other side of the coin, and demonstrating that Europe was never the only 'grand narrative' in town. Furthermore, when attention *has* focused back on the last century or so in Europe itself, what scholars have found there is often dark and grim: the idea of ineluctable liberal, democratic progress in Europe has come under serious question from historians.

However, there remains another area that has not yet been sufficiently examined: the *process* of what the authors in this volume call 'Europeanization'. For Europe remains one of the most fascinating examples of a transnational entity, which can be examined both in geographical and historical terms. The former has come in for plenty of scrutiny in the era of the European Union – as the EU has expanded its reach, the question of 'whither Europe' continues to exercise the minds of policymakers and peoples from Dublin to Lublin. But far less work has been done on the historical process and trajectory of Europeanization. One of the many factors that distinguishes this brilliant collection of essays is its refusal to be bounded by traditional chronological boundaries in the historiography of Europe, whether 1945, 1958 or 1989. This is just as it should be: transnational history does not stop at the borders of nations, and nor should it unthinkingly respect chronological barriers. The role of international organizations in defining Europe is just one of the powerful threads that runs across Europe's twentieth century: over and over, in areas of governance, finance, or economic production, norms, ideas, and institutions that emerged in the aftermath of the first global war re-emerged, changed but recognizable, in the aftermath of the second, and on into the supposedly post-ideological era of a united European project. The role of ideas and culture as drivers of 'Europeanization' also makes an important contribution. London – always a European city, sometimes despite itself – turns up in very different guises just a quarter-century apart, first as a 1940s wartime refuge for political thinkers in Europe's darkest hour, and then in the mid-1960s as an emitter of the most powerful popular cultural phenomenon of the era, the Beatles. Elsewhere, the volume takes scrupulous care to remind us that the interaction between Europe and the non-European world has never been a one-way process; essays in this collection show this for phenomena from the inspiring (colonial architecture) to the chilling (colonial violence).

This collection of essays is driven by a powerful and explicitly transnational theme: the examination of the process of breaking down national boundaries in a continent which, above all others, has until recently been obsessed by importance of frontier-based sovereignty. This is questioning, provocative history of the best kind; it takes a topic that one might have considered exhausted and makes it fresh and new.

RANA MITTER
AKIRA IRIYE

# Notes on Contributors

**Christian Bailey** is a Postdoctoral Researcher at the History of Emotions Center at the Max Planck Institute for Human Development, Berlin. He wrote his dissertation on 'The European Discourse in Germany 1926–1950' and is currently doing comparative research on honour in modern Britain and Germany.

**Tom Buchanan** is Reader in Modern History and Politics at the University of Oxford's Department for Continuing Education. His most recent publications are *Europe's Troubled Peace, 1945–2000* and *The Impact of the Spanish Civil War on Britain: War, Loss and Memory*. He is currently writing a book on China and the British Left, 1925–1976.

**Patricia Clavin** is a Fellow and Tutor in Modern History at Jesus College Oxford and a member of the History Faculty of The University of Oxford. She taught previously at the universities of Keele and London. She has published on modern European history, the history of the Great Depression, including *Europe and the Great Depression, 1929–1939*, and the history of transnational relations in the mid-twentieth century. She is currently working on the history of the League of Nations.

**Martin Conway** is Fellow and Tutor in History at Balliol College in the University of Oxford. He recently published (with Peter Romijn) *The War for Legitimacy in Politics and Culture*, and is also the author of *Collaboration in Belgium* and a forthcoming history of the liberation period in Belgium.

**John Davis** has been Fellow in History at The Queen's College, Oxford since 1989; he specializes in the history of modern London. His book *Reforming London. The London Government Problem, 1855–1900* was published by Oxford University Press in 1989. He is currently working on a study of London in the 1960s and 1970s, and has recently published essays on race and housing, planning, inner-city education and the drug scene in post-war London.

**Volker Depkat** is a historian and Professor of American Studies at the University of Regensburg. He has published widely on German and US–American history of the eighteenth, nineteenth and twentieth centuries. His most important recent publications are *Lebenswenden und Zeitenwenden. Deutsche Politiker und die Erfahrungen des 20. Jahrhunderts* and *Geschichte Nordamerikas. Eine Einführung*. He is currently working on a project on transatlantic constitutional history and the representation of legitimacy.

**Robert Gerwarth** teaches modern European history at University College Dublin. He is currently writing a biography of Reinhard Heydrich.

**Henning Grunwald** is DAAD Visiting Assistant Professor of History and European Studies at Vanderbilt University, having held postdoctoral positions at the Free University of Berlin, and as assistant to the president at Humboldt University in Berlin previously. He is the editor (with Manfred Pfister) of *Krisis! Krisenszenarien, Diagnosen und Diskursstrategien* and is currently working on political justice in interwar Europe.

**Jose Harris** was, until her retirement, Fellow and Tutor in Modern History at St Catherine's College in the University of Oxford. She has written widely on the social, political and intellectual history of Britain in the nineteenth and twentieth centuries. Among her principal publications are *William Beveridge: A Biography* and *Private Lives, Public Spirit: A Social History of Britain 1870–1914*.

**Ulrike von Hirschhausen** is currently senior lecturer in European history at the University of Hamburg and has held visiting professorships at the University of Leipzig and Bielefeld. She is the author of *Liberalismus und Nation. Die 'Deutsche Zeitung' 1847–1850, Die Grenzen der Gemeinsamkeit. Deutsche, Letten, Russen und Juden in Riga 1860–1914* and (with Jörn Leonhard) *Empires und Nationalstaaten im 19. Jahrhundert*. Together with J. Leonhard she edited *Nationalismen in Europa. West- und Osteuropa im Vergleich*. She is currently working on a larger monograph on European empires in the nineteenth and early twentieth centuries.

**Ruth Leiserowitz** is Deputy Director of the German Historical Institute in Warsaw. Her main fields of research are Modern and Contemporary History, European History, especially Baltic, Polish, and Russian history, cultural and social history as well as Jewish history. She is currently finishing a history of Polish War memories.

**Veronika Lipphardt** is director of a research network at the Max Planck Institute for the History of Science. She is the author of a number of publications including *Biologie der Juden. Jüdische Wissenschaftler über 'Rasse' und Vererbung*. She is currently writing a history of knowledge about human biological diversity.

**Stephan Malinowski** is currently a teaching and research fellow at University College Dublin. He has held teaching and research positions at universities in Berlin, Cologne, Cambridge MA, the EUI in Florence, and Freiburg. He is the author of *Vom König zum Führer. Deutscher Adel und Nationalsozialismus*. He has also published on French elites and the radical right, on 1968 and on the comparison of colonial wars and the Holocaust. He is currently writing a book on the simultaneity of forced modernization and military violence in late colonial wars, particularly in the French–Algerian War (1954–62).

**Kiran Klaus Patel** is Professor of EU History and Transatlantic Relations at the European University Institute in Florence. His latest publications include: *Europäisierung wider Willen. Die Bundesrepublik Deutschland in der Agrarintegration der EWG; Fertile Ground for Europe? The History of European Integration and the Common Agricultural Policy since 1945* (ed.); and *The United States and Germany during the Twentieth Century: Competition and Convergence* (ed. with Christof Mauch).

**Guido Thiemeyer** is associate professor for European Studies at the University of Kassel. He has published a study on the beginnings of the Common Agricultural Policy of the EEC in the 1950s and a major study on international monetary relations in the late nineteenth century.

**Jessica Wardhaugh** is a Junior Research Fellow at Christ Church, Oxford. She is the author of *In Pursuit of the People: Political Culture in France, 1934–1939* and the editor of *Paris and the Right in the Twentieth Century*. She has also published a number of articles on street politics and theatre, and is currently writing a history of popular theatre during the French Third Republic.

**William Whyte** is fellow, tutor, and university lecturer in history at St John's College, Oxford. He is the author of *Oxford Jackson: Architecture, Education, Status, and Style, 1835–1924* and co-editor of *Redefining Christian Britain: Post-1945 Perspectives*. He is currently writing a book on British universities and co-editing another on nationalism in the nineteenth century.

# Europeanization in History: An Introduction

*Ulrike v. Hirschhausen and Kiran Klaus Patel**

Europeanization has turned into a 'growth industry'. Now a catchword in political as well as academic realms, the term has enjoyed rapidly increasing usage, driven principally by the growing importance of the European Union. Its predominant connotation stems from the process of Europe's contemporary political integration: since the early 1990s, Europeanization has been most often associated with new forms of European governance and the adaptation of nation-state legal and administrative procedures to the pressures associated with EU membership. Consequently, the term has been used primarily in the fields of law and political science.[1] In recent years, however, a few anthropologists have weighed into the debate and begun to analyse the reconstruction of collective and personal identities brought about by processes of European integration.[2] In these ways, Europeanization has become one of the central concepts by which social scientists conceptualize the accelerating processes of change that have transformed Europe's recent past and present, and that will define its near future. However, all of these variations of literature share the same point of reference: the organizational structure and spatial dimension of the European Union. For historians concerned specifically with the EU's history, this approach might be fruitful – even if few such historians of European integration have so far chosen to enter into this cross-disciplinary debate.[3] At the same time, this whole strand of research restricts and scales down 'Europeanization' to a process closely linked to recent political and institutional developments.

There seems to be a need, therefore, for a broader historical approach to the phenomenon of Europeanization, one seen not in terms of the origins of a present-day reality, but rather as a more flexible analytical tool that seeks to explore to what extent the history of Europe can be conceptualized in terms of processes of Europeanization. This is, however, a task that historians have been slow to undertake. Their apparent reluctance to do so of course reflects the instinctive distrust with which historians tend to regard concepts derived from political science or from contemporary political debates. Fears about such present-mindedness are, perhaps, particularly evident in the case

1

of Europeanization. With its resonances of a remorseless and positive process by which Europeans transcended their national frontiers (and thereby their national conflicts), it appears to be unavoidably tainted by its contemporary associations. Moreover, it stands in stark contrast to the emphasis which historians have placed on the murderous and genocidal conflicts that have characterized European history, especially during the first half of the twentieth century. Be it Ernst Nolte's 'European civil war', Mark Mazower's 'dark continent' or Ian Kershaw's 'age of ultra-violence',[4] historians have resolutely focused on the national, ethnic and ideological divisions that made possible the mass violence that cost so many millions of European lives. What one might describe as the 'Sarajevo to Sarajevo' paradigm has many strengths, but it has arguably tended to stand in the way of appreciating more diverse and long-term processes of change. In that respect, it is perhaps significant that, whatever the reluctance of twentieth-century historians to use the term Europeanization, it has been adopted much more readily by historians of earlier centuries.[5]

This volume is therefore intended as a first step towards the application of the idea of Europeanization to the history of twentieth-century Europe. In so doing, we do not wish to abandon the scepticism with which many historians have approached the term. Instead, this volume assumes that Europeanization in the twentieth century is not a fact (and still less a cause), but rather a thesis which needs to be tested against the history of the century. At the same time, however, we do believe that it constitutes a fruitful way of approaching the overly familiar contours of twentieth-century European history. In particular, it provides a means of linking together what are often tacitly regarded as the self-contained sub-periods of the twentieth century (inter-war, post-war, the 1960s, etc.) in order to investigate changes that took place over longer or less defined time periods. In addition, Europeanization has the advantage of bringing together those working on different areas of history: Europeanization may indeed be inherently multi-disciplinary but it also emphatically crosses the boundaries between the fields of political, economic, social and cultural history, suggesting a more integrated approach to processes of historical change.

But what, then, might this broader definition of Europeanization look like? Perhaps unsurprisingly, while definitions of Europeanization have been much debated in other disciplines, there has been relatively little discussion among historians of how the term might be applied to periods of history.[6] Addressing this issue of definition is one of the principal aims of this introduction, and indeed of the volume as a whole. In short, we understand Europeanization as a variety of political, social, economic and cultural processes that promote (or modify) a sustainable strengthening of intra-European connections and similarities through acts of emulation, exchange and entanglement and that have been experienced and labelled as 'European' in the course of history. However, Europeanization is not limited to integrative elements such as these, but also encompasses parallel processes of delimitation and 'othering', as well as fragmentation and conflict. It is the sum of these transnational processes that constitutes Europeanization. In this definition of Europeanization it is, in our view, essential to avoid a process of selection – conscious or otherwise – whereby generally peaceful or progressive phenomena are identified as somehow inherently European, while those that are less palatable are dismissed as anti-European. Such value structures impede an historical understanding of Europeanization, which must encompass the ways in which the darker sides of European history also often constituted aspects of Europeanization. Similarly, it is essential that Europeanization is not viewed in teleological terms: Europeanization has not been a process of inexorable development, but rather a dialogical one which, over the course of the century, has also given rise to forms of de-Europeanization.

In order to elaborate on this rather broad definition, this introductory chapter will first develop three characteristics of what Europeanization means for historical research and elucidate the analytical tools that can help to narrate these processes. Then, using these three theses as a basis, the main approaches to studying Europeanization will be explored, and the concomitant opportunities and difficulties highlighted. Finally, we will consider the various forms of Europeanization that can be detected over the course of the twentieth century, and will introduce the ways in which the essays in this volume shed light on these processes.

## Three theses on Europeanization

1. *Europeanization is not a uniform, unidirectional and teleological process.* Phases and forms of enhanced intra-European connections have often been followed by periods of abatement or even retreat. Consequently, there has been no steady rise of Europeanization. Before 1914, for example, it was possible to travel from Paris to Bucharest in one train; not only did national boundaries subsequently prevent this, but new modes of transportation – such as aeroplanes – gradually eclipsed older ones. As this example demonstrates, several processes of Europeanization – in this case via different means of transportation – can and often did coexist; they might coalesce, compete, complement or compensate each other. Moreover, very often, processes of intensification had paradoxical side effects or gave way to contradictory movements which subsequently weakened intra-European connections. In this respect, the history of the European constitutional treaty between 2001 and 2005 might serve as an instructive example: intended as a beacon of Europeanization, it failed because of its rejection in French and Dutch referenda in May and June 2005. Thus, a move towards greater political and structural integra-tion prompted reactions that ostensibly articulated an alternative view of

Europe, but which in practice protected national or regional autonomy. On the other hand, this constitutional crisis also precipitated a surge in Europeanization: in the immediate aftermath of the two 'No' votes, not only were the French and Dutch positions fervently discussed throughout Europe, but so too was the project of European integration more generally. In this way, Europeanization can involve both intensifications and retreats; indeed, at times the two tendencies are deeply intertwined.[7]

This conception of Europeanization as a non-teleological process suggests what Norman Davies has described in a rather different context as a 'tidal Europe', the ebbs and flows of which have varied according to changing historical contexts.[8] Such a metaphor defies any linear development towards greater European integration. Rather, it critically reflects the fact that, although all terms describing processes, including Europeaniz*ation*, have some teleological element inscribed within them, Europeanization for us denotes a complex, multidirectional and open process of intra-European entanglement, exchange and cooperation that also comprises counter-tendencies to these developments.

2. *Europeanization has no fixed geographical boundaries.* The metaphor of 'tidal Europe' has not only a temporal but also a spatial dimension. Conceptually, while Europeanization can help to overcome the obstinate fixation of modern historiography on national histories, it cannot dispense with territoriality as a major factor in history.[9] Europeanization was (and is) a phenomenon which is most evident on the borders of Europe, and these borders have moved markedly over the course of the twentieth century. Nor are these frontiers only external. Tacitly or explicitly, much of the historical writing on Europe has privileged certain areas of the European continent as more important than others. This is especially true in the case of the latter half of the twentieth century. The Cold War divide has shaped not only the *grands récits* of that specific epoch, but also the historiography of modern Europe in general.[10] Even after the disappearance of the Iron Curtain from Europe's contemporary political reality, it continues to exist in historiography. Very often, the eastern half of Europe's past is shaved off or contained in unconnected, separate narratives implying backwardness and delay in comparison with western Europe.[11] Against this background, Michael Geyer has pleaded for a 'Europeanization of European history' by integrating and interweaving the histories of the entire continent.[12]

This raises a further question: what is meant by the 'continent'? Most historians would agree that, over the course of history there has been no stable or enduring notion of a geographically-defined Europe. The delineation of Europe's eastern frontier as the Ural Mountains was an eighteenth-century invention, intended to bolster Russia's claim to be one of the great European powers.[13] Indeed, the conception of Europe's borders has been contested since antiquity; the continuing debate surrounding the admission of Turkey into the EU illustrates that even in the twenty-first century, it is impossible to establish a consensus on the issue. European history – and hence Europeanization – must therefore avoid any essentialist geographical definition. As there is no general, simple solution to the instability and ephemeral quality of Europe, a historical study of Europeanization must acknowledge and incorporate an understanding of the continent's evolving frontiers.

The geographical vagueness of Europe serves to reinforce that, just as there is no 'natural' shape to Europe, so too does easy definition of Europeanization remain elusive. As frontiers have changed, so has the nature of Europeanization. The consequent complexities can appear intimidating: any attempt to 'map' Europeanization in terms of the rise or fall of particular forms of integration is necessarily undermined by the changing nature of the object (Europe) which it seeks to measure. For historians, however, this vagueness – or, more exactly, the changing nature of the object of the study – serves as a challenge. It is only by identifying the ways in which Europe has changed its meaning that we can begin to understand the nature of Europeanization. Or, to put it less modestly, history is not merely another way of looking at Europeanization, but rather is an essential means of doing so.

3. *Europeanization is not just about Europe*. For a long time, the term was primarily used with regard to non-European spaces, to conceptualize the Europeanization of the world, mainly as part of the European processes of expansion which took place from the early modern period onward.[14] This use of the term would appear more straightforward or even commonsensical; but it, too, presents problems of definition. How, for example, should the Europe being exported be defined? Moreover, these particular forms of Europe were, in turn, transformed as part of the process of their appropriation by, or imposition on, non-European societies. The 'exportation of Europe' was therefore anything but a simple process, and one made even more complex when this externally-defined Europe was subsequently refracted back into the history of the continent through, for example, the adoption of 'colonial' practices during the mid-century conquest of areas of central and eastern Europe.[15]

This issue of 'which Europe?' also serves to demonstrate the self-referentiality of the term. The existence (or otherwise) of Europeanization relies heavily on the definition that one chooses to give to Europe. This creates the danger of a circular argument, by which a definition of Europeanization is advanced which determines in advance the answer to the question of its existence. This problem is not, of course, unique to Europeanization; it haunts all attempts to apply ideal-type criteria to the past. It is, however, especially acute in the case of Europeanization because of the absence of a recognizable 'other'. While the Americanization of Europe, for instance, describes the moulding of an entity by a relatively well-defined external force, in the case of the Europeanization of Europe, the 'other' is the same as the object being influenced. Thus, institutions and identities, processes and perceptions which are being 'Europeanized' themselves constitute that which supposedly produces them. There is no easy solution to this problem: Europeanization cannot be measured as the rise of one thing at the expense of the other. Instead, it needs to be perceived as a changing historical factor which has taken different shapes at different times.

As the imperial influence well demonstrates, however, this process of Europeanization never occurred in isolation. The frontiers of Europe have never been closed, and this was especially true during the twentieth century. The presence of Muslim populations in Europe or of American popular culture uniting the peoples of the Old World via jazz and jeans exemplifies why Europeanization cannot be analysed adequately without taking the non-European dimension into account. Further, research in imperial history and other fields has demonstrated the extent to which non-European experiences and practices have affected and shaped Europe and its integration. Crucial forces of Europeanization, such as urban planning, bureaucratic routines or modern art, developed in a dialogue with places such as Savannah, Georgia, New Delhi or Papeete, Tahiti. This refers back to 'tidal Europe' and, more importantly, it also reminds us that Europe has not only left its imprint on other parts of the world but that the inverse is often also true. Even if one concentrates on the 'Europeanization of Europe', as we do here, the explanation of factors and motives cannot come to a halt whenever blue water or roughly the 60th degree of longitude are reached.[16]

The conceptual problem of dealing with the boundaries of Europeanization also applies to the internal frontiers of Europe. Dipesh Chakrabarty's plea to 'provincialize Europe' acquires a particular relevance when applied to areas of central or eastern Europe which have often been described as 'backward' in comparison with some implicit or explicit European norm.[17] Traditional categories of Western scholarship, such as modernization and backwardness, therefore not only fall short when explaining structures, processes and experiences in Africa or Asia. They are also far from satisfactory when applied to Romania, Ruthenia, Rioja, or any other place within Europe labelled as the periphery by the dominant, north-western part of the continent. Thus, if studies of Europeanization are to move beyond an oversimplified narrative of pioneers, model pupils and backwardness, much work has to be invested in order to carve out appropriate categories for diverse experiences and for plural paths to modernity.[18]

Taken to their logical conclusions, each of these three theses therefore serves to demonstrate the dangers inherent in any simplistic use of the term Europeanization. Every definition of Europeanization tends to result in a circular argument involving elements that are hard to define and a geographical space with vague borders. As Kevin Featherstone has rightly observed, the term is one that has often been applied as 'a loose epithet' to highly diverse forms of political, economic or cultural convergence.[19] One might therefore think that Europeanization is too elastic to be meaningful; this, however, would be unduly pessimistic. 'Europeanization' can be infused with real meaning when it is accepted as a flexible term that has always been plural, and which refers to different processes over the course of European history. Indeed, it is precisely the complexity of the term that serves to illuminate its richness as a historical topic. It is only by examining simultaneously what Europeanization meant in history and what it means when applied to history that the term acquires true significance.

## Approaches to Europeanization

A common way of dealing with the dilemmas of Europeanization has been a normative approach. If one works, for example, with strict categories such as the spread of Roman law, human rights, or Christianity, it is possible to analyse and frame processes of Europeanization quite clearly. According to this approach, phenomena thought to be constitutive of Europe are investigated in terms of their emergence and dissemination. The research which has been undertaken on peaceful plans of European integration – from Dante to Kant, from Rousseau to Schmidt-Phiseldek, and from Churchill to Spaak – might serve as another example of such a normative approach. At the core of this narrative very often lies a notion of peace (the transcending of national conflict in the name of a wider European idea) as a key element of Europeanization. As such, this perennial idea, or utopian ideal, has travelled across European societies, from one era to the next, never entirely extinguished and, as one approaches the present, gradually gaining in intellectual and political influence.

However, this normative take has serious drawbacks: the reduction of Europeanization to one abstract concept reduces the multifariousness of the past and marginalizes all those experiences that do not fit into its narrative framework.[20] Furthermore, many such norms were not exclusively European inventions but rather were developed and shared in a global environment. In adopting such a normative approach, there is therefore the danger of repeating, at a European level, notions of national distinctiveness, of a European *Sonderweg* which have too often characterized national narratives within European history.[21] In addition, because such a normative approach is always based upon selection, it must be capable of being challenged. Is, for example, Europeanization really about peace, given that the continent has, over the course of the twentieth century, seen some of the bloodiest wars in history? Or about democracy, in a part of the world deeply divided throughout most of the twentieth century by competing political ideologies and systems? Or about Christianity, during a century when Christianization waned as a formative influence on various parts of Europe? Indeed, such arguments serve only to demonstrate that attempts to define Europeanization in terms of a core set of values present more difficulties than solutions.

If, on the other hand, one accepts a non-essentialist approach to Europeanization, how then can we carry this forward as a viable project? In our eyes, there is no single master path to achieving this. However, a certain quantum of social constructivism seems unavoidable if one is to bypass the problems of essentialist or normative approaches described above. Building upon the work of Benedict Anderson and others on nationalism and modern nations, one can understand Europe as an 'imagined community' – that is, an artefact of particular cultural and social formations and not as a natural, obvious and perennial entity, neither unchanging nor self-contained.[22] At the same time, it would be incorrect to take this constructivist approach to the extreme. *Imagined communities* are more than mere figments of the mind. Discourses as well as material practices have turned Europe into a *lived community* that also needs to be researched through analysis of economic and political structures as well as cultural discourses. Europeanization has happened at different times for a reason, or more often for plural reasons; the task of the historian is to unravel its various constitutive elements and to trace their interactions. The advantage of such an approach is that it avoids many of the complexities of definition. It enables one to set aside questions such as: What is Europe? What are its constituent norms and what are their boundaries? In this way, we can ignore 'the Turkey in the room' (i.e., contemporary debates about the frontiers of Europe), and instead perceive Europe – and hence Europeanization – as a category of practice which has been projected and performed, experienced and exported, labelled and legitimized, appropriated and emulated in a range of contexts. We thereby understand Europe as a highly malleable concept, which has taken different shapes and acquired different contents in response to the actions of a variety of actors but also to the broader circumstances of the time.[23]

Under this umbrella, three approaches can be differentiated, all of which will be used in the empirical chapters of this volume. First, some scholars have highlighted the discursive side of these processes, that is, what can be summed up as *'Europe Imagined'*. Accordingly, Europeanization can be found wherever people talk, write, sing about or memorialize Europe. Such a cultural history of Europeanization, highlighting the role of language, imagination, visualization and memory, constitutes a distinct and coherent approach to the subject. Research of this kind – most importantly the ground-breaking work of Wolfgang Schmale – has shown that 'Europe' is in fact a relatively modern idea, replacing earlier concepts of Christendom after generations of religious conflict and filling the need for a more neutral designation of a common point of reference and identity. Despite the fact that the term has a history that can be traced back to antiquity, as a driving force of Europeanization in the sense defined above this use of the term 'Europe' has essentially developed since the beginning of the early modern period.[24]

This approach to Europeanization is conceptually convincing and has considerable potential for empirical research. In many respects, it remains surprising how little we know about the way in which the term Europe was constructed and employed within European cultural debates from the French Revolution onwards.[25] In future, it could be expanded and gain additional depth through a dialogue with a certain strand of the research on nationalism: expanding on Michael Billig's concept of 'banal nationalism',[26] one could frame this as a form of 'banal Europeanism', whereby figures and maps, tables and statistics as well as other forms of discourse were increasingly structured and presented according to 'European' lines in order to produce a specific vision of Europe. As ethnological research has emphasized, the permanent production of these standards and surveys not only served to shape a specific mode of representing Europe, but also, through 'fixing' Europe in a certain way, had a much wider impact on conceptions of Europe. Analysing such forms of 'banal Europeanism' would have the added advantage of widening cultural representations of Europe beyond the focus on the cultural artefacts of the middle class that have hitherto dominated the literature.[27]

Such a cultural approach, however, can only take one so far. It was not only ideas, representations or visual artefacts which transcended boundaries and strengthened or re-oriented intra-European connections but also more material and social factors. Hence the need for a second approach, which one might term '*Europe Constructed*': Through studying the nexus of pilgrims and paths, jugglers and journals, doctors and diseases within which the cultural representations of Europe emerged, it is possible to identify the diverse forms of social practice which have given rise to spaces of Europeanization. Not only must this material approach encompass a wide range of phenomena which go beyond the sphere of cultural history, but other subfields of history must also be introduced and incorporated. Johan Schot and Thomas Misa, for instance, have focused on the role of technology as a means of Europeanization. They analyse how 'actors design and use technology to constitute and enact European integration (or fragmentation)'. They see technology as a set of Europe-building practices 'in which specific concepts and visions of Europe became embedded in particular designs for artefacts and systems.'[28] Thus, European railway systems, television regulations or engineers' congresses imply specific notions of Europe that time and again have been put into practice. Technology in this context serves as one possible means of comprehending a Europe in action, and through two international research projects, on 'Inventing Europe' and 'Tensions of Europe', Schot and others have demonstrated not only the importance of this approach, but also the potential for its extension to analogous fields.

Thirdly, there is a more pragmatic approach, which combines the analysis of discursive and material practices and which focuses on '*Europe Emergent*'. Implicitly, it is this approach which has shaped most of the work undertaken so far. There are important arguments in favour of this flexible methodology. A purely discursive or material approach often leaves little room for integrating the unlabelled and unintentional aspects of Europeanization. Sometimes, actors carried out Europeanization without articulating it as such: from today's perspective, for example, there can be no doubt that Gothic architecture was a Europeanizing factor in European history, even if it did not know its name at the time. The decades between 1850 and 1880, to give another example, were a period when a growing number of transnational networks, both formal and informal, were created.[29] Many of them, such as the Red Cross or the International Statistical Congress, had a strong European focus and can also be seen as drivers of Europeanization – even if they were not referred to as such when they were created.

In many cases, therefore, it did not require a vision of Europe to initiate processes of Europeanization. This unintended facet becomes most obvious if one turns to the dark sides of Europeanization which necessarily constitute an explicit element of research of this kind. Violence and war have been major forces of transnationalism and of Europeanization throughout most of the continent's history.[30] They led to fragmentation as well as to exchange and new connections, as illustrated by the intense and durable cross-boundary experiences of soldiers or nurses, forced labourers or displaced persons during the era of the Second World War. In their memoirs, these actors very often framed their experiences as a period of *European* exchanges and contacts – thus constructing a specific landscape of actions and memories.

Analysis of Europeanization can therefore go beyond the focus on *Europe Imagined* – the deliberate and explicit reference to Europe – and of *Europe Constructed* – the establishment of European political, technological or other institutions.[31] The further one moves into the analysis of a *Europe Emergent,* however, the greater the danger of succumbing to an essentialist, normative and selective view of Europeanization. In the case of an emergent Europe, actors set up structures and initiate processes which subsequently stabilize and sediment. Over time, they may be experienced, labelled and used in different ways, but at some point, they are perceived as specifically *European.* Only then (if one follows the social-constructivist approach that we have adopted) do they enter the realm of Europeanization research because, without this caveat, anachronism, essentialism and teleology cannot be avoided.[32] Therefore, this kind of research is particularly interested in the moments when Europe turns into the denominator of these structures and processes – and of all the changes that follow from them.

Europeanization, however, never occurred in isolation. Discourses on Europe must be viewed in relation to alternative but often overlapping concepts of loyalty and identity – especially national and regional feelings of belonging, but also notions of cosmopolitanism.[33] Technologies, as well as political and economic integration projects, almost always emerged in larger regional settings, often spanning the North Atlantic or the Mediterranean, and these connections serve to underscore yet again how Europeanization was often embedded within contexts that were, at the same time, both geographically larger, and emotionally smaller. The degree of interconnection between Europeanization and these other processes varied. Some of the waves and ebbs of 'tidal Europe' have remained quite distinct, whereas in some cases, they have overlapped with other processes – notably those of regionalism, nationalization and globalization. In the twentieth century, for example, the United States of America has been an especially important influence on European history. This does not necessarily mean that Americanization or other such processes were the antithesis of Europeanization, but rather that such processes could develop in tandem. There is therefore no need to construct false dichotomies between Europeanization and these other wide-ranging processes of change. Instead, Europeanization has to be perceived as a multifarious phenomenon which took various forms and which developed in interaction with other forces.

## Europeanization in the twentieth century

The three varieties of a social constructivist approach that have been differentiated in this introduction will be taken up in the empirical chapters of this volume. In so doing, all of the contributions focus on twentieth-century history. Obviously, Europeanization is not exclusively a phenomenon of contemporary history; the decision to restrict ourselves to one century was essentially a pragmatic one. At the same time, the twentieth century is a particularly interesting research field for Europeanization because during this 'age of extremes',[34] processes of Europeanization – and their destruction – reached an unprecedented level of intensity, thereby highlighting its ambivalence and complexity.[35] Another consequence of focusing on the twentieth century has been that it has enabled us to emphasize the interconnectedness between processes of Europeanization and larger global ones. As such, although most of the essays have inner-European developments as their primary focus, we have been careful to highlight that Europeanization was never an internal or isolated process: the volume contains essays that look beyond Europe, and which emphasize that those processes of Europeanization 'out there' which formed part of empire-building also contributed to Europeanization 'back here'.

At this stage in the research, it is too early to trace how Europeanization changed over the course of the century; however, a number of general themes can be identified. Obviously, the era preceding the First World War that was characterized by a European sense of superiority over the rest of the world was, in many respects, a period of intense Europeanization. More than in subsequent decades, Europeanization during this time was an imperial endeavour aimed at wielding power over, or even projecting it on to, areas of the world perceived to be non-European. In contrast, what one may term the Europeanization of Europe only came to the fore during the second half of the twentieth century. At that time, the relative demise of European power on a global scale, coupled with the economic and political integration of Western Europe (after 1945, and particularly since the 1980s) were driving forces: With 'Europe' increasingly identified with Western Europe, and even more so with the integration process carried out under the auspices of the EEC/EC/EU, actors of all kinds had to reposition themselves – as attendants, allies, alternatives or aspirants to this new reality. The consequent conflicts and clashes over competing notions of Europe and Europeanization which emerged have strengthened rather than weakened the importance of this point of reference. So, the existence of the controversy surrounding the development of the EU, especially since the 1980s, has helped to normalize and stabilize the reference to Europe, and has transformed it from a discrete entity into the basis for both discourse and material practice, as well as for combinations of the two. Against this backdrop, any binary logic of increase and decline seems unduly simplistic. Instead, the manifold forms of Europeanization and their quality of constant change need to be considered and given credence. Rather like blood, what matters are the situations in which these different forms of Europeanization coalesce and clot.

By focusing on Europeanization during the twentieth century, we hope that this volume will contribute to wider inter-disciplinary debates. Given the undeniable political and economic influence of the EU, our work can, we believe, contribute to an understanding of the contemporary shape of Europe. But the deeper value of an historical perspective on Europeanization lies in the way in which historians can re-orientate attention away from an exclusive focus on the post-1989 expanded European Union, and emphasize instead the different configurations of Europe, and meanings of the word 'European', which have flourished over the past century. Thus, although many of the essays in this volume have a contemporary resonance, they are emphatically historical in nature, and include many subjects that have not been hitherto viewed in the context of Europeanization. Rather than seeking to provide an alternative narrative account of the twentieth century, our concern is to emphasize the plurality of forms of Europeanization which have arisen (and in some cases disappeared), as well as warning against overly facile uses of the term.

During the course of developing our approach to Europeanization, the authors of this volume time and again felt that they were entering a *terra incognita*. It should be made clear from the outset that we aim only to provide select case studies that reflect the general ambition of our approach; we do not claim to map comprehensively all aspects of Europeanization in twentieth-century Europe. Hence, the empirical chapters of the book are fundamentally tentative in character. While some areas and issues will be dealt with in more detail than others, any attempt to define our objectives more narrowly would have prejudiced the overall goal of the project; consequently, we see our task more in terms of proposing a putative agenda than of providing definite and final empirical answers.

The contributions to the volume reflect this purpose, encompassing disparate periods and areas of twentieth-century European history. In a manner perhaps appropriate to its topic, this book itself is an exercise in Europeanization because it is a product of primarily British–German cooperation (with some American, Irish and Italian outposts). In particular, the four co-authored chapters, co-produced by British and German writers, epitomize our attempt to move not only beyond national history but also beyond national ways of writing history. Furthermore, all of the chapters adopt distinct versions of the three approaches delineated above. To this end, we have chosen to divide the chapters into the three sub-headings outlined above; in doing so, however, we have been conscious that many of the chapters combine two (or even all three) of these approaches, and that their allocation to one of the three sub-groups must therefore be somewhat arbitrary.

A first group of texts is clustered around the idea of *Europe Imagined*. The chapter jointly written by Jessica Wardhaugh, Ruth Leiserowitz and Christian Bailey contends that intellectuals have been important agents of cultural Europeanization in the twentieth century, particularly in their construction of European spaces of imagination, communication and conviviality. Three case studies of Western, Central and Eastern Europe explore the creation of 'dream-Europes' by intellectual dissidents, drawing out their search for moral and social authority and their determination to bridge European division by creating transnational networks. The chapter reveals a close connection between imagined Europe and its physical geography, and suggests the need for a long-term perspective on Europeanization, since its cultural importance in times of political tension often emerges most clearly in retrospect.

The chapter by Jose Harris examines the debates over the past, present and future of Europe which took place during the Second World War in the United Kingdom. Despite Britain's intellectual isolation from the continent for much of the war, and the intense celebration of 'Englishness' apparent in many aspects of wartime culture, interest in the identity and fate of Europe among politicians, economists, social scientists, creative writers and artists was surprisingly widespread. Using three contrasting examples of people who engaged in such discussions, the chapter explores the multifarious views and conceptions of Europe, and demonstrates that it was mainly the perception of a crisis of European civilization that spurred the increased interest of British elites.

This 'Europeanization of the mind' is also evident in the chapter by Veronika Lipphardt, which looks at how concepts of a *Homo Europaeus* have developed in the life sciences. Anthropologists in particular investigated and described the figure of 'European man' as biologically different from 'Non-Europeans' for more than two centuries, albeit with evolving intensity and motives. The chapter argues that one can therefore speak of a Europeanization of knowledge production, evident through the scientists' 'willingness' to denote certain objects under study as 'European'. This was not, however, a fixed phenomenon, but rather one which underwent substantial change over the course of the twentieth century.

A second group of chapters deals with *Europe Constructed*. Ulrike von Hirschhausen describes the European Nationality Congress between 1925 and 1945 as a phenomenon revealing moves towards Europeanization as well as towards de-Europeanization. While its founding members tried to safeguard the newly emerging 'minorities' all over Europe, a generational change and its financial dependency on the German government turned the Congress during the 1930s into an instrument of German revisionism. The very process of reinterpreting the – formerly democratic – idea of securing minorities' rights into an argument that legitimized expansive and revisionist policies underlines the ebbs and flows of a 'tidal Europe' in an age of extremes.

The chapter by Patricia Clavin and Kiran Klaus Patel explores the history of two international organizations, the League of Nations and the European Economic Community. Taking the negotiations about agricultural trade and production as an example, they interpret both the League and the EEC/EU as sites of Europeanization. In propitious political, social, and intellectual contexts, these international organizations generated shared causal and normative conceptions of 'Europe', which subsequently provided a resource essential for collective action. The process examined demonstrates how these agencies were both Europeanizing and Europeanized.

In their chapter, Martin Conway and Volker Depkat explore the ways in which non-Communist political elites in Western Europe thought and talked about democracy in the first 15 years following the Second World War. What emerges from their empirical analysis is the substantial convergence which occurred in the ways in which democracy was defined, experienced and practised by leading politicians of France, Germany, the Benelux countries and Italy. As these political elites were increasingly speaking in the same political language, democracy as a set of commonly shared values and a political system developed into a key element of notions of 'Europeanness' and European identity. In this way, political democracy also became a site of Europeanization.

In a somewhat similar vein, Tom Buchanan analyses the history of human rights from the early post-war years to 1975. By focusing on the interaction between different actors – such as states, international organizations and voluntary campaigning bodies – within the context of the Cold War, European integration and decolonization, he demonstrates the incremental process by which this set of values and legal norms developed into a cornerstone of European identity, and thus came to be seen as a conscious attempt to invest Europe with distinctive meaning.

Guido Thiemeyer's chapter discusses Europeanization in the monetary sector between 1958 and 1999. By focusing on the interplay between economic and social 'forces profondes', including their unintended effects on political behaviour on the one hand and political plans and attempts at monetary integration on the other, he stresses that Europe and Europeanization meant completely different things for the various actors involved. In addition, Thiemeyer emphasizes that integration was accompanied by fragmentation and delimitation, not only vis-à-vis the Eastern bloc, but in this case also with respect to the United States.

A third and final cluster of chapters focuses on *Europe Emergent*. In their chapter, Robert Gerwarth and Stephan Malinowski investigate the largely unplanned Europeanizing effects of two violent projects of epic dimensions: European colonialism and the two world wars. Their chapter engages with what one might call the 'dark side' of transnational history in order to promote an ambivalent concept of 'Europeanization' that weaves together histories of extremely violent encounters and border-crossings and those of economic success, democratic reorientation and collective recovery. In doing so, they aim to highlight multiple dynamics and to complicate the 'happy' image of Europeanization that continues to dominate scholarly and political debates.

William Whyte's chapter uses debates about architecture in Nigeria and Ghana between the mid-1940s and the 1990s as a way of exploring Europeanization. Modernism, he argues, was seen as synonymous with modernization, and modernization was equated with Europeanization. For some writers, modernism was necessarily European and therefore bad. For others, it was evidently modern and therefore good. Ironically, of course, these arguments rested upon assumptions which had been articulated by European writers for centuries. Whyte's chapter thus highlights the ambiguous relationship between Europeanization and modernization while also exposing a wider Europeanization of discourse more profound than the architecture that was its ostensible subject.

In contrast, the contribution by John Davis focuses on an even more unexpected and certainly unintentional form of Europeanization. Taking British beat music of the 1960s as a point of reference and departure, he looks at the ways in which European pop musicians emulated English style and language of music; in doing so, they in fact effected a Europeanization of popular music, as opposed to simply perpetuating a derivative of the English model.

The final contribution returns to the dark side of Europeanization. Drawing on examples from East and West Germany, Poland and France, Henning Grunwald examines the impact of Holocaust remembrance on European collective memory and identity. Critically surveying the way in which these concepts are framed in political science, sociology and legal history, the chapter explores the waxing and waning (and waxing again) of Holocaust memory as a Europeanizing force. From the earliest, idealistic notions of a European community of suffering and solidarity forged in the camps and embodied in camp memorials via the nationalization and instrumentalization of memory in the Cold War, to the disputed emergence of the Holocaust as a 'European founding myth' after 1989, this chapter eschews teleological accounts for an exploration of Europeanization through violence and its remembrance, a Europeanization *malgré soi*.

As Martin Conway argues in the concluding contribution, the evident heterogeneity of the subject matter and the multifarious processes of Europeanization explored in this volume indicate that the history of Europeanization defies any finite definition. While it can be perceived as 'a thing in itself' – that is, a process (or processes) that *happened* – it also denotes a discourse which, by influencing the way in which actors have seen the world, has had an impact on the shape of the European twentieth century.

## Notes

* Apart from the other contributors to this volume, we would like to thank Johan Schot and Cornelius Torp for their helpful remarks on earlier versions of this text. Martin Conway deserves special thanks. Only the two of us know how much we owe to his comments and suggestions on matters large and small.

1. E.g. see Paolo Graziano and Maarten Peter Vink (eds), *Europeanization: New Research Agendas* (New York, 2007); Gunnar Folke Schuppert (ed.), *The Europeanisation of Governance* (Baden-Baden, 2006); Robert Harmsen and Thomas Wilson, 'Introduction: Approaches to Europeanization', *Yearbook of European Studies* XIV (2004), 132–6.

2. E.g. see Irène Bellier and Thomas M. Wilson (eds), *An Anthropology of the European Union* (Oxford, 2000); Cris Shore, *Building Europe: The Cultural Politics of European Integration* (London/New York, 2000); Marc Abélès, 'La communauté européenne: une perspective anthropologique', *Social Anthropology* IV (1996), 334–5.

3. W. Kaiser, B. Leucht and M. Rasmussen (eds) *The History of the European Union. The Origins of a Trans- and Supranational Polity* (London, 2008) is a first step towards such a debate.

4. Ernst Nolte, *Der europäische Bürgerkrieg, 1917–1945: Nationalsozialismus und Bolschewismus* (Frankfurt/Main, 1987); Mark Mazower, *Dark Continent: Europe's Twentieth Century* (London, 1998); Ian Kershaw, 'War and Political Violence in Twentieth-Century Europe', *Contemporary European History* XIV (2005), 1072–3. See also Mark Levene, *Genocide in the Age of the Nation-State* 2 vols (London, 2005).

5. Robert Bartlett, *The Making of Europe: Conquest, Colonization and Cultural Change 950–1350* (London, 1993); Stuart Woolf, *Napoleon's Integration of Europe* (London, 1991).

6. As one of the few exceptions: Hartmut Kaelble, 'Europäisierung', in Matthias Middell (ed.), *Dimensionen der Kultur- und Gesellschaftsgeschichte* (Leipzig, 2007), pp. 738–9.

7. See Maurizio Bach, Christa Lahusen and Georg Vobruba (eds), *Europe in Motion: Social Dynamics and Political Institutions in an Enlarging Europe* (Berlin, 2006).

8. See for this concept Norman Davies, *Europe: A History* (Oxford, 1996), p. 9; W.H. Parker, *A Historical Geography of Russia* (London, 1968). The metaphor also has its limits: the tidal Europe we envisage is not caused by the forces of the moon or any other single, 'natural' actor.

9. See e.g. Charles S. Maier, 'Consigning the Twentieth Century to History: Alternative Narratives for the Modern Era', in *American Historical Review* CV (2000), 807–31; Kiran Klaus Patel, *Nach der Nationalfixiertheit: Perspektiven einer transnationalen Geschichte* (Berlin, 2004).

10. As attempts to overcome this divide, see e.g.: Bernard Wasserstein, *Barbarism and Civilization: A History of Europe in Our Time* (Oxford, 2007); Mazower, *Continent*; Davies, *Europe*; also see Stuart Woolf, 'Europe and its Historians', *Contemporary European History* XII (2003), 323–38.

11. See Manfred Hildermeier, 'Das Privileg der Rückständigkeit: Anmerkungen zum Wandel einer Interpretationsfigur der Neueren Russischen Geschichte', *Historische Zeitschrift* No. 244 (1987), 557–603.

12. Michael Geyer, 'Historical Fiction of Anatomy and the Europeanization of National History', *Central European History* XXII (1989), 316–42, quote 334.

13. See Larry Wolff, *Inventing Eastern Europe* (Stanford, 1994); Maria Todorova, *Imagining the Balkans* (New York, 1997).

14. See e.g. the entry in the Oxford English Dictionary.

15. See e.g. Williard Sunderland, *Taming the Wild Field: Colonization and Empire on the Russian Steppe* (Ithaca, 2004); Daniel Brower and Edward Lazzerini (eds), *Russia's Orient. Imperial Borderlands and Peoples 1700–1971* (Bloomington, 1997).

16. See e.g. Ann Laura Stoler and Frederick Cooper (eds), *Tensions of Empire: Colonial Cultures in a Bourgeois World* (Berkeley, 1997).

17. See Dipesh Chakrabarty, *Provincializing Europe: Postcolonial Thought and Historical Difference* (Princeton, 2000).

18. See, For example, Ulrike v. Hirschhausen and Jörn Leonhard (eds), *Nationalismen in Europa: West- und Osteuropa im Vergleich* (Göttingen, 2001).

19. Kevin Featherstone 'Introduction: "In the Name of Europe"' in Kevin Featherstone and Claudio M. Radaelli (eds), *The Politics of Europeanization* (Oxford, 2003), p. 12.

20. See e.g. Marie-Louise von Plessen (ed.), *Idee Europa: Entwürfe zum 'Ewigen Frieden'* (Berlin, 2003); Heinz Duchhardt, 'Was heisst und zu welchem Ende betreibt man – Europäische Geschichte?', in Heinz Duchhardt and Andreas Kunz (eds), *'Europäische Geschichte' als historiographisches Problem* (Mainz, 1997), pp. 191–202.

21. See notably S. Berger (ed.), *Writing the Nation: A Global Perspective* (Basingstoke, 2007) and S. Berger and C. Lorenz (eds), *The Contested Nation: Ethnicity, Class, Religion and Gender in National Histories* (Basingstoke, 2008).

22. See Benedict Anderson, *Imagined Communities: Reflections on the Origin and Spread of Nationalism* (London, 1983).

23. For a similar conceptual approach, though not on Europeanization but on the figure of 'European man': Lorraine Bluche, Veronika Lipphardt and Kiran Klaus Patel (eds), *Der Europäer – ein Konstrukt. Wissensbestände, Diskurse, Praktiken* (Göttingen, 2009).

24. See e.g. Wolfgang Schmale, *Geschichte Europas* (Vienna, 2001); some of the contributions in Bo Stråth (ed.), *Europe and the Other and Europe as the Other* (Brussels, 2000); on memory and Europeanization Konrad H. Jarausch and Thomas Lindenberger (eds), *Conflicted Memories: Europeanizing Contemporary Histories* (New York, 2007); from the perspective of anthropology Wolfgang Kaschuba, 'Europäisierung als kulturalistisches Projekt? Ethnologische

Betrachtungen', in Hans Joas and Friedrich Jaeger (eds), *Europa im Spiegel der Kulturwissenschaften* (Baden-Baden, 2008), pp. 204–25; e.g. on music, Philipp Ther, 'Das Europa der Nationalkulturen. Die Nationalisierung und Europäisierung der Oper im "langen" 19. Jahrhundert', *Journal of Modern European History* v (2007), 39–66.

25. See e.g. Wlodzimierz Borodziej et al. (eds), *Option Europa. Deutsche, polnische und ungarische Europapläne des 19. und 20. Jahrhunderts*, 3 vols (Göttingen, 2005).

26. Michael Billig, *Banal Nationalism* (London, 1995).

27. See e.g. Reinhard Johler, '"Europa in Zahlen". Statistik–Vergleich–Volkskunde–EU', in *Zeitschrift für Volkskunde* xcv (1999), 246–63; Maryon McDonald, '"Unity in Diversity". Some Tensions in the Construction of Europe', *Social Anthropology* iii (1996), 47–60.

28. See Johan Schot and Thomas J. Misa, "Inventing Europe: Technology and the Hidden Integration of Europe", *History and Technology* xxi (2005), 1–19, quotes 8, 9; e.g. also see: Johan Schot and Vincent Lagendijk, 'Internationalism in the Interwar Years. Building Europe on Motorways and Electricity', in: *Journal of Modern European History* vi (2008), 196–217. Schot and Misa use the term 'European integration' but by this they mean basically the same as when we talk about Europeanization.

29. See Akira Iriye, *Global Community: The Role of International Organizations in the Making of the Contemporary World* (Berkeley, 2002).

30. See e.g. Kiran Klaus Patel, 'In Search for a Transnational Historicization. National Socialism and its Place in History' in Konrad H. Jarausch and Thomas Lindenberger (eds), *Conflicted Memories*. pp. 96–116.

31. See for this concept Kaelble, *Europäisierung*.

32. For the somewhat analogous case of nationalization, John Breuilly has pointed at the pitfalls of all alternatives: John Breuilly, 'Nationalismustheorien und kritische deutsche Gesellschaftsgeschichte', in Sven-Oliver Müller and Cornelius Torp (eds), *Das Deutsche Kaiserreich in der Kontroverse: Eine Bilanz* (Göttingen, 2009).

33. See e.g. Heinz-Gerhard Haupt, 'Erfahrungen mit Europa. Ansätze zu einer Geschichte Europas im langen 19. Jahrhundert', in Duchhardt and Kunz, *Europäische Geschichte*, pp. 87–104; Achim Trunk, *Europa, ein Ausweg: Politische Eliten und europäische Identität in den 1950er Jahren* (Munich, 2007).

34. See Eric Hobsbawm, *The Age of Extremes. A History of the World, 1914–1991* (New York, 1994).

35. We do not agree with Wasserstein, *Barbarism*, viii, who argues that Europe, even during the twentieth century, was not even a meaningful category for most of its inhabitants.

# Part One
# Europe Imagined

# 1
# Intellectual Dissidents and the Construction of European Spaces, 1918–1988

*Jessica Wardhaugh, Ruth Leiserowitz and Christian Bailey\**

The French writer Julien Benda was renowned for his controversial assertions on the role of European intellectuals. In 1927, he denounced the political engagement of fellow writers as a betrayal of their duty to defend the abstract principles of truth and justice. His speech to the 'European nation' in 1933 encouraged intellectuals to become self-denying evangelists, abandoning homes, families, goods, salaries, and status in order to spread the gospel of European fraternity. And in 1948 he anticipated the birth of a European spirit through the rewriting – and relearning – of European history, whereby the emphasis would shift from nationalism to internationalism, from cynical nation-builders to the 'dreamers' whose grandiose projects of unity had ultimately foundered. Roman emperors and medieval popes would be the heroes of this new curriculum, to be taught in the only truly European language: French.[1]

Benda's proposals were idiosyncratic, yet many intellectuals in the twentieth century shared his determination to build Europe in the hearts and minds of Europeans. Defying national differences, writers and journalists imagined unity across geographical boundaries, exchanging ideas and forging friendships. Against the often troubled background of a political Europe, they discerned a Europe of shared culture and experience. Intellectual dissidents were of particular significance in imagining 'dream-Europes': fraternal utopias that deliberately challenged the political or social orthodoxies of their times. In the 1920s and 1930s, pacifists such as Romain Rolland promoted Franco-German reconciliation in conscious opposition to growing tensions, while Prinz Rohan's *Europäische Kulturbund* championed the cause of a common European aristocracy against the perceived divisiveness of national democracies. From the 1940s onwards, the German periodical *Merkur* drew on this pre-war cultural network to strengthen European thought and thinkers against American and Soviet influence, urgently confronting the increasing fragmentation of the European communication space. And it was against this fragmentation that eastern European dissidents began to re-imagine Europe and recreate networks of solidarity and dialogue in the Cold War period, their efforts gaining impetus after the Helsinki Conference of 1975.

This chapter contends that intellectual dissidents have been both dreamers and activists in the Europeanization of Europe. The intellectuals here discussed were European writers with a strong sense of public – and often political – engagement, and a conviction that they were morally responsible for the formation of literary and public opinion. They were dissidents in that they felt ill at ease with the political regimes in which they lived, and in that their advocacy of an ideal or 'dream' Europe was often in deliberate opposition to the status quo. For such writers, the tracing of Europe as a mental map was also inseparable from the creation of European spaces of sociability and communication. Through their writing, meetings and networks, they contributed to the creation and strengthening of intra-European ties and to the discernment of European boundaries and values – in brief, to a process of cultural Europeanization that has ebbed and flowed with the passage of time.

The case studies at the centre of this chapter are underpinned by a threefold concept of European space that spans imagination, conviviality and communication. Within this conceptual framework, our aim has been to determine the nature and boundaries of these European spaces: to examine intellectual representations of Europe, intellectual agency in the creation of European networks, and the rise and fall of such Europeanization during the twentieth century. Through a chronological and thematic analysis of the Paris-based *Europe, revue mensuelle* in the 1920s and 1930s, the German periodicals *Europäische Revue* and *Merkur* in the 1930s and 1940s, and the activism of Eastern European dissidents in the 1970s, we explore the creation of European spaces in Western, Central, and Eastern Europe. This exploration leads, in turn, to a number of conclusions concerning Europe's global role, the search for European authority, and the distinction between Europe as an imagined and lived experience. Both conceptual and empirical in character, this chapter offers a composite contribution to the understanding of cultural Europeanization in the twentieth century.[2]

## The cordial geography of *Europe, Revue Mensuelle*

For the writers of *Europe, revue mensuelle* – a Paris-based periodical with a world-wide readership in the inter-war years – one of the most important roles of the intellectual was the creation of a 'cordial geography of Europe'. The phrase was coined by Georges Duhamel,[3] a French doctor, poet and essayist whose commitment to Europe and knowledge of its geography had been forged through both youthful idealism and wartime suffering. Before the First World War he had walked across the continent with his student friends, a notebook of poetry as his passport and European fraternity as his goal. During the war itself he had served as a doctor near the front line, witnessing soldiers turning to pacifism and nationalists to pessimism, and a dying man singing to forget his pain.[4] Remembrance of both pain and pleasure shaped Duhamel's post-war commitment and not least his determination to tend the sick continent as once he had tended its soldier-sons. In 1923 Duhamel contributed to the first edition of the *Europe, revue mensuelle*, describing with characteristic fervour the 'poet's mission' to encourage European dialogue, understanding, and fraternity.

Like Duhamel, other contributors to the review were also concerned to redraw Europe as a mental map and to re-establish European spaces of conviviality and communication that had existed before the First World War. Created with the support of the controversial pacifist Romain Rolland and published monthly until 1939,[5] *Europe* was sustained by a central group of French writers including René Arcos, Jean-Richard Bloch, Jean Guéhenno, Jean Cassou, and Paul Colin, while also providing a forum for intellectuals from other European countries. The latter comprised some of the most renowned and controversial of their day: the German authors Thomas and Heinrich Mann, the Austrian short story writer Stefan Zweig, the Italian diplomat Carlo Sforza, the Spanish philosopher José Ortega y Gasset, and the Hungarian poet Tivadar Raith. *Europe, revue mensuelle* was generally – but not exclusively – left-wing in the inter-war years, and shared concerns with a number of other reviews with similar titles: *L'Europe nouvelle*, *La Revue européenne*, the *Europäische Revue*, *Europäische Gespräche* and *Paneuropa*. As a case study for Europeanization, it provides a valuable insight into an intellectual community whose ideal of cordiality – a Europe of the heart – was both a weakness and a strength, and whose influence was to be felt throughout the twentieth century. These intellectuals may not have built the Europe of their dreams (indeed no single idea of Europe emerges from the review), but they clearly contributed to an expansion of Europeanization in discourse and practice.

Such writers were concerned with the creation of Europe because they could see little evidence of genuine European collaboration and fraternity in the international politics of their times. *Europe* was founded against the inauspicious background of the *Bloc National* government in France and the military occupation of the Ruhr, and received none of the financial support accorded to its more patriotic counterparts. Indeed, the editor René Arcos was even refused a visa when he announced his intention to discuss the project with Romain Rolland in Switzerland, and was eventually obliged to cross the border clandestinely, and in heavy snow.[6] The new literary review was therefore intended as an expression of dissidence: a mirror held up to the aggression and cynicism of nationalist politics, and a suggestion of an 'other Europe' founded on moral authority and a network of intellectual exchanges and mass associations. *Europe* wanted to succeed where politicians and diplomats had failed, rejecting even the work of the League of Nations and the promises of President Wilson in its European mission.[7] Of necessity, its contributors recognized the importance of the boundaries resulting from the First World War, with Carlo Sforza ruefully observing that Europe had entered the war with 26 customs areas and 13 monetary systems, and emerged with 35 and 27 respectively (not to mention a further 6000 kilometres of customs barriers).[8] But such boundaries were perceived to be an unnatural and undesirable aspect of the European continent, and these intellectuals believed in tracing the contours of a more permanent and fraternal Europe, patterned not by customs barriers but by cultural associations. 'Frontiers may change,' wrote Duhamel in February 1923, 'nations may be made or unmade by arbitrary treaties. (...) But, stable as the geography of mountains and rivers, there is another geography: that of great men. They mark out space as they mark out time. One country is the land of Cervantes, another is the land of Dante. There is the century of Shakespeare and the century of Voltaire.'[9] Likewise, as Heinrich Mann insisted later the same year, 'It is in the minds of thinkers that Europe is most deeply alive, and they transmit this inheritance from generation to generation, even at times when most Europeans have almost forgotten the name of Europe.'[10]

From the beginning, the intellectuals of *Europe* considered it to be their duty to speak in the name of Europe, to further the ties between Europeans and their awareness of a common culture. They aimed to Europeanize both themselves and the peoples of the continent, and their contribution to Europeanization must therefore be seen as one of discourse and practice. Although these writers of *Europe* did not propound a single concept of Europe (the diverse articles, reviews, poems, and political commentaries in the periodical were rarely directed towards such a definition), some important common themes nonetheless emerge.

Essentially, Europe was portrayed as a continent, a civilization and a religion. Early issues of the review defined the continent as the single inheritance of its many peoples: editor René Arcos described it as the 'unique fatherland of the Indo-European race',[11] while Heinrich Mann identified Europe as a 'supreme state' demanding a supra-nationalist allegiance.[12] For Romain Rolland, European unity and fraternity should ideally prefigure a fraternity as broad as humanity itself.[13] Aspiring towards such ideals, the writers of *Europe* were nonetheless conscious of the cultural boundaries of their continent, as their articles on America and Asia demonstrate. Although there were a number of American contributors to the review, there were many more who criticized the increasing Americanization of Europe. Andrée Jouve, one of the few female writers in *Europe*, saw America as a terrifying mirror of the future towards which Europe appeared to be heading: a nation that scorned artisan crafts and European *joie de vivre* in order to promote capitalism and materialism.[14] Carlo Sforza observed that America had forged a defensive sense of European identity, and that a European returning from a prolonged visit to the United States would feel equally at home whether he landed at Cherbourg or at Genoa.[15] Writers in *Europe* were also conscious of a division between East and West, and between Europe and Asia. Divided in their interpretations of the Russian Revolution, they described Russia and the Orient as indubitably alien, not least in their relative neglect of the individual in favour of the collective.[16] Even writers such as Tivadar Raith, who recognized that European civilization had origins in the East, were concerned that the mentalities of East and West had become irreconcilable.[17]

Civilization was seen as an essential bond between Europeans, even if its past development had been furthered by coercive rather than cordial means. Luc Durtain described European civilization as, 'despite its lacunae, the supreme effort of the world',[18] while Georges Duhamel claimed to feel at home wherever this civilization was venerated.[19] Civilization was in their eyes the cumulative expression of intellectual and artistic achievement, but also of political, legal, judicial and religious structures and administration. The secular Jewish writer Jean-Richard Bloch thus described with wistful admiration the establishment of common European structures and practices: the *pax romana*, the unity of Christendom and of Islam, and even the unity forged by French revolutionary and Napoleonic imperialism.[20] Pierre Drieu la Rochelle, a future convert to fascism who wrote for *Europe* in its early years, was similarly nostalgic for the bond of religious unity between medieval Europeans.[21] 'Have we not sufficient energy to provide, as in the twelfth and thirteenth centuries, an effort towards universalism?' he demanded. 'Can we not embrace life as well as death?'[22]

Most fundamentally, indeed, the writers of *Europe* wanted Europe itself – their ideal of a cordial, fraternal continent and community – to become their new religion. 'Our faith is Europe', declared Heinrich Mann, 'and our salvation its unification.'[23] If these intellectuals saw themselves as moral authorities committed to the definition and realization of a new Europe, they also described themselves as evangelists, spreading the good news of a fraternity that would bring about final peace. Sceptical of the merits of coercion over cordiality, they imagined their role as one of teaching through word and example. Jean Guéhenno and Julien Benda therefore considered schoolteachers to be fundamental to the creation of a new Europe, and encouraged them to appeal to the imagination of their pupils with the history of great Europeans, and with more prosaic tales of the common experience of so-called 'enemies' in the First World War.[24]

This discourse on Europe as a continent, civilization, and religion was also a practical form of Europeanization. The practice of contributing to *Europe* and the common exchange of ideas within and around the review reinforced and extended a network of friendships on a European scale. Indeed, one of the most important precedents for the review was the European circle of friends who had met before the First World War for the monthly *Dîner des amis* in Paris, discussing German romanticism and French poetry, and picturing a new Europe amid debate, laughter and clouds of cigarette smoke.[25] After the war, many of the former participants in these monthly meetings were to become central to *Europe*'s foundation and development. Like other contemporary reviews with similar titles, *Europe* thus revived and sustained a European communication space, offering to writers unable to speak freely in their own countries the opportunity to disseminate their ideas of an 'other Europe' to a European – even world-wide – audience. As the ideal of European peace came increasingly under threat in the 1930s, *Europe* appeared, albeit briefly, as a reassuring fortress in the Republic of Letters. In April 1938, for example, the musicologist Wolf Franck reported to *Europe* that German and Austrian literary societies were defying political violence with a mutual concern to defend their common culture against the National-Socialist assault, hoping in this way to serve 'the cause of Europe'.[26] More broadly, *Europe* contributed to the creation and strengthening of intra-European ties by supporting literary societies such as the PEN association,[27] and anti-fascist organizations such as the CVIA (*Comité de Vigilance des Intellectuels Anti-Fascistes*), which sought to unite intellectuals and the masses in a common front.[28] In this way, the Europeanization promoted by *Europe* moved beyond the intellectual elite who read and contributed to the review to the citizens of Europe itself.[29]

The 'cordial geography' promoted by *Europe* was, of course, problematic. By the late 1930s there were increasing tensions between contributors to the review, and the violent imposition of a totalitarian vision of Europe seemed to leave little space – or justification – for their largely pacifist ideals. Increasingly French rather than European in character, the review was described by its new editor Jean Cassou in 1936 as devoted primarily to the rehabilitation of French thought and French glory. Before it ceased publication in 1939, a number of articles advised the defence of the nation and its literary traditions as the most effective bulwark against the imposition of a fascist 'monoculture',[30] and Europe was described more frequently as a tortured continent than as a fraternal ideal. Jean Guéhenno voiced a wide-spread anxiety when he began to wonder if the writer could not fight more effectively with a gun than with a pen. Yet, cordiality could be a strength as well as a weakness, and the history of *Europe, revue mensuelle* between the wars cannot be fully encompassed within a linear narrative of declining Europeanization. It was the apparent dearth of European fraternity in the political sphere that had provided the review with its initial impetus, and even the increasing focus on the nation in the later 1930s was, paradoxically, the only means by which these writers could safeguard their earlier vision of a composite, European civilization against an encroaching mono-culture. Some lost faith – even their lives – during the Second World War. Nonetheless, the contribution of these writers to Europeanization should not be judged only by its most immediate results. Georges Duhamel saw his works banned by the Gestapo, but in the post-war years he promoted inter-national cultural relations as president of the *Alliance Française*, with his moral authority – and ideal of cordiality – reinforced by their earlier decline.

The cordial geography of Europe seemed, indeed, to have a chronology of its own.

## The *Europäische Revue* and *Merkur*: A search for authority

While *Europe, revue mensuelle* was seeking a Europe of the heart, the German *Europäische Revue* was concurrently envisaging a Europe of the head, discerning a European elite whose authority would be social and political as well as moral and intellectual. Published from 1925 to 1944, the *Revue* was founded by Prinz Rohan – 'a scion of one of the most famous dynasties of European aristocrats'[31] – and attracted a readership of 7000.[32] It emerged from the *Europäische Kulturbund*, which Rohan had created in Vienna in 1922, and which also established centres in Paris, Milan, Frankfurt and Heidelberg between 1924 and 1926. Indeed, the *Kulturbund* became a network stretching from Portugal to the Baltic, with a 'membership list [that] (...) reads like a *Who's Who* of European celebrities'. Members included the mayors of Cologne and Hamburg Konrad Adenauer and Carl Peterson, the president of the *Allgemeine Elektrizitäts Gesellschaft* (AEG) Hermann Bücher, the jurist Carl Schmitt, the painter Max Bechmann, and the future Chancellor of Austria Ignaz Seipel. With annual meetings attended by 300 members, regular local meetings in more than fifty branches across Europe, and the *Europäische Revue* as its mouthpiece, the *Kulturbund* was 'the most important intellectual network on the continent' before its collapse in 1934.[33] Its influence continued in the post-war years through the periodical *Merkur: Deutsche Zeitschrift für Europäisches Denken*, to which a number of former members of the *Kulturbund* contributed.

The *Europäische Revue* may seem, at first sight, an unlikely space for the expression of intellectual dissidence. Indeed, the mainstream history of European discourse identifies European thought as emerging out of 'a spirit of resistance' associated with left-wing exiles from Nazi Germany.[34] Yet, an analysis of inter-war European discourse clearly reveals ideas of an 'other Europe' among right-wing dissidents as well, many of whom advocated an alternative to the Europe of nation-states and parliamentary democracies that was emerging from the Treaty of Versailles. Studying the *Europäische Revue* and the post-war *Merkur* in parallel to *Europe, revue mensuelle* demonstrates that European concerns were shared by dissidents of left and right alike, and also that these concerns continued to develop in the post-1945 years.

The prominence of the *Europäische Revue* among European elites, and its continued relevance after the Second World War, suggest that its Europeanist agenda spoke to the hopes and fears of a significant community of European intellectuals. European elites who had, before 1914, holidayed in each other's resorts, been educated in each other's intellectual centres, and conducted business across each other's borders, experienced the post-Versailles period as an era of de-Europeanization.[35] After 1918, continental populations appeared to have been segregated from each other within the newly created nation-states. There were specifically German causes for the discontent with the nation-state expressed in the journal: whereas the three-class franchise in Imperial Prussia had ensured aristocratic predomi-nance and made parliamentarianism palatable for the nobility, the Weimar Republic offered aristocrats no such privileges. Furthermore, reductions in the size of the German army after Versailles blocked a further career path for young nobles in Germany.[36] However, the *Europäische Revue* also echoed and responded to a widespread dissatisfaction with parliamen-tary democracy and a yearning for 'leadership' that was evident across Europe, and particularly pronounced in the Weimar and French Third Republics. The preponderance of anti-republican French authors suggests the *Revue*'s agenda was not perceived as significant only to Germans. Such authors included the future Vichy minister Lucien Romier, an advocate for the anti-parliamentarian *Redressement français* and the author of *Who Will be Master, Europe or America?*; Alfred Fabre-Luce, who also became active in the Vichy regime and was a supporter of Jacques Doriot's fascistic *Parti populaire français* (PPF); and Pierre Drieu La Rochelle, a PPF member and enthusiastic supporter of the Nazi occupation of northern France, and who later became the director of the *Nouvelle Revue Française*.[37] These authors joined forces with some of the most prominent anti-democrats in Germany and Austria in their role as contributors to the journal.

In response to the politicization of life and the crisis of authority in inter-war Europe, contributors to the *Europäische Revue* advocated a European polity led by a new aristocracy, transnational as the old version had been. While observing that 'the nobility, as a political class, is dead', Prinz Rohan appealed for a regeneration of the aristocracy, if only 'as an ethical community'.[38] When he discounted the return of a pre-democratic aristocracy, Rohan was stating a belief shared by the Central European nobility. Like writers for the *Deutsches Adelsblatt*, he recognized that the elite 'now want to be leader, not lord', and noted that the old word *Herrschaft* had disappeared from aristocratic publications after 1918, to be replaced by *Führung*.[39] In common with many members of the German aristocracy, Rohan therefore believed that the European aristocracy could rejuvenate itself by making transnational alliances with New Right movements such as Italian Fascism, which had in his view 'present[ed] the first successful counter-revolution since the French Revolution'.[40]

It may seem contradictory that Europeanists would look to such hyper-nationalist regimes as allies. However, as research by Arnd Bauerkämper (among others) has demonstrated, the nationalism of New Right regimes and their transnational connections were not contradictory but 'comple-mentary and even dialectical'. The subsidizing of minor fascist parties by Mussolini, along with exchanges between European fascists at all levels, and official conferences of European fascists such as the one held at

Montreux in 1934, suggest the pan-European dimensions of the New Right movement.[41]

Clearly the discourse of Europe in the *Europäische Revue* was pointedly dissident: its authors overwhelmingly supported a revision of the Treaty of Versailles and welcomed movements that threatened the integrity of pre-existing regimes in Europe.[42] And the dissident European discourse in the journal was by no means an isolated phenomenon: rather, it intersected with significant critical currents in European thought. When Rohan advocated the German *Anschluss* of Austria as a step towards European unity, for example, he was speaking for Austrians who 'strive[d] to return home to the greater Germany [*Grossdeutschland*], from which they had been excluded for the last 60 years'.[43] The former (and future) Austrian Chancellor, Ignaz Seipel, also expressed the widespread dissatisfaction with the status of Austria after 1871 and particularly after 1918. Writing in the *Europäische Revue* he explained that: 'We Austrians, perhaps, feel most keenly what it is like when a formerly great economic area is torn apart for political reasons'.[44] Even German left-liberals such as Karl Spiecker could advocate an *Anschluss* in the name of European peace, arguing that this would create a better Germany and check the influence of Prussian forces intent on revenge upon France and Italy.[45] Similarly, when Rohan denounced the creation of an Austrian crown by Metternich and a Berlin crown by Bismarck as revolutionary acts that had desacralized the *Kaiserkrone*,[46] he was echoing the beliefs of numerous south-western German aristocrats, who were, according to Graf Neipperg-Schwaigern of Bavaria, 'completely Holy Roman Empire–German Nation' in their mentality.[47] Thus, Europeanism functioned for many rightist German circles as a means of advocating a different kind of Germany to the post-Bismarckian nationalist (and thus de-Europeanized) version.

Echoing contemporary concerns in *Europe, revue mensuelle*, the *Europäische Revue* also addressed a widespread anxiety regarding Europe's place in the world order, confronted both by the United States' rapidly rising economic and military power and by the emergence of Soviet Russia. Oswald Spengler may have expressed this concern most starkly in his *Decline of the West*, but he was by no means an isolated prophet of doom.[48] Contributors to the *Europäische Revue* were well represented in the glut of works decrying the march of Americanism and Sovietism, with Lucien Romier's *Who Will be Master: Europe or America?* and Pierre Drieu La Rochelle's *Geneva or Moscow* being two particularly prominent examples.[49] Within the pages of the *Europäische Revue*, the liberal academic Alfred Weber positioned Europe in an ever-tighter space between 'the colossus of western civilization' and 'the second Leviathan, of the East'. The First World War had demonstrated the strengths of the Anglo-Saxon and Russian powers and, Weber believed, offered a vision of Europeans as either 'slaves of the East or West' or as living in 'a battleground between the two'. Heinz Ziegler commented that American leaders had supported a form of democratic nationalism that amputated European traditions and communities from one another. 'Wilson [was], as a result of his nation-state democratism, an enemy of international law (...) The consequences of the destruction of the Habsburg monarchy proves it.' What remained was 'the war between sovereign nations', which was, 'in principle, unending'.[50]

This complicated relationship between the United States and Europe was a significant theme in the post-1945 legacy of the *Europäische Revue*. The legacy was most evident in the journal *Merkur*, one of the very few cultural journals founded in the decade after 1945 that continues to thrive, and which attracted such contributors as Martin Heidegger, Theodor Adorno, Hannah Arendt, Jean-François Lyotard, and Ralf Dahrendorf. *Merkur: Deutsche Zeitschrift für Europäisches Denken* was founded in 1947 by Hans Paeschke and Joachim Moras (editor of the *Europäische Revue* between 1933 and 1944). Paeschke described its mission thus: 'it strives (...) for the (...) diversity that the *Europäische Revue* – unique among the German journals – possessed at the beginning and also never quite lost.'[51] Certainly it would be misleading to describe *Merkur* as simply a successor journal to the *Europäische Revue* as from the mid-1950s it became a more squarely liberal publication, even going on to support the student movements of the 1960s. Yet in its first decade the *Revue*'s influence is unmistakable.

*Merkur* relied not only on the *Europäische Revue* editor Joachim Moras, but also on other *Revue* contributors such as Jürgen von Kempski, Herbert von Borch, and Leopold Ziegler. Indeed *Merkur's* editor Hans Paeschke echoed the aspiration of the *Europäische Revue* to build a new European elite, urging that at 'the first meaningful European conversation after the war, the Geneva *Rencontres Internationales* of 1946, we were able to show (...) a new elite of European minds that was beginning to form (...) aware of the impurity of all existing ideologies [and] (...) beginning to think beyond these old opposi-tions.'[52] Although *Merkur* did not specifically advocate the cause of the old aristocracy, the editor's call for a new European elite certainly recalled the support among *Europäische Revue* writers for a new aristocracy. Furthermore, in spite of censorship, *Merkur* was marked by a scepticism towards democ-racy and nationalism that echoed the *Revue* agenda. Guglielmo Ferrero's inter-war writings were, for instance, used to discredit post-1918 forms of parliamentary democracy. He had, in stark terms, contended that: 'When the great monarchies of 1917 and 1918 fell, then the Idea that the peoples should rule themselves (...) which had been collecting (...) for 50 years like an explosive gas (...) caught fire. Everywhere, clever minorities have (...) foist[ed] democratic republics on the people, who were suddenly declared sovereign.'[53]

Again like the *Revue*, *Merkur* advanced a distinctively German case for European integration. It sought to represent the interests of Germans who had been marginalized by the Prussian-led unification of Germany, and advocated a form of European integration that would afford them a greater voice. Jürgen von Kempski argued, for example, that 'from the point of view of foreign policy, everything seems to indicate that an association of German states should take the most politically loose form possible. (...) Such a formation would be more conducive to a European federation, and would, in fact, be an incentive to create such a federation.' Equally importantly, southern Germans would regain the voice they had lost during the Bismarckian unification. 'It is important', claimed Kempski, 'that the [federal] question is decided not by the German people as a whole but rather by the *Länder*, and it is clear that the southern Germans, especially the Bavarians, want a federal state.' Kempski was not, however, anticipating the break-up of Germany but rather its reconfiguration. As he concluded: 'the federal solution is the only one that leaves room for the hope of German reunification'.[54]

The arguments put forward for European integration were, however, not merely proposals for Germans, by Germans. With regards to the increasing threat of American and Soviet dominance in Europe, *Merkur* represented a common European fear, expressed by a variety of Europeans such as the Swiss intellectuals Denis de Rougement and Gonzague de Reynold, the Austrian Franz Klein and the British journalist Henry Noel Brailsford.[55] Its authors conceived of European integration as a way of protecting European sovereignty from these emergent empires and expressed it largely in traditionalist terms strongly reminiscent of the *Europäische Revue*. As Leopold Ziegler (another former contributor to the *Revue*) insisted, it was necessary to establish an '*Imperium Europaeum*': a genuine '*Dritte Reich*' to follow the *Imperium Romanum* and the *Imperium Sacrum*, which would also be a Third Empire between the two empires of the East and West.[56]

These two journals provide evidence not of a European discourse following a linear trajectory but rather of an ebbing and flowing. The *Europäische Revue* was, unsurprisingly, most lively as an agent of Europeanization in the years before the National Socialist takeover. Although the journal depended chiefly on right-wing Germanic authors, the diversity of its contributors attests to its aspirations to be European and to transcend traditional ideological divides. Certainly, prominent Fascists from Italy such as Enrico Corradini and Giuseppe Bottai, as well as future collaborators from France such as Lucien Romier and Alfred Fabre-Luce, were well represented in its pages. But space was also created for those on the European left such as Ramsay MacDonald and Harold Laski, and for German liberals such as Alfred Weber and Karl Spiecker. After 1933, however, the journal bore traces of the National Socialist *Gleichschaltung*. The first issue in 1934 opened with Josef Goebbels' speech on 'National Socialist Germany as a factor in European peace', and continued with writings from leading Nazi functionaries. From this date onwards, contributions from foreign authors critical of German actions disappeared. Editorial freedom was further eroded in 1936 when control of the publication was handed over to the Nazi jurist Axel Freiherr von Freytagh-Loringhoven.[57]

The European discourse that developed in the *Europäische Revue* and re-emerged in the pages of *Merkur* was part of a remarkable efflorescence of the print media in Germany in the early post-war years. *Merkur* was joined by a number of other Europeanist journals such as *Die Wandlung, Der Ruf, Frankfurter Hefte*, and *Der Monat*, most of which achieved circulation figures in excess of 50 000 before the currency reform of 1948, after which they struggled to retain more than 10 000 subscribers.[58] The challenges faced by such ventures after the early post-war years were not, however, merely financial. The *Dritte Kraft* agenda animating most of these publications had promoted Europe as a non-aligned community of nations that could steer a middle path between Anglo-Saxon capitalism and Soviet totalitarian statism. Yet, this seemed increasingly implausible after the successful implementation of the Marshall Plan, the imposition of the Soviet Berlin Blockade, and the conclusion of the North Atlantic Treaty Organization (NATO) defence pact. While *Merkur* continued to bear witness to a European unity that cut across the Cold War divide, it became a journal of – and for – West Germany and Western Europe rather than a self-consciously Central European organ such as the *Europäische Revue*.

## The (re-)construction of European spaces: Eastern European dissidents in the 1970s

In bridging the divided Europe of the Cold War era, a particularly important role was played by the intellectual dissidents of Eastern Europe, and however banal the resurgence of the concept of 'Europe' may appear to us today, its relevance for these writers should not be underestimated. During the 1960s it had been virtually impossible for an Eastern European to refer to 'Europe' as a concept, for the East–West division of the continent had effectively blocked the representation of Europe and its history. 'Europe' – as defined by a shared culture and civilization – was a thing of the past that had seen its last florescence between 1918 and 1939, a period now viewed by ideologues in the Eastern bloc as politically discredited.[59] The numerous and multi-faceted events in Europe in 1968 and the reactions they elicited had, moreover, reinforced the conviction of Eastern European intellectuals that the continent was divided, and that its two halves were now living different histories. In 1975 the convention of European states in Helsinki thus marked the first step towards the return of 'Europe' as a concept. For the observer of current affairs, the Helsinki document cemented the treaties of Yalta and Potsdam, and consequently the division of Europe. Yet with a more long-term perspective, the Final Act of the Conference on Security and Co-operation in Europe also brought the concept of Europe as a common value back into the public eye, and this in itself represented a renewed sanctioning of a single, common, communication space.[60]

The impact of this conceptual shift was immediate. When considering European concepts developed by Eastern European dissidents in the wake of Helsinki, it is the writings of Milan Kundera and the essays of György Konrád in the 1980s that come most immediately to mind.[61] Yet these texts had been preceded in the 1970s by important efforts to rethink an apparently moribund concept of Europe, and to devise a new framework of reference more suited to current concerns. In his Nobel Prize lecture of 1975, the Lithuanian human rights activist Andrei Sakharov responded to the Helsinki Conference by promoting the idea of Europe as a single geographical space within which Europeans should be free to travel, unhindered by Soviet restrictions. 'You all know, even better than I do', he addressed his audience, 'that children from Denmark, for example, can get on their bicycles and cycle off to the Adriatic. No one would even think of suggesting that they were "teenage spies".'[62] At the same time, images of Europe were frequently constructed in articles by Polish intellectuals in underground journals, such as those by Adam Michnik in *Puls*.[63] Similarly, the editorial of the quarterly *Res Publica* (published in Warsaw from 1979 to 1981) declared that the periodical would focus on official and unofficial culture both in Poland and also in the Polish emigrant community, promoting its survival and development in close association with Europe and the world of Christian culture, 'because Europe is, *in a wider sense, our home*'.[64]

To reconstruct a European space, it was necessary both to re-imagine Europe as a concept and also to establish a network of European contacts and dialogues. Re-imagining Europe demanded a reconsideration of national identity and allegiance; and the question of national identity within a European framework was consequently central to the debates of all dissident groups. The nature and state of Europe figured prominently in the discussions of the various Helsinki groups in Russia and the Baltic Soviet Republics, as well as in *Charta 77*[65] and in Polish dissident groups such as the workers' defence committee KOR (*Komitet Obrony Robotnikow*). Here, in both internal and semi-public debates, as well as in the dissidents' samizdat publications,[66] the decisions made at Yalta and the self-experienced deconstruction of Europe became issues of vital importance. For Eastern Europeans, 'Europe' emerged as a counterpoint to the Soviet Empire, a concept which gained further impetus in the 1980s as the dream of 'Europeanization' became linked to the desire for a return to 'normalcy' after many years of Socialist domination.[67]

The imagined relationship between Europe and the nation varied according to national context, and there were sharp differences between Polish and East German experiences. The 1976 Polish opposition group *Polskie Porozumienie Niepodległościowe* (Polish League for Independence/PPN) developed an early vision of a free Poland within a free Europe, the latter being conceived outside the Soviet Empire. After extensive debate, the dissident group published

*Polska a Niemcy* (Poles and Germans) in late 1977, in which the Polish struggle for independence was linked to a European level of action. What was new was the PPN's explicit criticism of 'rigid either-or categories' that made Europe's future dependent on the existence of the Soviet Empire.[68] In the authors' opinion, increasing European integration would make the existence of a united and Europeanized Germany possible. The text states:

> If this reunification clearly takes place within the context of European unification, and if the territory of the current GDR is integrated within a federal Europe and not merely within the German Federal Republic, thus strengthening the European community as a whole rather than merely one of its member states, then Polish resistance could subside. German reunification within the framework of the European Community would result in Poland's gaining direct contact with the West, with which it is already linked through tradition and contemporary culture, and would also bring an opportunity to co-operate with the European Community – and so, ultimately, the prospect of a real choice between alliances and economic communities.[69]

Such opposition was not yet characteristic of dissidence within the Czechoslovak Socialist Republic (CSSR) in the late 1970s, where other topics were of greater relevance. Equally, the topic remained too sensitive for discussion by East German opposition circles in that it was inextricably linked to the question of German reunification, which most East German civil-rights activists preferred not to address. Not only did they doubt the possibility of a successful solution, but they also eschewed such discussions for fear of being labelled nationalistic or revanchist.[70]

Linked to the representation of Europe as a single space was the active development of networks of communication and exchange within a European framework – and Eastern Europeans were particularly concerned to emphasize the limited and asymmetrical nature of communication across the continent. Creating and defending such networks was by no means straightforward. Only those privileged enough to travel outside the Eastern bloc could broaden their horizons sufficiently to see beyond the confines of Socialist society, and figures such as Zdzisław Najder, Vladimir Bukowski, Milan Kundera, and Tomas Venclova were not only subjected to massive defamation by the governments of their native countries and in some cases even persecuted abroad, but were also branded as 'deserters' by numerous intellectuals.[71] In retrospect, however, it is clear that their familiarity with both worlds gave them the necessary intellectual force and expertise to initiate and fuel desperately needed debate. Their experiences also enabled them to establish and expand the lines of communication between exiles and their supporters (one of the most prominent of these figures was Karol Wojtyła, the future Pope John Paul II).[72] In addition to such direct interaction, there was a considerable amount of cross-influencing of a more indirect nature, as any kind of non-conformist or oppositional behaviour was immediately picked up by the highly sensitive 'radar' of those living under Socialism. One aspect of this acutely honed awareness was the fact that language barriers were practically non-existent. Many involved in the civil rights movement learned Czechoslovak, Polish or Hungarian in order to read samizdat publications or to communicate with political associates in other countries. Publications were also translated in order to communicate shared concerns across linguistic borders: one example being Lithuania's most important underground periodical, *Chronicle of the Lithuanian Catholic Church*, which was published in both Lithuanian and Russian from the outset.[73]

This process of Europeanization reveals a number of common strategies, notably personal contacts, symbolic visits, statements of solidarity, and protest declarations. Dissident organizations endeavoured to publish increasingly in the foreign press and to hold press conferences, and a popular tactic was to invite guest professors from Western Europe to attend lectures given in underground adult education courses (a method employed by *Charta 77*).[74] Dissidents also pursued official contacts with politicians in the hope of winning their support – although in this case there was a distinct difference in practice between Poland and Czechoslovakia on the one hand, and the Soviet Union on the other. Dissidents in the former contacted politicians in Western Europe: in 1976, for example, Jacek Kuroń wrote an open letter to the Italian politician Enrico Berlinguer,[75] and in March 1977 the Minister of Foreign Affairs in the Netherlands (Max van der Stoel) attended an official meeting with Jan Patočka, the spokesman for *Charta 77*. Meanwhile, dissidents in the Soviet Union relied less heavily on Europe and more on the United States. Jimmy Carter sent a telegram to Anatoli Sharansky in October 1976, and the first press conference of the Lithuanian Helsinki group was held in the apartment of a Moscow dissident in December the same year.[76]

A further example of the judicious utilization of personal contacts was the trip to Vilnius by Andrei Sakharov in December 1975 to follow the trial of the Lithuanian dissident Sergei Kovaliov.[77] Since Sakharov had recently been awarded the Nobel Peace Prize but not been granted a travel permit to attend the award ceremony, he was a centre of attention for the entire Western press, and took advantage of this media interest to gain publicity for his Lithuanian 'colleague'.[78] Polish–Czechoslovak contacts were also significant, and members of KOR and *Charta 77* – including Adam Michnik, Jacek Kuroń, and Václav Havel, among others – met in 1978 in the mountainous area bordering both states. Contacts were also maintained between Hungary and Poland: the planned visit to Poland by György Benes and four other Hungarian dissidents (whose passports were confiscated at Budapest airport on 27 August 1980, while negotiations were taking place with *Solidarność* in Danzig) being one such example.[79]

Declarations of solidarity with foreign groups and movements were also essential 'interfaces' in the recreation of a European space. These may appear marginal today, but in the 1970s it was a courageous step to generate publicity both for one's own group – the undersigning group – and for the group to be supported; courageous to sympathize openly with political and social activism, and to vouch with one's name for non-conformist beliefs when such activity was generally countered with state repression. The number of drafted declarations of solidarity for foreign groups also demonstrates that there was a striking awareness of transnational values at this time. Particular examples are the support of Romanian intellectuals for the writer Paul Goma,[80] the activity of the Polish KOR, and the explicit support of the Helsinki Group for Lech Wałęsa and *Solidarność* in 1980.[81] The joint signing of appeals for solidarity with foreign movements frequently had a 'feedback' effect as well, triggering the formation of a new group 'at home'. Many civil-rights activists took a decidedly transnational view; there was a sense of sharing the same experiences, and an acute awareness that the Eastern bloc had a common destiny. As Hungarian dissidents insisted in a statement to *Charta 77* in 1977, 'We are convinced that the defence of human and civil rights is a common concern of all Eastern Europe'.[82] Even sarcastic jokes, such as references to the differences between the 'barracks in the Socialist camp', reflect a transnational perspective.

A considerable number of protest declarations were also sent by various groups to the governments of other Eastern bloc states. Important examples include the letter from the Lithuanian Helsinki Group to the government of the CSSR in 1979, in which the group denounced the repeated violation of human rights,[83] and Sakharov's appeal in the same year on the occasion of the sentencing of members of *Charta 77*. Occasionally there were also 'copycat' actions. The demonstrations by Estonian student in Tallinn and Tartu in 1980 and the strike in Tartu on 1 October 1980 were, for instance, directly connected to developments in Poland and to the founding of *Solidarność*,[84] as was the pamphlet issued by the outlawed Latvian Social Democratic Party on 1 May 1981.

The cumulative effect of dissident dialogue and activity was to reform a communication space on a European scale. With the easing of travel restrictions after 1975 as a result of superpower *détente*, the imbalance in communication between East and West gradually diminished, and new networks began to form. Governments in the Eastern Bloc even contributed to this process, typically by offering Western European scholarships for research abroad that allowed potential civil-rights activists to travel more frequently. (The objective was not altruistic, but rather to disconnect brilliant thinkers from emerging political groups, thus stopping nascent social movements in their tracks).[85] This increasing participation of Eastern Europeans in a Western context led to the emergence of a new European society. At first this fell far short of the hopes of friends and compatriots in Eastern Bloc countries, and there was indeed some stagnation in these intellectual processes in the 1980s, particularly with the deployment of troops and the imposition of martial law in Poland. But we now know that the changes that occurred were frequently of much vaster and more lasting significance than was once predicted.[86]

## Conclusions

The meaning and impact of 'dream-Europes' within the broader process of Europeanization should certainly be viewed with a long-term perspective. As this chapter demonstrates, the construction of European spaces by intellectual dissidents can take place on a number of different levels: as a reaction to specific international tensions and with pointed political engagement, but also in deliberate rejection of contemporary power structures and with a broader, more consciously apolitical desire to map out utopian European communities of the past or future. The influence of these intellectual constructions may be explicit within their own networks of communication, but it may also be implicit, radiating through wider circles of readership or solidarity with effects not necessarily realized or visible as an immediate consequence.

This chapter reveals both continuity and change in intellectual preoccupations with Europe during the twentieth century. Three particular concerns emerge through these chronological case studies: an anxiety regarding Europe's place in the world order, a search for European authority, and a determination to preserve Europe as a space of conviviality and communication, regardless of its fragmented political reality. Though working in different contexts, the intellectual dissidents described in these studies shared a deeply felt concern at the prospect of a decline in European influence and power (whether political or intellectual), and were committed to the defence of a specifically European space between the invasive empires of the United States and Soviet Russia. They were concerned, sometimes explicitly, with the realization of a third Empire to succeed the Roman and Holy Roman Empires, and with a European internationalism to combat the visions for world order proposed by Anglo-Saxon or Russian powers. They were, in short, concerned with the problem of European authority – for how could such a sphere of European control and influence be realized without a political and moral authority to define values, boundaries, and aspirations?

Dissident writers were equally conscious of their own role in the creation and regulation of this European space. For the intellectuals of *Europe, revue mensuelle*, these preoccupations were expressed through the image of Europe as a geography of the mind and heart, and as a utopian, fraternal community with an almost numinous dimension. For the elites writing in the *Europäische Revue* and subsequently in *Merkur*, the solution to the problem of Europe lay in the regeneration of a European aristocracy, offering a guidance that would be moral and intellectual, but also political and social, restoring to Europe the strength and structure necessary to the maintenance of a European Empire between its American and Russian counterparts. For the dissidents in Eastern Europe in the 1970s, caught in the midst of this imperial rivalry, the realization of Europe required the identification of a single geography and communication space outside Soviet control, the assertion of rival, transnational values in support of civil and human rights, and the voicing of an alternative moral authority to that of the USSR.

Mental maps were of central importance to these intellectual dissidents: images of Europe that projected ideals of unity and authority in reaction to contemporary divisions. But the physical geography of the continent was also significant. For both Georges Duhamel and Andrei Sakharov, European peace and fraternity were symbolized by young people travelling across the continent on foot or on bicycle, exploring the geography of the continent as they crossed its political boundaries. Physical and cordial geographies were thus closely interrelated. The crossing of political boundaries was also important for other Eastern European dissidents, whether this involved the invitation of Western professors to participate in clandestine educational courses, or, latterly, travel to the West for the purpose of study with the apparent encouragement of government authorities. Even impediments to travel could serve to highlight the desirability of free movement and communication between Europeans, and to promote a strengthening of European understanding and allegiance: the publicity generated by the refusal to authorize Sakharov's journey to receive his Nobel Peace Prize is one such example.

Through such publicity, as well as through circles of readership and wider networks of support, these intellectual dissidents succeeded in making some of their projected authority a reality. This was perhaps a by-product in the pursuit of unrealized 'dream-Europes', but it was nonetheless an important contribution to the uneven process of Europeanization. The *Europäische Revue* sustained a readership of 7000, the post-war *Merkur* achieved nearly 50 000 readers, and both gave expression to social groups that felt otherwise deprived of a political voice. *Europe, revue mensuelle* and the Eastern European dissidents forged connections with wider political groups, from the anti-fascist organizations of the 1930s to human and civil-rights associations and Polish *Solidarnos´c´* in the 1970s and 1980s. By offering forums for the expression of alternative visions of Europe, intellectual groups and periodicals encouraged the development of intra-European ties and transnational values.

To discern a clear rise and fall of Europeanization in this period is by no means straightforward. Eastern European dissidents of the 1970s identified the inter-war years as a period when the idea of Europe flourished, and perceived their own time as one lacking in Europeanization – yet this was not necessarily the experience of those writers active in the 1920s and 1930s. Indeed, contributors to *Europe, revue mensuelle* and the *Europäische Revue* committed themselves to the creation of European spaces precisely because these spaces appeared to be particularly under threat. Writers in *Europe, revue mensuelle* even referred nostalgically to the *Dîners des amis* before 1914 as a time of greater freedom of communication on a European level. While cultural Europeanization could be described as rising in the 1920s and 1930s, briefly flourishing after 1945, and then re-emerging in conscious opposition to Cold War divisions in the 1970s and 1980s, this would not fully represent the lived experience of those involved in these processes. 'Dream-Europes' have an ability to flourish even when they appear to be least justified by the pattern of European development.

## Notes

* The authors gratefully acknowledge the valuable advice offered by other members of the network, as well as by Antonella Romano at the European Institute in Florence, during the preparation of this chapter.

1. Julien Benda, *La Trahison des clercs* (Paris, 1927), 'Discours à la nation européenne' (Paris, 1933), and *Deux Croisades pour la paix: juridique et sentimentale* (Brussels, 1948). Benda was here responding to the *Rencontres Internationales* held in Geneva in 1946.

2. As the introduction to this volume has emphasized, studies of Europeanization as a concept and process have often neglected its cultural aspect. The most widely cited definitions of Europeanization – notably those of Claudio Radaelli – define the process as the construction, diffusion, and institutionalization of discourses, policies, rules, and procedures, particularly in the post-1945 period and in the European Union. There is a growing recognition that Europeanization is cultural as well as political and economic, but this has received limited attention. Some recent analyses recommend the consideration of 'ideas and interests' as well as institutions and policies, while studies of the EU accession states of 2004 have described the experience of Europeanization as an adaptation to European values. Yet cultural studies of European-spirited intellectuals in the twentieth century have often paid little explicit attention to the concept of 'Europeanization' (Robert Bartlett's consideration of the 'Europeanization of Europe' in the middle ages could serve as an excellent template for such research), and much therefore remains to be explored. See Claudio Radaelli, 'Whither Europeanisation? Concept stretching and substantive change', *European Integration Online Papers* (EIoP) 4.8 (2000); Kevin Featherstone, 'In the name of Europe' in Kevin Featherstone and Claudio Radaelli, *The Politics of Europeanization* (Oxford, 2003); Martin Brusis, 'European Union enlargement and the Europeanisation of Eastern Europe: research and policy issues' in Zdenka Mansfeldová and Vera Sparschuh (eds), *Patterns of Europeanisation in Central and Eastern Europe* (Hamburg, 2005), and Robert Bartlett, *The Making of Europe: Conquest, Colonisation and Cultural Change, 950–1350* (London, 1993), especially Chapter 11.

3. Georges Duhamel, *La Géographie cordiale de l'Europe* (Paris, 1931).

4. Georges Duhamel, 'Anniversaire', *Europe, revue mensuelle* (hereafter *Europe*), 15 July 1934. For further discussion of the role of *Europe* in creating Europeans, see Jessica Wardhaugh, 'Europäer erschaffen: die Rolle der Zeitschrift *Europe – Revue Mensuelle*, 1923–1939' in Kiran Patel et al. (eds), *Der Europäer – ein Konstrukt. Wissenbestände, Diskurse, Praktiken* (Göttingen, 2009), pp. 97–117.

5. *Europe, revue mensuelle* was published by Rieder, and subsequently by Denoël, in the inter-war years, and was revived in 1945 as *Europe, revue littéraire mensuelle*. In the inter-war period the review was, for a literary periodical, widely read – there were 2000 subscribers by 1929, compared with 2500 for the *Nouvelle Revue Française*. Its intellectual importance has therefore been much discussed, although its ideas of Europe have received relatively little attention. See Nicole Racine and Michel Trebitsch, 'Dossier: la revue *Europe'*, *Lendemains* 86–7 (1997), 93–107, Nicole Racine, 'La Revue *Europe* et le pacifisme des années vingt' in Maurice Vaïsse (ed.), *Le Pacifisme en Europe des années 1920 aux années 1950* (Brussels, 1993), pp. 51–69, and Nicole Racine, 'La Revue *Europe* et l'Allemagne, 1929–36' in Hans Manfred Bock, Reinhart Mayer-Kalkus and Michel Trebitsch (eds), *Entre Locarno et Vichy: les relations culturelles franco–allemandes dans les années 1930* (Paris, 1993), pp. 631–58.
6. Joseph Kvapil, *Romain Rolland et les Amis d'Europe* (Prague, 1971), p. 88.
7. Maxime Leroy, 'La Société Professionnelle des Nations', *Europe*, 15 June 1924, and Stefan Zweig, 'Le Visage énigmatique de Wilson', *Europe*, 15 April 1924.
8. Carlo Sforza, 'l'Avenir de l'Europe', *Europe*, 15 January 1937.
9. Georges Duhamel, 'Mission du poète', *Europe*, 15 February 1923.
10. Heinrich Mann, 'L'Europe, état suprême', *Europe*, 15 July 1923.
11. René Arcos, 'Patrie européenne', *Europe*, 15 February 1923. This article also formed the basis for the speech that Arcos gave at the Peace Conference in Wiesbaden, reprinted as 'Quelques Paroles de paix' in *Europe*, 15 September 1924.
12. Mann, 'L'Europe, état suprême'.
13. Romain Rolland, 'Une Réunion internationale d'écrivains à Londres', *Europe*, 15 June 1923.
14. Andrée Jouve, 'Notes sur l'Amérique', *Europe*, 15 October 1924. Georges Duhamel was to echo these sentiments in his anti-American diatribe, *Scènes de la vie future* (Paris, 1930). On the effects of such comparisons on French self-perception, see Jackie Clarke, 'France, America, and the Metanarrative of Modernisation: from post-war social science to the new culturalism', *Contemporary French and Francophone Studies* VIII No. 4 (2004), 365–77.
15. Sforza, 'Avenir de l'Europe'.
16. Elie Faure, 'Les Trois Miracles', *Europe*, 15 February 1928.
17. Tivadar Raith, 'L'Europe occidentale, terra incognita', *Europe*, 15 July 1926.
18. Durtain, 'Fritz von Unruh'.
19. Duhamel, *Géographie cordiale*, p. 80.
20. Jean-Richard Bloch, 'L'Unité du monde', *Europe*, 15 March 1932.
21. Pierre Drieu la Rochelle, *Le Jeune Européen* (Paris, 1927), p. 103.
22. Drieu la Rochelle, *Le Jeune Européen*, pp. 201–2. On the paradoxical penchant for action rather than reflection among such right-wing intellectuals, see Pascal Balmand, 'L'Anti-intellectualisme dans la culture politique française', *Vingtième siècle* XXXVI No. 4 (1992), 31–42.
23. Mann, 'L'Europe, état suprême'.
24. Jean Guéhenno, 'Notes de lecture: réflexions sur Europe', *Europe*, 15 May 1933, and Benda, *Deux croisades*. On Guéhenno's utopianism, see Jessica Wardhaugh, *In Pursuit of the People: Political Culture in France, 1934–39* (Basingstoke, 2009), pp. 25–6.
25. The *Dîners* were vividly described by Luc Durtain in his article 'Fritz von Unruh et l'esprit européen', *Europe*, 15 November. On the particular importance of Paris as a focal point for European intellectuals, see Michel Trebitsch, 'Paris, "capital

culturelle" de l'Europe centrale?', *Vingtième siècle, revue d'histoire* XLVII No. 3 (1995), 201–5.

26. Wolf Franck, 'Questions allemandes', *Europe*, 15 April 1938.

27. The PEN (poets, playwrights, essayists and novelists) association was founded in London in 1921 by the novelist, playwright, and future Nobel Prize winner John Galsworthy.

28. On the importance of intellectuals in the anti-fascist Popular Front in France, see Stéphane Courtois, 'Les intellectuels et l'antifascisme' in Jean-Paul Rioux (ed.), *Le Front Populaire* (Paris, 2006), pp. 41–6.

29. Practical solidarity between Europeans had also been encouraged by the review in the 1920s, when Romain Rolland issued appeals for direct donations for those suffering from hunger in German cities. See *Europe*, 15 January 1924.

30. Louis Aragon, 'Nouvelles du vaste monde, réunies par l'Association Internationale des Écrivains pour la Défense de la Culture,' *Europe*, 15 August 1938.

31. Guido Müller, 'France and Germany after the Great War: Businessmen, Intellectuals, and Artists in Nongovernmental European Networks' in Jessica Gienow-Hecht and Frank Schumacher (eds), *Culture and International History*, (New York and Oxford, 2003), p. 103.

32. According to Hans Paeschke's estimates in a letter to Ernst Robert Curtius on 30 July 1948 in 'D: Merkur: Briefe von ihm an Curtius, 1946–1949', (Deutsches Literaturarchiv, Marbach, hereafter DLA).

33. Müller, 'European Networks' in Gienow-Hecht, *Culture and International History*, pp. 103–4.

34. For instance, Frank Niess, *Die Europäische Idee – aus dem Geist des Widerstands* (Frankfurt am Main, 2001).

35. Ute Frevert, 'Europeanizing Germany's Twentieth Century', *History and Memory* XVII (2005), pp. 92–3.

36. Stephan Malinowski, *Vom König zum Führer. Deutscher Adel und Nationalsozialismus* (Frankfurt am Main, 2004), p. 201.

37. See Julian Jackson, *France: The Dark Years 1940–1944* (Oxford, 2001), pp. 53, 78, and 205.

38. Karl Anton Rohan, 'Adel', *Europäische Revue* (hereafter *ER*), 2.1 (April–September 1928), pp. 19–20.

39. Malinowski, *König zum Führer*, p. 116.

40. Rohan, *ER* 8.11 (November 1932), p. 666 and 'Fascismus und Europa', *ER* 2.1 (January–June 1926), p. 122.

41. Arnd Bauerkämper, 'Ambiguities of Transnationalism: Fascism in Europe between Pan-Europeanism and Ultra-Nationalism, 1919–39' in *German Historical Institute London Bulletin* XXIX No. 2 (November 2007), 44, 53–4, 56, and 58.

42. See for instance Alfred Fabre-Luce, 'Frankreichs Politik gegenüber Deutschland', *ER* 1.1, pp. 152–4 and Otto Hoetzsch, 'Von der Deutschen Rechtsbewegung, von Deutsch–Französischer Aussenpolitik, und von Europäischer Verständigung', *ER* 1.1, pp. 214–17.

43. Rohan, 'Zukunftsfragen deutscher Aussenpolitik', *ER* 5.6 (September 1929), p. 375.

44. Ignaz Seipel, 'Wege zum Frieden', *ER* 1.1, p. 4.

45. Karl Spiecker, 'Österreichs Anschluss an Deutschland', *ER* 1.2 (January–June 1926), p. 100.

46. Rohan, 'Vom Mythos der Totalen Nation im Dritten Reich', *ER* 9.4 (April 1933), p. 195.

47. Letter of September 1928, cited in Malinowski, *König zum Führer*, p. 256.

48. Oswald Spengler, *Der Untergang des Abendlandes. Umrisse einer Morphologie der Weltgeschichte*, (Munich, 17th ed., 2006).
49. See also Margaret Beale, *The Modernist Enterprise: French Elites and the Threat of Modernity 1901–40* (Stanford, 1999).
50. Heinz Ziegler, 'Nation und Politik', *ER* 2.7 (October 1926), p. 41.
51. Paeschke to Ernst Robert Curtius, 17 August 1947, 'D: Merkur. Briefe von ihm an Ernst Robert Curtius, 1946–49' (DLA).
52. Paeschke, *Retrospective of 1949*, p. 4, and 'A: Merkur: TNL Paeschke'.
53. Guglielmo Ferrero, 'Die legitime Demokratie', *Merkur* 6.1 (1947–48), pp. 803–4.
54. Jürgen von Kempski, 'Föderalismus und Unitarismus', *Merkur* 6.1 (1947–48), p. 819.
55. See Denis de Rougemont, 'Die Krankheiten Europas', *Merkur* 6.1 (1947), pp. 18–25; Gonzague de Reynold, 'Was ist Europa?', *Merkur* 7.2 (1948), pp. 121–4; Robert Ingram (Franz Klein), 'Amerikas Europäische Politik', *Merkur* 9.1 (January 1950), pp. 2–12.
56. Leopold Ziegler, 'Imperium Europa', *Merkur* (1948), p. 117.
57. Hans Manfred Bock, 'Das "Junge Europa", das "Andere Europa" und das "Europa der weissen Rasse". Diskurstypen in der *Europäische Revue* 1925–39', in Michel Grunewald and Hans Manfred Bock (eds), *Der Europadiskurs in den Deutschen Zeitschriften (1933–39)*, (Bern, 1999), pp. 324–5.
58. See Grunewald and Bock (eds), *Der Europadiskurs in den deutschen Zeitschriften*, and John Spalek, Konrad Feilchenfeldt and Sandra Hawrylchak, *Deutschsprachige Exilliteratur seit 1933, Band 3, USA, Teil 3* (Bern and Munich, 2002).
59. See also *Res Publica* 2 (1979).
60. To evaluate the significance of this turning point, it is also necessary to consider the nature and form of the repressive domestic policies introduced by Eastern bloc governments in the 1970s to counter the resolutions of the CSCE. Particularly important in this context are the 1976 amendment of the Polish constitution and the ensuing protests. See Andrei Sakharov's discussion of the Helsinki Conference and its consequences in his Nobel Prize Lecture, 'Frieden-Fortschritt-Menschenrechte', in Andrei D. Sakharov and Ute Baum, *Andrei Sakharov* (Leipzig, 1991), pp. 41–55, here p. 49.
61. Milan Kundera, 'Un occident kidnappé oder die Tragödie Zentraleuropas' (1983). http://www.europa.clio-online.de/DesktopModules/VlibArticles/ArticlesView.asp x?tabID=40208281&alias=europa.clio-online&lang=de&ItemID=87&mid=11373 (accessed on 15 November 2009), and György Konrád, *Antipolitik. Mitteleuropäische Mediationen* (Frankfurt am Main, 1985).
62. Sakharov, 'Frieden-Fortschritt-Menschenrechte', in Sakharov, *Andrei Sakharov*, pp. 41–55, here p. 49.
63. Adam Michnik, 'Intelektualis´ci i komunizm w polsce po 1945 roku', *Puls* (1978), pp. 4–5.
64. Marta Fik, *Kulturs Polska po Jałcie. Kronika lat 1944–81* (London, 1989), p. 633 (emphasis in original).
65. *Charta 77* was the title of a petition published in January 1977 to protest against the violation of human rights by the Communist regime in the Czechoslovak Socialist Republic (CSSR), and was also the name of the resulting civil-rights movement.
66. Samizdat literature (from the Russian for 'self-publisher') was non-conformist and unofficially distributed.
67. Tony Judt, *Geschichte Europas von 1945 bis zur Gegenwart* (Munich, 2006), p. 656. Kundera's essay may have been influential in this context, but similar discussions were taking place concurrently in the Soviet Union.

68. For example, Xaver Mooshütter, 'Polens Nachbar im Westen: Deutschland', *Osteuropa* 29 (February 1979), pp. 137–46, here p. 145.
69. 'Polen und Deutschland. Gedanken polnischer Oppositioneller zur deutschen Wiedervereinigung', *Osteuropa* 29 (February 1979), pp. A101–5, here p. A104.
70. See also Basil Kerski, *Die Rolle nichtstaatlicher Akteure in den polnisch-deutschen Beziehungen vor 1990* (Berlin, 1999), p. 31.
71. Judt, *Geschichte Europas von 1945*, p. 656.
72. Philipp Ther, 'Milan Kundera und die Renaissance Zentraleuropas', *Themenportal Europäische Geschichte* (2007), URL: http://www.europa.clio-online.de/2007/Article=153 (accessed on 15 November 2009).
73. Eitan Finkelshtein, 'Old hopes and new currents in present-day Lithuania', *Lituanus. Lithuanian Quarterly Journal of Arts and Sciences* XXIII No. 3 (1977), 47–58.
74. Barbara J. Falk, *The Dilemmas of Dissidence in East–Central Europe: Citizen Intellectuals and Philosopher Kings* (Budapest, 2003), pp. 92–3.
75. *Liberation*, 28 July 1976.
76. *Lietuvos Helsinkio grupė* (Vilnius, 1999), p. 620.
77. Andrei Sakharov, *Furcht und Hoffnung. Neue Schriften bis Gorki 1980* (Vienna, 1980), p. 37.
78. It was this visit that laid the foundation for the special relationship between the Baltic and Russian civil-rights movements, which was to continue for many years.
79. Falk, *The Dilemmas of Dissidence*, p. 128.
80. Judt, *Geschichte Europas von 1945*, p. 659.
81. Thomas Remeikis, 'Dissent in the Baltic Republics. A Balance Sheet', *Lituanus* XXX No. 2 (1984), 5–25.
82. Quoted in RFE Report, 'Thirty Hungarian intellectuals express solidarity with Charter 77' (Munich, 20 January 1977), and György Dalos, *Archipel Gulasch. Die Entstehung der demokratischen Opposition in Ungarn* (Bremen, 1986).
83. 'Protestas Čekoslovakijos vyriausybei dėl žmogaus teisių pažeidimų, 17 November 1979', *Lietuvos Helsinkio grupė* (Vilnius, 1999), pp. 46–7.
84. Remeikis, 'Dissent in the Baltic Republics'.
85. Dalos, *Archipel Gulasch*, p. 34.
86. It is not possible to provide full details here on the comparative development of civil-rights movements or on their opportunities to harness foreign media for their own causes. A few examples should, however, be mentioned, not least the Paris-based exile newspaper *Kultura*, the radio station Radio Free Europe, and Hamburg's *Der Spiegel*. Radio Free Europe was founded in 1950 by the National Committee for a Free Europe (based in Munich), and Radio Liberty was established in 1964 by the American Committee for the Liberation of the Peoples of Russia, headquartered in the German city of Lampertsheim and associated with Radio Free Europe from 1973 onwards. These two radio stations gave nightly broadcasts and served as important disseminators of information, thus projecting the vision of a common European space.

# 2
# 'A Struggle for European Civilization': T.S. Eliot and British Conceptions of Europe during and after the Second World War

*José Harris*

## I

Contemporary perceptions and imaginative portrayals of Great Britain's role in the Second World War often interpreted it as a defence, not just of particular 'British' interests, nor of 'universalist' values against fascist tyranny (though both of these were recurrent themes), but as representing an intermediate position, loosely depicted as a 'struggle for European civilization'.[1] Such disparate figures as Winston Churchill, T.S. Eliot, Bishop Bell of Chichester, Cyril Connolly, Julian Huxley, Harold Laski and J.M. Keynes, all talked of 'European civilization' in order to conjure up a picture, not just of specific war aims, but of a much more intangible commitment to a certain kind of social, political, religious and philosophical 'culture', embodied in the cumulative experience of two thousand years of European history. A conception of Europe, past, present and future, was invoked to describe 'not just a geographical or economic entity' but 'a system of beliefs and ideas, an outlook, a culture, a way of life'.[2] Such a vision of Europe and its history was often portrayed at the time, not just as a good in itself, but as a stark antithesis both to the nationalist and ethnic 'separatism' artificially created by the Treaty of Versailles, and more recently to the mechanistic 'uniformity' being forcibly imposed on conquered territories by the 'New European Order' of Adolf Hitler. This alternative vision, of Europe as the cradle of shared civilized values, was seen by some as a vision waiting to be fully realized only in a post-war future; but to others it appeared as a way of life and a set of religious, moral and humanistic ideas that needed to be resuscitated from the more distant past.[3]

From the historian's perspective, however, this 'Europeanist' vantage-point and its relation to a wider understanding of the mid-twentieth-century epoch poses a number of problems. Not least among these is the question of whether the earlier history of 'European civilization' had really been quite

44

so distinctive, coherent, and free from Hitlerite tendencies as some of the pro-Europeanist rhetoric seemed to imply: a note of scepticism that was sounded early on in the war, though from two very different perspectives, in the writings of Michael Oakeshott and E.H. Carr.[4] And a more finite problem is just how far this ambitious Europeanist perspective fitted in with the day-to-day political and social realities of a Britain struggling, in almost total isolation from Europe, for its own national survival. In the sphere of high policy, Britain's strategic priorities for much of the war period were heavily concentrated on home defence and preservation of the British empire rather than engagement on the European continent (often a cause of much frustration and annoyance to Britain's military allies). Cabinet records and other contemporary sources suggest that from a very early stage in the Churchill coalition, there were recurrent disputes among ministers, between those who were pressing for German territories and their industries to be incorporated into a newly modernized 'federal Europe', and those who wanted them ruthlessly razed to the ground.[5] But in practice it was only towards the end of the war – with the Soviet armies rapidly advancing upon Berlin – that serious attention was given at the level of high policy to the future of 'Europe' as anything more than a random collection of defeated or 'failed' nation states. At a rather lower level of political activity, within all major parties in wartime Britain there were many theorists and activists campaigning for various models of political, economic and cultural 'internationalism'. But not all such groups placed 'Europe' at the centre of their concerns and goals (indeed to many the perceived failure of the Geneva-based League of Nations suggested a quite different perspective). Most Conservatives and many Labour 'moderates' were much more interested in promoting various models of a 'revitalized' British empire or commonwealth, rather than the regeneration of post-fascist Europe as the main focus for a progressive internationalism of the future.[6] Even campaigners who favoured greater British identification with a unified Europe were careful to distance themselves from pan-European movements in exile, for fear of being seen as promoting even indirectly the ideas of Hitler's 'New Order'.[7] And for much of the war, and particularly after the German attack on Russia in June 1941, a modified version of the ideals of the Soviet Union seemed a much more compelling vision than a revival of 'European civilization' to many on the British left.[8]

Commitment to 'Europe' as either a political or a cultural idea was even more muted and ambivalent at the level of popular consciousness. At a very basic and personal level, familiarity among the wider British populace with day-to-day life in Europe was probably more limited during the early-1940s than at any previous period since the time of the Napoleonic wars.[9] Below the level of the upper-middle classes, very few English, Welsh, Scots, or Northern Irish people in 1940 had ever set foot on the continental mainland, except as soldiers on the battlefields of the Great War, in republican Spain, or, more recently, in the retreat from Dunkirk; while personal encounters with individual Europeans were largely limited to migrants and refugees escaping from continental tyrannies. Both kinds of experience tended to confirm the view among many that, far from being the 'cradle of civilization', Europe was a peculiarly violent, dangerous and uncivilized place. Moreover, at both 'high-brow' and more popular levels the war brought in its train the sudden explosion of an intense culture of 'Englishness'. Books, films, paintings, music, drama, poetry and strip cartoons of the early-1940s all accentuated themes drawn from the English countryside, the romance of the sea, and epic turning-points in earlier English history. Wartime trends in popular culture also included a wave of interest in all things Russian (after Hitler's attack on the Soviet Union in 1941), and an even greater vogue for all things American (after the arrival of the US Army in 1943).[10] By contrast, popular interest in the wider culture of Europe was largely confined to 'stars' of European origin who had made their careers in Hollywood, such as Greta Garbo and Charlie Chaplin. Public-opinion surveys of the war period occasionally included a question on respondents' attitudes to foreign nations, which registered a consistent but modest level of British affection for France. But the only European nation ever to score highly in such a poll (albeit briefly, during the siege of Stalingrad) was the Soviet Union. The most admired nations revealed by these surveys were almost invariably Canada, Australia and New Zealand; suggesting that by comparison with sentiments of kinship, commonwealth and empire, any imaginative identification with Europe among the wider British populace was very shadowy and remote.[11]

Despite its frequent invocation by British politicians and intellectuals, the rhetoric of 'Europe' and 'European civilization' in speeches and writings of the war period can therefore be quite misleading. Close analysis of famous occasions when the phrase, or its synonyms, were deployed suggests that, even when invoked by the same individual, the idea of 'European civilization' often implied quite different things in different contexts. Winston Churchill, for example, had first used the term at the time of Munich to highlight the paganism and barbarism of Adolf Hitler. At various stages during the war he had voiced support for some kind of future European 'confederation' or 'Zollverein'; but it was not until after the end of the war, when he was once again out of office, that Churchill in his famous Zurich speech of September 1946 came to attach the cause of 'civilization' to a rallying-call for a 'United States of Europe'.[12] J.M. Keynes likewise linked 'Christian civilization' to the cause of European reconstruction – partly as a 'moral' ideal, but partly also for the more pragmatic end of reassuring suspicious Americans that Britain had a 'wider mission' than mere national self-interest and that war loans would not be used simply to bolster up the beleaguered British empire.[13] When it came to practical details about post-war reconstruction, however, the ideal of 'Europe' throughout the war was in constant tension with what were believed to be the much more advantageous prospects offered by closer ties with the Empire.[14] Even among those who were unequivocally committed to Europe, not just as a strategic gambit but as an imaginative ideal, there was clearly a world of difference between those who saw the continent as the historic site of culture, liberty, classicism and Christianity, and those who viewed it in much more bureaucratic and functional terms as ripe for various models of institutional 'reconstruction' and 'modernization'.

## II

Nevertheless, since the notion of 'Europe' has proved surprisingly tenacious (while the rival internationalisms of the 1940s have largely waned or vanished), it is worth taking a closer look at why 'European civilization' was such a recurrent reference point in British public debate of that period, and what it meant in the minds of those who invoked the term – even though its immediate impact on the substance of power politics at this time may have been relatively limited. The subject is enormous and can be broached only very selectively here; but in this paper I shall aim to identify and look more closely at the ideas of certain individuals and coteries in the early 1940s who took 'Europe' seriously. These were to be found among senior politicians, among numerous academic and reformist pressure-groups, and among various individual writers, political thinkers and creative artists committed to rescuing Europe from totalitarian oblivion.

An important example of the first kind was the coterie of cross-party (though predominantly Conservative) politicians, headed by the radical imperialist and controversial Secretary of State for India, Leo Amery. Amery's group throughout the war maintained close contact with Count Coudenhove-Kalergi's 'Pan-European Union' movement; a body earlier based in Geneva, but after 1940 living in voluntary exile in New York. This movement, often seen in retrospect as an important germ in the genesis of the eventual European Union, laid strong emphasis on the 'cultural', 'spiritual' and 'philosophical' identity of Europe as well as on economic, strategic and political goals.[15] But, though Leo Amery's cross-party followers expressed strong support for all these aims, there was little suggestion among them during the war period (or even in 1946 after Churchill's 'Zurich speech') that Britain itself was, or may become, an active and integral participant in that shared European identity.[16] On the contrary, the group's aim was to encourage European states to evolve into a voluntary union of 'free peoples'; a body that would be linked together by history, economic interests and common culture, both on the model of and parallel to – but nevertheless quite separate from – the evolving British commonwealth, with Britain relating to this new revitalized Europe merely as a benevolent guide, neighbour and friend.[17] It was only much later, in the early 1950s, with the waning possibilities of empire and commonwealth as a cohesive power bloc, that some members and supporters of Amery's group would begin to shift their ground towards seeing the United Kingdom as a potentially integral part of that future European identity. They thus contributed to a momentous, though at the time almost imperceptible, shift in the real and imagined identity of Great Britain itself.

Another wartime pro-Europeanist outlook that likewise gained support from senior politicians, among them the Labour leader Clement Attlee, was the Federal Union movement. This body was founded in 1939 as an off-shoot from the League of Nations Union and in response to a similar initiative in North America. Its members included both democratic socialists and members of the 'Right Wing Book Club' (the latter an 'anti-censorship' body rather than the bastion of reaction that its title led some to assume). The Federal Union strategy was initially envisaged by its north American founders as a campaign for promoting closer union between European continental democracies and the USA.[18] But its British wing rapidly became much more closely concerned with schemes for linking Europe to Great Britain – the latter seen as including, in the vision of some of the movement's supporters, the whole of the self-governing territories of the British commonwealth.[19] Among its other notable ideas, canvassed by such luminaries as Lionel Robbins, Barbara Wootton, C.E.M. Joad and William Beveridge, were proposals that what they called 'economic and financial sovereignty', together with 'collective security' or 'external' sovereignty, should be transferred to a single pan-European authority with domestic, constitutional and cultural matters being retained in the hands of the separate nation-states. This likewise signalled a further seminal shift in British liberal political thought, which for more than two centuries had viewed control of defence and public finance as constituting the very essence of a modern nation-state. But in the eyes of many federal unionists the state itself was an increasingly transient and evolutionary category, with 'ethics' destined ultimately to displace 'power' as the chief determinant of 'the soul' of 'Western European civilization'.[20]

Such movements and perspectives were ultimately to play an important role in reshaping and redefining British conceptions of Europe at the level of high politics. But in the immediate and practical context of wartime a much more detailed focus on European affairs came to the fore, not in the macro-political or philosophical spheres but at the 'expert' and sub-political levels of the wartime reconstruction movement and in economic and social planning. An interest in the 'European' dimension of planning was evident here, not just in the thought and writings of many British economic and social reformers of the period, but in the contributions of the substantial body of emigré and exiled European economists, lawyers, statisticians, psychologists, political philosophers and even theologians who became involved in reformist pressure groups and actively contributed to wartime planning movements in Britain.[21] In discussions of education, social security, unemployment, health care, architecture and community planning, these continental migrants very substantially enhanced the European dimension of such debates, not simply by drawing upon continental problems and examples, but also in the ideological sphere. Historians of the British planning movements of the 1930s and 1940s are familiar with the role of dissident European socialists, both Marxian and non-Marxian, in flight from both fascism and Soviet communism, in all these fields. But a relatively neglected, though arguably more pervasive and influential group, was the substantial body of heirs to the European 'managerial' and 'positivist' traditions of Saint-Simon and Auguste Comte: figures who contributed to wartime planning debates, not just as refugees but often as representatives of European governments in exile. This was a group, moreover, whose members – unlike many Marxists – had every intention of returning to their homelands to pursue and implement policies of reconstruction as soon as the war would come to an end.[22] Recent writing on the history of wartime political and economic thought has suggested that it was members of this European positivist tradition, inspired by the doctrines of Comte and Saint-Simon rather than by Marxian socialism, that F.A. Hayek had in mind when he composed his famous 1944 polemic against 'planning' in *The Road to Serfdom*.[23] And certainly it was not classical Marxism, but something much closer to the Saint-Simonian and Comtean vision – of Europe as a single integrated 'great western republic', governed by bureaucracy, managerialism, and technical expertise – that seemed to permeate many aspects of the British planning and reconstruction movements during the wartime and early post-war years.[24]

The extent of such 'Europeanist' themes was often largely invisible to contemporaries (particularly at a time when continental states and cultures seemed so enfeebled, while Great Britain despite its wartime and post-war economic crises seemed relatively stable and strong). But such continental influences may nevertheless be detected as a powerful practical and intellectual presence in many strands of the British wartime planning movement. They can be found, for example, in the writings of William Beveridge (the son of a devout Scottish disciple of Comte), who – despite proclaiming his famous social-insurance report as a 'British revolution' – was nevertheless well aware that many of his key proposals on social security were Swiss, Belgian, French, German and Scandinavian as well as British in origin.[25] Such continental influences were also apparent in the writings of the health and population reformers, Richard Titmuss and David Glass, both strongly influenced by the moral and biological doctrines of the Positivist movement. And, above all, they may be seen in the thought of Julian Huxley, scion of England's most eminent scientific family in the domestic English positivist tradition, whose end-of-war appointment as Director-General of the Paris headquarters of UNESCO seemed to many (including Huxley himself) to signal the triumph of humanistic positivism over more traditionalist ways of thought in science, education, social policy, and all aspects of the wider planning movement.[26]

Such connections may perhaps most clearly and revealingly be found, however, in settings where representatives of emigré governments and their staffs themselves directly participated in discussions about the social, economic and cultural futures of both Britain and Europe. In the series of post-war reconstruction conferences, jointly organized by Chatham House and Nuffield College, Oxford, between 1941 and 1945, representatives of the governments-in-exile of Holland, France, Belgium, Luxembourg, Denmark, Norway, Poland, Yugoslavia and Czechoslovakia, together with members of the cross-national 'New Europe Circle', regularly debated problems of post-war European development with British academic and professional representatives and experts.[27] Topics discussed included not merely economic and technical issues, but more macroscopic questions such as the dissolution of sovereignty, the political implications of the Atlantic Charter, the creation of a continent-wide 'common currency' and a 'common civil law', and 'What might be done if Europe were a single political territory?'. Papers presented at such meetings clearly revealed the depths of under-development and below-subsistence living conditions prevalent in many parts of Europe, particularly its eastern and south-eastern agricultural regions.[28] But they also bore witness to an unexpected degree of routine, cross-national, technical and organizational co-operation that had been evolving in central Europe over the previous hundred years, in fields such as transport, river-navigation, customs agreements, frontier-policing and postal and telecommunications, much of which appeared to have been carried on regardless of revolutions and regime-changes, economic booms and recessions (and, in some cases, even of invasions and wars).[29] They also revealed what to British eyes was a range of unexpected factors. These included a degree of admiration for many substantive aspects of Hitler's New European Order and a desire that many of its 'unified structures' should be retained into the post-war era; together with strong hints of continuity and coherence in certain quarters between modern 'positivist' thinking about pan-European planning and the more traditional 'corporatist' policies of European conservatism (including some of the more progressive elements in the socio-economic doctrines of the Catholic Church). 'Imaginings' of the future (a term explicitly used at these meetings) included the evolution of a single European geo-political unit stretching from Russia to Spain; the construction of a unified pan-continental transport network; and the replacement of 'capitalist cartels' by Europe-wide 'public corporations'.[30] And they also envisaged a continent of unlimited migration from poorer to richer countries, a process seen as leading to the transformation of Great Britain and its dominions into a largely finance-based 'consumer economy', drawing its 'service workers' from the surplus agricultural populations of Europe's south and east.[31]

At one of the Nuffield and Chatham House meetings in October 1942, the chairman declared that not just administrators and planners but also intellectuals and poets alike shared this vision of the future of Europe, as a unified, modernized, 'federalized' state, that would adapt the experience of wartime controls and planning to peaceful, benevolent, and 'reconstructionist' ends.[32] Just how far British 'intellectuals and poets' in fact envisaged the post-war revival of Europe in these technocratic and administrative terms is open to question; but certainly it was true that many of the literary and artistic avant-garde in wartime Britain had a much more positive interest in, and identification with, the European continent and its culture than most of the population at large. This perspective stemmed partly from the strongly 'European' identity of all branches of the early twentieth-century 'modernist' movement in literature and the arts, and partly from a widespread disgust and disenchantment with domestic British culture and politics in all its aspects that had prevailed within intellectual and artistic circles during the pre-war decade. The story of the prolonged mental and moral crisis generated among artists and writers in Britain by events of the 1930s has been told many times and need not be recounted here.[33] But developments during the early years of the war left many such figures, particularly those on the 'far left', in total disarray, with their Soviet heroes in alliance with the Nazi enemy, European civilization apparently in ruins, and British resistance to fascism being led predominantly by political conservatives.

Personal responses to this crisis varied, with some prominent cultural figures relocating to the USA, some swallowing their scruples and joining the armed forces or various forms of government service, while others were to become major contributors to the widespread flowering of the wartime culture of 'Englishness' mentioned above. A significant role in mediating these dilemmas was played by the arch-Europhile, Cyril Connolly, whose wartime magazine *Horizon* struggled valiantly to maintain contacts with dissident aesthetic movements on the continent and to give a British platform to European writers and artists in exile – even though Connolly himself had reached the despairing conclusion that European civilization was doomed, and that the torch of high culture, transmitted by highly-cultivated emigrés from both Britain and Central Europe, was now inexorably passing to north America.[34] Other progressive literary outlets, such as Penguin New Writing, the Hogarth Press and publications of the Left Book Club, likewise continued to give prominence to dissident continental writers and to underground literary and aesthetic movements in occupied Europe. Quite unexpectedly, however, the key figure in the cultural and imaginative reconfiguration of Europe in wartime Britain turned out to be neither Cyril Connolly nor the disenchanted spokesmen of the pre-war far left, but a writer perceived by many radicals of the period as a fellow-traveller of the forces of political reaction, namely T.S. Eliot. Eliot's wartime picturing of continental Europe – as a unique treasure-house of both 'high' and 'popular' culture, but also as in grave danger, not just from war, fascism, and totalitarian tyranny but from many other gigantic and destructive forces of contemporary history – will be the main focus of the rest of this chapter.

# III

I have referred to T.S. Eliot's role in this debate as 'unexpected'; but a case could also be made for seeing it as highly predictable. This is a point that highlights both the shifting and elusive character of what was understood at the time by 'Europe' and the complex identity and outlook of T.S. Eliot himself. Eliot, although a naturalized British subject, was not a native Briton but a former United States citizen, who had shot to fame during the 1920s with 'The Wasteland' and other poems, as one of the great stars of European literary modernism, on a par with figures such as Paul Valéry, Marcel Proust, James Joyce and Luigi Pirandello. From 1922 until the brink of the Second World War Eliot had also been editor of the *Criterion*, a literary and philosophical magazine for an English-speaking audience, that was dedicated to the advance of the 'European mind', to establishing in London 'a local forum of international thought', and to stressing the common roots of both British and European thought in Graeco-Roman and Judaeo-Christian culture. These tasks Eliot had seen as closely complementing the work of other very similar cosmopolitan and trans-cultural 'little magazines', published on the continent during the inter-war years in Germany, France, Spain, the Netherlands, Italy and Czechoslovakia. From the mid-1930s, however, Eliot's confidence in this project had gradually waned, as sister-magazines in continental countries had been successively closed down by authoritarian governments, and as the very notion of 'Europe' – as an entity embodying two millennia of creative evolution from classicism into intellectual modernity – had collapsed in the face of fascist, communist and even 'liberal' totalitarian oppression. This 'closing down of the mental frontiers of Europe' had been accompanied by a partial drying-up of Eliot's own poetic voice, as the cosmopolitan milieu on which it had previously depended had contracted and shrivelled away.[35] Moreover, Eliot's personal role as an expositor of the European avant-garde had not been helped, in the eyes of some, by his deeply serious conversion to 'catholic' Christianity: a move that was particularly puzzling to many contemporaries because it was a conversion, not to Catholicism in its 'universalist' Roman mode, but to the much more localized, low-key, and historically ambivalent form practised by a minority of 'Anglo-Catholics' within the Church of England. Cyril Connolly, when reviewing Eliot's 'East Coker' for *Horizon* in May 1940, never for one moment doubted Eliot's continuing status as one of the great stars of international literary modernism (indeed, the poem in question was judged to be 'one of the finest long poems of the twentieth century').[36] Nevertheless, Eliot's views on British and European culture were portrayed in *Horizon* circles as resembling those of 'the bald head of some Bishop (...) seen as emerging from the egg-shell of a lifetime's complacency'. 'Mr Eliot, although disturbed by Munich, seems curiously out of touch. (...) the trouble with Eliot is that (...) like Henry James he is at once impressed and confused by the European tradition'.[37]

Eliot's re-emergence during the early 1940s as a major protagonist of what he identified as 'the cultural economy of Europe' was therefore not out of keeping with his intellectual past, and was indeed accompanied by his resurgence as a major poet; nonetheless, it surprised and even shocked many of his literary contemporaries. To some, his concern for Europe seemed particularly puzzling because it coincided with the composition of his 'Four Quartets', a sequence of poems that in content if not in style seemed to encapsulate the passionate feeling for small-scale, localized 'Englishness' that was such a pervasive feature of British insular and domestic culture during the Second World War.[38] Commentators on Eliot have largely glossed over the seeming paradox of his passionate championship of 'European civilization' at a time when his poetic writing was so deeply imbued with echoes of intensely 'English' themes; and they have also neglected the historical aspects of what it was that Eliot meant by 'Europe' at this time (other than something vaguely 'Christian' and 'retrospective'); so I shall try to address both questions here. Eliot's anxiety for the future of European culture in the late 1930s and early 1940s was certainly stirred by its fate at the hands of pagans, barbarians, and belligerent nationalists in the guise of Nazis, fascists and other totalitarians. However, this could not have been its sole trigger, since, as editor of *Criterion*, he had been gloomily aware of the onset of such trends for more than a decade before 1939. Nor does it seem to have been in any way linked to the protests of his close friend, Bishop Bell of Chichester, against the blanket bombing of ancient German cities, since it antedated Bell's campaign by several years. A more immediate trigger was almost certainly Eliot's horror and disbelief at Cyril Connolly's prediction in February 1940 that 'European' culture could survive only by an irreversible transplantation of the carriers of high art to north America. Such an outcome, Eliot declared, was 'the most insidious form of defeatism', it being well-nigh inconceivable 'that civilization should pass from Europe to such a conservative country as the United States'.[39] And a less dramatic but much more long-lasting catalyst was a mounting conviction that the survival of Europe as a 'civilization' was threatened, not just by the blatant barbarism of Europe's Nazi and fascist enemies, but by what he saw as the lesser but more insidious and unintended barbarism of many of its well-meaning friends. Indeed, it increasingly appeared to Eliot that the destructive impact of Nazism was likely to be not reversed but intensified by certain aspects of the European 'social reconstruction' agenda being mooted in many quarters in Great Britain over the course of the war.[40]

Thus the long-term implications of large-scale bureaucratic planning, in both its national and international aspects, seemed to Eliot to threaten the 'organic' character of communities throughout Europe much more permanently, if less violently and horrifically, than the short-term impact of fascism; although, as he was quick to point out, there was also plenty of 'large-scale planning' going on under National Socialism, with Hitler's 'Neuropa' being a 'hideous metamorphosis' of the 'holistic' social engineering so much admired by planners on the Allied side.[41] And likewise, while strongly emphasizing what he saw as the inherent underlying unity of 'European culture', he was strongly opposed to measures designed to impose that unity by legalistic and institutional means. In other words, Eliot's views about what was needed to rescue 'European civilization', and indeed his conception of what that 'civilization' itself entailed, were in many ways diametrically opposed to that of many of the British and continental protagonists of a 'new Europe' whose views I have outlined above. It would be a mistake to see Eliot as an out-and-out opponent of social planning in all its forms. On the contrary, he was surprisingly sympathetic to 'sociology' as a scholarly and analytical discipline, and was a close friend and admirer of the educational sociologist Karl Mannheim, who was a major theorist and protagonist of the British wartime planning movement. Eliot himself certainly favoured some degree of educational planning; and he shared Mannheim's view that where 'organic' communities had broken down there should be well-thought-out interventionist policies to sustain and revive them.[42] But such policies should be based on 'regeneration' rather than wholesale replacement, and they should focus on families, communities, voluntary organizations, and small self-governing municipalities or districts, rather than on uniform national or international programmes; while schools in particular, according to Eliot, should be treated as cultural 'organisms', each with its own distinctive spirit and institutional character, rather than as units in a monolithic national scheme.[43] The goal should be not a trans-national continent of 'abstract Europeans', but a multiplicity of mutually interacting local cultures, that would combine broad cosmopolitan sympathies with deep communitarian 'roots', in a manner explored by the French philosopher Simone Weil. In Eliot's eyes Weil's teachings embodied a conjunction of Christian and Judaic moral theology, community and cosmopolitanism, spirituality and practical social action, classical and avant-garde philosophy, to a quite exemplary degree.[44]

There may seem to be certain practical affinities here with the celebrated model of 'piecemeal social engineering' recommended at this time by Eliot's younger contemporary, Karl Popper.[45] But in fact Eliot came to his vision of a well-ordered society not through Popper's model of rationalistic trial and error, but through a quite different route. Indeed, his interest in such matters, and in the wider question of what constituted a 'good ' or 'just' society, was not primarily that of a political, economic, or social theorist at all. Rather it was that of a poet and critic, trying to conjure up a picture of the social relations most conducive to the flourishing of a cohesive and creative culture among human beings. Thus Eliot had almost no interest in the technical problems of federalism, local self-government, national sovereignty and so on, that engaged other participants in the European reconstruction movement; and, although he was certainly concerned with the question of 'social justice', this was primarily in relation to certain specific policies – such as support for communities, education, and family life – which he saw as having a wider bearing on the character of national and local cultures (rather than on 'justice' as a goal in its own right). Likewise his ideas about economic reconstruction, in which he gave priority to the revival of small-scale agriculture and village and small-town communities, were driven almost entirely by the belief that such arrangements were indispensable to the continuing life-cycle of both high and popular culture.[46] These themes were only very indirectly concerned with the issues of mass unemployment, poverty, and wider economic development, with which most other participants in European reconstruction movements were primarily concerned. Instead, Eliot suggested (perhaps unsurprisingly!) that planners should cease taking 'engineers' as their model and should act more like 'poets'; the planner should remember that 'the plan must be transformed by the material, as much as the material is transformed by the effects of his plan'.[47]

What was Eliot's theory of culture and how did it connect with his concern for the wider flourishing of European civilization? Clearly millions of his contemporaries shared the view that 'saving Europe' was a worthwhile goal, but few did so for the same reasons or for the same goals as Eliot's, which were in many respects highly personal, counter-intuitive, and idiosyncratic. They centred in particular on his ideas about the intrinsic unity of 'Europe' as a deep-rooted historic culture, about the importance of language and religion, and about the mutual relation between 'high' culture and the habits of everyday life. Europe's over-arching cultural unity was for Eliot not a matter of highbrow debate, but simply an incontestable 'given' fact ('culture' in Eliot's view being a 'mysterious social personality', antecedent to any views or conscious intentions that participants could have about it).[48] It had been generated organically over two thousand years of European history, out of the inheritance of Greece, Rome and Judaeo-Christian monotheism, and honed by the logical and scholastic legacy of Roman law. Such a culture could not possibly be replicated or artificially created, although in the hands of holistic planners of both totalitarian and democratic persuasions it could only too easily and rapidly be destroyed. And languages too had a life of their own, extraneous to the human will, that could be continually shaped and adapted but not 'invented' by creative human beings.[49] Eliot was fond of recalling how, when he had first arrived in Europe as an 'adolescent' in 1910, he had been astounded by the amazing technical achievements of young French and Italian poets of that epoch, writing at a time when nothing at all of any poetic significance seemed to be happening in the immensely richer and more varied language of English.[50] He had decided on the spot to abandon philosophy and devote his life to doing for English what Laforgue and Valéry had done for French, with the aim of forging English poetry into a much more subtle and ambitious instrument of meaning than it had been for several centuries. The moral that Eliot drew from this tale was that different languages with common roots constantly inspired and nourished each other, with the flourishing of one bringing about the flourishing of all; and that nothing could be more disastrous for Europe than its progressive evolution into a single homogenous monoglot culture, whether its inhabitants were to speak Esperanto, Basic English, or the artificially invented new languages of 'business' and 'planning'.[51] And in Eliot's view the same was true of religion. Diversity of belief within a common monotheistic framework generated a much richer flowering of transcendental experience than any superimposed uniformity: while what he called 'bickering' between different religious and cultural groups was often not a weakness but an intellectual strength, that actively enriched both religious and secular culture.[52]

Tying all this together was Eliot's distinctive theory of how cultures worked as a 'frame' within which elites and masses, educated and demotic speech, and civic and rural life all needed constantly to interact with each other in order to stay alive. It was an outlook exemplified in the writing of his own poetry, where popular music, slang, and idioms of the street were all constantly imported into high art, with images of 'Derby Day (…) dog races, the pin table, the dart board, a Wensleydale cheese, a boiled cabbage cut into sections' being used to 'deflect the mind from a misleading concentration on perpendicular Gothic and the music of Elgar'.[53] This was more than merely an aesthetic theory, however; it also casts significant further light upon Eliot's understanding of the distinctive socio-economic characteristics of 'European civilization'. To Eliot it seemed that throughout continental Europe during the earlier twentieth century, daily life had been (and to a large extent still was) characterized by an age-old 'culture', or collection of cultures, in the anthropological conception of that term. This was a culture of peasant cultivation, small market towns, popular sports, dignified civic centres and cathedral cities, all of which continued to survive and interact with the great capitals of cosmopolitan modernism, like Paris, Amsterdam, Munich and Berlin.[54] It was the co-existence of these many different layers of productive life within a unified common framework, that in Eliot's view had made possible the 'Modernist' movement of the early twentieth century, where artists and writers reared in the deep-rooted structures of the pre-modern era had been able to step outside those structures and thus to see and interpret them as they had never been seen before. (This cycle of archaic inheritance, creative tension, and dynamic innovation was exemplified, Eliot believed, in the life and work of James Joyce.)[55] Of Eliot's own commitment to this new revolutionary aesthetic there can be no doubt; nevertheless, he saw it as wholly dependent upon the continued material and imaginative input of the older way of life, which was vanishing all too quickly under the pressures of 'modernization'. In this respect England itself, no less than Adolf Hitler's Neuropa, offered a dire warning and example – and not just to Europe, but ultimately to 'all the races of the world'.[56] In England, Eliot believed, much of the multi-layered common culture which he so much admired in continental Europe had been dwindling and dying under the progressive onset of 'modernity' ever since the eighteenth century – leaving the poet and would-be creative writer with no sources of inspiration other than 'social commentary' or his own fragmented ego. Moreover, this collapse into imaginative banality had gone much further among the 'educated classes' than in cinema, tabloids, or demotic speech ('I am less alarmed about the decay of English when I read a murder story', Eliot told an audience of classicists, 'than when I read the first leader in "The Times".').[57] From this perspective, the preservation and revival of classic 'European' culture in all its multi-layered diversity was as important, or even more so, to the revival of 'English' culture as it was to Europe itself.[58] Seen in this light, Eliot's voluminous wartime writings, speeches and broadcasts on 'European' themes appear as much more than simply a pious and public-spirited contribution to the post-war continental recovery programme. They should also be seen as celebrating a European way of life that, despite the temporary frightfulness of fascism, offered an inspiration and way of salvation for twentieth-century British culture, at least as much as vice versa.

## IV

What if anything do my examples indicate about British perceptions of continental Europe during a period when, for a time at least, Britain was an isolated and besieged off-shore island fighting a battle, not so much for 'culture' or 'civilization' as for basic national and physical survival? Unsurprisingly, for many British people living at the time, thinking about 'Europe' as anything other than a source of near and present danger from hostile powers, was not to the forefront of their minds. Given the circumstances of the period, however, the extent and degree of interest shown by 1940s Britons, not just in the fate of Nazi Germany but much more widely in the survival and resurgence of a 'free' Europe, seems perhaps unexpected. At the level of high politics, invocation of the defence of 'European civilization' was only very selectively linked to any clearly-defined vision or strategic plan for Europe's long-term future; nonetheless it was more than just a gambit for winning allies or for extracting money from gullible Americans (as had been claimed early on in the war by suspicious American isolationists).[59] A significant element in political debate over the course of the war period was a perceptible shift in thinking about how far Britain itself was an integral part of Europe, or merely an off-shore neighbour with European roots. In 1939 the latter view was widespread, whereas by 1945 it had become much more common to see Britain as a part (albeit an unusual part) of the wider continent. The possibility of Britain playing a much more active role (not just as a 'paymaster' but as a constructive partner) in various cross-national continental institutions had also become much more thinkable by 1945. And views about Britain's long-term political relations with Europe had also evolved, partly as an intuitive response to Hitlerism, but also partly in response to more pragmatic factors (such as rising unease about the long-term future of the British commonwealth, dislike of ever-expanding American hegemony, and the incipient onset of the Cold War).

At the lower political level of pressure-groups and social reformers there was a wide range of people, including a substantial group of refugee administrators and intellectuals from Europe, who held strongly articulated views about what the future of Europe should entail. Members of this latter group played an important role in inseminating a 'Europeanist' dimension into British domestic reconstruction debates (particularly in relation to the built environment and town-and-country planning), but their impact within Europe itself was limited until after the end of the war. In retrospect it appears that their influence on popular perceptions of Europe in Britain may in some respects have been a mixed or negative one. This was partly because the passionate enthusiasm of some European activists for wholesale 'reconstruction' programmes (including in some cases admiration for the technical achievements of the 'New European Order') tended to reinforce ancient Anglo-Saxon prejudices about Europe as the homeland of bureaucracy and officious regimentation. They thus provoked a critical reaction not just among libertarian intellectuals, but from certain sections of broader public opinion, popular culture and the national press.[60] On the other hand, the very fact of wartime severance from the European 'mainland' appeared in some quarters positively to revive British interest in European ideas and culture: in Eliot's words, it made Britons more aware in a way they had not been conscious of before that severance from the Continent meant living in an iron lung, by 'artificial respiration'.[61]

Wartime thinking among British writers and intellectuals about the past and future of 'European civilization' deserves much wider and more detailed examination than there is space for here, as do the ideas on this subject of T.S. Eliot himself. Many aspects of Eliot's social and political interpretation of the historic evolution of Europe were by no means peculiar to himself, being in part adapted from continental social and religious theorists such as Mannheim and Jacques Maritain, and (more indirectly) from the sociologists Emile Durkheim and Ferdinand Tönnies.[62] But Eliot's attempt to construct a cross-national cultural anthropology of how social structures and religious beliefs impinged upon human creativity at all levels, from high art through to the minutiae of everyday life, invites much closer attention, as does his very challenging claim that great art is impossible without continuous creative interaction with a deep-rooted popular culture. Particularly striking was his specific claim that the 'Modernist' explosion of the early twentieth century in both 'high' and 'popular' culture had been wholly dependent for its roots and inspiration upon the continuing existence of an older, deeper, and more static, 'pre-modern' civilization (with artificial programmes of institutional 'modernization', sponsored from above, being frequently not the complement but the antithesis of 'Modernism' in the creative arts). Moreover, to passionate Europeanists of the wartime and post-war periods Eliot threw down a dramatic challenge. This was his claim that wholesale strategies of 'reconstruction' and 'unification' (including large-scale 'cultural programmes') were themselves destroying the very civilization they were meant to save: a civilization that Eliot himself believed was 'the greatest the world had ever known'.[63] Were these genuine intellectual hypotheses about the past, present and future of the continent of Europe, and about the pre-conditions for a flourishing creative life? Or were they merely the expression of more diffuse and incoherent concerns – widely shared though less articulately expressed by many of Eliot's contemporaries – about the confused relations of community and identity, efficiency and democracy, religion and creative art, endemic in all modern industrial and bureaucratic societies?

## Notes

1. On the genesis of this debate, see Pierre van Paassen and James Waterman Wise (eds), *Nazism: An Assault on Civilization* (New York, 1934). The essays in this collection, and particularly that of Dorothy Thompson, the celebrated American journalist and anti-Nazi campaigner, were widely cited by British commentators during the war.
2. Amery mss (Churchill College, Cambridge), AMEL 1/7/39, draft statement on 'The Purpose of the Proposed Council for European Union', autumn 1946.
3. Winston Churchill, *Thoughts and Adventures* (London, 1932 and 1947); George Bell, *The Threat to Civilisation: a speech delivered to the Upper House of the Convocation of Canterbury* (London, 1942); Harold J. Laski, *Faith, Reason and Civilisation* (London, 1944); T.S. Eliot, *Notes towards the Definition of Culture* (London, 1948); *Collected Writings of John Maynard Keynes*, ed. Donald Moggridge, vol. XXII (London, 1978), pp. 24–5.
4. Michael Oakeshott, *The Social and Political Doctrines of Contemporary Europe* (London, 1940), pp. xi–xxiii; E.H. Carr, *Conditions of Peace* (London, 1942), pp. 187–275.
5. Huxley papers (Rice University, Texas), 14, 5, Harold Nicolson to Julian Huxley, 23 Oct. 1940; Martin Gilbert, *Finest Hour: Winston Churchill 1939–1941* (London, 1989), pp. 801–2.
6. Amery MSS, 1/7/39, 'Draft statement of Aims. European Union (British Sector)', n.d.; and 'The Purpose of the Proposed Council of the European Union', n.d.
7. A response that greeted E.H. Carr's famous, or notorious, *Conditions of Peace* (1942), pp. 187–275, where Carr argued for a 'European' planned economy.
8. E.g. G.D.H. Cole et al. *Plan for Britain: A Collection of Essays Prepared for the Fabian Society* (London, 1943); Harold J. Laski, *Reflections on the Revolution of our Time* (London, 1943).
9. Before 1914 it had been a common experience among skilled and semi-skilled working-men to be employed on the continent in industrial projects, but this had largely died out as a result of the Great War and inter-war depression. Likewise, holidays in resorts in France and Germany had been not uncommon among the better-off Edwardian working and clerical classes, but declined in popularity after 1918.

10. Jose Harris, 'To Russia with Love: Anglo-Russian cultural relations 1941–45' (forthcoming).
11. Hadley Cantril, *Public Opinion 1935–1946* (Princeton, 1951), p. 369; *BIPO Survey*, 16 January 1942; R.B. McCallum, *Public Opinion and the Last Peace* (1944). Mass-Observation reports of the war period likewise appear to suggest a widespread lack of interest among diarists, observers, and ordinary British citizens in anything to do with Europe, other than matters that concerned the actual fighting of the war: Dorothy Sheridan, *Mass-Observation File Reports, 1937–1972: An Annotated Chronological List with Subject Index* (1981); Angus Calder and Dorothy Sheridan (eds), *Speak for Yourself* (London, 1984).
12. Martin Gilbert, *Finest Hour. Winston S. Churchill*, Vol. VI, p. 943; *Road to Victory, Winston S. Churchill*, Vol. VII, p. 1026; *Never Despair, Winston S. Churchill*, Vol. VIII, p. 285; Amery mss, AMEL 1/7/ 73; AMEL 1/7/394–6.
13. *Collected Writings of John Maynard Keynes*, vol. XXII (1978), pp. 24–5; vol. XXV (1980), pp. 11–16.
14. Amery mss, AMEL, 1/6/ 4; Leo Amery to Sir Herbert Williams, 20 Nov. 1940.
15. Amery mss, AMEL, 1/7/39, paper on 'Pan-European Union', n.d.; Richard Coudenhove-Kalergi, *Europe must Unite* (1939); Jan Werner-Müller, '"Our Philadelphia"? On the Political and Intellectual History of the "European Constitution"', *Journal of Modern European History*, VI (2008), 139–41.
16. Amery mss, AMEL, 1/6/2; AMEL 1/ 7/ 39, 'The Purpose of the Proposed Council for European Union, n.d. (September 1946).
17. Amery mss, AMEL, 1/6/3, speech by Amery in *Empire Industries Association Monthly Bulletin*, December 1942; AMEL, 1/6/4, Amery to Sir Herbert Williams, 20 November 1940; AMEL, 1/7/40(2), typescript on 'United Europe', August 1938.
18. Clarence Streit, *Union Now. A Proposal for a Federal Union of the Democracies of the North Atlantic* (New York, 1939); W.B. Curry, *The Case for Federal Union* (1940); Clarence Streit, *Union now with Britain* (London, 1941).
19. William Beveridge, *Peace by Federation* (April 1940); Barbara Wootton, *Socialism and Federation* (London, 1941).
20. Barbara Wootton, *Socialism and Federation*; C.E.M. Joad, *The Philosophy of Federal Union* (London, 1941); Lionel Robbins, *Economic Aspects of Federation* (London, 1941).
21. Nuffield College Private Conferences (Nuffield College, MssNCPC), particularly International Private Conference on European reconstruction (18–19 April 1942); Research conference on international agencies for economic reconstruction, 16–17 October 1942); and Ninth Private Conference on the international aspects of post-war employment policy in Great Britain, 11–12 September 1943; Bishop Bell mss (Lambeth Palace Library), correspondence on 'Reconstruction of Germany', vols. 43, 50 and 63.
22. E.g. Pierre Laroque, *Au Service de l'Homme et du Droit* (Paris, 1993), pp. 134–93.
23. H.S. Jones, 'The Era of Tyrannies: Elie Halevy and Friedrich von Hayek on Socialism', *European Journal of Political Theory*, I, 2002, 53–69.
24. On the Europeanist and 'planning' strands in positivist thought, see Auguste Comte, *Discours sur l'ensemble du positivisme*, (trans. J.H. Bridges, ed. F. Harrison, 1909); and Ghita Ionescu (ed.), *The Political Thought of Saint-Simon* (London, 1976), pp. 42–7, 83–98, 147–52.
25. W.H. Beveridge, *Social Insurance and Allied Services*, Appendix F, 'Some Comparisons with Other Countries' (London, 1942).

26. D.V. Glass, *Population Policies and Movements in Europe* (Oxford, 1940); R. and K. Titmuss, *Parents Revolt: A Study of the Declining Birthrate in Acquisitive Societies* (London, 1942); J. Huxley and A.C. Haddon, *We Europeans: A Survey of Racial Problems* (London, 1939); J. Huxley, *Memories* (Harmondsworth 2 vols, 1970, 1972).

27. MSSNCPC, 3/3/1–130, 'Research Conference on International Agencies for Economic Reconstruction', held at Chatham House, 16–17 October 1942.

28. MSSNCPC, 2/1/20–23, Dr J. Lowy, 'Questions relating to health-standards of nutrition and standards of living', 18 April 1942.

29. MSSNCPC, 2/1/37–40, 'Industrial Reconstruction, including the development of communications of all kinds, including Electric Power', 19 April 1942.

30. MSSNCPC, 2/1/ 1–57 (April 1942); 3/ 3//36–98, (October 1942); 6/2/27–132, (September 1943); 7/3/3–23 (February 1944), 10/4/1–99 (July 1947).

31. MSSNCPC, 2/1/33, International Private Conference, 18 April 1942, 'Agricultural Reconstruction'.

32. MSSNCPC, 3/3/73, Dr F.A. Burckhardt, 'Notes on international shipping agencies', 16–17 October 1942.

33. Peter Stansky and William Abrahams, *Journey to the Frontier* (London, 1966); David Caute, *The Fellow-travellers: Intellectual Friends of Communism* (2nd ed. London, 1988); Valentine Cunningham, *British Writers of the Thirties* (Oxford, 1989).

34. Cyril Connolly, *Horizon,* 2 February 1940, pp. 68–70. This article also suggested that the only thing that could save Europe at this point was a permanent merger of Britain and France into a single unitary state – an idea that interestingly anticipated Winston Churchill's equally radical (though equally abortive) proposal to Marshall Pétain on the same theme four months later.

35. 'Last Words', *Criterion*, xxx, 1939, pp. 269–75; T.S. Eliot, 'A Commentary', *New English Weekly*, 5 October 1939, pp. 331–2; T.S. Eliot, *Notes towards a Definition of Culture*, pp. 115–16.

36. *Horizon*, I, 5 (May 1940), p. 314.

37. Stephen Spender, 'How shall we be saved?', *Horizon*, I, 1, (January 1940), pp. 55–6.

38. This was true even of the third poem in the sequence, *The Dry Salvages* (published September 1941), whose conjuring-up of remote New England communities, small boats, rugged survival, the sea and its deep mysteries and perils, exactly coincided with many of the images of quintessential 'Englishness' prevalent during the war epoch.

39. T.S. Eliot, 'News and Reviews. On Going West', *New English Weekly*, 15 February 1940, p. 251.

40. *The Times*, T.S. Eliot to the editor, 20 September and 17 October 1947.

41. T.S. Eliot, 'A Commentary', *New English Weekly*, 8 October 1939, pp. 631–2.

42. T.S. Eliot, 'Man and Society', *Spectator*, 7 June 1940, p. 782; 'The Classics and the Man of Letters', *Presidential Address to the Classical Association*, 15 April 1942 (Oxford, 1942), pp. 16–24.

43. T.S. Eliot, 'On Reading Official Reports', *New English Weekly*, 11 May 1939, pp. 61–2.

44. On Eliot's debt to Simone Weil's political thought, see his preface to the English translation of her posthumous *L'enracinement: prélude á une déclaration des devoirs envers l'être humain* (Paris, 1949).

45. Karl Popper, *The Open Society and its Enemies* (1945, London 1962 ed.), pp. 158–9 and 162–7.
46. T.S. Eliot, 'Notes towards a Definition of Culture', *Partisan Review*, XI, 2 (Spring 1944), p. 150.
47. *Hamburger Akademische Rundschau*, 1950.
48. T.S. Eliot, 'The Social Function of Poetry', *The Norseman*, I, 6 (November 1943), pp. 455–6.
49. T.S. Eliot, 'That Poetry is made with Words', *New English Weekly*, 27 April 1939, pp. 27–8.
50. *Listener*, XXXVII, 9 January 1947, p. 72.
51. T.S. Eliot, 'What France Means to You', *La France Libre*, viii, 44, 15 June 1944, pp. 94–5. This view lay behind his refusal to support publishing projects for translating great works of European literature into English, and his claim that readers got more out of reading non-English poetry in its original language, even if they only had little knowledge of that language, than in English translation: T.S. Eliot, 'Talk on Dante', *Adelphi*, xxvii, 2 (1951), pp. 106–14.
52. 'The Church and the World', report in *The Times*, 17 July 1937; T.S. Eliot, 'The Responsibility of the Man of Letters in the Cultural Restoration of Europe', *Norseman*, II, 4 (July/August 1944), pp. 243–8. Eliot's views thus bore little relation to the claims of critics who saw him as favouring a monolithic ecclesiastical hegemony based on the Roman Catholic church (e.g. Harold Laski, *Faith, Reason and Civilisation*, pp. 197–8). A similar point might be made about his views on the teaching of Latin, which he defended, not as a 'mental discipline' for a 'snobbish elite', but as 'good for rich demotic everyday speech' (*Classics and the Man of Letters*, London, 1942).
53. T.S. Eliot, 'The Music of Poetry', *Partisan Review*, IX, 6, Nov.–Dec. 1942, pp. 450–65; 'Cultural Forces in the Human Order', in Maurice Reckitt (ed.) *Prospect for Christendom* (London, 1945), p. 65.
54. T.S. Eliot, 'Cultural Forces in the Human Order', pp. 57–69; 'Reflections on the Unity of European Culture (III)', *Adam International Review*, XIV, 161 (August 1946) pp. 20–2; *Notes Towards a Definition of Culture*, pp. 110–24.
55. T.S. Eliot, 'The Approach to James Joyce', *The Listener*, 14 October 1943, pp. 44–67.
56. *Partisan Review*, XI, 2 (1944), p. 153.
57. T.S. Eliot, 'That Poetry is made with Words', *New English Weekly*, 27 April 1939; T.S. Eliot, 'The Classics and the Man of Letters', address to the Classical Association, 15 April 1942, p. 13.
58. *Partisan Review*, 1944. Space precludes any detailed discussion of Eliot's apparent lack of interest in the modern British empire. But there are many hints that he would have viewed the monoglot global Anglo-Saxon culture favoured by many progressive imperialists as no less culturally distasteful than the 'New Order' of the Third Reich.
59. Amery papers, AMEL, 1/6/3, draft of speech by Leo Amery, December 1942.
60. Most famously in F.A. Hayek, *The Road to Serfdom* (London, 1944); but see also Ernest Benn, *Murmurings of an Individualist* (London, 1941), and *Benn's Protest* (London, 1945); Osbert Lancaster, *More and More Productions* (1948); John Jewkes, *Ordeal by Planning* (London, 1948).
61. *Oxford Magazine*, March 1949.

62. The unusually precise way in which he used the terms 'community' and 'society', as two quite distinct categories of social analysis, suggests some familiarity with the thought of Tönnies and Durkheim, though this would have almost certainly been mediated through more sociologically-minded friends such as Canon Demant and Philip Mairet (T.S. Eliot, *The Idea of a Christian Society* (London, 1939); John Hayward (ed.), *T.S. Eliot: Selected Prose* (London, 1953), pp. 212–6.

63. 'Social Function of Poetry', *Norseman*, II, 1944, p. 457; T.S. Eliot, 'Reflections on the Unity of European Culture (I)', *Adam International Review*, XIV, 158 (May 1946), pp. 2–3; T.S. Eliot, 'UNESCO and its Aims', *The Times*, 17 October 1947.

# 3
# Knowing Europe, Europeanizing Knowledge: The Making of 'Homo Europaeus' in the Life Sciences

*Veronika Lipphardt*

## I De/Europeanization: A labelling process?

Europe has often been imagined as the cradle of modern science and knowledge production. It is therefore not surprising that in the context of the European Union and its research agenda, the notion of a *knowledge-based society* has become a central focus. In fact, infusing knowledge production with Europeanness, on the one hand, and basing notions of Europe on knowledge, on the other, can been seen as two sides of the same coin: the Europeanization of knowledge production.

But how can 'Europe' or 'Europeanness' be conceived of in order to show how knowledge production has been Europeanized? Is it a given constant, a stable value? And, if so, what is it about it that is unmistakably European, and that distinguishes it from all other geographical, regional or political influences on knowledge production? In order to answer these questions, I suggest that, rather than seeking an objective essence of Europeanness, we should instead see 'Europeanization' as referring to any activity when the respective actors intentionally name it as 'European' – regardless of whether they perceive 'Europeanness' to be a cultural, legal, political or biological quality. By redefining the problem of 'Europeanness' as a subjective category, I hope to show how the label 'European' has evolved in the hands of the various historical actors who have appropriated it.

The approach outlined in the Introduction to this volume helps to overcome the classical divide between constructivist and essentialist standpoints by regarding 'being' and 'constructing' as intertwined elements of the same process. It captures the contingency of *Sinngebungen* as well as the 'concreteness' of Europe. In the case of knowledge production, this process might be described as a looping interplay between 'experiencing' or 'practising Europe', and 'labelling' or 'knowing Europe'. Actors can initiate, practise and organize structures and routines without intending to create something European, and only afterwards reflect on them as 'European'. Conversely, in wanting to 'know more' about Europe and Europeanness, actors may initiate inquiries into what they believe to be European. In addition, by applying knowledge about Europe or Europeans to achieve standardization – in public health-care systems, for example – a new level of practising Europe is reached. The Europeanization of knowledge production can thus be seen as a spiral looping process, oscillating between practice and representation. Despite what this metaphor might initially suggest, it does not necessarily take place in Europe, nor does it teleologically tend towards a concentration of what we call 'European'. Conversely, removing 'Europe' or 'Europeanness' from knowledge production and knowledge representation – that is, effecting 'de-Europeanization' – can, in fact, be a motive for actors to start their inquiries or build new structures.

To analyse such processes, I draw on the example of the production of biological knowledge about 'the European', or 'Homo Europaeus'.[1] Around 1700, scholars started to classify human diversity, as they had been doing for animals and plants. Since that time, 'Europeans' have been treated as a biological object in the life sciences – as a race, a subspecies, or a population. They are not, of course, the only subgroup of the human species that has occupied the attention of life scientists; most classificatory schemes are based on three, four or five races, with a varying number of ancillary categories. One of those main categories was labelled 'European' by many scholars; its vague, imagined contours comprised humans whose primary identifying physical features were light skin complexion, eyes and hair, and whose ancestors were believed to have had the European continent as their place of geographical origin. One might argue that life scientists used the term 'European' less often than (and, indeed only as a synonym for) the terms 'Caucasian' or 'White'. Certainly, many scientists – particularly in Anglo-American circles – viewed Europeans as the 'White race', 'Caucasians', or the 'Nordic type'. Such terms, however, were neither interchangeable nor ever perfectly congruent with the term 'European'. Europeanness meant more than just being white: it also connoted notions of cultural belonging and commitment. Biological concepts of a 'European race' implied the inclusion or exclusion of certain national, ethnic or political groups, and these boundaries were not coterminous with those of 'Caucasian', 'White' or 'Nordic'. This aspect has been neglected by the otherwise convincing and comprehensive studies of Bruce Baum or Matthew Jacobson of the use of 'Caucasian' and 'White' in the context of US immigration policy;[2] and my aim here is to illuminate the conceptual differences behind the terminological uses of 'European' and 'Caucasian', respectively.

While this article focuses primarily on German anthropology, it is set against the backdrop of related discussions in the USA and the UK.[3] In the United States, physical anthropology has been marginalized – though not replaced – by cultural anthropology. This is not the case in Germany. As German anthropology has always been synonymous with physical anthropology, the prefix 'physical' would have been tautological. Although German anthropology was deeply discredited after the Second World War, the discipline was nonetheless perpetuated by 'human geneticists' or 'anthropologists' in West Germany.[4] Because the history of the biological category 'European' is so closely linked to that of the biological term 'race', this chapter will view the history of both together as an intertwined development. The Anglo-American context also serves as an interesting foil because, despite the fact that the history and meaning of the term 'race' differs significantly from the German equivalent *'Rasse'*, they are nonetheless used as the translation for each other. Whereas *Rasse* denotes a biological concept of human diversity, 'race' – at least in its current usage in the USA and UK – is understood as a social construct that remains a valid category in the census; at the same time, however, the term 'race' carries biological notions, and a social construct can be subject to reification.

## II   De/Europeanization of knowledge production

In order to trace processes of Europeanization with respect to knowledge production, I will investigate the willingness of actors to label things as *European* (as opposed to alternate names), and to practise or perform something *European*; or, conversely, their resistance to labelling or performing something as *European*. If we understand knowledge production not only as a scientific undertaking but also in a broader sense, we can discern three levels on which Europeanizing and de-Europeanizing effects may be observed. First, elements of knowledge production – such as 'facts', artefacts, papers, routines, practices, persons or discourses – are exchanged among places, institutions and actors. In this sense, Europeanization describes the process that intentionally brings together networks and institutions under the label 'Europe' or 'European'. De-Europeanization, in contrast, signifies a process that breaks up networks and institutions which had been labelled European. This first definition represents a rather nebulous form of Europeanization: while travelling scholars may have liked the idea of belonging to Europe, they were not necessarily concerned with effecting Europeanization through their networks.

Europeanization on the other two levels requires effort that is much more cognitive and intentional. On a second level, 'Europe' can be seen as a category of knowledge production in an epistemological sense. That is, if actors attach the labels 'Europe', 'Europeans' or 'Europeanness' to the 'reality' under investigation, or if those labels appear in various epistemic places (for example in categories, classifications, research designs, concepts, descriptions, theories, and so on), this may be considered to be a Europeanizing process. Conversely, de-Europeanization occurs if European labels disappear from such epistemic places. Thirdly, knowledge representations help to disseminate knowledge in Europe and elsewhere. Institutions or networks cooperate in order to enhance knowledge dissemination; if those institutions are called 'European', and if they promote knowledge about Europe and Europeans, we can even speak of a double effect of Europeanization. Similarly, one can observe de-Europeanization if actors in European institutions cease cooperation, if they change the institution's name from 'European' into 'International' or 'National', or if the label 'European' disappears from the institution's agenda and from the knowledge representation itself.

One may conclude that the second level follows the first, and that the third follows the second. However, the three levels are not necessarily always linked in a linear, chronological relationship. Europeanization of epistemic places can take place without the Europeanization of networks; likewise, cooperation with respect to knowledge dissemination in European institutions is not necessarily a corollary of knowledge about Europe.

Why this preoccupation with labelling processes which occurred in the past? Can we not simply call European those things that are commonly viewed as European all over the world? Is not the *Res publica literarum*, for example, widely considered a European phenomenon – that is, an intense exchange of ideas, artefacts and scholars within Europe – and, at the same time, as a shaper of Europe and Europeanness? For analytical as opposed to ontological reasons, however, this chapter seeks to distinguish between current and historical notions of Europeanness. In this way, I hope to illustrate where and when these forms of Europeanization came together, and the synergetic effects this might have had. Where Europeanness is not a subjective category attributed by the actors themselves – as in the case of the *Res publica literarum* – but rather is used today to describe historical processes, we risk losing sight of an interesting historical phenomenon: that is, for example, when and why scholars appropriated certain labels of belonging, and when and why they started calling their networks 'European'. (I would suggest that Europeanization was a result of the *Res publica literarum*, rather than a precondition of its existence. As the early modern period was an era of *national* academies, to speak of a European *Res publica literarum* merely obscures processes of identification, and cannot signify more than the extension of a banal geographical network.[5])

## III  The making of Europeans in the life sciences

While many outstanding works on the biological construction of *national* identities through anthropology have been written,[6] the history of the biological understanding of *Europeanness* has not yet been studied; the category of Europeanness has thus far been neglected by historians of anthropology. There is a good reason for this neglect: while the nationalistic undertone of anthropological work undoubtedly contributed to the atrocities of discrimination and murder undertaken in the name of the nation, the idea of Europe has appeared in contrast to be relatively innocent and harmless. But it bears paying special attention to the labelling process itself: when and how was the national label challenged, completed or paralleled by the European one?

### 'Homo Europaeus' in the early modern period

The first scientific attempts to classify different kinds of humans took place in the late seventeenth century.[7] Since that time, bioscientists around the world have repeatedly attempted to define the unique aspects of their respective biological make-up, behaviour and needs; notions of human biodiversity were inevitably tied to bio-historical narratives of the origins of the human group in question. For example, in 1735, Carl Linné coined the name 'Homo Europaeus' for Homo sapiens with supposedly European features. He distinguished four races of 'Homo nosce te ipsum': *'Homo Europaeus albese*; *Homo Americanus rubese*; *Homo Asiaticus fuscus*; and *Homo Africanus nigr'*.[8] In the tenth edition (1758) of his *Systema Naturae*, 'Homo Europaeus' was characterized as 'white, sanguine, muscular. Hair: flowing, long; Eyes: blue. Gentle, acute, inventive. Covered with close [-fitting] vestments. Governed by law.'[9]

Johann F. Blumenbach was unsatisfied with Linné's classification system in general, and with that of the European in particular. Consequently, he based his classification of 1775 strictly on physical criteria, and not on character traits or clothing. He further divided mankind into five races: Mongolian, Ethiopian, American, Malay and Caucasian. He thereby coined the term 'Caucasian', which comprised both Europeans and West Asians. Caucasians, according to Blumenbach, were the ancestors of all humans and had originated in the Caucasus. Accordingly, 'Europeans' constituted only one subcategory of Caucasians; namely, they were the inhabitants of the continent Europe, with the exception of 'people from Lappland'.[10] Although criticized by some contemporaries, his classification proved very successful in the following centuries. Indeed, his term 'Caucasian' is an example of a migrating discourse: it became the official term for whites living in the USA.[11]

How did Linné and Blumenbach practise science, and how did they produce knowledge? Blumenbach had measured skulls but neither had conducted empirical studies of living humans. While both had encountered 'non-Europeans', most of their knowledge was derived from travel reports gathered from colonial activities. For both men, aesthetic criteria were very important, and they both considered Europeans – or Caucasians – to be the most beautiful of all races. Following the analytical framework suggested above, Linné and Blumenbach were Europeanizing knowledge by virtue of their use of the label 'European'. Blumenbach, however, disagreed with Linné regarding the relevance of that very label: Europeans had only a secondary place in Blumenbach's categorization. He was less willing than Linné to label something European; indeed, neither seemed that concerned with establishing networks under the label European.

## The European race around 1900

In the late nineteenth century, the classification of human beings required much more than theoretical speculation and travel reports. Against the backdrop of the nation-state, immigration restrictions, and military-service recruitment, it became a primarily empirical undertaking. Bodies of living humans were scrutinized and the results carefully reported in complex registration programmes. Large-scale investigations of many thousands of probands were carried out in schools and barracks.[12] Since the release of Darwin's theory of evolution, biologists had narrated the history of human beings in biological terms – that is, as a history of racial crossing, inbreeding, selection, development, inheritance and environmental influences; thus, the so-called 'Homo Europaeus' was seen as a product of European history. Accordingly, new forms of representation emerged, reflecting the bio-historical thinking of evolutionary theory: pedigrees were compiled, and maps drawn to trace migration routes in order to demonstrate the origins of racial ancestors.[13] These provide a striking example of the Europeanization of knowledge through the visualization of bio-historical narratives about Europeans.

'Europeans' were either labelled 'European race' or – particularly in US American contexts – 'Caucasians' or 'Whites'.[14] There is a certain paradox apparent in the history of knowledge about Europeans: although scholars considered the 'European' superior to other human races throughout the nineteenth and much of the twentieth century, Europeans were not, in fact, the primary objects of anthropological interest; most anthropologists simply took for granted that Europeans existed as a clearly distinct biological group. Hence, the 'Europeans' enjoyed the primary places in knowledge representations of human diversity, but not necessarily in the research design of empirical studies. Although textbook classifications of humankind before 1900 cited Linné's or Blumenbach's system of four or five races,[15] investigations *within* Europe increasingly focused on differences between subgroups of Europeans, often claiming differences between 'national' or 'regional' 'types' and 'races', and sought to distinguish Northern, Eastern, and Southern Europeans.[16] This focus on subdivision differentiation did not, of course, challenge the assumption that the subgroup under scrutiny was still considered to be European; nor did it undermine the traditional classification of mankind into four or five primary races.

There was, however, a revealing exception to this rule: William Z. Ripley, an American economist with anthropological interests, claimed that 'there is no single European or white race'. He collected all available findings from anthropometric investigations in his influential book *The Races of Europe, a Sociological Study*.[17] In the introduction, Ripley gave a detailed description of his methodology, whereby he compared head shape, hair and eye colour, and stature, and assumed the existence of three European races: Teutonic (called

Nordic by others), Alpine and Mediterranean. These, Ripley assumed, were prevalent in all European nations to varying degrees, and in the empirical part of his book the chapters were sorted according to certain groups of nations.

Why did Ripley organize his book along national lines instead of his three racial categories? To his own regret, Ripley was forced to take a national approach owing to the information on which he relied: statistics and anthropometric data were derived from *national* sources because they were intended for *national* purposes. Measurements could only be taken in national institutions where great numbers of probands were readily available. While Ripley complained about these restrictions, he saw no alternative.[18] Indeed, from Ripley's dissatisfaction one can infer the resistance to Europeanization he faced: national boundaries made it difficult to produce 'European' knowledge in the late nineteenth century. We can also see from his example how the attention of anthropologists shifted towards subdivisions of Europeans at the end of the nineteenth century. Nonetheless, in trying to differentiate between certain types of Europeans, he implicitly accepted that there was a clear difference between Europeans and non-Europeans.

What about Ripley's willingness to undertake something European? As a US citizen, Ripley certainly understood his work to be that of an unprejudiced non-European, free from national bias. But in the case of American scientists, the situation is more complicated. The terminological question of 'European', 'White' or 'Caucasian' had implications for every white American's own descent, and for the relationship between the respective colonies and the European land of origin.[19] Around 1900, heated discussions about immigration restrictions for Europeans were widespread in the USA, and anthropologists engaged in the fervent debates as experts and political advisers.[20] Disagreement centred on the question of how many and, above all, *which* European immigrants should be admitted. Each expert came from a family 'of European descent', and was therefore influenced and affected in his own right. The two main sides of the argument were represented on the one hand by Franz Boas, a German Jew who had immigrated in the 1880s and who considered the idea of European racial types to be completely unfounded, and on the other by Madison Grant, a white Anglo-Saxon Protestant who adhered to a scheme similar to Ripley's, and had a strong preference for the Nordic type.[21]

The use of the terms 'Caucasian' or 'European' in immigration and naturalization cases in the USA is revealing. 'Caucasian', as Jacobson points out, 'brought the full authority of modern science to bear on white identity'.[22] Nevertheless, its use was paralleled and challenged by the terms 'White' and 'European' in courts. When four Armenians applied for naturalization in 1909, the distinctions between 'Caucasian', 'European' and 'White' puzzled the court, because neither geographical origin, nor complexion or nationality provided any clear criteria. It was stated that the Armenians were less white than Norwegians, but whiter than Portuguese. Armenians were certainly

Caucasians, but were they Europeans? Who, in fact, should be considered European (and therefore admissible)? People from all European nations, or only those from countries whence the first American settlers had come?[23] In the many naturalization cases in that decade, all three terms were used successfully as means of both inclusion and exclusion.[24]

## Europeans in colonial contexts

After 1900, new methodological approaches were applied to human diversity, and investigations were carried out in new environments outside of Europe. Especially with research endeavours in the colonies, anthropologists and physicians were eager to distinguish and compare human groups according to their physical constitution. This trend of Europeanization in the colonies reached its peak between 1900 and 1914. The *Archiv für Schiffs- und Tropenhygiene*, a medical journal, provides a rich source for knowledge about Europeans and non-Europeans: it reported on 'European hospitals' and 'European quarters', discussed the adaptation of 'Europeans' to tropical climates and the effects of 'race mixture' between 'Europeans' and 'Natives'. Rarely do articles and reviews refer to 'Whites' instead of 'Europeans', and never to 'Caucasians', and we may consider the journal itself, published in Germany, to have been a Europeanizing institution. Articles were published in German or English and dealt with medical findings from all over the world – though mainly from colonial contexts. Reviews appeared in English, French, Italian and German, and principally covered publications by European authors. Scholars from many European nations appeared on the board of editors. However, the actors did not label their undertaking 'European'; their intention was probably simply to publish a scientific journal with an international agenda that would support colonial interests. However, since it primarily brought together scholars from Europe, and certainly enhanced European medical networks, this should be considered a case of unintentional Europeanization.

The primary sorting mechanism of such studies relied on the difference between 'Europeans' and natives, and this terminology clearly outweighed the use of 'White' versus 'Coloured'. Some scientists focused on the European's capability to cope with tropical climates – an important question for colonial rulers.[25] Others, rather than making the 'homo europaeus' an object of their research, used him instead as a point of reference and control in the investigation of non-Europeans. In addition to anthropometric measurements, all parts and functions of the body were scrutinized and compared. One doctor, for example, studied the digestion of both Europeans and Chinese in Shanghai; others discussed the differences between the brain anatomies of various 'races'.[26] Where serological methods were available for large-scale investigations, blood samples were taken and analysed in laboratories in order to find 'racial differences'.[27] The methods and findings of such research into the materiality of human diversity might not seem very convincing to today's reader, but at the time they enjoyed the prestige of objective and empirically sound scientific practices.

Another topic that attracted the attention of European researchers in tropical regions was the so-called 'race mixture', that is, marriages between 'natives' and 'Europeans'.[28] Especially in cases where the skin colour of the two spouses contrasted, these marriages and their offspring were seen from a Mendelian perspective: as a crossing of representatives of two 'pure lines'. When raising the theoretical issue of race mixture in publications, scientists preferred to use the analogy of Mendel's flower colours and speak of 'white' and 'black'. Conversely, where 'race mixture' was the epistemic object studied empirically, scientists used the category 'European' more often than 'white'. What logic informs such terminological patterns? Obviously, the daily work of research brought the scientists into contact with humans who embodied not just race, but also culture, hygiene, and a certain style of living. They met their European probands in European quarters, European hospitals or European houses; in short, in surroundings that had been built for Europeans. Distinguishing between 'Europeans' and 'natives' therefore seems to have been the most obvious approach in empirical studies, whereas theoretical approaches drew on biological aspects only – as with the Mendelian colour schemes – and not on cultural features or geographical origin.

In order to maintain colonial order, it seemed necessary to apply cultural techniques to the European body, that is, in terms of food, hygiene, physical and mental discipline, daily routine and contact with 'natives'.[29] Informed by medical studies, researchers recommended medical measures explicitly for Europeans, while 'natives' were treated differently, for example in the case of the sleeping sickness in Africa or the hookworm in Australia.[30] Europeanization was both an infrastructural way of establishing order and a system of knowledge production and application which allowed the maintenance of that very order.

After 1914, the term 'European' disappears from the articles and reviews published in the *Archiv für Schiffs- und Tropenhygiene*, and no substitute appeared; at the same time, the focus turned to specific medical or biochemical problems. Discussions about human diversity, European lifestyle in the colonies, and methods to help Europeans cope with tropical climates came to an end. Obviously, there was no longer a common interest between the German editors and their European colleagues. In terms of the journal's content and mission, this process may be considered as a case of de-Europeanization, and it seems evident that the editors' diminished willingness to perform and to label things 'European' coincided with the First World War.

### The Europid between the two world wars

In the first half of the twentieth century, scientific notions of 'race' and of human diversity were dominated by nationalistic attitudes; this was as true elsewhere as it was in Germany. While the notion of an 'Aryan race' was much more influential in Germany than that of a 'European race', the division of mankind into four or five races persisted and ran parallel to national classifications. After the First World War, however, the conditions for German anthropological research changed dramatically. Anthropologists were confronted with difficult circumstances: not only were there no colonies or prisoner-of-war camps where diversity could easily be studied at a single site, but there were also no more resources for expensive expeditions. German academics were internationally isolated, and the intensification of nationalism and societal disintegration had left their imprint on anthropological inquiry.

These various factors had paradoxical effects. First, we should consider the position of Jewish anthropologists in the German scientific community. At a time when German anthropology increasingly tended towards racist and anti-Semitic positions, German anthropologists with a Jewish background used the 'European race' as an integrative figure: they claimed that Jews belonged to the 'European race', and were not a foreign race in Europe.[31] Had they used the term 'white race', it would have put them in the same position as, for example, North-African Muslims. In contrast, the term 'European race' expressed not only a physical, but more importantly a cultural belonging.

Secondly, because empirical studies were difficult to carry out, many essayistic, non-empirical books on race appeared; one example was the work of Hans F.K. Günther, which was enthusiastically welcomed by the public and like-minded scholars. Moreover, scientific publications focused even more than had been the case previously on the 'racial composition of the nation', and those who were critical about race science – such as Rudolf Martin and his students – published mainly methodological reflections.[32] In spite of the focus on the racial composition of the nation, however, 'Europe' and 'European' remained meaningful categories in anthropological publications as well as in popular writings. Most authors referred to it as a 'mixed race', that is, a race consisting of various racial types which had undergone synthesis. Some authors, like Günther, believed that mixture was an inferior condition, and that the 'Nordic type' especially should abstain from marriages with other types. In his book *Deutsche Rassenkunde*, Günther assumed that there were five European types more or less present in Germany and in all other European nations. Because the problem obviously 'transgressed national borders', Günther published a *Kleine Rassenkunde Europas* that dealt with Europe's racial composition.

Although Ripley had established a similar system of classification, his had been based on empirical study and was free from such obviously racist motivations. Others, such as German-Jewish anthropologists who regarded themselves as integrated into European society, considered the Jews to belong to the 'European race', which was a homogenous, indivisible unit. Their opponents, on the other hand, held that the 'Jewish race' was an ancient, mixed race in its own right, alien to the European mixed race with respect to the quality and the proportions of its elements. Zionists took a yet different standpoint, believing as they did that the Jews were naturally suited to Palestine.[33]

In 'sound' scientific literature – meaning that which was acknowledged as such by international scholars at the time – the European found an even more elaborate consideration. In *Menschliche Erblehre*, a standard German textbook, Fritz Lenz and Eugen Fischer claimed to have coined the term 'Europid', in contrast to 'Mongolid' and 'Negrid'.[34] Of course, the general sketch of the Europid was much more favourable than those of the other two groups. The term 'Europid' was taken up by Egon von Eickstedt in 1934 and, from there, found its way into European anthropology after the Second World War.[35] Obviously, it was fine for Fischer, Lenz, Günther and Eickstedt to attach a European label to a certain detail of the knowledge they disseminated. Regarding their involvement with National Socialist bio-politics, one might conclude that their willingness to practise something *European* must have come a distant second to their willingness to practise something *national*.[36] Even if it is discordant with our current understanding of Europeanization, their interest in Europeanness can nonetheless be seen as a reflection of the Nazi regime's willingness to dominate Europe, and therefore as a manifestation of Europeanization in its own right. Moreover, because of its international success, the category of 'Europids' might also ultimately be seen as a form of Europeanization. Ironically, the German anthropological community had introduced a new classification of mankind that accounted for the European. But we should not be misled: the focus of its work was not on European, but rather on national unity. Indeed, the de-Europeanizing effect of German racial biology extends to the institutional level: cooperation was halted and networks interrupted – despite the fact that Eugen Fischer, especially, had enjoyed international recognition.

In the 1930s and 1940s, the new classification scheme devised by Fischer, Lenz and Eickstedt, together with Günther's view of Europe's racial composition, was influential. Not only did they advocate the National Socialist view of German predominance, but also the ideal of Nordic-type pre-eminence both within and outside Europe. However, today's history lessons have pared them down to their nationalistic agenda and to Günther's tradition; after the Second World War, only the *nationalistic* dimension was discredited, whereas the 'Europaeistic' dimension of their knowledge production not only remained unchallenged, but actually became quite influential.

### The European in anti-racist campaigns

From the beginning, many European and American contemporaries perceived the German racial biology sponsored by the National Socialist regime to be pseudo-scientific, inhuman, and strongly biased.[37] However, if we take a closer look, their reactions were sometimes ambivalent and half-hearted.[38] The understanding of humankind as a species with three, four or five races was internationally acknowledged and remained unchallenged. The notion that races differed in their capacities, in biological quality, and in cultural achievement was equally widespread. Anthropologists around the world were involved in the ethnic conflicts of their own nations, and some of them even held views not that different from those of their German colleagues.[39]

Nevertheless, biologist scientists launched and supported anti-racist campaigns, most notably Franz Boas and W.E.B. Du Bois.[40] As early as 1936, three British biologists published a book entitled *We Europeans* that accused German racists of drawing on 'pseudo-scientific' work, and on a perverted nationalism which threatened to de-Europeanize Europe.[41] The book was aimed at a broader European public and sought to convince Europeans that they all belonged to the same European race, and should therefore live together in peace. The authors tried to oppose the 'brutalization of European conscience', as George Mosse put it.[42] In their remarkable attempt to Europeanize knowledge about Europeans, the authors also itemized the tripartite classification of humankind; Europeans were accounted for as an indivisible biological unit subordinated to that larger classification. Their complaints were directed against the glorification of the Nordic or Aryan type, and not against biological subdivisions of humankind per se. Thus, even in egalitarian approaches we see subdivisions of humankind into 'Europeans' or 'Caucasoids'.[43] It was not until the early 1970s that new findings in human population genetics would challenge this common assumption.

## Europeans and Europids after the Second World War

After the Second World War, Eickstedt's classification and his new category of 'Europids' found their way into European textbooks, encyclopedia, and popular science books, even outside of the two Germanies.[44] As noted above, in anti-racist advocacy by UNESCO and in books by well-known geneticists, classifications of humans into three, four or five races – of which 'European' was still one – received broad acceptance.[45] From the 1970s, however, population geneticists started to point out that the genetic diversity of the human species did not permit coarse race classifications. Rather, they explained, each species can only be divided into manifold subgroups – populations – separated by continuous transitions instead of sharp breaks. In addition, intragroup variation was now found to be more extensive than intergroup variation.[46] Nonetheless, there remained physical anthropologists who held on to racial classification. Among them, the US scientists Carleton Coon and Stanley Garn publicly promoted their idea of nine 'geographic races' from 1974 (*World Book Encyclopedia*) until 1998 (*New Encyclopedia Britannica*). Garn maintained that the 'Caucasians' should be called a 'European geographical race', because thereby 'the original geographic centre is defined, and the inclusion of purely local races is more clearly understood'.[47] In his view, the 'Caucasian' was an inadequate term because it did not signify the place of origin of those humans who best represented the Whites of today – that is, the 'Nordics'.

In Germany both the term 'race' and the category 'European' persisted. Knowledge about human diversity was further Europeanized, on both the content and the institutional levels. Eickstedt's student Ilse Schwidetzky, a professor at Mainz University, launched a cooperative of European physical anthropologists working on 'European populations'.[48] Meanwhile, thanks to the pioneers of human population genetics, the term 'population' had replaced the unsatisfying and misleading term 'race',[49] and Schwidetzky used this new approach in the English proceedings of the group. At the same time, however, she published a popular science book in German entitled *Rassen und Rassenbildung beim Menschen*, in which 'race' is still the term for distinguishable groups in human diversity (in 1988 she stated that the term 'race' had been unfairly discredited by the National Socialists, and that she was satisfied with the new popularity those 'old concepts' had regained recently[50]). One long chapter in the book is devoted to 'Europe', and another of equal length to the rest of the world. In the Introduction, Schwidetzky informs the reader that her publisher had been approached by an English publishing house with the suggestion of translating an American textbook about human diversity into German. She had then decided to write a book herself because she thought the 'German reader' would like to learn more about 'Europe'.[51]

Schwidetzky's student Rainer Knußmann, professor of physical anthropology at the University of Hamburg, published a textbook on *Comparative Biology of Humans* in 1986 with a long chapter on 'race' and 'racial systematics'. In a four-page-long table, he compares 'Europids' with 'Mongolids', 'Negroids' and 'Australoids', and lists dozens of characteristics – blood group alleles, body measurements, pigmentation, body odour, and so on – which are presumed to differ from 'race' to 'race'.[52] The 'Europids' are the first group listed in the table, implying that all others are measured against their standards; a careful reading of the columns of numbers reveals that the table suggests that Europeans have light complexion, well-proportioned and sexually-attractive bodies, a delicate body odour, and certain gene alleles exclusively. Knußmann's table shows that in the second half of the twentieth century, the classifications proposed by early modern scholars had finally been filled out with empirical data, just as national classifications had been empiricized in the nineteenth century. A second edition of Knußmann's book appeared in 1996 with only minor changes; however, the book was withdrawn because students at his institute in Hamburg protested successfully against his teaching *Rassenkunde*.[53] Since that time, the term 'race' had disappeared from German publications on human biodiversity as well as from textbooks and encyclopedia.

### The European in human diversity studies today

For the moment, molecular genetics seem to have issued the final word on the race question. The 'population paradigm', as one might term it, has allowed for impressive public and political proclamations about the biological meaninglessness of race.[54] Humankind, the message suggests, consists of hundreds of thousands of populations and does not allow for coarse classification. One could therefore assume that the category of the 'European' should simply disappear from the map of human biodiversity. Nonetheless, even genetic classifications work with large group names such as 'European'. Since molecular genetics have taken over the knowledge production relating to human biodiversity, the 'genetic distance' between 'Europeans' and, for example 'Asians' or 'Africans' is measured exactly[55] – and, of course, each large group presumably consists of many smaller populations. The 'European' label in human diversity representations has proved to be even hardier than the term 'race'.

Today, human diversity is studied in large international research networks and also in EU-funded cooperative research projects.[56] The category 'European' is still prevalent in knowledge production and representation; it is often used interchangeably with 'Caucasian', 'White', or, in the USA, 'European Americans'. In the present situation, the uses of knowledge about human biodiversity are revealing. The main field of usage today is the medical sector. In Germany the approval procedure for new medications requires the recording of the ethnic descent of test subjects; one of the four or five default categories is 'White', 'European' or 'Caucasian'. Obviously, it is assumed that the doctors completing such documents know how to handle the ambiguity of these classifications. In German society, with its comparatively low ethnic diversity, the diversity itself is not the focus of the study and the respective information is considered irrelevant – although the fact that it is collected at all shows that its existence is not negated entirely. This corresponds with the handling of diversity in the political and administrative contexts in Germany as well as in the EU: in laws and regulations, the term 'race' is still used in a rather essentialist way. Recently, the German Institute for Human Rights has therefore claimed that the term 'race' should be abandoned in all governmental, juridical and public acts, and substituted by 'ethnic descent' or avoided by using the term 'racist discrimination'.[57]

In the USA the situation is more complex. The American census accounts for ethnicity in a very elaborate manner – ethnic categories are deliberately established and viewed as social constructs – and gives individuals the right to self-identify as the category that fits best. The collected data then help to frame policies against discrimination. But census categories also are the basis for recruiting a diverse population of probands in medical studies, and by law all minority groups must be considered in order to avoid discrimination. That means that the socially constructed census category might be reified in medical studies, especially in pharmacogenetics which aim at discerning the importance of genetic differences as causes of diverse drug responses.[58] The term 'European American', 'White' and 'Caucasian' are, at least according to the intention of researchers, considered to be interchangeable. However, whether a patient would regard them as congruent is highly questionable because it would require prior knowledge about the historical connotations of these terms. While patients from the USA might occasionally have acquired such knowledge in the course of daily life, for patients from European countries it is in no way self-evident that they should consider themselves Caucasians.[59] No system of classification of human diversity, we may conclude, can be valid in all places around the globe.

Another field of application is that of genetic ancestry. Since molecular genetics have become the primary access point for human diversity, geneticists claim to be able to trace the history of diverse groups by DNA testing and by comparing DNA sequences in terms of mutations that are allegedly typical for certain regions. Large research collaborations, human genome database projects, and genetic ancestry tracing companies have all undertaken to explore the biological history of humans down to its finest detail.[60] Multi-ethnic societies and nations with high immigration, especially the United States, have proven to be a good market for genetic ancestry testing services, which are sold to people who want to find out about the geographical origins of their families. This new sort of self-reassurement is paralleled by research efforts into the history of certain groups, such as, for example, Europeans. As the authors of respective studies emphasize, their genetic approach is meant to contribute decisively to the old discussion about the place of origin of Europeans. For example, a German team from Mainz University claims that Europeans are not, as most anthropologists believed, descended from Neolithic farmers who emigrated from the Near East and replaced the older resident hunter-gatherers.[61] The team compared the DNA of skeletons from Neolithic farmers with that of 'modern Europeans' and found no congruence in critical components of their DNA. The classification of 'modern Europeans' used by the team in their research is revealing: in the supplementary material, a list of the 'modern individuals' tested shows that there was a proband category 'European/Eurasian branch', in contrast to the 'Central Asian' and 'African/South Asian' branch. Even individuals from the same geographic origin were put into different categories, which implies that there were sorting criteria other than geographic origin that were not revealed in the publication. Historical and cultural notions of what it means to be European have obviously entered the research unnoticed, and the discussion about cultural achievements and survival success of 'farmers' and 'hunter-gatherers' still impinges on debates about genetic ancestry.

## IV   Conclusions

Knowledge production about the biological make-up of the inhabitants of Europe has, one may conclude, from its beginning in the early modern period, undergone processes of Europeanization which proved to be stronger than those of de-Europeanization. There were certainly significant drawbacks in the heyday of nationalism, but fewer with respect to categories than with respect to collaboration and positive identification.

Europeanization, in the sense suggested here and in terms of human diversity studies, occurred across Europe. Even in the anthropological discourses of the Soviet Union, the 'Europid' represented a figure of integration.[62] As a closer study of Germany reveals, there was a peak of Europeanization in physical anthropology between 1900 and 1914 – on the content level as well as on the institutional level – due to colonial medical research endeavours. This was followed by a phase of de-Europeanization on the part of those predisposed to nationalism; ironically, however, these scientists were the ones who introduced the new label 'Europid', which would prove so successful after the Second World War. Against this trend of de-Europeanization, anthropologists with a Jewish background or with other political agendas held on to their view that the Europeans represented a single, united and indivisible 'race', thereby – although without discriminatory intentions – reinforcing the boundaries between Europeans and non-Europeans.

Even more important than tracing the ups and downs of Europeanization, however, is to consider the nature of the Europeanization that was at work. Four variations can be found in the examples provided above. First, some protagonists drew on 'Europe' and 'Europeanness' as an invocation of European solidarity within Europe, as the examples of German-Jewish and British scientists have shown. They referred to Europe as an indivisible unit, believing that only European solidarity could help to overcome nationalism and war. Secondly, Europeanization could be centred on the idea of European subgroups. Many supported this idea and, at the same time, suggested a certain hierarchy of European 'types': a 'Nordic' or 'Aryan' type that was seen as naturally prone to dominate in Europe and, as the principal European type, elsewhere also. Hence, their call for unity still viewed 'Nordics' as the representatives of Europeans. Thirdly, Europeanization occurred when scientists attempted to classify humankind. Often – but not always – this was done under the unspoken assumption that Europeans were naturally prone to dominate all other humans. Certainly some biologists tried hard to establish objective categories that would preclude discrimination; but intentional or otherwise, no classification system can escape the logic of sorting, belonging, and ascribing, nor the cultural assumptions which precede even the most unprejudiced research design. No classification scheme, we may conclude, exists without the implicit act of distinguishing the 'other' from the 'self'. Finally, as Knußmann's example shows, standardization and making those standards universal was a form of Europeanization which used the 'European' as the point of reference, be it for comparison or for medical, economic, and administrative purposes.

From Linné to Knußmann, and even today, the label 'European' continues to be meaningful in human diversity studies. In many bio-anthropological publications the underlying message includes both notions of solidarity among Europeans, and, at the same time, ideas of predominance: that is, the predominance of Europeans (both within Europe and overseas), but also the predominance of respective nations or groups within a wider European population. Indeed, studies of human biodiversity are always deeply entangled in social constellations: in dealing with diverse groups, they are at times implicated in dramatic social and political conflicts, and thus in power relations – these are sometimes even embedded in their research design. This holds true for colonial medicine as well as for military screenings in Western nations. Regardless of the context, the 'European' always plays a crucial role in human biodiversity studies, be it as a reference point for measuring and comparing, for identification, or for standardization.

While the 'European' of the life sciences is not necessarily the same as the 'European' in political discourse, biological notions of 'Europeanness' may nonetheless resonate in the political realm; indeed, the relationship between these bears further study in the future. To date it seems these two discourses – that of the political sphere and that of the life sciences – converged most closely in colonial contexts, far away from Europe, where the differences between 'Europeans' and 'non-Europeans' seemed much more obvious than the distinction between various European types. In recent years, Europeanizing initiatives have been tackling European history school textbooks. Given what we have seen of the centrality of colonial scientific endeavours in shaping European identity, the message to prospective young European readers should be that if we can appropriate classical antiquity, the Enlightenment, and the moniker of a 'knowledge-based society', if we can label these as 'European' and deem them constituent parts of European identity, then we must also include colonialism in this list.

## Notes

1. Cf. W. Schmale, 'The construction of Homo Europaeus', in: *Comparative European History Review* I (2001), 165–84.
2. B. Baum, *The Rise and Fall of the Caucasian Race. A Political History of Racial Identity* (New York, 2006); M.F. Jacobson, *Whiteness of a Different Color. European Immigrants and the Alchemy of Race* (Cambridge, MA, 1998).
3. N. Stepan, *The Idea of Race in Science: Great Britain 1800–1960* (Basingstoke, 1984); E. Barkan, *The retreat of scientific racism. Changing concepts of race in Britain and the United States between the world wars* (Cambridge, 1992).
4. U. Hossfeld, *Geschichte der biologischen Anthropologie in Deutschland. Von den Anfängen bis in die Nachkriegszeit* (Stuttgart, 2005); D. Preuss, '"Zeitenwende ist Wissenschaftswende". Egon Freiherr von Eickstedt und die Neuanfänge der "Breslauer Tradition" in Leipzig und Mainz 1945–1950', in D. Preuss et al. (ed.), *Anthropologie nach Haeckel* (Stuttgart, 2006), pp. 102–24.
5. Cf. K. Garber and H. Wismann (eds), *Europäische Sozietätsbewegung und demokratische Tradition: Die europäischen Akademien der Frühen Neuzeit zwischen Frührenaissance und Spätaufklärung* (Tübingen, 1996).
6. To name but a few: H.-W. Schmuhl, *The Kaiser Wilhelm Institute for Anthropology, Human Heredity and Eugenics, 1927–1945: Crossing Boundaries* (Berlin, 2008);

B. Massin, 'From Virchow to Fischer. Physical Anthropology and "Modern Race Theories" in Wilhelmine Germany', in G.W. Stocking (ed.), *Volksgeist as Method and Ethic: Essays on Boasian Ethnography and the German Anthropological Tradition* (Madison, 1996) pp. 79–154; G.L. Mosse *Towards the Final Solution: A History of European Racism* (London, 1978); P.J. Weindling *Health, Race and German Politics between National Reunification and Nazism 1870–1945* (Cambridge, 1989); S.F. Weiss 'German Eugenics' in D. Kuntz (ed.), *Deadly Medicine: Creating the Master Race* (Washington DC, 2004), pp. 15–39.

7. For a detailed account of human diversity in Enlightenment science cf. Baum, *Caucasian Race*, pp. 58–94.

8. C. Linneaus, *Systema Naturae* (Stockholm, 1735).

9. C. Linneaus, *Systema Naturae* (10th ed. Stockholm, 1758–59), pp. 20–2.

10. Baum, *Caucasian Race*, pp. 73–82.

11. Cf. Baum, *Caucasian Race*, pp. 109–17 and 135.

12. For example, R. Virchow, 'Gesammtbericht über die von der deutschen anthropologischen Gesellschaft veranlaßten Erhebungen über die Farbe der Haut, der Haare und der Augen der Schulkinder in Deutschland', *Archiv für Anthropologie* XVI (1886), 275–434.

13. For example: E. Haeckel, *Unsere Ahnenreihe. Kritische Studien über Anthropologie* (Jena, 1908), p. 54.

14. Baum, *Caucasian Race*. See also: M.F. Jacobson, *Whiteness*.

15. An early example: C. Bertuch, *Bilderbuch für Kinder* (Weimar, 1830), vol. 12, no. 76.

16. Cf. Baum, *Caucasian Race*, pp. 119–60.

17. W.Z. Ripley, *The Races of Europe. A Sociological Survey* (London, 1899). Cf. Baum, *Caucasian Race*, pp. 144–51.

18. Ibid., pp. 27–9.

19. Cf. D.A. Segal, '"The European". Allegories of racial purity', *Anthropology Today* 7.5 (1991), 7–9.

20. Baum, *Caucasian Race*, pp. 128–51; A. Zolberg, *A Nation by Design: Immigration Policy in the Fashioning of America* (Harvard, 2006).

21. Boas did refute the idea of 'European races' but not the division of humankind into three larger races. Cf. Baum, *Caucasian Race*, pp. 157–60.

22. Jacobson, *Whiteness*, p. 94.

23. Jacobson, *Whiteness*, pp. 231–4.

24. Ibid.

25. Cf. P. Curtin, *Disease and Empire: The Health of European Troops in the Conquest of Africa* (Cambridge, 1998).

26. W. Fischer, 'Über Stuhluntersuchungen bei Europäern und Chinesen in Shanghai' *Archiv für Schiffs- und Tropenhygiene* XVIII 18 (1914), 124–51.

27. C. Bruck, 'Die biologische Differenzierung von Affenarten und menschlichen Rassen durch spezifische Blutreaktionen' *Berliner klinische Wochenschrift* XXVI (1907), 793–7.

28. E.g. E. Fischer, *Die Rehobother Bastards und das Bastardisierungsproblem beim Menschen. Anthropologische und ethnographische Studien am Rehobother Bastardvolk in Deutsch-Südwestafrika* (Jena, 1913).

29. Cf. B. Barth and J. Osterhammel, *Zivilisierungsmissionen. Imperiale Weltverbesserung seit dem 18. Jh.* (Konstanz, 2005).

30. W. Anderson, *The Cultivation of Whiteness: Science, Health and Racial Destiny in Australia* (Melbourne, 2002).

31. V. Lipphardt, *Biologie der Juden. Jüdische Wissenschaftler über 'Rasse' und Vererbung (1900–1935)* (Göttingen, 2008), pp. 75–86.

32. E.g. R. Martin, *Richtlinien für Körpermessungen und deren statistische Verarbeitung Zusatz mit besonderer Berücksichtigung von Schülermessungen* (Munich, 1924).

33. R. Falk, 'Zionism, Race and Eugenics' in G. Cantor and M. Swetlitz (eds), *Jewish Tradition and the Challenge of Darwinism* (Chicago, 2006), pp. 137–65; Lipphardt, *Biologie der Juden*, pp. 213–22.

34. E. Baur, E. Fischer and F. Lenz, *Grundriß der menschlichen Erblichkeitslehre und Rassenhygiene* (München, 3rd ed., 1927), pp. 135f. 'Mongoloid', 'Caucasoid' and 'Negroid' had been used in US classifications before.

35. V. Lipphardt, 'Von der "europäischen Rasse" zu den "Europiden". Wissen um die biologische Beschaffenheit des Europäers in Sach- und Lehrbüchern, 1949–1989' in L. Bluche, V. Lipphardt and K.K. Patel (eds) *Der Europäer – ein Konstrukt. Wissensbestände, Diskurse, Praktiken* (Göttingen, 2009); E. v. Eickstedt, *Rassenkunde und Rassengeschichte der Menschheit* (Stuttgart, 1934). This development has remained completely unnoticed by Bruce Baum and others.

36. Preuss, *Eickstedt*.

37. Barkan, *Scientific Racism*.

38. Cf. Baum, *Caucasian Race*, pp. 173–81.

39. S. Kühl, *The Nazi Connection: Eugenics, American Racism, and German National Socialism* (New York, 2002).

40. Cf. Baum, *Caucasian Race*, pp. 152–60.

41. J. Huxley et al., *We Europeans: A Survey of 'Racial' Problems* (New York and London, 1936), p. 235.

42. Mosse, *Final Solution*, p. 172.

43. L.C. Dunn and T. Dobzhansky, *Heredity, Race and Society* (New York, 1947); idem, *The Race Question in Modern Science: Race and Biology* (Paris, 1951). For more examples: Baum, *Caucasian Race*, pp. 173–91.

44. Lipphardt, Von der 'europäischen Rasse'; Baum, *Caucasian Race*, pp. 200–3.

45. Ibid.; P. Weingart, J. Kroll and J. Bayertz, *Rasse, Blut und Gene. Geschichte der Eugenik und der Rassenhygiene in Deutschland* (Frankfurt am Main, 1988), pp. 602–22; S. Müller-Wille, 'Was ist Rasse? Die UNESCO-Erklärungen von 1950 und 1951' in P. Lutz (ed.), *Der (im-) perfekte Mensch. Metamorphosen von Normalität und Abweichung* (Köln, 2003), pp. 79–93; E. Barkan, 'The Politics of the Science of Race: Ashley Montagu and UNESCO's Anti-racist Declarations' in L.T. Reynolds and L. Lieberman (ed.), *Race and other Misadventures: Essays in Honour of Ashley Montagu in his Nineteenth Year* (New York, 1996), pp. 96–105. The original texts are reprinted in: L.C. Dunn et al. (ed.), *Race, Science and Society* (Paris/London, 1975), pp. 343–64.

46. Cf. Baum, *Caucasian Race*, pp. 207–11.

47. Ibid., pp. 200–4.

48. I. Schwidetzky et al. (ed.) *Physical Anthropology of European Populations* (The Hague, Paris and New York, 1980).

49. Most notably R. Lewontin and, though more ambivalent, L.L. Cavalli-Sforza. Cf. Baum, *Caucasian Race*, pp. 207–13.

50. I. Schwidetzky, 'Geschichte der Anthropologie' in R. Knußmann *Wesen und Methoden der Anthropologie* vol. I (Stuttgart and New York, 1988), 98f.

51. I. Schwidetzky, *Rassen und Rassenbildung beim Menschen. Typen – Bevölkerungen – Geographische Variabilität* (Stuttgart and New York, 1979), pp. 1–55 (Introduction).

52. R. Knussmann, *Vergleichende Biologie des Menschen* (Stuttgart and New York, 1980), pp. 328–31.

53. Arbeitsgemeinschaft gegen Rassismus in den Lebenswissenschaften, *Deine Knochen – deine Wirklichkeit. Texte gegen rassistische und sexistische Kontinuität in der Humanbiologie* (Hamburg and Münster, 1998).
54. For detailed critics of population genetics: J. Marks, *Human Biodiversity: Genes, Race, and History* (New York, 1995); cf. J. Reardon, 'Decoding Race and Human Difference in a Genomic Age' *Differences* xv (2004), 38–65; idem, *Race to the Finish: Identity and Governance in an Age of Genomics* (Princeton, 2005).
55. See, for example, the world map in: W. Buselmaier and G. Tariverdian, *Humangenetik für Biologen* (Heidelberg, 2006), p. 339.
56. Such as the Human Genome Diversity Project (until 2000) and the HapMap Project. See B. Koenig, S.S.-J Lee and S.S. Richardson (eds), *Revisiting Race in a Genomic Age* (New Brunswick/New Jersey/London, 2008); AG gegen Rassismus (ed.), *Gemachte Differenz. Kontinuitäten biologischer 'Rasse' Konzepte*, (Münster, 2009); Reardon, *Race to the Finish*.
57. H. Cremer, '*…und welcher Rasse gehören Sie an?' Zur Problematik des Begriffs 'Rasse' in der Gesetzgebung* (Berlin, 2008).
58. S. Epstein, *Inclusion. The Politics of Difference in Medical Research* (Chicago and London, 2007).
59. See a recent account of critics of 'race-based medicine': P. Ng et al., 'Individual Genomes Instead of Race for Personalized Medicine', *Clinical Pharmacology & Therapeutics* 84.3 (2008), 306–9.
60. M. Sommer, 'History in the Gene: Negotiations between Molecular and Organismal Anthropology', *Journal of the History of Biology* xli (2007), 473–528.
61. W. Haak et al., 'Ancient DNA from the First European Farmers in 7500-Year-Old Neolithic Sites', *Science* 310 (2005), 1016–18; see particularly the supplementary material.
62. M.F. Nesturch, *Menschenrassen* (Leipzig and Jena, 1959); cf. Lipphardt, 'Von der europäischen Rasse'.

# Part Two
# Europe Constructed

# 4

# From Minority Protection to Border Revisionism: The European Nationality Congress, 1925–38

*Ulrike v. Hirschhausen*

## I  Introduction: The Congress as a symbol of Europeanization

The First World War and the break-up of Europe's continental empires marked not only a triumph of democratic principles, but also one of nationalism.[1] While the erstwhile empires had relied on dynastic, historic and religious loyalties that allowed them a flexible policy towards their many ethnic groups,[2] the new countries emerging after 1918 legitimized themselves by equating 'state' with 'nation', and defined their population as homogeneous, regardless of its actual degree of heterogeneity. Due to the complexity and multi-ethnic structure of the distribution of the population, particularly in Central and Eastern Europe, the Allies' redrawing of the political map at the Paris Peace Conferences of 1919–20 did not realize Woodrow Wilson's vision of the 'self-determination of peoples'.[3] Rather, the cessation of large territories and their inhabitants to ethnically different nation-states suddenly created a group of approximately 35 million people who were defined as 'minorities' in their new or remodelled countries. While nine million of these lived in Western Europe (mostly in Germany, Italy and Spain), about 26 million were spread across Eastern Europe – primarily in Poland, Czechoslovakia, Yugoslavia and Romania.[4] The Allies tried to safeguard them by imposing upon the new host states treaties which placed ethnic minorities under international rule and were guaranteed by the newly founded League of Nations.[5]

The League's subsequent failure to live up to this difficult responsibility led some minority leaders, whose status was still at risk in the new states, to establish the 'European Nationality Congress' in 1925. In contrast to the League, which represented states, the Congress aimed to represent the people who felt marginalized by these states. The very name of the Congress – combining the European dimension with the national one – underscores the inherent tension between national rights and the idea of protecting their status everywhere in Europe. Indeed, the Congress's ambivalent history of both liberal principles and revisionist strategies, its diverse membership (ranging from staunch democrats and liberal Jews, to conservatives and National Socialists), and the time frame of its existence between democracy and dictatorship, has inspired very divergent assessments of its activities by successive generations of historians. They have oscillated between viewing the Congress as an instrument of German imperialism on the one hand,[6] and as a democratic forerunner of European integration politics on the other.[7] Only the most recent works have overcome such a polemical approach by accentuating both its European and national politics; yet in these instances the history of the Congress has been examined primarily in terms of its concrete actions or as an object of international relations.[8] Looking instead at the Congress's development as an aspect of Europeanization in the twentieth century can fruitfully challenge long-held assumptions on this theme and contribute to a new understanding about what Europeanization means from a historical perspective.

In particular, three major premisses of Europeanization are brought to the fore. First, the binary model of a Europe of nationalism, violence, and destruction before 1945, and a Europe of political integration, peace, and prosperity thereafter has implicitly contributed to a diametrical categorization of the processes of Europeanization and de-Europeanization: on the one hand, a linear process of intensifying political, economic, and cultural links that endured from the end of the Second World War until today, and on the other, a comparably linear process of fragmentation, fascism, and total war that reached its nadir in 1945.[9] The new approaches tested in this volume posit instead that processes of Europeanization can no longer be neatly separated and assigned to certain time periods, but rather comprised ambivalent and contradictory forms of both entanglement and fragmentation, for example through violence, forced migration, or the experience of war.[10] Both aspects of Europeanization – that is, intensification as much as fragmentation – crystallized in the European Nationality Congress, and therefore contradict any attempt at diametrical distinction. The Congress's history forces us to ask how and why these processes could occur, and where to locate those of Europeanization in a 'tidal Europe', whose ebbs and flows varied with a changing historical context.

Secondly, the spatial dimension with which the term Europeanization has thus far been associated seems to be thrown into question given the history of the European Nationality Congress. Europeanness, as Wolfgang Schmale has pointed out, has until now been almost automatically considered to be a characteristic of Western Europe; as such, Europeanization has correspondingly been regarded as a process of entanglement between Western states and societies.[11] In contrast to this dominant view, the idea of the Congress, with its aim of Europeanizing minority rights, was conceived of by politicians in Central-Eastern Europe and enjoyed particular resonance in that area of Europe. Examining the role of the Congress in inter-war European history can therefore contribute to overcoming the spatial reduction of Europeanization (which still reflects the former Cold War division), and to stimulating a new concept of place when approaching the history of the continent as a whole.

Finally, the Congress's history points to the necessity of engaging critically with the question of boundaries. There are several sound reasons, as explained in the Introduction to this volume, why we must sufficiently take into account the many non-European influences that shaped the processes of Europeanization. At the same time, agents of Europeanization have consistently set boundaries to distinguish their projects from the non-European world. Thus, the members of the European Nationality Congress restricted their activity to Europe because they sharply distinguished between minorities by migration, most common in the non-European world, and minorities emerging from the political reconfiguration of Europe after 1918. Inflating the definition of Europeanization to include all possible transactions with non-European contexts neither corresponds to the historic reality nor provides the clear analytical tool which is so needed. Instead, it merely makes Europeanization interchangeable with processes such as Westernization, transnationalism or imperialism, and thereby strips the concept of any analytical value. As such, an appreciation of the impact of non-European influences must go hand in hand with a clear understanding of the distinct boundaries within which Europeanization took place in the minds of contemporary players.

Having located the European Nationality Congress within this context, this chapter proceeds in four parts. Using the Congress's minutes, publications, and memoirs of its members, it first examines the reasons for the organization's foundation and its programmatic aims. Secondly, it analyses the membership of the Congress in terms of their geographical, ethnic, and social composition. It then goes on to investigate how the Congress implemented its programme and to assess how successful it was in a time of growing nationalism. Finally, we grapple with whether we can identify a turning point at which the politics of Europeanization gave way to patterns of de-Europeanization. If so, what were the reasons for this? The chapter concludes by returning to the arguments introduced here, and seeks to locate the Congress within the larger concept of a history of Europeanization.

## II  'A parliament of minorities'? The founding motives and programme of the Congress

The complete alteration of Europe's political landscape after the First World War had given rise to entities which were called nation-states, but in fact were not. Most of the states – particularly in Central-Eastern Europe – were composed of multi-ethnic populations, with national minorities making up about 30 per cent of the total population. At the Paris Peace Conferences of 1919–20, the Allies had settled treaties with most of these states that were intended to safeguard the rights of minorities in terms of citizenship, legal equality, property relations, schooling and cultural identity.[12] Some states with minority populations – namely Germany and Italy – were, however, excluded from these enforced stipulations.[13]

The Allies were primarily interested in the consolidation of those new states which could form a *cordon sanitaire* against the Soviet Union, and therefore made individuals, as opposed to collective groups, the subject of the minority treaties. This initial decision resulted in minorities being legally hindered in how far they were able to sue for their guaranteed rights. The main shortcomings of minority protection, however, lay in the absence of effective enforcement; the League of Nations, as guarantor of the treaties, had established extremely complicated procedures for any appeal by minorities, and this effectively precluded cases being referred to the Council (the highest appellate body).[14] In most cases the League tended to support the position of the accused government and therefore did not transfer complaints, for example, to the Permanent Court of International Justice in The Hague.[15] This imbalance notwithstanding, resentment towards the treaties in many of the new states grew, not least because the treaties had only been enforced in certain countries. Above all, the rise of nationalism across Europe triggered a tendency in most states to view their minorities less as citizens than as the 'fifth column' of another state and, therefore, as a security risk.

The discrimination against minorities that had been growing since the 1920s – for example in Fascist Italy, Poland, Czechoslovakia, Romania or Hungary – and the increasingly visible failure of the League to safeguard their rights, precipitated the idea of organizing a European representation of national minorities: 'The question of national minorities is a European question.'[16] The impulse came mainly from Baltic Germans in the newly founded Baltic States, who looked back on a long tradition of cultural autonomy,[17] Hungarians who were dispersed among many neighbouring countries due to the large territorial losses experienced by the Hungarian state after the First World War,[18] and Jews from Central-Eastern Europe where they had long suffered from repression and inequality.[19] Correspondingly, members of these groups took the lead in establishing an official representation of minorities in Europe; first among these was Dr Paul Schiemann, a Baltic German journalist and member of the Latvian parliament,[20] Dr Josip Wilfan, a Slovene lawyer and member of the Italian parliament, Geza v. Szüllo, representing the Hungarian groups in the parliament of Czechoslovakia, and the head of the Committee of Jewish delegations in Paris, Leo Motzkin.[21]

Owing to the indefatigable efforts of Ewald Ammende, a Baltic German lawyer from Estonia with excellent connections to many governments and non-German minorities across Europe,[22] minority groups from all over the Continent attended the formal founding ceremony of the European Nationality Congress in Geneva on 14 October, 1925.[23] About 60 representatives of minorities from 14 European states took part in the inaugural session, wherein French and German were the main languages of communication.[24] Certain membership criteria were established with a view to eliminating any separatist tendencies and making the Congress a respectable institution that would constitute a serious partner for governments, international institutions, and minorities alike. These conditions included: a) restriction to minorities within Europe; b) a strict rule that only questions of general relevance – not specific cases – were to be negotiated; c) a requisite declaration of loyalty to the country of citizenship combined with a promise to eschew separatist aims; d) a certain degree of organization and representation in their own countries; and e) tolerance towards co-minorities in the same country.

From the assumed basis of loyalty to the state of citizenship – notwithstanding its later corrosion – the members developed a variety of ideas and activities in the first decade of the Congress's existence. As this chapter is interested primarily in the Europeanizing impact and its limits, it concentrates on four separate goals and examines how they were implemented. First, a European communication network was to be developed to bring together leading representatives of various minorities and to give them a forum in which to meet and to develop and exchange ideas on minority rights. A second aim of the Congress was to bring the minority cause effectively to the attention of the European public. Thirdly, its members intended to build up a 'proto-diplomacy' which would influence supranational decision-makers (such as the League of Nations) in order to effect tangible improvements in the situation of minorities. Concrete plans consisted, for example, of establishing a permanent commission for minority rights at the League and of providing the Permanent Court of International Justice in The Hague with greater authority in minority issues. Fourthly, the Congress sought to give minority rights a scientific grounding by developing legal concepts and empirical material which would support the cause in the public and political realms. In particular, at the heart of this endeavour lay the internationalization of minority rights, which, it was hoped, would make them an integral part of the constitution of each state. The history of the Congress over the following years serves as evidence of the extreme difficulty in achieving such aims during a time of growing nationalism in many European states, and in translating the specific national interests of discrete groups into an abstract supranational principle to which all minorities could subscribe.

## III   Transcending borders and ethnicity: The Congress's European membership

This brief glimpse at the members of the European Nationality Congress has already shown that the problems faced by minorities were by no means confined to Eastern Europe. As General Secretary Ewald Ammende pointed out at the fifth session in 1930, 'Our problem is not only one of this or that

*Table 4.1* Geographical distribution of Congress members, 1925–1938

| Country of origin | Number of delegates |
|---|---|
| Poland | 51 |
| Romania | 29 |
| Czechoslovakia | 29 |
| Spain | 23 |
| Germany | 13 |
| Yugoslavia | 12 |
| Latvia | 12 |
| Estonia | 11 |
| Austria | 11 |
| Italy | 9 |
| Hungary | 9 |
| Other | 10 |
| Total | 219 |

single state but concerns all parts of our continent, and is therefore a matter of the entire Europe. The nationality issue is particularly urgent and relevant in Central and Eastern Europe, but, as the example of Spain, where 25% of the population belong to the minorities, teaches us, this is valid to a certain degree also for Western and Southern Europe.'[25]

The range of countries whence the 219 delegates originated from confirms this contemporary assumption and underlines the fact that the membership was not compartmentalized along an East–West divide. Table 4.1[26] gives a numerical account of the European home countries of the delegates.[27] What the table does not show, however, is the gradual dominance attained by ethnic Germans, particularly after Northern Frisian, Poles and Sorbs from Germany left the Congress in 1927, and after all Jewish minorities withdrew in 1933.[28] While each delegate carried the citizenship of his country, his ethnic or cultural identity differed from this citizenship, thus giving him the status of a 'minority'.

Table 4.2 lists the largest ethnic groups represented among the delegates, with 'ethnicity' defined as that which the individual considered himself to be. Among the 'Others' were Basques, Lithuanians, and Slovenes who, in the early years, formed quite a substantial group; later on, German minorities – primarily from Poland, Czechoslovakia and the Baltic countries – gained the upper hand.[29] This later development notwithstanding, the diversity of the membership confirms the impression that the Congress did, in fact, comprise both East and West European groups. Jews were integrated from the very beginning as an ethno-religious minority, and served prominently on the Board until 1932. This cross-section shows that, despite the notion of a 'Christian Occident' ('Christliches Abendland') popular in Central European

Table 4.2 Ethnic composition of Congress members, 1925–1938[30]

| Ethnicity | Number of delegates |
|---|---|
| Germans | 74 |
| Jews | 25 |
| Catalans | 17 |
| Ukrainians | 17 |
| Hungarians | 16 |
| Russians | 13 |
| Poles | 11 |
| Czechs | 8 |
| Bulgarians | 6 |
| Other | 32 |
| Total | 219 |

public discourse of the time, Europe was imagined by the Congress not as a Christian continent, but rather as a multi-religious one that included Protestants, Catholics, Orthodox and Jewish groups alike.[31] While in geographical and ethnic respects diversity was high, in social terms homogeneity dominated. Almost all delegates came from the middle class and the free professions – lawyers, journalists, professors, businessmen, to name but a few. In addition, homogeneity was also the rule in terms of gender, with only four women among the 219 delegates participating in the Congress's sessions.[32] Table 4.3 outlines the social profile of Congress members.

The reasons for such an overwhelmingly middle-class composition were manifold. Above all, one of the admission criteria – that is, to be able to undertake a certain degree of organization and representation in one's home country – resulted in leadership by the intelligentsia. Moreover, many of the minority leaders were at the same time members of parliament in their home countries, where they represented the interests of their respective ethnic group. In most cases this type of political affiliation went hand in hand with a requirement for a university diploma. Finally, the broad subject of minority law was a highly sophisticated and complicated matter requiring fairly substantial juridical, political and ethnographic knowledge; this in itself minimized the participation of lower- or working-class members, who were, in fact, essentially absent from the sessions of the European Nationality Congress throughout its existence.

In sum, the idea of defending minority rights as a form of European representation did not remain merely notional. Rather, it was employed and practised by actors from a variety of European countries (albeit somewhat dominated by Central-Eastern Europe). The social reality behind the ideal shows that while the protagonists may have been restricted to the middle class, they nonetheless established personal networks that

*Table 4.3* Social composition of
Congress members, 1925–1938[33]

| Occupation | Number of delegates |
|---|---|
| Lawyers, judges | 37 |
| Journalists | 27 |
| Entrepreneurs, businessmen | 16 |
| Pastors | 10 |
| Farmers | 7 |
| Teachers | 3 |
| Politicians | 5 |
| Other | 6 |
| Total | 111 |

successfully transcended geographical, ethnic and religious boundaries, and which proved capable of initiating and channelling Europeanization as a social and communicative process.

## IV    Realizing minority protection and its limits: Congress activities 1925–32

In the first years following its foundation the European Nationality Congress gradually developed into a well-functioning and visible advocate of national minorities in Europe.[34] Already the successful and well-publicized opening session in Geneva in the autumn of 1925 had garnered a fair amount of publicity and led to the entry of several additional minorities in subsequent years.[35] With its goal of constituting a counterbalance to the state-dominated League of Nations, the European Nationality Congress successfully represented the civil interests of groups otherwise excluded by the state-to-state organizations of the time. The rhetoric of a 'parliament of minorities' made discernible the original democratic idea of detaching minorities from Europe's political geography and opposing borders which seemed ruthlessly to identify state and nation.[36] The separation of these was at the heart of the concept of an 'anational State', developed by the Congress's leading intellectual, Paul Schiemann.[37] In his keynote address at the inaugural session in October 1925, he argued that, although the state should remain responsible for the entire political realm, it should grant its minorities autonomy in all cultural affairs: 'And we do foresee the day, which in earlier times the champions of religious freedom had fought for. The state has no right on the nationality of its citizens (...) as much as the national identity of the citizen must not influence his loyalty to the state (...) Citizens of different nationality will without problems work together for the state and the public weal, as long as they can freely develop their own cultural development.'[38]

This idea of cultural autonomy superimposed a new, contemporary interpretation on the Baltic German estate tradition, which had prevailed since the early modern period, as well as on concepts of Austrian Social Democracy and Zionism dating from the early twentieth century. With the main focus on reforming the relations between minority and majority within a single state, it reflected the philosophy of the Congress's liberal and democratic wing and remained the framework for their various activities throughout the 1920s. In contrast, a rival group consisting of right-wing Germans, nationalistic Ukrainians and a few Slovenes and Hungarians, saw the main purpose of minority politics as strengthening the 'inseparable bond' between an ethnic minority and its national 'homeland' abroad. As long as the influence of the liberal wing was strong, and favoured by a political climate relatively interested in minority issues, such ideas did not resonate much in the Congress, which instead pursued its original aims (with varying success).

As has already been shown, probably the most successful aspect of the Congress was the ability of its members to *develop a communication network* between ethnic minorities all over Europe. The number of groups represented in the Congress rose steadily until the early 1930s, quickly covering large parts of Central and Eastern Europe as well as some territories in Western Europe. Together, Russians from Poland and Estonia, Catalans and Basques from Spain, Poles and Bulgarians from Romania, Czechs and Croats from Austria, and Jews from Bulgaria – to name but a few – participated in the annual meetings and communicated with each other in the interim.[39] The experience of jointly defending minority rights against what were essentially uninterested or hostile states did, for a limited time, effect a personal network whose members across Europe thought and acted according to similar principles. As the delegate of the Lithuanians in Germany, Vydunas emphatically stated in 1930, 'We told each other that this is something completely new; here not alliances between states are concluded, but representatives of the peoples come together and reach out to each other with their hands.'[40]

The second aim, that of *publicizing minority issues to the European public,* proved only partly successful. While the Congress's proceedings were only meant for the participants and certain interested journalists, the journal *Nation und Staat* ('Nation and State'), established in 1927, was intended for a larger audience. Although not formally linked to the European Nationality Congress, *Nation und Staat* became the main vehicle for communicating Congress ideas, reflections and activities to a larger middle-class audience in Europe.[41] The fact that it was published only in the German language restricted its resonance to a certain degree, although many non-German minorities in Central-Eastern Europe could read German. Since its inception, the German Ministry of Foreign Affairs had subsidized the journal with the aim of making it an advocate of Foreign Minister Gustav Stresemann's revisionist policies.[42] As long as the predominantly liberal editorial board under

Paul Schiemann remained responsible for the content, however, these secret subsidies did not really diminish the journal's character as a sophisticated forum for European minority questions.[43]

Besides *Nation und Staat*, the Congress supported the publication of various empirical and legal analyses. The so-called 'Lageberichte' (situation accounts), published in 1931, collected detailed accounts on almost every larger minority in Europe and described their respective political, economic and cultural contexts.[44] Despite its subjectivity and several empirical flaws, the novel character of the work earned high praise and led to the volume being used by many international organizations as a scientific basis for dealing with minority causes.[45] While the grand vision of founding a European institute for nationality politics was never realized,[46] a number of members and friends of the Congress published ground-breaking studies, mostly of a legal nature, on the question of minority rights as an aspect of international law. In addition to the Hungarian law professor Artur von Balogh's work *Der internationale Schutz der Minderheiten*, published in Hungarian, German and French, Congress-member Carl Georg Bruns published *Grundlagen und Entwicklung des internationalen Minderheitenrechts* with support of the Congress. The Catalan member, Joan Estrich, also concentrated his study 'La questió de les Minories nacionals i les vies del dret' on similar questions of how to integrate cultural autonomy into the constitutions of respective European countries.[47]

Probably more effective in drawing the attention of a larger public to minority issues than these academic publications with their restricted readership was the influence wielded in their home countries by the many journalists among the Congress members. More than 25 per cent of members were journalists; not only did most of them work for reputable newspapers in their own countries, but they also had access to a variety of non-minority newspapers as well. Indeed, the public outrage expressed in many serious newspapers across Europe after Italian Fascists arrested Congress President Josip Wilfan in 1929 exemplifies the publicity that members themselves were able to harness within and beyond their own national context.[48]

The third aim, that of *developing a proto-diplomacy* that could influence the relevant international institutions, proved particularly difficult to achieve.[49] The Congress was successful at establishing good working relations with other international organizations pursuing comparable pacific lobbying work. The cooperation, for example, with the International Association of Leagues of Nations Unions became so close, that its president, the well-known British politician, Sir Willoughby Dickinson, gave the keynote address at the European Nationality Congress session in 1929.[50] Such working relations – other examples include the 'Deutsche Liga für Völkerbund' and the 'Interparliamentary Union' – led to a petition to the League of Nations in 1928 demanding the creation of a permanent commission on minority issues.[51] It was hoped that such a commission would replace the ineffective 'Committees of Three' with a permanent body, and put the existing 'Minority Section of the Secretariat' under pressure; indeed, this had been one of the central aims of the Congress since its inception.[52] Another petition in 1928, again in cooperation with other organizations, sought the expansion of minority treaties to all League members. The idea of internationalizing minority rights seemed all the more necessary because only 15 of the 55 members of the League had formal minority treaties with the League.[53] Both efforts, however, were in vain. The League neither agreed to change its procedure (despite growing international pressure in 1929), nor was able to convince its member states (many of which had made the transition to authoritarian regimes) to introduce minority treaties at home.

Another long-term aim of the Congress's proto-diplomacy was the transfer of more juridical and executive power in minority issues to the Permanent Court of International Justice in The Hague. An example of the potential effect of such power-sharing occurred in 1928, when the League of Nations had been unable to solve a German–Polish conflict on schooling in Upper Silesia.[54] This incident and the surrounding publicity prompted the German government – which was keen to present itself as a 'defender of minorities' – to turn to the Court of International Justice. This appeal and the resulting judgment remained an exception, however, and no further steps were taken to strengthen the Court's authority in controlling League decisions.

The Congress's lack of success in all three aspects of lobbying work must, however, be seen in the larger context of European inter-war politics. Most of the Allies both tacitly favoured assimilation of minorities within the new states on the one hand, but did everything possible to stop any intervention in their own minority policies on the other. Growing discrimination in the new states of Central-Eastern Europe was not only due to rising nationalism, but also thanks to the liberal idea of modernizing the state anew. Only a fundamental change in the governments' attitudes towards the League could have eventually brought about the reforms that civil organizations did not have the power to enforce.[55] The very fact, however, that such reforms were pursued in concert with other international organizations illustrates that the Congress conceived of proto-diplomacy as a multilateral act of exchange and collaboration – not just with governments, but also with other civil organizations; this, in turn, promoted intra-European connections both on the personal and programmatic levels.

## V  Turning Europeanization upside down: generational and programmatic change, 1932–38

The particular concern of this volume in understanding Europeanization as a multidirectional and non-teleological process with ebbs and flows evokes the question of when and why integrative processes of Europeanization change direction.[56] Such questions are particularly relevant in relation to the

European Nationality Congress because they highlight its conversion from a movement that strengthened intra-European ties into one that weakened them. The growth of nationalism and the turn towards authoritarianism entrenched a general tendency throughout Europe to equate the concepts of nation and state, and this critically undermined the Congress's fundamental principle of distinguishing between the two. With the concept of minority politics being interpreted in very different ways, the Congress became, from the early 1930s, a pawn on the diplomatic chessboard of inter-war Europe – with National Socialist foreign policy emerging as the ultimate victor. This section of the chapter identifies four major reasons why and how an international organization dedicated to minority rights could, within few years, transform into a tool of nationalistic and expansive German politics.

A first problem was the Congress's growing *financial dependence* on the German Foreign Service.[57] Initially the German government had seen the Congress as a rather unwelcome rival in its approach to foreign policy.[58] With Gustav Stresemann's policy of peaceful revisionism, from 1927 this scepticism gradually gave way to new hopes to enhance the political control of German minorities abroad through financial incentives. In a memorandum of April 1928, the responsible attaché in the Foreign Ministry, v. Weizsäcker, wrote: 'Germany in particular has an interest in supporting all movements aiming to wake up the League from its former phlegmatic attitude and induce positive action. Because of the pivotal role, which German minorities played at the past sessions of the Congress, its dissolution would mark a victory of the Poles and the defeat (Niderlage) of Germandom.'[59] Weizsäcker concluded with a recommendation to 'negate any regular subsidies', but to favour 'a support from time to time to keep the receivers under tighter control'.[60] Despite ongoing conflicts between the Congress's General Secretary Ewald Ammende and the German Foreign Ministry, the subsidies quickly rose to 30 000 Reichsmark in 1929, thereby accounting for more than a third of the entire budget.[61] As the Foreign Ministry was gradually taken over by National Socialists after 1933,[62] its response to the loss of all Jewish payments and the growing difficulty of non-German minorities in making their payments was to provide an opportunity for even greater coverage by the German authorities of the Congress's annual costs. This continuous support resulted in the Congress having unprecedented financial stability between 1933 and 1938, at the same time as its political independence gradually but steadily diminished until it ceased to exist.

Apart from financial dependency, one of the most decisive reasons for the Congress's transformation was a broad *generational change* in its membership. In the years between 1928 and 1935 many of the active members who had personally experienced pre-war discussions and compromises on multi-ethnic coexistence in the Habsburg Monarchy and Tsarist Russia passed away. While the experience of war and its aftermath had often evoked nationalistic or revanchist sentiments in the younger generation,[63] many of their surviving elders – those born between 1860 and 1890 – had come home with pacifist convictions, and this latter group dominated the Congress until the early 1930s. An example is the Hungarian state secretary and university professor of German origin, Jakob Bleyer. Bleyer had grown up in the Habsburg monarchy, was pro-Hungarian and worked for democratic compromise between the Hungarian majority and German minority; his views provoked nationalistic German students to boycott his lectures in Budapest shortly before his death in 1933.[64]

With the shrinking presence of Bleyer's generation in the Congress,[65] new delegates stepped in who had a different political outlook and were strongly influenced by the turn to authoritarianism occurring in many of their home states. At the forefront of this new group was Werner Hasselblatt, a German lawyer from Estonia who, in 1932, became the permanent delegate of the 'Verband der deutschen Volksgruppen' (Association of German national groups abroad),[66] Johannes Schmidt-Wodder, a German pastor from Denmark who, long before 1933, had welcomed the ideology of National Socialism,[67] Dr Dmytro Levyc'ky, the nationalistic leader of the Ukrainians in Poland, and Dr Engelbert Bednjartz, an anti-Jewish Slovene in the Italian parliament. Key anti-democratic concepts of the time, which Kurt Sontheimer has analysed for the Weimar Republic, were shared by many of these new men, who instrumentalized German terms like 'Volk' (nation), 'decision', 'new politics', 'organism' or 'Gemeinschaft' (community) in their own national contexts. It was therefore not only Germans who now displayed an acceptance of separatist solutions; both Ukrainians from Poland and Catalans from Spain also elaborated openly on such ideas, despite the fact that they stood in fundamental opposition to the Congress's founding principle of complete loyalty to the state of citizenship.

The political change which the generational shift had introduced was in part also an ethnic one, with Germans gaining the upper hand numerically. After 1932 dedicated democrats were absent from the Congress's Board, and non-German participation dropped considerably from 75 per cent in 1931 to 58 per cent in 1934.[68] By the time charismatic democrat Paul Schiemann argued one last time against 'the new nationalistic wave', the institution he had founded was already well on its way to inverting the founding principles:

> If we meet in the next days, all of us undoubtedly will still be under the strong impression that the ideology of our movement (...) is now confronted with a growing tendency, which is opposed to our standpoint and strives instead for exacerbating the tensions in the political realm (...) It is the spirit of war which considers peace only as a continuation of war by different means, that has seized power now (...) But the transfer of concepts of community which in war were necessary into peace is the core of

what in contrast to a normal national identity we call nationalism. It is coined by an equation of 'Volksgemeinschaft' [national community] and 'Staatsgemeinschaft' [state community].[69]

With the dominance of right-wing members the Congress's basic *concept of 'minority'* also underwent a profound change. Although at first glance it seems a purely semantic change, in fact it represented a shift in practice evolving from a new meaning. The term 'minority' had appeared in European public discourse since essentially 1918, when the new democracies had started to differentiate their populations in terms of majority and minority. In the Versailles Minority Treaties the term was defined as a group which 'differed from the majority of the inhabitants of these states by language, religion and race'.[70] With race as an equivalent of nationality in the French and English languages, this definition considered minorities primarily as a numerical group and acknowledged the factual existence of minorities and majorities within democratic states.

The nationalists who were gaining power in the Congress after 1932, however, favoured a very different interpretation of such groups. With their particular focus on German minorities in Central and Eastern Europe, they sought to replace 'minority' as the key definition of these groups with the term 'Volksgruppe' or 'Volkstum'.[71] 'Volksgruppe' (inadequately translated here as 'national group'), like 'Volk' ('nation') and 'Volksgemeinschaft' ('national community'), had become a central concept of anti-democratic thought in Central Europe after 1918.[72] The term 'Volksgruppe' evaded numeric definition on a democratic basis and its defenders viewed the word 'minority' as being discriminatory. They insisted instead on the holistic and inseparable connotation of 'Volk', whose body included all ethnic members ('Volksgruppen') regardless of where they lived.[73]

Defining all ethnic minorities in Europe as members of a given 'Volk' cast minority problems and politics in a critical light, particularly for those who wanted to equate state borders with ethnic lines. These younger members of the Congress, often affiliated with right-wing organizations like the 'Deutscher Schutzbund', 'Sudetendeutsche Heimatfront' or 'Verband der deutschen Volksgruppen in Europa',[74] quickly dismissed the supranational and internationally compatible term 'minority', and instead tried to introduce the term 'Volksgruppe' into the Congress's language: 'The term 'minority' should be applied to Volksgruppen only in such contexts where the arithmetic element is relevant (…) the term 'Volksgruppe' needs to be adopted everywhere where the context points to the German parts of a country's entire population, as well as to the regional part of the entire German nation. The word, and this is its great advantage, relates both to the homeland as to the entire nation.'[75]

The conceptual change that had begun in 1933 later became further institutionalized with the renaming of the Congress's flagship journal *Nation und*

*Staat*. Between 1927 and 1932 the subtitle of the journal had been 'German journal for the European minority problem', which had clearly indicated the scope of its content as well as its language of communication. Until 1932 *Nation und Staat* had openly listed the names of the editors, but after April 1933 it simply noted that the editor was the 'Verband der Deutschen Volksgruppen in Europa'. This change of nomenclature was significant. Even prior to 1933 this organization had demonstrated an affinity with certain aims of National Socialism, and in 1937 the journal's title was changed to 'German Journal for the European Nationality Problem', thereby finally dropping the despised term 'minority'.[76]

While most of the non-German members of the Congress seemed indifferent to the shift in concept, some reacted by replacing 'minority' (which they also considered discriminatory) with 'nationality' – a term intended to neutralize the ethnic exclusivity of the German 'Volksgruppe'. The Catalan delegate, Batista i Rocca, was one of the few who openly discussed the changing semantics in 1936:

Our respected Dr. E. Ammende was one of the first who opposed the somewhat disputable term 'national minority'. The term 'Volksgruppe' was proposed and has soon found broad acceptance and wide distribution. This term however could well appear as going somewhat too far and causing confusion. Driven by the wish for clarity and exactness, the Catalan delegates consider it an advantage to differentiate between various specific types within the general denomination 'national group' or 'Volksgruppe.'[77]

The Congress's proceedings clearly show that the term 'minority' – used heavily for self-description in the 1920s – was eclipsed from the early 1930s by either 'Volksgruppe' (used primarily by the German delegates) or by both 'Volksgruppe' and 'nationality' (used by the other delegates). This gradual decline of the supranational, ethnically neutral term 'minority', which carried a democratic connotation, in favour of the concept of 'Volksgruppe', which had an explicitly non-democratic and ethnically exclusive meaning further illustrates how, on the semantic level, a language of Europeanization was gradually replaced by a terminology of de-Europeanization.

Words, however, were more than just a description of things. In the case of the European Nationality Congress, they were also verbal symbols of political orientation and stimulants for political action. The fourth and final pivotal reason for the transformation of the Congress into a movement fostering processes of de-Europeanization was the *fundamental change in the political function of minority rights* that accompanied the semantic change. Under the dominance of liberal and democratic minority politicians, the Congress's central focus had been on reforming the relationship between minority and majority within a state. Cultural autonomy had been the key concept negotiated by Congress members, albeit in diverse ways and with varied success. Minority politics which combined cultural autonomy with strict loyalty to the state had always been considered in the exclusive domain of domestic politics and separate from the broader aim of internationalizing related legal standards across Europe. With the new right-wing orientation and change in personnel within the Congress, this former focus on minority rights as a domestic issue shifted towards mobilizing minorities as an instrument of the foreign policy of their 'homelands'. Legitimized by the semantic change from 'minority' to 'Volksgruppe,' this perspective saw minorities less as members of the state they lived in, and more as extensions of their 'homeland nation' – and therefore as an object of the foreign policy of the latter.

This new philosophy dovetailed nicely with the new regime's increasing willingness to use the Congress as an instrument of National Socialist foreign policy. In particular, Werner Hasselblatt – who replaced Paul Schiemann in 1933 as the leading figure in the Congress and on the Board of *Nation und Staat* – was responsible for advocating this new ideology and practice. After being promoted to the position of permanent delegate of the 'Verband der deutschen Volksgruppen', he worked closely with Joachim v. Ribbentrop (who became Hitler's foreign minister in 1938) and helped to instrumentalize minorities as a tool of expansionist foreign policy.[78] This redefinition of 'minority protection' was a decisive factor why an international network devoted to Europeanizing minority rights changed so quickly into a German-dominated organization enforcing national autonomy only for German groups and working towards a complete overhaul of borders within Europe.

The fact that such a fundamental conversion – from Europeanizing ideals into de-Europeanizing politics – could take place peacefully was not openly discussed. This perhaps accounts for the surprising, conspicuous silence with which the non-German members of the Congress met this semantic and political change. Another reason for their outward compliance was that some minorities had structurally similar interests, insofar as they were dissatisfied with the Versailles-dictated borders and hoped for their revision. In particular, both the Ukrainian minorities in Poland and the Hungarians in Romania and Czechoslovakia favoured separatist solutions in their own national contexts which they assumed to be compatible with the new foreign policy of Nazi Germany.[79]

The programmatic change of the Congress's basic principles was not just a theoretical one. Its practical consequences became apparent as soon as Hitler's regime introduced a new policy of violence towards the Jewish population in Germany, which the Congress had thus far considered a minority like any other. Prior to the meeting in Bern in September 1933, Leo Motzkin, leading representative of the Jews at the Congress and one of its founding members, had demanded from the delegates a public resolution condemning the repression of Jews in Nazi Germany as a clear violation of minority rights: 'Such a resolution can not carry a vague character, but needs to call the relevant country by its name as much as the Jews in particular.'[80] When the Board members refused this request by arguing that concrete cases were not to be discussed, all Jewish groups withdrew from further participation and left the Congress.

The subsequent debate on the repression of Jews clearly revealed the extent to which anti-Jewish sentiments had already permeated the Congress community. The delegate Hans Otto Roth, a German from Romania, explicitly claimed to speak for all German minorities when he eloquently defended the theory of 'dissimilation' as opposed to 'assimilation' and introduced terms like 'Volksgemeinschaft' (national community) and 'Rasse' (race) into the forum of the Congress: 'The dissimilation of people of different origin in particular of different race, from a national culture (Volkskultur), which could be observed in recent times, we consider basically legitimate.'[81] While Russians, Lithuanians, Ukrainians, Catalans and Hungarians publicly refrained from supporting such views, all others expressed their solidarity. The refusal to criticize publicly the measures of the National Socialist regime led to ongoing conflicts between the Congress's few remaining democrats and the numerous adherents of the new politics, and ultimately resulted after 1933 in most of the former retreating from the Congress.

In addition to the refusal to defend Jewish citizenship rights, the gradual take-over of the Congress by members of the so-called 'Sudetendeutsche Bewegung' further cemented the smooth transformation of the organization into a tool of Nazi foreign policy. More and more of the German delegates who replaced the ones who either left or passed away adhered to the separatist ideal of uniting the Czech territories populated by Germans with Nazi Germany.[82] Their dominance became so strong that in the years that followed they systematically used the Congress (with its multi-ethnic character) as an outwardly neutral platform for marketing expansionist propaganda to the European public. After the tenth meeting in 1935, Ewald Ammende lauded the success of this strategy: 'The start of this first international demonstration of the Sudetendeutsche Partei worked out excellently and would without the platform of the Nationality Congress have been almost impossible.'[83] This general line of propaganda, supported by the Ukrainian and Hungarian minorities with interests in revising the Versailles order, dominated all further sessions until 1938. At the last session in Stockholm, in 1939, a drastically reduced number of delegates passed a resolution which stood in direct opposition to the anti-separatist founding principles of the Congress and instead advocated border revision and a new territorial order across Europe: 'The European Nationality Congress urgently appeals to the governments of the European states to initiate a new order which only can secure the right of the nationalities on political and cultural equality.'[84]

## VI   Conclusion

The history of the twentieth century is itself an example of Europeanization having come full circle: after an age of extreme violence and total war, we are, in a way, back at square one. Travelling from Paris to Bucharest in a direct train, or selling machines made in Manchester to people in the Urals, was just as possible around 1900 as it is again in 2000. Such historic cycles are simply a reminder of the variety of forms, contents and directions that Europeanization can assume.

The manifold nature of the possible forms has been illustrated in this chapter through a case study of the European Nationality Congress (1925–38). Established by politicians and intellectuals of various ethnic and religious origins, the Congress strove to internationalize minority rights throughout Europe. Its subsequent evolution reflected the enormous difficulty in translating the specific interests of discrete minorities into an abstract, supranational principle. Minorities, whose right to cultural autonomy had been considered an object of domestic reform within each state, were transformed after 1932 into an instrument of expansionist foreign policy, above all by Nazi Germany. The close relationship between integration and fragmentation illustrated by the Congress's history underscores once again the need – as argued throughout this volume – to redefine Europeanization as an open process of both promoting and limiting intra-European connections.

Three implications seem to be particularly relevant. First, the redefinition proposed here points to the need for longer-term perspectives when approaching Europeanization. For example, it was due only to the 'de-Europeanizing' experience of the First World War and its consequences that 'Europeanizing' organizations like the Congress were born. Similarly, it was the experience of total destruction in the Second World War that resulted in a new, longer wave of Europeanization, which in itself has also experienced its own ups and downs. Indeed, the fact that the Congress's short-lived journal *Nation und Staat* has retrospectively been acknowledged as the forerunner of *Europa Ethnica* (founded by the Federal Union of European Nationalities in 1958) is a fitting anecdote supporting our argument about the rhythms of Europeanization.[85] Only such a longer term perspective allows us to recognize these ambivalent shapes and contradictory directions as part of a broader, integrated process of Europeanization, and to locate them adequately within the twentieth century.

Secondly, redefining Europeanization stimulates a new sense of place. Despite its fall 20 years ago, the Iron Curtain still exists in the historiography. In most fields of academic research and public discourse, Europeanization still, for the most part, is used to describe Western European processes of interconnection and exchange. An organization such as the Congress, fighting for the introduction of democratic minority rights all over Europe, might therefore be assumed to have had its origins in the western half of the continent. The manifest surprise at finding its roots in the East reveals the long shadow cast by the continental divide. By thinking instead of Europeanization as a process that can happen anywhere in Europe, we can start to move – albeit slowly – out of this shadow.

Finally, Europeanization has many forefathers from both within and beyond the continent. The 'new imperial history' is shaping our sensibility of the impact of non-European influences in Europe, and this chapter has underscored that non-European transfers must be considered alongside intra-European processes of entanglement as constituting factors of Europeanization. This is not, however, to ignore the boundaries inherent in the terms 'Europe' and 'Europeanization'; the process of Europeanization – as opposed to Westernization, transnationalism or imperialism – can only remain a useful analytical tool if the realm where such transfers unfold and become appropriated can be clearly distinguished from others. In the case of the European Nationality Congress, activity and admission were explicitly restricted to European countries; this decision was based on the rationale that minorities in countries subject to recent immigration (such as the USA or Canada) faced different challenges than those in the older, multi-ethnic societies of Europe. Once again, the historical reality reminds us of the need for a clear-cut and rather narrow definition of Europeanization as a multifarious process unfolding within the borders of the continent; indeed, the constant shifting of these borders is, in itself, a central element of this very process.

## Notes

1. See M. Mazower, *Der dunkle Kontinent. Europa im 20. Jahrhundert* (Berlin, 2000), pp. 69–116; D. Diner, *Das Jahrhundert verstehen. Eine universalgeschichtliche Deutung* (Frankfurt, 2000), pp. 79–134; A. Roshwald, *Ethnic Nationalism and the Fall of Empires: Central Europe, Russia and the Middle East 1914–1923* (London, 2001).
2. See D. Lieven, *Empire. The Russian Empire and its Rivals* (London, 2000); A. Kappeler, *Russland als Vielvölkerreich. Entstehung, Geschichte, Zerfall* (Munich, 1992); G. Hosking, *Russia. People and Empire 1552–1917* (London, 1997); A. Wandruszka and P. Urbanitsch (eds), *Die Habsburgermonarchie 1848–1918*, 12 vols (Vienna, 1973–2006); R.A. Kann, *A History of the Habsburg Empire 1526–1918* (Berkeley, 1974); D. Quataert, *The Ottoman Empire 1700–1922*, (Cambridge, 2000); P.F. Sugar, *Nationality and Society in Habsburg and Ottoman Europe* (Aldershot, 1997).
3. See M.F. Boemeke et al. (eds), *The Treaty of Versailles. A Reassessment after 75 years* (Cambridge, 1998).
4. See the classic work: C.A. Macartney, *National State and National Minorities* (London, 1934); R. Pearson, *National Minorities in Eastern Europe 1848–1945* (London, 1983); P. Smith (ed.), *Ethnic Groups in International Relations* (New York, 1991); Mazower, *Kontinent*, p. 90.
5. See B. Dexter, *The Years of Opportunity: The League of Nations 1920–1926* (New York, 1967); F.P. Walters, *A History of the League of Nations* (Oxford, 1960); for the relationship between Germany and the League, see J. Wintzer, *Deutschland und der Völkerbund 1918–1926* (Paderborn, 2006); C. Raitz von Frentz, *A Lesson Forgotten. Minority Protection under the League of Nations. The Case of the German*

*Minority in Poland 1920–1934* (Münster/New York, 1999); for a concise overview on the minority problems, see B. Schot, *Nation oder Staat? Deutschland und der Minderheitenschutz. Zur Völkerbundspolitik der Stresemann-Ära* (Marburg, 1988).

6. See M. Rothbart, 'Der Europäische Minderheitenkongreß als Instrument imperialistischer deutscher "Revisionsstrategie". Grenzrevision und Minderheitenpolitik des deutschen Imperialismus (1919–1932)', Diss. B. (Rostock, 1983).

7. See R. Michaelsen, *Der Europäische Nationalitäten-Kongress 1925–1928. Aufbau, Krise und Konsolidierung* (Frankfurt, 1984); E. Kelmes, 'Der Europäische Nationalitätenkongreß (1925–1938), Phil. Diss. (Cologne, 1958).

8. See X.H. Nunez Seixas, 'Internationale Politik, Minderheitenfrage und nationale Autonomie. Der Europäische Nationalitätenkongreß (1925–1938)', in H. Timmermann (ed.), *Nationalismus und Nationalbewegung in Europa 1914–1945* (Berlin, 1999), pp. 39–72; S. Bamberger-Stemmann, *Der Europäische Nationalitätenkongreß 1925 bis 1938. Nationale Minderheiten zwischen Lobbyistentum und Großmachtinteressen* (Marburg, 2000).

9. See A. Pagden (ed.), *The Idea of Europe: From Antiquity to the European Union* (Cambridge/New York, 2002); T. Judt, *Postwar. A History of Europe since 1945* (New York/London, 2005); J. Sheehan, *Where Have All the Soldiers Gone? The Transformation of Modern Europe* (New York, 2008).

10. See U. Frevert, 'Europeanising German History', *Bulletin of the German Historical Institute* xxxvi (2005), 9–31.

11. See W. Schmale, 'Die Europäizität Ostmitteleuropas', in *Jahrbuch für Europäische Geschichte* iv (2003), 198–214; M. Geyer, 'Historical Fiction of Anatomy and the Europeanization of National History', in *Central European History* xxii (1989), 316–43.

12. See the collection of the treaty texts: *Protection des minorités de langue, de race et de religion par la Société des Nations. Recueil des stipulations contenues dans les différents instruments internationaux actuellement en vigueur. Publication de la Société des Nation* I.B. Minorité 1927 (Geneva, 1927); Boemeke, *Treaty of Versailles*.

13. See Frentz, *Lesson*, pp. 21–33; Schot, *Nation oder Staat?*, p. 4ff.

14. See Frentz, *Lesson*, S. 126; for a legal account on the procedures: H. Pieper, *Die Minderheitenfrage und das Deutsche Reich 1919–1933/34* (Frankfurt, 1974); C. Gütermann, *Das Minderheitenschutzverfahren des Völkerbundes* (Berlin, 1979).

15. See Mazower, *Kontinent*, p. 88; for a detailed account on the procedures see Schot, *Nation oder Staat?*, p. 7ff.

16. Paul Schiemann, 'Sitzungsbericht des Kongresses der organisierten nationalen Gruppen in den Staaten Europas', Genf 25–27 August 1926, p. 37. (In all further annotations the Congress annual minutes, published in Vienna since 1925, are abbreviated as 'Sitzungsbericht'.)

17. See M. Garleff, 'Baltische Minderheitenvertreter auf den Europäischen Nationalitätenkongressen 1925–1938, in *Jahrbuch des baltischen Deutschtums*, xxxiii (1986), 117–31; for an analysis of such pre-war traditions see U. v. Hirschhausen, *Die Grenzen der Gemeinsamkeit. Deutsche, Letten, Russen und Juden in Riga 1860–1914* (Göttingen, 2006).

18. See M. Ormos, *Hungary in the Age of the Two World Wars 1914–1945* (New York, 2007); J.C. Swanson, *The Remnants of the Habsburg Monarchy: the Shaping of Modern Austria and Hungary 1918–1922* (Boulder, 2001).

19. See J. Klier and S. Lambroza, *Pogroms: Anti-Jewish Violence in Modern Russian History*, (Cambridge, 1992); J. Klier, *Imperial Russia's Jewish Question 1855–1881* (Cambridge, 1995).

20. See his autobiography P. Schiemann, *Zwischen zwei Zeitaltern. Erinnerungen 1903–1919*, (Lüneburg, 1979); now his biography by J. Hiden, *Defender of Minorities. Paul Schiemann (1876–1944)*, (London, 2004).
21. See 'Sitzungsbericht' (1926), p. 8.
22. See Schot, *Nation*, pp. 101–5.
23. See Europäischer Nationalitäten Kongress, 14–16 October 1925.
24. See above, p. 12.
25. 'Sitzungsbericht' (1931), p. 17.
26. Table 4.1 comprises the detailed account given in Bamberger-Stemmann, *Nationalitätenkongreß*, p. 111.
27. The number of 219 refers to all delegates who had participated in the congress sessions between 1925 and 1937. For sources see the annual minutes of the congress (Sitzungsberichte) listing all delegates with their country of origin and their ethnic identity.
28. For the reasons for this retreat see Bamberger-Stemmann, *Nationalitätenkongreß*, chapter 6.2.
29. Ibid., p. 135.
30. Table 4.2 comprises the detailed account given in Bamberger-Stemmann, *Nationalitätenkongreß*, p. 118.
31. Muslims were not mentioned in the Congress' minutes. See for the discourse on the "Christian occident" J. Pieper, *Was heißt "Christliches Abendland?"* (Munich, 1960).
32. Bamberger-Stemmann, *Nationalitätenkongreß*, p. 104.
33. Table 4.3 comprises the detailed account given in Bamberger-Stemmann, *Nationalitätenkongreß*, p. 117. A clear proof of the occupation according to Bamberger-Stemmann was possible only for 111 out of 219 delegates, ibid., p. 116.
34. See Michaelsen, *Nationalitäten-Kongreß*, pp. 106–333; Nunez, *Internationale Politik*.
35. See 'Sitzungsbericht' (1926, 1927, 1928).
36. See e.g. Schiemann on the Congress in 1926: 'Gentlemen, the right of national autonomy is not a right of nationality, it is a democratic right, a political right, the realization of the volonté générale', 'Sitzungsbericht' (1926), p. 35.
37. See P. Schiemann, 'Volksgemeinschaft und Staatsgemeinschaft', in *Nation und Staat* I (1927/28), 21–41; M. Dörr, 'Paul Schiemanns Theorie vom "Anationalen Staat". Ein Beitrag zur europäischen Nationalitätenbewegung zwischen den beiden Weltkriegen', in *Geschichte in Wissenschaft und Unterricht* VIII (1957), 407–21; Hiden, *Defender of Minorities*.
38. Schiemann at the first session of the Congress in 1925, 'Sitzungsbericht' (1925), p. 18.
39. See 'Sitzungsbericht' (1926, 1927, 1928, 1929). A step back was the retreat of minorities from Germany, that is Poles, Danes and Sorbs who left the Congress in 1927; for reasons see Bamberger-Stemmann, *Nationalitätenkongreß*, pp. 233–48; Michaelsen, *Nationalitäten-Kongreß*, pp. 387–547.
40. 'Sitzungsbericht' (1930), p. 13.
41. See for an extensive account of the journal Bamberger-Stemmann, *Nationalitätenkongreß*, pp. 233–48.
42. For a description of German foreign policy between 1918 and 1933 see G. Niedhart, *Die Außenpolitik der Weimarer Republik* (Munich, 1999).
43. See *Nation und Staat. Zeitschrift für das europäische Minoritätenproblem* (Vienna, 1927/28–1931/32); for the change of concept and editors see Part V of this chapter.

44. See Die Nationalitäten in den Staaten Europas. Sammlung von Lageberichten des Europäischen Nationaliäten-Kongresses, hg. im Auftrag des Europäischen Nationalitätenkongresses von Generalsekretär E. Ammende (Vienna, 1931).

45. See for the history of the publication Bamberger-Stemmann, *Nationalitätenkongress*, pp. 216–24.

46. 'See Sitzungsbericht' (1929), pp. 147–61.

47. See 'Sitzungsbericht' (1929), p. 13.

48. See Michaelsen, *Nationalitäten-Kongreß*, pp. 280–5.

49. See for the concept and realization of 'Proto-diplomacy': I.D. Duchacek, *The Territorial Dimension of Politics. Within, Among and Across Nations* (London, 1986); A. Heraklides, *The Self-Determination of Minorities in International Politics* (London, 1991).

50. See 'Sitzungsbericht' (1929), pp. 26–9. See also the participation of Christine Bakker van Bosse, a leading Dutch member of the International Association of Leagues of Nations Unions, 'Sitzungsbericht' (1930), p. 4.

51. See 'Sitzungsbericht' (1929), p. 18, text of the resolution, p. 142; Mazower, *Kontinent*, p. 90.

52. See 'Sitzungsbericht' (1928), p. 30; 'Sitzungsbericht' (1929), p. 142; 'Sitzungsbericht' (1926), p. 132.

53. See Schot, *Nation oder Staat?*, p. 4.

54. See Frentz, *Lesson*, pp. 129–240; Schot, *Nation oder Staat?*, pp. 187–200.

55. See on this problem Mazower, *Kontinent*, p. 102.

56. See the Introduction in this volume.

57. For the financial aspects see Bamberger-Stemmann, *Nationalitätenkongress*, pp. 147–61; Michaelsen, *Nationalitäten-Kongreß*, pp. 243–54.

58. See Schot, *Nation oder Staat?*, pp. 132–60.

59. Memorandum of the Referat Völkerbund, Auswärtiges Amt, from 7 April 1928, quoted in Bamberger-Stemann, *Nationalitätenkongreß*, p. 150.

60. Quoted in Michaelsen, *Nationalitäten-Kongreß*, p. 253.

61. See Bamberger-Stemmann, *Nationalitätenkongreß*, p. 151ff.

62. See H.-A. Jacobsen, *Nationalsozialistische Außenpolitik 1933–1938* (Frankfurt, 1968), pp. 16–44.

63. See for the German context K. Sontheimer, *Antidemokratisches Denken in der Weimarer Republik. Die politischen Ideen des deutschen Nationalismus zwischen 1918 und 1933* (Munich, 1994, first ed. 1962); for the Hungarian context see M. Zeidler, *Ideas on Territorial Revision in Hungary 1920–1945* (New York, 2007); I. Németh, 'Die ungarischen Revisionsbestrebungen und die Großmächte (1920–1941)', in H. Timmermann (ed.), *Nationalismus und Nationalbewegung in Europa 1914–1945* (Berlin, 1999), pp. 73–100; I. Deak, 'Historiography of the Countries of Eastern Europe: Hungary', in *American Historical Review* XCVII (1992), 1041–63.

64. See for sources Bamberger-Stemmann, *Nationalitätnkongreß*, p. 143, footnotes 149 and 150; M. Fata, 'Jakob Bleyer, politischer Vertreter der deutschen Minderheit in Ungarn (1917–1933)', Phil. Diss. mss (Freiburg, 1991).

65. Among them liberal delegates such as Wilhelm v. Medinger (1935) or founding member and Jewish representative Leo Motzkin (1935).

66. See M. Garleff, 'Nationalitätenpolitik zwischen liberalem und völkischem Anspruch. Gleichklang und Spannung bei Paul Schiemann und Werner Hasselblatt', in J. v. Hehn und J. Kenez (eds), *Reval und die baltischen Länder. Festschrift für H. Weiss* (Marburg, 1980), pp. 113–32.

67. Among his publications were: *Volk und Völker. Der Angelpunkt der europäischen Probleme* (Vienna, 1930); *Deutschland gestern und heute* (Vienna, 1934).

68. Numbers on the ethnic representation of each annual meeting gives Bamberger-Stemmann, *Nationalitätenkongreß*, p. 123.
69. Paul Schiemann, 'Die nationalistische Welle', in *Nation und Staat* v (1931/32), 800.
70. Michaelson, *Nationalitäten-Kongreß*, p. 25, footnote 2; Frentz, *Lesson*, ch. 1.3.
71. See W. Hasselblatt, 'Geistige Verkehrshindernisse': in *Nation und Staat* I (1927/28), 330–7.
72. See for the Weimar context Sontheimer, *Antidemokratisches Denken*, pp. 244–78; W. Oberkrome, *Volksgeschichte. Methodische und völkische Ideologisierung in der deutschen Geschichtswissenschaft 1918–1945* (Göttingen, 1993).
73. See for the intellectual development of these thoughts Sontheimer, *Antidemokratisches Denken*, and for their institutionalization Oberkrome, *Volksgeschichte*.
74. See for an overview of these organizations Schot, *Nation oder Staat?*, pp. 86–117; H. v. Rimscha, 'Zur Gleichschaltung der deutschen Volksgruppen durch das Dritte Reich', in *Historische Zeitschrift* CLXXXII (1956), 29–63.
75. Protokoll 'Ergebnis der Herbsttagung am 17.12.1929' of the 'Verband der Deutschen Volksgruppen in Europa'; there was an attempt also for this term to be introduced in the European Nationality Congress, see for the context and quote Bamberger-Stemmann, *Nationalitätenkongreß*, p. 251.
76. Ibid., p. 245.
77. Batista i Rocca on the XI session of the Congress, quoted in: 'Sitzungsbericht' (1936), p. 33.
78. See note 66.
79. See Jacobsen, *Nationalsozialistische Außenpolitik*.
80. Motzkin to Wilfan, 'Sitzungsbericht' (1933), p. 2.
81. Roth, 'Sitzungsbericht' (1933), p.26; see for the origins of this theory in the German right-wing circles above all M.H. Boehm, *Europa Irredenta. Eine Einführung in das Nationalitätenproblem der Gegenwart* (Berlin, 1923); idem, *Volkstheorie und Volkstumspolitik der Gegenwart* (Berlin, 1935); Oberkrome, *Volksgeschichte*.
82. See M. Cornwall and R.J.W. Evans (eds), *Czechoslovakia in a Nationalist and Fascist Europe 1918–1948* (Oxford, 2007); R. Jaworski, *Vorposten oder Minderheit – Der sudetendeutsche Volkstumskampf in den Beziehungen zwischen der Weimarer Republik und der CSR* (Stuttgart, 1977); H.H. Hahn, *Hundert Jahre Sudetendeutsche Geschichte: eine völkische Bewegung in drei Staaten* (Frankfurt, 2007); R. Gebel, *'Heim ins Reich'. Konrad Henlein und der Reichsgau Sudetenland (1938–1945)* (Munich, 1999).
83. Ammende to the German Foreign Service in September 1935, quoted in Bamberger-Stemmann, *Nationalitätenkongreß*, p. 272.
84. Ibid., p. 381.
85. Ibid., p. 234, for the problems of this tradition.

# 5

# The Role of International Organizations in Europeanization: The Case of the League of Nations and the European Economic Community

*Patricia Clavin and Kiran Klaus Patel* *

Europeanization is a given of twentieth-century European history. At the level of social and economic history in particular, many studies emphasize an increased level of intra-European exchange, transfer and in some fields even convergence when compared to that of other centuries.[1] Very few published accounts, however, explore the role of international organizations in this process. This chapter will argue that some of these institutions have served both as agents and semi-public playgrounds for several forms and processes of Europeanization. The focus will not be on the economic, social or political impact on European societies of the various international agreements struck in these institutions. Rather, it concentrates on the organizations themselves as sites where knowledge was produced and as places where policies were developed. We argue that these organizations served as clearing-houses for intelligence, expertise and experience, and as hubs that *generated, contained, stabilized* and *modified* specific 'European' positions and mindsets, networks and policy outcomes.

The conceptual foundation of our chapter is the sociologically-based, institutionalist literature that claims that organizations socialize their members. It argues that in propitious political and intellectual environments, international organizations have the potential to generate shared causal and normative understandings, and these agreements form prerequisites and resources adequate and necessary for collective action.[2] Accordingly, 'Europe' emerged as the central episteme of these debates, and in this sense, these agencies were both Europeanized and Europeanizing.

In order to explore these issues, we have chosen to adopt a long-term perspective. Covering the period from the 1920s to the 1970s, the chapter will primarily highlight two organizations: the League of Nations (LON) and the European Economic Community (EEC). Conventionally, the League is presented as a part of what Akira Iriye has called the 'Global Community'.[3] However, much of its work was dominated by European powers and their preoccupations.[4] At the same time, the interaction in the LON shaped a certain sense of European identity and an impression of European (imperial) unity vis-à-vis the League's non-European members. In the case of the EEC, the European focus is obvious but the issue of Europeanization as conceived here has rarely been researched from a historical perspective. We also draw out the EEC's connections to other international organizations, the role of which is essential to fully appreciate the Community's contribution to shaping the character and process(es) of Europeanization.

The empirical focus of this chapter is the various negotiations that have taken place concerning agricultural production and trade within these organizations. Despite the wide economic remit of both the LON and the EEC, agriculture is particularly apposite for the study of Europeanization. Both organizations have produced a huge amount of information within this sector of the economy; and in so doing they have developed a shared and rich vision as to the nature and value of European agriculture. In the case of the EEC, this has also led to very concrete forms of political action. In the history of agricultural policy it is possible to chart the evolution from national and international conceptions of the phenomena, to ones that were identified *with* Europe and thus came to *define* Europe. The long chronological range of this chapter also affords the perspective necessary to identify longer continuities in the history of Europeanization, question the caesura of 1945, re-evaluate the role of the LON in European history and, finally, gain a better understanding of the success of the EEC.

## The League of Nations, Europeanization and agriculture

Established in 1919, the LON was the world's first inter-governmental organization intended to prevent war. In the words of its founding covenant, the League sought to 'promote international co-operation and to achieve international peace and security'.[5] Despite its global aspirations, the League was in many ways dominated by European powers and their preoccupations, built – as it was – out of the ashes of a world war that had begun in Europe: the governments of Britain and France were, until the middle of the 1930s, its chief financial backers (with Europe as a whole providing the majority of its financial contributions). They also provided its leadership. The General Secretary of the League was always a European: the Briton, Sir Eric Drummond, followed by the Frenchman, Joseph Avenol and then the Irishman, Sean Lester, and many of the permanent and non-permanent members of the Council of the League of Nations were European. Although the pro-active side of the League's work in the so-called 'technical' organizations (so-called because technical implied cooperation with the politics taken out although, in reality, this was impossible) were devoted to facilitating economic and financial, transportational and social cooperation on a global scale, the reactive dimension of their efforts meant that much of their work was focused on Europe. The point was underlined by the League's social and physical space, too: the European-style architecture of the purpose-built *Palais des Nations*, the official languages and the habits which governed its diplomacy. Indeed, part of the Secretariat's mission was to school the untutored non-Europeans in the finer points of diplomatic engagement.

In 1919 there had been no plans for the League to become involved in international economic and monetary cooperation, but the difficult economic climate prompted financiers and economists to lobby for policy coordination through the League and for nation-states to support the creation of an Economic and Financial Organisation (EFO) within the League. The organization took life at first as a section within the Secretariat of the League and was primarily dedicated to collating economic and financial statistics. The officials who came to work for it, however, demonstrated ambition and independence of mind from the outset, pressing for special expert advisory committees on economic and financial questions to help the LON and to fortify the role of the League in the world economy. The officials of the EFO were among the most pro-active groups in the Secretariat. By 1945, the Economic and Financial Organisation had amassed more than 25 years' worth of expertise in the field of international economic and financial relations, drawing into its orbit a huge range of divergent know-how, predominately from Europe, which was sustained by a regular and diverse programme of meetings and a voluminous publication record. During the course of its history, the EFO became the first ever intergovernmental organization dedicated to promoting economic and financial cooperation. It is, therefore, a pertinent site from which to explore the dynamics of Europeanization.

EFO's interest in agriculture developed gradually, and became of real significance in the wake of the Great Depression. By 1934 the influential heads of the Economic and Financial Sections of the EFO, namely the Briton, Alexander Loveday, and the Italian, Pietro Stoppani, became convinced that their efforts were better directed against trade protectionism, and increasingly within this, agricultural cooperation. The Secretariat was the primary means by which policy was driven forward within the EFO, and during the course of the 1930s the EFO became increasingly central to the League's activities.[6] Its role was further heightened during this period as other elements of the League's international programme stalled, notably in the field of peace-keeping. Its staff swelled, too, as it became a self-conscious and sophisticated generator and disseminator of information and ideas. As Loveday put it, the intention was not so much to draft plans or blueprints as to assess 'past experiences and failures and the collection and comparison of data' conducive to economic growth.[7] This was to be a pattern that would be emulated by the EEC and, while the EFO could never boost the same successful track record in agricultural negotiations, its long history in facilitating failed negotiations helped to clarify different interests and positions that laid a path to new forms of European cooperation after the Second World War.

There were several distinct strands to EFO's approach to the collation and dissemination of data and ideas that are important to understanding its contribution to Europeanization. It had a scholarly approach to data collection, which initially centred on developing the networks and procedures by which data could be secured, correlated and disseminated. Some of this information was published in title series such as the annual *Statistical Yearbook of the League of Nations*, the *Monthly Bulletin of Statistics*, *Money and Banking*, the *Review of World Trade* and the *World Economic Survey*. In each publication Europe appeared as a distinct category and sometimes intra-European interactions were measured. It was not easy work. League officials consistently complained of countries' unwillingness to supply the data requested, or that they provided it in a way that was of limited use.[8] But it became such an important part of EFO's work that its statistical division came to form a separate institution within it, known as the Economic Intelligence Service. These statistical compilations were supplemented by annual reports from the Economic and Financial Section on the general economic situation, notably the reports of the *Delegation on Economic Depression* and the *World Economic Survey*. What was important to the process of Europeanization was not just that this was – in many cases – the first time that this material was collated, but also that it explicitly sought to draw comparisons (in the hope of facilitating coordination and ultimately cooperation) between countries. As in Michael Billig's concept of 'banal nationalism', the arrangement of these figures, tables and statistics created a structured and stabilized meaning of the term 'European' under which the League organized and presented its findings along 'European' lines.[9]

This statistical work was supported by a remarkable network of European economists whom the EFO employed over the duration of its lifetime. Its members included Jan Tinbergen, Gunnar Myrdal, Tjalling Koopmans, Ragnar Nurkse, Jean Monnet, Wilhelm Röpke, James Mead, and Per Jacobsson to name but a few. Supported by a sophisticated Secretariat and Economic Intelligence Service, the EFO also developed a range of publications, experience and ideas that played a crucial role in shaping Europeanization after 1945.[10]

After 1933, European trade and its relationship with agricultural production became central to EFO's programme of work, in part because there was little chance of the League effecting cooperation on other questions any time soon. As the EFO became more important within the League, so agriculture became more important to the EFO. The battle against protectionism had always been a part of the League's economic programme. This was evident in the 1927 World Economic Conference, which was dedicated to fighting tariffs and quotas, and where the EFO had limited success, notably with negotiations for commodity agreements begun in 1933 that resulted in the Wheat convention of 1933 and the Sugar agreement of 1937. Moreover, the 'second wave of protectionism' that swept the world economy in 1930 and 1931 largely originated in agrarian markets – witness the Smoot–Hawley Tariff in the USA, the imperial preference agreements concluded between Britain and its empire in 1932 and a grand total of some 3000 quotas imposed to protect French agriculture in the same year. Germany was by no means the only offender but Nazi Germany's determined exploitation of trade and clearing controls moved the battle against protectionism into the heart of Europe and made it a more striking and immediate priority that was linked to the preservation of peace in Europe.[11] Liberal democratic governments, notably those of Britain and the United States but also the EFO, recognized the threat that German autarky presented to liberal capitalism. Not only was Nazi Germany singularly determined and able to use trade protectionism to penetrate and exploit central and eastern Europe; protection also insulated it from pressure which open markets might exert, as well as enabling it to exploit suspicions between the capitalist powers. In light of the failed Disarmament Conference and the crisis over Ethiopia, the EFO argued that a League-sponsored effort to coordinate the reduction of protectionism in Europe would provide an opportunity to reaffirm the value of the League.

It is revealing what comprised 'Europe' in EFO's work on European agriculture in the 1930s. As in any kind of border-drawing, Europeanization was a process also characterized by the geographical limits of participation and cooperation. In the 1930s, the most important, non-cooperative power was Germany and there was an expressed acknowledgement by all that Europe's future economic and political health depended on German re-engagement with Europe. In the period after the Second World War, first the USSR and then the whole Eastern Bloc fulfilled this same function of 'othering'. But when it came to agriculture, the EFO excluded the Soviet Union from 'its' Europe: the USSR's avowed hostility to capitalism, of course, was the main reason behind this ostracism from initiatives that were partly focused on securing the restoration of liberal capitalism. But at the time, EFO's position was differently cast. The argument came in two parts. The first part underlined that only 19 per cent of the world's population resided in Europe (excluding the USSR) on a landmass that comprised no more than four per cent of its total land area, but that 'in normal years, the value of Europe's total trade (imports plus exports) was about equal to the trade of the whole of the rest of the world'. The second aspect of the case centred on showing how the inclusion of the USSR would distort the picture: 'if the USSR is included in Europe, these figures are naturally increased somewhat, but the effect of that inclusion is slight for the USSR is largely a self-contained economic unit, and her trade is very small in comparison with her area or population.' Of course, these arguments could barely hide the political motivation behind this vision of Europe and its borders.

But who, then, was in? EFO's Europe included the following countries: Albania, Austria, Belgium-Luxembourg, Bulgaria, Czechoslovakia, Denmark, Estonia, Finland, France, Germany, Greece, Iceland, Ireland, Italy, Latvia, Lithuania, Malta, the Netherlands, Norway, Poland-Danzig, Portugal, Romania,

Spain, Sweden, Switzerland, and Turkey, and a number of other minor territories, including Gibraltar, Svalbard, and assorted free ports. But, although not commonly included in the geo-political definition of Europe in this period, Britain was part of EFO's Europe. EFO's main reason for including it was because of the huge amount of foodstuffs and raw materials imported to the United Kingdom, although there is no doubt that Britain's role as one of the League's key paymasters and political leaders was also an important, if unspoken, influence.[12]

One non-European power which, nevertheless, was attributed a central role in the development of these trade and agricultural negotiations, was the United States. The American Secretary of State, Cordell Hull's commitment to the Reciprocal Tariff Act Agreement of 1934 played a fundamental role in shaping American relations with the League (as well as with Latin America) in the 1930s, and it went on to form the political and intellectual bedrock of the General Agreement on Tariffs and Trade (GATT) in 1947. In the 1930s the USA was interested in supporting EFO's initiatives in the fields of trade and agriculture because, as it put it in 1935: 'the administration is anxious to effect a radical change in its commercial policy and desires occasions for establishing contact with persons concerned with commercial policy in Europe.'[13] The significance here is that American officials referred not to particular nations, nor categories of nations, but to Europe as a whole. As will also be demonstrated in the exploration of Europeanization and European agriculture in the European Economic Community below, the process can be shaped and defined by nations and actors who are not in Europe, but whose political sympathies and security interests are aligned with it.

EFO's enquiries during the second half of the 1930s also drew attention to the important, yet vulnerable, position of European agricultural production and trade. The process of quantification and categorization of European trade drew out, more than ever before, that 'with the exception of Greece, the agricultural countries of southern and eastern Europe were net exporters of foodstuffs although their unit yields were low' and their farms small.[14] In fact, agricultural countries in Europe differed from the majority of those in other continents 'by their limited resources of arable land. In a sense, the pressure of population in Europe is greatest, not in the densely populated highly industrialized regions, but in the least developed agricultural countries'.[15] Moreover, this pattern of disadvantage that typified the relations between European 'agricultural' and 'industrial countries' also operated within individual countries. In almost every aspect of European life in the 1930s, the EFO argued, the agricultural producer was disadvantaged. The economic and financial vulnerability of agriculture was clear, and explained these population groups' recourse to the extreme Left (in parts of Spain), and more apparently, the Right (almost everywhere else in Europe) of the political spectrum. The anomaly of agriculture's situation came from the fact that its political importance in national and international affairs far outweighed its significance in the performance of the European economy as a whole.

Having helped to identify the problem, the EFO believed it carried a particular responsibility to highlight the problems facing countries dependent on a feeble agriculturally-based economy because their comparative economic weakness militated against their effectiveness as cooperative international actors. This vulnerability, moreover, put them at risk of falling into the orbit of powerful predators. In the 1930s, of course, this was typified by the development of Germany's exploitative trading relations in Central and Eastern Europe; in 1945 the next potential predator was the USSR.[16]

By 1938 the condition of Europe's agriculture came to dominate EFO's preoccupations: while industrial Europe[17] had important trading relations with the wider world, the 18 leading agricultural states in Europe were very largely dependent on the industrial European states. 'They obtained approximately two-thirds of their imports from them and consigned three-quarters of their exports to them.' In other words, poor European countries were especially dependent on intra-European trade for their survival, whereas richer, predominately industrialized European countries traded successfully beyond Europe's frontiers.[18] To save Europe as a whole, the problems of small peasant farmers now needed to be addressed as a matter of urgency.

The sustained examination of intra- and extra-European trade in relation to agriculture, and the codification of comparisons and tools of measurement that accompanied it coincided with an important epistemic shift within the EFO and the League more generally, in the face of the almost complete breakdown of the latter's authority and international relations more generally after 1937. This approach, formulated during the course of the late 1930s, was embodied in what became known as the Bruce Report published on the eve of war in August 1939. It contained two principal strands, one practical and the second intellectual. The first centred on a re-configuration of what was deemed to be the League's central role in international relations. It now argued that many of the 'really vital problems' of international cooperation did 'not lend themselves to settlement by formal conferences and treaties'. In language of globalization and transnationalism more typically associated with the twenty-first century, it argued that 'the primary object of international cooperation should be rather mutual help than reciprocal contract – above all, the exchange of knowledge and the fruits of experience'.[19] It was a recognition born of its own 20-year experience as an international organization, but also of the desperate struggle for survival which faced the League in 1939. Reasonably enough, the organization was anxious to underline its genuinely pioneering contribution to the creation and dissemination of technical expertise on a huge range of economic and social questions, and to shift criticism of its work away from what it regarded as a '1920s' mentality that 'assumed international co-operation necessarily implied international contractual obligations, and that success could be measured by the [number of] new obligations entered in to'.[20]

The second key shift that was central to the future of international cooperation on questions of agriculture was its emphasis that, if regional and international economic agreements were to be secured, it was essential to address questions of social welfare too. The structure and priorities of the League of Nations were redesigned to reflect this recognition. The EFO argued that economic and social policy should be developed together and that a common emphasis on 'living standards', far more than the 'abstract' topics of monetary and trade diplomacy, could revive the interest and enthusiasm of what they called 'common people' in the work of the League and international cooperation more generally. This elitist language suggests there were likely to be limits on what this approach could achieve.[21]

This development was articulated most clearly in the League's mixed report on 'The Relation of Nutrition to Health, Agriculture and Economic Policy' published in 1937. Widely known as 'The Nutrition Inquiry', it came to form an important part of EFO's wider policy agenda, and helped to generate a remodelled policy language that focused on agricultural production and trade policy. Key officials within the League argued that the needs of primary producers had to be integrated more effectively into international relations. In particular, industrialized countries should concentrate their agricultural production on milk and fruit to meet their domestic markets for perishables, but for the good of their own economies and the wider world they should produce less wheat, sugar and cereals. If the League's recommendations were to be taken up, the benefits to the world economy would be obvious: increased levels of imports for Europe's primary producers and increased levels of exports for the world's industrialized economies, because as the poor became wealthier they would be able to buy more exports. Tariff barriers and quotas would gradually fall and the world would resume the virtuous circle towards democracy and free trade.

Although these issues were posited in global terms, there was no mistaking this episteme's focus on Europe. Moreover, the knowledge it had produced and the experience it embodied were Euro-centric too. All this was underlined and brought together in a Conference on European Rural Life that was to be held in Europe in September 1939. (The fact that almost no one has ever heard of it, of course, was because the conference was postponed owing to the outbreak of war.) The hitherto ignored materials prepared for the conference in the spring and summer of 1939 are a revelation.

A few subsidiary themes embedded in the preparatory materials are of particular relevance to our consideration of the role of international organizations in the history of Europeanization and to the links between the inter-war and post-war periods. First, in the words of the preparatory report, there were 'profound differences between the manner of life of the rural populations of Eastern and Western Europe'. The latter, of course, became the environment in which the

EEC *de facto* had to operate. Secondly, the EFO argued that the challenge of dealing with Europe's rural communities had to be understood in its most ample definition. In the conference materials, the EFO uses the all-embracing phrase 'rural life' because it wanted delegates to explore the standard of living of European farmers, while at the same time arguing that the terms 'economic situation' and the 'manner of living' were not synonymous.[22] Holding these categories apart, the EFO believed, would enable the specialness of European rural life to thereby become clear.

Thirdly, for the process to work, nations needed to provide intelligence in categories which were clearly specified by the EFO, but in so doing should not allow the flavour of national particularities to be lost. The conference thereby adopted an interesting and new methodology: countries prepared individual monographs on their conditions under League-determined headings that were to form the 'living matter of the conference's discussions'.

Fourthly, it was argued that deliberations at the conference should be sensitive to non-governmental and governmental views, in its consideration of 'the part that the public authorities play, or should play, in any endeavour to bring about an improvement in any aspect of the life of the rural populations'. It was to be a conference of government representatives because they had the power to effect change, but at the same time it was recognized to be highly desirable for delegations to include members with special knowledge of the various subjects on the agenda.[23]

Finally – and this theme speaks most directly to the place of agricultural policy in the EEC – the monographs for the conference themselves emphasized the particular importance of the family farm in 'European Rural Life'. The central role attributed to the family farm by the League when considering European agriculture was an early indication of its importance; one that came to form a central theme in the work of the EEC. This was evident on the front covers of the national monographs prepared for the conference. The similarity of the illustrations and many of the messages contained within these volumes underlined how far the League had helped to create, sustain and coordinate a sense of European solidarity.[24] This was undoubtedly a 'Europeanizing process' that was borrowed from, and found echoes in, the (western) Europeanization of agriculture in the period after 1945. It is to this that we now turn.

## The EEC, Europeanization and agriculture

The EFO spent most of the Second World War based at the Institute for Advanced Study in Princeton from where it sought to shape American plans for European and global reconstruction for the post-war world. Much of this work took it away from longer term preoccupation with European agriculture broadly defined in favour of more urgent worries about food supplies and population figures in the immediate aftermath of the war, as evidenced by its work for United Nations Relief and Reconstruction Administration. This hiatus in the history of agriculture as a site of Europeanization continued into the immediate post-war years when the problems that had shaped the negotiations on agricultural cooperation during the inter-war years seemed to have disappeared. Instead of a structural crisis leading to surplus production and to decreasing prices, at war's end the main problem was one of shortage. All across Europe there was a consensus in 1945 that the best institutional framework to solve these problems was the nation-state and not forms of international or transnational cooperation along European or other lines. Highly interventionist agricultural policies thus became important means and forms of restoring or reinforcing the power of the nation-state. Agriculture returned to the role of a bulwark of nationalism and state-formation that it had played since early modern times. On the eastern side of the Iron Curtain, this led to the collectivization of agriculture; in Western Europe, nation-states prolonged, reinstituted or perfected the interventionist and most often also protectionist measures of the inter-war years.[25]

And yet, the importance of state action and economic nationalism should not be exaggerated. Unlike the inter-war years, the bipolar context of the Cold War and of open US-American hegemony over Western Europe acted as a counterweight to protectionism. On a concrete level, the main difference between the inter-war and the post-war years was that now more influential institutional settings were developed in order to balance out nation-centred policies and frameworks. Some of them – like GATT or the Marshall Plan institution, the OEEC – highlighted the liberalization of (agricultural) trade. GATT and the OEEC drew on the lessons of the damaging history of inter-war economic nationalism and the practical legacies (notably publications) of the EFO to make its case for trade liberalization. More importantly, many of the key architects of the structure of international economic relations after 1945, notably the Nobel Prize-winning economist James Meade, had been heavily involved in EFO's work.[26] These new institutions aimed at reducing existing tariff barriers, trade quotas and other distortions of the market. Thus, they challenged the protectionist systems the European nation-states were putting into place at the very same time. Under US leadership, these organizations had some liberalizing effects.

In addition, this claim of liberalization brought about paradoxical consequences. In the long run, it put the wider role of agriculture as a defining feature of Europe back on to the political agenda and, once more, the discussions and negotiations over such projects turned into important Europeanizing forces. In these processes, the very meaning of Europe changed again its contents, especially due to the emerging Cold War divide. As in the case of the inter-war period, the role of external actors, notably the United States, continued to loom large. As a counter-reaction to this pressure to liberalize trade, West European agro-political elites were increasingly attracted to ideas of regional cooperation. Integration, they hoped, would help to fend off or balance out the American position as well as other agricultural competitors in the global arena. This new interest, however, was connected to another even more important task: to find and save markets for one's own surplus production. Therefore, it was the export-oriented agricultural producer countries, most importantly France and the Netherlands, that pushed for a deeper form of European agricultural integration from around 1950 onwards. By divesting themselves of their surpluses, these two nations also endeavoured to solve their pressing foreign exchange account problems, to Europeanize the high costs for their subsidized agricultural production and to keep their increasingly productive farmers happy. This kind of cooperative perspective had been found in more limited measure in the 1920s and 1930s in Western and Central Europe. Now it was elaborated further and became a major political force in Western Europe.[27]

The first important attempt of such an agricultural integration within Western Europe was the *Pool vert* project, which was discussed between 1952 and 1954. This project failed, however – mainly because Western European countries could not agree on a model of integration. Evidently, it was not that easy to raze the political, economic and mental fortresses of nationalism and state sovereignty. While they had failed in much the same way as EFO's efforts at economic diplomacy in the 1930s, the intense negotiations of the *Pool vert* played an important role in clarifying the different interests and positions. At first glance the impact of this unsuccessful attempt at integration was rather negative with regard to Europeanization: owing to these debates, states now had a clearer picture than before as to the diverse character of European agriculture and a recognition that a strongly integrated common policy would pose a major challenge for most nation-states.[28]

Examining the role of non-state actors further reinforces this interpretation. Building upon legacies of their cooperation in the inter-war period, agricultural interest groups were quick to form transnational networks after 1945. After the creation of the United Nations system, and the FAO (the UN's Food and Agriculture Organization) in particular, farmers searched for a form of representation at the international level. In 1946 the *International Federation of Agricultural Producers* (IFAP) was founded in order to secure the cooperation of national organizations. Whereas IFAP included many Commonwealth countries, the *Confédération Européenne de l'Agriculture* (CEA), instituted in 1948, was geared more towards continental European countries. But, even within these two bodies, it was extremely difficult to reach an agreement over any substantive issues; therefore, the effects of these exchanges should not be overstated. This was partly because some transnational bonds actually impeded integration. Most importantly, German, French and Belgian farmers' organizations cooperated closely during the *Pool vert* negotiations but their joint action was focused on torpedoing this attempt at agricultural integration. Transnational exchange thus led to a shared view that the existing national regulations as well as bilateral trading agreements were more opportune than any form of European unity.[29]

In a longer term perspective, however, these new institutional settings generated important forces of Europeanization. First, it was from the late 1940s onwards, and especially in the context of the OEEC and the FAO, that huge amounts of data on the situation of European agriculture began to be collected. This included a discussion about statistical parameters and standards, about systems of census as well as about the forms and effects of political action.[30] Partially building on norms and practices established by the EFO (which also sought to reform the statistical practices of the International Institute of Agriculture that had been established already before the First Word War) and its subsidiary organization the Economic Intelligence Service, they produced a steady stream of statistical surveys on the situation of agriculture in Europe, as well as on many other issues.[31] Later, the EEC/EU surpassed the OEEC's importance in this context, and alongside this development came a narrowing down of the geographic realm of 'Europe'.[32]

In both the inter- and post-war periods, data production was central because it changed the way in which scientists, bureaucrats and politicians perceived their nations and their nation-states' relations with other countries as well as with regional and international entities. The newly generated information was characterized by its relational character, i.e. by its explicit and codified emphasis on comparison of European countries within a Western European context. Colonial systems or a truly global perspective and comparison no longer organized the statistical evidence. Focusing on Europe instead, a specific regional context was created which also served as a framework for interpretations of relative backwardness, of structural advantages and of common goals.[33]

Even the most cursory scrutiny demonstrates that these statistics ordered Europe in a particular manner. For example, FAO's 1949 *Yearbook of Food and Agricultural Statistics* had – under the heading 'Europe' and in what had been the *lingua franca* of European diplomacy for the longest time – listed countries in alphabetical order: 'Albanie' was followed by 'Andorre', 'Autriche' by 'Belgique' and 'Bulgarie'. As during the inter-war period, the USSR did not fall into Europe but the emerging Cold War had not yet led to an exclusion of all the states on the eastern side of the Iron Curtain.[34] This was to change: by 1958, 'Europe' only comprised the states of the western half of the continent and Yugoslavia.[35] Other organizations, such as the OEEC, the often-neglected UN's Economic Commission for Europe (ECE) or the EEC had their own systems, and the future head of the statistical office of the EEC insisted as early as 1952 that it would not suffice 'to look at the O.E.E.C. and E.C.E. materials and use some of it for our report'.[36] Rather, the EEC needed its own studies. So, the statistical representation of Europe remained contested and changed several times. Still, these conflicts and deliberations were a sign of an emerging consensus that Europe mattered and that it formed a special entity. The debates drew upon the earlier versions of this banal 'Europeanism', such as that fostered by the Economic Intelligence Service of the League of Nations. Thus, a new language and mode of understanding developed – a fresh way of seeing the nation-state, agriculture and also Europe.

Secondly, the *Pool vert* negotiations implied and furthered a specific regional focus – including processes of delimitation and otherization. Very often, the international organizations mentioned above are seen simply as starting points of Europe's integration. According to the standard narrative, the Marshall Plan was one of the first of these initiatives, and the historical literature only disagrees on its importance and its precise effects. However, the Marshall Plan also had another side: *de facto*, it reinforced the division of Europe into a Western and an Eastern Bloc; Europeanization thus also entailed fragmentation. So, the history of German autarky and security policy, which had challenged the values of the League and brought Europe and Europeanization to the heart of its agenda by the 1930s, continued to play an important role. Germany had once been the 'other' from which Europeanization had delimited itself. Now at least the western part of the country was part of the integration process, and Europeanization was perceived as an answer to the 'German question'. On the other hand, there was not a single serious attempt at regional integration that transcended the emerging border of the Cold War from the late 1940s onwards. Therefore, the overarching context of the reorganization of post-war Europe into two conflicting and separate camps heavily impinged on all attempts at integration and redefined the limits and boundaries of Europeanization. Also, the relationship to the United States remained ambivalent – with the USA supporting and accepting European (agricultural) integration, mainly for overarching political reasons, and the Europeans welcoming the United States' hegemony, while at the same time using integration as a means to challenge American global economic superiority.

Thirdly, Europeanism was not confined to banalities. From the late 1940s onwards, a discussion re-emerged about the family farm. Accordingly, it deserved special attention and protection because it epitomized the particular qualities of Europe's agriculture, but also of the continent's heritage and culture. The idea of the European family farm was nourished by earlier debates which occurred in the second half of the nineteenth and the first half of the twentieth centuries. Back then, farming had developed into a source of national identity and ideology in many European countries. The link to nationalism continued to loom large in the period after 1945. However, now the European element gained in importance. The intensification of exchange during the post-war era in arenas such as the OEEC or transnational farmers' organizations such as the CEA strengthened the European dimension of these ideologies. For example, the CEA's first president, Ernst Laur from Switzerland, claimed that 'European agriculture differed significantly from the one overseas'. The 'European family farm with its diversified economy, its strong share of self-sufficiency and the role of women and children' were epitomized as specifically European traits. Again, 'othering' was an important factor in the Europeanization of a common ideological point of reference. The family farm sometimes delimited itself from American capitalist large-scale farming and much more from collectivization in the Eastern Bloc. International and transnational contacts, the economic difficulties of farming in Western Europe as well as the need to find a shared vision demanding and justifying joint action were important driving forces accounting for the emergence of this concept.[37]

All this does not explain why some West European countries eventually decided to turn agriculture into the pioneering feature of European integration. In the mid-1950s, the idea of the European family farm as a shared project did not mobilize the masses. The Cold War divide might have been a precondition for more intense forms of integration but European unity did not follow from the East–West divide automatically. Nor did the change of the arrangement of statistics bring about European integration. And, more seriously, the economic and political interests and preferences of Western European states continued to point in different directions.

We argue instead that the single most important factor for the emergence of the EEC's agricultural policy was the robustness of the institutional framework in which the integration of this sector was being negotiated, and this despite the fragility and polyphony that had characterized early European integration history. The so-called Spaak committee and a subsequent intergovernmental conference paved the way to the European Economic Community and its Common Agricultural Policy (CAP). The politicians, bureaucrats and experts negotiating here were well aware of the divergent viewpoints and other obstacles that had turned the *Pool vert* into a failure. Therefore, they included the idea of agricultural integration in their agenda but delegated all concrete and hence controversial issues to later negotiations. It was only *after* the signature of the Treaties of Rome, within the context of an emerging supranational organizational setting, that the EEC's Common Agricultural Policy was born and a consensus found as to the format and content of its agricultural policy.

From this point on, ideology production gained new momentum. The rather vague concept of the family farm found an institutional framework in which it was propagated systematically. At the Stresa conference of 1958, the starting point of concrete negotiations over the CAP, the EEC's six original member states decided that the family farm should become the role model of their common agricultural policy. This concept was stabilized and reinforced a few years later, when a papal encyclical emphasized this form of farming. During the 1960s, the formative period of the CAP, the concept of the family farm was fostered by the integration process as much as it helped to legitimize it.[38]

On the level of political negotiations, a strong alliance consisting of France, the Netherlands and the European Commission pushed in favour of a supranational form of agricultural integration; and obviously the latter of these partners owed its sheer existence to the very fact of European integration. The other, more reluctant partners among the six original members of the EEC would not have been won over without the possibility of compensation deals which related agriculture to other policy areas such as the wider Common Market project or the Fouchet plans. This is particularly true for Germany and Italy. Additionally, although this lay beyond the realm of the EEC itself, the wider context of other international negotiations embodied in such organizations as NATO, GATT, the UN and its special agencies by and large stabilized the cooperation within the narrower framework of the six EEC member states. In contrast, it is worth remembering that the League contained no additional international organizations that might have worked to support its efforts. (The International Institute of Agriculture was held in considerable disrepute by the EFO which believed it had fallen largely under the sway of an Italian Fascist government uninterested in economic cooperation.) All in all, we therefore argue that the organizational framework of the CAP, the EEC and the western alliance as a whole were co-constructed.[39]

At the same time, the role of institutions in this process should not be overstated. Other projects, such as the integration of the transport sector, which were also part of the Treaties of Rome, enjoyed a similar institutional environment and yet the transport project failed to take off – at least it was not the umbrella of the EEC that saw its integration.[40] It took the combination of a propitious institutional and international environment of a strong alliance pushing for this project, together with the weakness of its opponents as well as the process's incremental quality – which in some ways reached back into the inter-war and wartime periods – that allowed for a whole host of package deals, compromises and trade-offs, to bring about the CAP.[41]

At first glance, the history of the CAP seems to contradict the emphasis on the role of institutions to socialize their members. The first few years of the CAP's existence were characterized by fierce negotiations over conflicting national interests, foot-dragging and open menaces, occasionally even dirty language. For example, the Dutch in 1960 pioneered the tactic of refusing integration steps in other fields unless their own wishes regarding the CAP had been fulfilled. Italy cultivated a disgruntled sulk from around 1963, when it learned that the CAP was less favourable for it than it had thought. And France even used the financing of the CAP as a central argument in the crisis of the 'empty chair' when it recalled its representative from the Community in 1965–66. All in all, the whole decade from 1958 to 1968 saw the clash of diverging positions, dissonance and division principally along national lines and a growing level of frustration among all partners.[42]

Yet, there was a second tier on which an unexpressed consensus emerged over time. More precisely, the mindsets of the key actors in the Agricultural Council of Ministers, the Special Committee on Agriculture as well as other EC bodies dealing with the CAP were increasingly 'Europeanized': as a result of the frequent and long-term participation in international negotiations, there emerged an 'epistemic community'; a network of agricultural politicians, bureaucrats and experts within the EEC/CAP structures that shared important interests and world views.[43] Against the rising criticism of consumers, taxpayers, the Commission, international trading partners such as the United States, the tendency of GATT negotiations as well as other parts of their national administrations, these agricultural politicians were increasingly connected by the recognition of a common problem, a shared framework of knowledge and a code of behaviour. Most importantly, from the second half of the 1960s onwards, their primary interest was to preserve the institutional status quo of the CAP and to secure high prices for the producers back home. Not least due to the high degree of their international interaction, the agro-political elites shifted allegiances away from their domestic colleagues, especially from those in the ministries of finance. And since it was the ministers of agriculture who formed the Agricultural Council of Ministers, this epistemic community could inhibit major changes. At a time when the costs for the CAP skyrocketed, their veto position was the main reason why the EEC's agricultural policy was not reformed until the early 1990s. At the same time, the emergence of this Europeanized epistemic community implied a fragmentation of pre-existing, primarily national loyalties and commitments.

The best example for this development was the discussion about agricultural prices which stood at the core of the CAP. The agricultural council had to decide on these prices on a yearly basis. In the late 1960s, no consensus could be found between the diverging positions of the member states – after long and substantial fights, they simply decided to perpetuate the status quo. In a decisive meeting on this issue in 1970, the ministers of agriculture explicitly agreed that no changes to this status quo were possible, and there emerged a real alliance in favour of high prices among them.[44]

Career patterns and informal networks played a large role in order to establish a consensus over time. The ministers of agriculture who came together in the first rounds of negotiations were very often national politicians with little or no earlier experience on an international stage. Rather, they were deeply embedded in their respective national agricultural arenas and often also in the rural world itself. It was the French minister of agriculture Edgard Pisani (1961–66) who exemplified the emergence of a minister of a different type: eloquent and well educated, clever and sleek; more an expert of administration and law than of agricultural production. Soon, other countries followed this example and searched for what they even called their own 'Pisani'. Also, networking became much more transnational. Private visits between the ministers of agriculture of the Six, family exchanges, hunting gatherings and the like: all these types of informal encounters on different levels between agricultural politicians helped to generate shared Europeanized world views.[45]

The importance of the institutional aspect of this process of identity and consensus building can also be highlighted by a side glance at alternative international organizations in the field. Most importantly, EFTA did not develop into a comparable organization with a shared set of beliefs and practices. There, the primary focus was put on trade liberalization. Agriculture was intentionally excluded from these negotiations. Consequently, no intense form of knowledge production, of exchange and decision-making characterized this rival of the EEC.[46]

At the same time, it is obvious that most of 'Europe' – however it might be defined – was not part of this emerging epistemic community. The EEC itself always stressed its links to the outside world, particularly to its partners in Western Europe. And yet its protectionist stance led to a serious reorganization of existing trade patterns; by and large, inner-EEC agricultural trade flourished. Others, especially agricultural export nations who now found themselves outside the Community, suffered. A good example of this is Denmark, suddenly and painfully situated on the other side of the fence: obliged to choose between a rock (EEC membership) and a hard place (EFTA membership), it reluctantly chose to participate in the framework led by Britain – but very soon, it had to learn that the protectionist stance of the EEC's agricultural policy was nothing short of a catastrophe for its agricultural exports until it joined the EEC in 1973.[47]

Finally, the emerging consensus among the 'Europeanized' political actors within the EEC formed a precondition for the immense impact of the CAP on the European Community as well as on other parts of the world. Under its auspices, farmers in the EEC were subjected to a tight structure of regulations, notably regarding their standards of production. This has to date impinged heavily on consumption patterns within the Community. For example, EEC standards have shaped European citizens' perception of how an apple or a banana should look. Because of its protectionist stance and the fact that the EU today is the second largest global exporter of agricultural commodities, it also shapes the fate of producers and consumers all over the world. All in all, these dynamics of Europeanization have leaped over from the restricted realm of experts and politicians in an international organization to much broader circles.

## Conclusion

We have tried to show the important role of international organizations in the 'Europeanization of Europe' in the middle decades of the twentieth century. At a general level, it is important to note that there were many continuities between the League of Nations and the European Economic Community. Recent years have seen a more positive reassessment of the League but the 'grand divide' of the Second World War is rarely bridged by historians and social scientists. Moreover, the existing studies primarily emphasize LON's role as a predecessor of the United Nations and thereby neglect the multifarious legacies of this institution. Because of its strong European focus, the League was also an important forerunner and source for all post-war efforts to unite Europe, even if the failure of the League's peace-keeping efforts prevented the 'founding fathers' of the integration process from referring to the LON too explicitly. These continuities have also been overlooked in research on the European integration process owing to an excessive present-mindedness.

More specifically, both the League of Nations as well as the European Economic Community became sites where specific forms of 'European' knowledge were negotiated, stored, reorganized and disseminated. There were also important continuities from the endeavours of the inter-war period to the post-war years. That Europe – and the family farm as its core symbol in the realm of agriculture – turned into a central episteme after 1945 was possible only thanks to earlier debates. This was partly a political process, but it was also because the pioneers of post-war Europeanization could lean upon the statistics, scholarly analyses and other forms of expertise compiled under the auspices of the LON. Indeed, we have shown that more distinctive traits usually associated with the process of Europeanization after 1945, notably the identification of a 'genuinely European' way of (family) farming, or the 'othering' and delimitation vis-à-vis the USSR point in this direction.

At the same time, it would be wrong to over-emphasize direct continuities. The Cold War divide created a different notion of 'Europe' than that generated by the more volatile and violent developments of the inter-war years. Non-state actors appear to have played a much more important role in Europeanization after 1945 than before. And, most importantly: in the context of the League, the effects of Europeanization was confined largely to the rather restricted realm of experts, bureaucrats and politicians; on the other hand, the successes of European integration under the auspices of the European Union both widened and deepened their impact.

Today, there is a continued and growing tendency in many debates to identify the EU with 'Europe' – for better and worse. For example, the 'No' in the Irish referendum on the Lisbon Treaty in 2008 is often interpreted as a 'setback', or a 'new opportunity' – but as much for the European Union as for Europe. It is interesting to see how, in keeping with the middle years of the twentieth century, in the early twenty-first century too, staunch opponents of the integration process contribute to Europeanization nonetheless. In short, international institutions are not just the subjects, the actors and sites, of the processes of Europeanization; they are also their very objects.

## Notes

\*   We would like to thank Ulrike Lindner, Diana Panke, Kenneth Weisbrode and all the team members for their helpful remarks on earlier versions of this text.

1.  See e.g. T. Judt, *Postwar: A History of Europe since 1945* (New York and London, 2007); H. Kaelble, *Sozialgeschichte Europas. 1945 bis zur Gegenwart* (Munich, 2007); B. Eichengreen, *The European Economy since 1945: Coordinated Capitalism and Beyond* (New York and Oxford, 2007).

2.  E.g. J.G. March and J.P. Olsen, 'The Institutional Dynamics of International Political Orders', *International Organization* CII (1998), 943–69; M. Finnemore, *National Interests in International Society* (Ithaca, 1996); for an overview, see A. Wiener, 'Constructivism and Social Institutionalism', in M. Cini and A. Bourne (eds), *Palgrave Advances in European Union Studies* (Basingstoke, 2006), pp. 35–55.

3.  A. Iriye, *Global Community: The Role of International Organisations in the Making of the Contemporary World* (Berkeley and London, 2002) pp. 20–3.

4.  P. Clavin, 'Europe and the League of Nations', in R. Gerwarth (ed.), *Twisted Paths. Europe 1914–1945* (Oxford and New York, 2006), pp. 325–54. This is not to suggest that the League's European focus should not be regarded critically and, in certain areas – health care, children's rights, disarmament and slavery – challenged. Susan Pedersen's recent article represents the League of Nations from almost an entirely European perspective yet it is remarkably unaware of it. See S. Pedersen, 'Back to the League of Nations', *American Historical Review*, CXII (2007), 1091–1117.

5.  The Covenant of the League of Nations available through the Avalon Project, Yale University: www.yale.edu/lawweb/avalon/leagcov.htm, consulted on 15 November 2009.

6.  P. Clavin and J.-W. Wessels, 'Transnationalism and the League of Nations: Understanding the Work of its Economic and Financial Organisation', *Contemporary European History*, XIV (2005), 465–92.

7.  Loveday to Janet Smith (League's Treasury Office London for circulation to HMG), 10 March 1941, The National Archives, Kew, London, General Correspondence of the Foreign Office (hereafter TNA FO371) TNA FO371/26661, C 3124/3124/98.

8.  For an example of Loveday's reflections on the problem see 'Improvement of the Statistics of Consumption' 2 September 1930, Records of the League of Nations, United Nations Library, Geneva, LN Box R2959, File 10E/19973/4346.

9.  See M. Billig, *Banal Nationalism* (London, 1995); also see L. Cram, 'Imagining the Union: A Case of Banal Europeanism', in H. Wallace (ed.), *Whose Europe: Interlocking Dimensions of Integration* (London, 2001), pp. 231–46.

10. An emphasis on lesson learning is surprisingly absent from the historiography of international economic relations during and after the Second World War, particularly with regard to American foreign economic policy. Structural change, interest-group politics or ideology form the dominant modes through which scholars have sought to account for the evolution of American foreign economic policy during the Second World War. For an example of the structural approach, see T. Zeiler, *Free Trade. Free World. The Advent of GATT* (Chapel Hill, 1999). For the role of interest-group constellations see T. Ferguson, 'Industrial Conflict and the Coming of the New Deal: The Triumph of Multinational Liberalism in America', in S. Fraser and G. Gerstle (eds), *The Rise and Fall of the New Deal Order, 1930–1980* (Cambridge, Mass., 1992). For the role played by key individuals and ideology see, for example, J.L. Harper, *American Visions of Europe. Franklin D. Roosevelt, George F. Kennan and Dean Acheson* (New York, 1994).

11. It is worth noting that the League Inquiry into clearing agreements launched in 1935, though not the focus of this chapter, foreshadowed the thinking that underpinned the European Payments Union of 1948 and became a central plank in the continent's economic revival. For the early League discussion see, Letter and attached note from Baumont to the French Foreign Minster, 21 July 1934, Quai d'Orsay, Série SDN, IJ – Organisation Economique et Financière de la Société des Nations, Comité Economique, no. 1184, 41e â 46e Session, Juillet 1934 – Septembre 1937.

12. Of course, New Zealand, Australia, Canada, and South Africa, Britain's Commonwealth partners and India were regarded as separate and entirely distinct nation-states under the membership rules of the League of Nations. For the figures, see League of Nations, *Europe's Trade: A Study of the Trade of European Countries with Each Other and with the Rest of the World* (Geneva, 1945), pp. 5–7. The volume of British international trade meant it also needed to be factored into non-European trade.

13. Loveday's report to Avenol on his Mission to Canada and the USA in October/ November 1934, 29 December 1934, LN R4605, 10C/13175/9854; Loveday (in Washington) to Stoppani, 19 November 1934, LN R4422, 10A/13878/13878.

14. *Europe's Trade*, p. 69.

15. *Europe's Trade*, pp. 69–70.

16. *Europe's Trade*, pp. 71–2.

17. Defined as Austria, Czechoslovakia, Belgium, France, Germany, Italy, the Netherlands, Sweden, Switzerland and the United Kingdom 'though it was recognized the dividing line between these industrialised countries and the others is necessarily somewhat arbitrary', *Europe's Trade*, p. 14.

18. *Europe's Trade*, p. 8.

19. League of Nations, *The Development of International Co-operation in Economic and Social Affairs: Report of the Special Committee* (Geneva, 1939), p. 11. For a further discussion of this integrated strategy, see League of Nations, *Report of the Co-ordination Committee on the Economic and Financial Questions* (Geneva, 1939).

20. *Development*, pp. 11–12.

21. Final Report of the Mixed Committee of the League of Nations, *The Relation of Nutrition to Health, Agriculture and Economic Policy* (Geneva, 1937). For the first time, the League of Nations' Health Organisation, the International Labour Organisation and the EFO worked together in a sustained way over the course of three years to produce a series of hugely influential reports.

22. The European distinction between the 'manner of living' and the American emphasis on the 'standard of living' was a contested field in European–American relations. See Victoria De Grazia, *Irresistible Empire. America's Advance through Twentieth-Century Europe* (Cambridge, Mass., 2005), pp. 75–129.

23. League of Nations, *European Conference on Rural Life: Report of the Preparatory Committee on the Work of its First Session* (Geneva, 1938), C 161.M.101. For the centrality of Europe to EFO's wartime work, see, Economic and Financial Committees, *Report to the Council on the Work of the 1943 Joint Session* (Princeton, NJ, 1948).

24. The monographs produced were on: Bulgaria, France, Poland, Finland, UK, Denmark, Belgium, the Netherlands, Luxembourg, Latvia, Lithuania, Yugoslavia, Norway, Sweden.

25. K.K. Patel (ed.), *Fertile Ground for Europe? The History of European Integration and the Common Agricultural Policy since 1945* (Baden-Baden, 2009); A. Milward, *The European Rescue of the Nation-State* (London, 1982); M. Tracy, *Agriculture in Western Europe. Challenge and Response, 1880–1980* (London, 1982).

26. Meade's studies of *The Theory of International Economic Policy – The Balance of Payments* (London, 1951) and *The Theory of International Economy Policy – Trade and Welfare* (London, 1955) marked but the culmination of series of hugely influential publications on trade liberalization in the 1940s and 1950s. See also A.M. Endres and G. Fleming, *International Organizations and the Analysis of Economic Policy, 1919–1950* (Cambridge, 2002), pp. 125–30, 235–54 and G. Lundestad, *The United States and Western Europe since 1945. From 'Empire' by Invitation to Transatlantic Drift* (Oxford, 2003).

27. G. Thiemeyer, *Vom 'Pool Vert' zur Europäischen Wirtschaftsgemeinschaft. Europäische Integration, Kalter Krieg und die Anfänge der Gemeinsamen Europäischen Agrarpolitik 1951–1957* (Munich, 1999), pp. 20–30; Milward, *Rescue*, pp. 265–84.

28. Thiemeyer, *Pool*; G. Noël, *Du Pool Vert à la Politique Agricole Commune. Les tentatives de Communauté agricole européenne entre 1945 et 1955* (Paris, 1988).

29. See Noël, *Pool*; Thiemeyer, *Pool*, pp. 31–126.

30. On the role of FAO and OEEC in this context, see Historical Archives of the European Union, Florence (HAEU), BAC 238/19801– and HAEU, OEEC, 1082.

31. As one of its earliest reports on agriculture, see OEEC, *Report of the Food and Agriculture Committee* (Paris, 1948); also the yearly publication of OECD, *Low Incomes in Agriculture. Problems and Policies* from 1964 onwards. The OEEC was reformed into the Organisation for Economic Co-operation and Development in 1961.

32. See on the inner-EEC debates on these statistics e.g. Bundesarchiv/Koblenz (BA/K), N 1266/1748, Thiede, Statistical Bureau of the EEC to Weinstock, 3 December 1962.

33. On this role of statistics for the British case: G. O'Hara, *From Dreams to Disillusionment. Economic and Social Planning in 1960s Britain* (Basingstoke, 2006).

34. FAO, *Yearbook of Food and Agricultural Statistics 1949*, p. 13.

35. FAO, *Yearbook of Food and Agricultural Statistics 1957*, p. 2; for further changes during later years see the successor of the Yearbook, i.e. FAO, *Trade Yearbook*, e.g. 1967, 1977.

36. HAEU, Pierre Uri Papers, 43, Letter Wagenführ to Uri, 2 September 1952, on the work of Wagenführ's office regarding agriculture, e.g. see HAEU, BAC 118/ 1986–1545; on UNECE, see G. Myrdal, 'Twenty Years of United Nations Economic Commission for Europe', in *International Organization* XII (1968), 617–28.

37. E. Laur, 'Rückblick und Ausblick', in Confédération Européenne de l'Agriculture/ CEA (ed.), *Festgabe zum Jubiläum des zehnjährigen Bestehens der CEA 1948–1958* (Brugg, 1958), pp. 30–1; L. Bluche and K.K. Patel, 'Der Europäer als Bauer. Das Motiv des bäuerlichen Familienbetriebs in Westeuropa nach 1945', in L. Bluche, V. Lipphardt and K.K. Patel (eds), *Der Europäer – ein Konstrukt* (Göttingen, 2009), pp. 135–57.

38. E.g. see *Dokumente der Landwirtschaftskonferenz der Mitgliedstaaten der Europäischen Wirtschaftsgemeinschaft in Stresa vom 3.–12. Juli 1958* (Cologne, 1959), especially pp. 227–30, EWG-Kommission, *Erster Gesamtbericht über die Tätigkeit der Gemeinschaft* (Brussels, 1958), p. 76; the encyclical 'mater et magistra' of 1961 (e.g. on http:// www.vatican.va, consulted on 15 November 2009); Bluche et al., *Europäer*.

39. Patel, *Fertile Ground*; for Germany K.K. Patel, *Europäisierung wider Willen. Die Bundesrepublik Deutschland in der Agrarintegration der EWG, 1955–1975* (Munich, 2009).

40. On transport, e.g. see J. Schot and V. Lagendijk, 'Technocratic Internationalism in the Interwar Years: Building Europe on Motorways and Electricity Networks', *Journal of Modern European History* VI (2008), 196–217 as well as

Schot's ongoing research project on the integration of the transport sector in the twentieth century.

41. C. Henrich-Franke, 'Europäische Verkehrsintegration im 19. und in der zweiten Hälfte des 20. Jahrhunderts', in Henrich-Franke et al., *Internationalismus und Europäische Integration im Vergleich* (Baden-Baden, 2007), pp. 133–75.

42. On these negotiations, e.g. see A.-C. Lauring Knudsen *Farmers on Welfare. The Making of Europe's Common Agricultural Policy* (Ithaca, 2009); N.P. Ludlow, *The European Community and the Crises of the 1960s. Negotiating the Gaullist Challenge* (London, 2006).

43. P.M. Haas, 'Introduction: Epistemic Communities and International Policy Coordination', in *International Organization* XLVI (1992), 1–35, also see A.-C. Lauring Knudsen and M. Rasmussen, 'A European Political System in the Making, 1958–1970. The Relevance of Emerging Committee Structures', in *Journal of European Integration History* XIV (2008), pp. 51–67.

44. HAEU, CM2 1970–40/ab, EEC, Council, Minutes Council of Ministers, Session 8/9 June 1970; Political Archives of the German Foreign Ministry, B 202–00/1536, German Embassy, Luxemburg to German Foreign Ministry, 9 June 1970.

45. See e.g. BA/K, B 116/14018, Note Federal Ministry of Agriculture, 26 November 1965; on the position of the German farmers' lobby HAEU, BAC 13/1969–6, DBV-Informationsdienst, 26 October 1965.

46. E.g. Wolfram Kaiser, *Using Europe, Abusing the Europeans. Britain and the European Integration, 1945–63* (London, 1999).

47. Morten Rasmussen, 'Joining the European Communities. Denmark's Road to EC-Membership, 1961–1973' (unpubl. diss., EUI, Florence, 2004), especially pp. 67–82.

# 6

# Towards a European History of the Discourse of Democracy: Discussing Democracy in Western Europe, 1945–60

*Martin Conway and Volker Depkat*

## Introduction

Democracy was everywhere in Western Europe after 1945. In contrast to the deep crisis experienced by parliamentary regimes during the preceding decades, the ideas and institutions of democracy gained a sudden and unexpected hegemony following the Second World War. With the discrediting of the authoritarian ideologies that had formed such a prominent element of Europe's political culture during the years since the First World War and the enforced marginalization of Communist political forces that occurred in Western Europe by the end of the 1940s, a new and rather broad centre-ground had emerged in European politics that enabled the construction of largely similar democratic political regimes in much of Western Europe.[1] As Raymond Aron noted in a perceptive comparative essay written at the end of the 1950s, the events of the Second World War had rather unpredictably brought about a 'stabilisation démocratique', whereby most of the regimes in Western Europe (he was cautious about the cases of France and Italy) had achieved a real stability based on their political legitimacy and their effective government.[2] At the same time, 'parliamentary democracy' came to be presented by a great majority of political elites in Western Europe as one of the central elements of 'European civilization' and a distinguishing feature of a common European identity.[3]

But, if all Europeans were now democrats, what did they mean when they used the term? As the Cold War developed, so 'democracy' became a concept contested between east and west as well as within the individual European nation-states. Was democracy 'liberal democracy' or was it 'people's democracy'? And what exactly was 'liberal democracy' and how was it to be institutionalized? Was democracy defined solely by the (Anglo-)American model or did Europe have its own traditions of democracy? And, if so, was that European democracy only an ensemble of diverse national democratic traditions or was there a distinctive European tradition? While a large majority of European political elites seemed eager to claim after 1945 that they were (and had always been) democrats, it is not at all clear whether they were actually speaking the same political language and meant the same things by 'democracy'.

This contribution, therefore, seeks to analyse the Western European discourses that surrounded democracy in the years from 1945 to 1960 as a site of Europeanization. It takes as its limited focus an exploration of the political rhetoric used by non-Communist European political leaders in the 15-year period following the end of the Second World War. By focusing on the level of political rhetoric, we are concerned to examine how far it is possible to identify a Europeanization of the concept of democracy in the post-war period; and, if so, to explore more exactly what might be meant by such a process. Does examination of the discourse on democracy demonstrate a convergence in the way in which political figures envisaged democracy or does it expose the continuing differences and cleavages between Western European countries and their ideological traditions? And, if there was convergence, does this imply simply that political leaders thought of democracy in broadly similar ways, or that a European identity became part of how these political leaders conceived of democracy? That European political leaders did indeed articulate common notions of democracy in this immediate post-war period appears to have long formed part of the rather tacit assumptions that historians have brought to the study of the period. However, despite the wealth of research that has been undertaken in recent years on post-1945 European history, it seems to us that there has been an absence of comparative empirical studies which have sought to analyse the discourses on democracy in the individual Western European nation-states in terms of convergence and divergence.[4]

This brief article has, of course, no pretension to arrive at definitive conclusions to these somewhat large questions. Our common interest in the subject arises out of our separate but overlapping interests in the democratic political culture of post-1945 Western Europe.[5] But we regard the conclusions that we draw in this chapter as no more than a tentative template: much remains to be done in terms of more systematic research on how democracy was understood in Europe during the immediate post-war era. For our part, in this chapter we have sought to draw upon a variety of primary material, which is intended to provide a survey of the ways in which European political leaders used the term and elucidated its guiding principles. In doing so, we have chosen largely to omit Communist statements and Soviet concepts of Europe's order. This should not be regarded as implying that European Communist thinking on democracy was no more than a pale reflection of Soviet-inspired propaganda. On the contrary, the nuances evident within the approaches to democracy adopted by European Communist parties provide an important alternative approach to understanding the aspirations for democracy within post-war Europe.[6] Furthermore, by the way in which Communist concepts of democracy and of Europe challenged non-Communist parties to articulate their own responses, it is evident that Communist statements also structured the discourses of the Western European advocates of parliamentary democracy. Our reasons for omitting Communist statements are therefore merely pragmatic. Instead we have sought to concentrate on a variety of non-Communist political figures, preferring to emphasize the points of convergence between their ideas, rather than differentiating them into separate Christian Democrat, Socialist, agrarian or liberal movements. This approach too can be questioned. Much writing on post-1945 Europe has rightly emphasized the durability of ideologically-inspired political traditions, which in turn reflected the way in which the intellectual formation and careers of political figures in many areas of Europe continued to take place within distinctive and relatively closed political traditions.[7] The political leaders who came to the fore after 1945, especially in Central Europe, were different from those who had been in power, at least at a national level, before the war; but they were neither especially young nor devoid of experience. On the contrary, they were to a large degree the products of well-defined political and social milieux. To suggest, therefore, a fundamental similarity of views between non-Communist politicians risks occluding the very different backgrounds from which they came. However, there are also pitfalls in such an ideologically-defined approach. In particular, it neglects the degree to which the concrete practice of democracy within the predominantly multi-party political systems of post-war Europe and the experience of functioning democracy drew political actors not merely into the compromises inherent in coalition government, but also – and more intangibly – into the sense of common purpose that came to be celebrated as one of the key characteristics of a mature parliamentary system.[8]

## True democracy

At first sight perhaps the most surprising element of Europe in the immediate context of 1945 was the relatively limited use that was made of the word democracy. 'Freedom', 'liberty' and 'justice' as well as the aspiration for a new and more just economic order were the slogans which predominated during the rather complex process whereby the populations of Occupied Europe regained forms of legitimate government at the national and especially local levels. Each liberation, or occupation, was different; but throughout this period attention focused not so much on democracy but on the restoration of a sense of legitimate order and normalcy.[9] In many respects, this was scarcely surprising. The collective euphoria of liberation as well as immediate demands for action against those guilty of collaboration and for an end to the material hardships of the war were uppermost in the minds of Europeans in 1945; politics, and more especially the construction of the formal panoply of democratic government, necessarily seemed rather more distant, both temporally and geographically, from many people's concerns.[10] Even so, it is remarkable how relatively limited was the role that discussions of democracy played in the politics of liberation. In so far as 'democracy' did emerge, it tended to be less in its own right and more as the antithesis of fascist or other discredited authoritarian regimes: the defeat of fascism must be the victory of democracy.[11] This subordination of democracy within a wider rhetoric of patriotism was not without consequences. In particular, it tended to pre-empt the articulation of alternative definitions of democracy, and contributed to the way in which in those states that had not been allied to the Axis cause calls for radical political change after 1945 tended to lose out in the later-1940s to the re-establishment of modified forms of the pre-war political order. Elsewhere, too, democracy did not emerge as an effective oppositional tool. In post-fascist Germany and Italy, although the cause of 'democracy' was espoused by some radical voices, it was predominantly appropriated as a means of legitimizing a more 'top-down' stabilization of the post-war order.[12] Democracy in that respect, in Europe after the Second World War, never signified an entirely new beginning, and was more often a tool used by the powerful to legitimate their rule, rather than the means whereby the weak or marginal challenged the powerful.[13]

The relative absence of discussion of the content or structures of political democracy was reinforced by what one might describe as the tendency to invest the term with wider, and at times almost metaphorical, meanings. Democracy was often used in immediate post-war Europe less as a description of a specific political system, than as a means of describing an aspiration for a new civic culture characterized by mutual respect and a shared morality. In the words of one Belgian Catholic periodical, there was a need to establish a 'démocratie vraiment humaine'[14], while Konrad Adenauer was convinced that the reconstruction of Germany would have to be inspired by a 'Christian and democratic spirit'.[15] There was also much rather vague reference to a 'new democracy',[16] although quite exactly what this meant, beyond the fact that it would mark a break with both authoritarianism and the democracy of the past, was far from clear. In so far as such rhetoric had any meaning, it was that there should be 'more' democracy. Thus, in a characteristic example of such rhetoric, the founding charter of the French Socialist Party, the SFIO, declared in 1946 that there was a need for 'libertés démocratiques étendues et développées'.[17] In concrete terms, such statements implied not so much a widening of the democratic political process as the need for a wider democratization of society. Calls for 'economic democracy' and a 'soziale Marktwirtschaft' were widespread in Europe in the years following the Second World War, and often took precedence over discussion of political structures. Once again, the nature of such an economic democracy was often defined only vaguely and encompassed multiple meanings, ranging from the radical ambition of some workers to take charge of their workplace, to the very different intentions of various employers and trade-union leaders to establish more structured forms of industrial corporatism.[18] Common to all of these ideas was, however, the sense that democracy should not be conceived in solely political terms, but as part of the wider social and economic framework of society. Land reform, full employment, decent housing and old-age pensions were in this respect more prominent elements of the post-1945 democratic agenda than the more fundamental issues of how a democracy might be organized.

With the consolidation of Western Europe during the later 1940s into a defined and inter-connected framework of nation-states, discussions of the content of democracy did, however, become both more prominent and more 'political'. This was especially so in France, Germany and Italy, where the highly contested debates surrounding the nature of the new constitutions to be introduced in each country necessarily focused attention on issues that were sometimes highly technical in nature (notably the relative merits of different voting systems) but also powerfully symbolic. Thus, the referendum in 1946 on the future of the monarchy in Italy, the parliamentary debates and referenda which eventually led to the establishment of the Fourth Republic in France in 1946 and the widely voiced calls for free and general elections to a national parliament in occupied Germany between 1945 and 1949 were all ways in which discussions of the form of democracy came to the fore in post-war Europe.[19] This was reinforced throughout Europe by the ritual (and self-congratulation) which accompanied the elections, both local and national, that served as symbols of the new democratic order. The enfranchisement of women in France, Italy and Belgium, as well as the return to a multi-party structure of elections in Italy, Austria and eventually Germany after a hiatus of more than a decade meant that by 1950 for the first time directly elected governments ruled all the states of Western Europe outside of the Iberian peninsula. As a consequence, the very concepts of 'Europe' and 'democracy' began to merge in political and intellectual discourse: Europe came to be seen as the 'home' of democracy, just as democracy was the expression of a shared European identity.

Once again, however, it would be wrong to exaggerate the extent of the debate provoked by this rather sudden democratic revolution. As historians have long remarked, the most tangible change in democracy – the introduction of female suffrage in those states which had not formerly adopted it – did not give rise to much public debate or celebration. It was perceived as little more than an adaptation to an unavoidable necessity, and one which on the political left was accompanied by ill-disguised unease at the electoral advantage that they assumed Christian Democrat parties would derive from female enfranchisement.[20] Moreover, in more general terms, the most distinctive element of the way in which the term 'democracy' was used by post-war political elites was the sense of unease and even of nervousness with which they approached it. For many of Europe's political leaders, the operation of a stable democratic politics was a complex task, and one replete with potential dangers.

Nothing better conveyed this unease than the repeated use by political and intellectual figures of the phrase 'true democracy'. This adjectival qualification rapidly became and remained, for much of the 1950s, a key element of European political discourse. It was one which also had several meanings. Most obviously, it formed part of the arsenal of anti-Communist language by which the political parties and leaders of Western Europe defined their concept of democracy against what they regarded as the caricature of democracy that operated in the 'people's democracies' of Central and Eastern Europe. The visible spectacle in the East of mass crowds, crude propaganda techniques and show trials provided an almost daily demonstration of what democracy should *not* be, and in doing so helped to solidify a Western definition of a true democracy based around the individual citizen, pluralist intellectual debate and the rule of law. Socialist political figures in particular hastened to emphasize how their definitions of democracy should not be confused with those of the Communists. Indeed, a commitment to democratic practice and values became the means by which the Socialist parties of post-war Europe defined themselves against the false democrats of the Moscow-directed Communist Internationale.[21] The case of the Belgian Socialist Party (PSB-BSP), undoubtedly one of the most powerful Socialist parties in post-war Western Europe, was typical in this respect. Though in many respects, the party remained loyal to its nineteenth-century Marxist heritage, and eschewed attempts by some intellectual groups to make it adopt a new and more 'liberal' programme after the Liberation, the Socialist political leaders were at pains to demonstrate that they were 'socialistes de l'Occident' who had inherited the democratic values of West European culture.[22] At the same time, however, most European Socialist parties remained sensitive, as they long had been, to accusations that participation in democracy was in some sense a retreat from their Socialist ambitions. Thus, Socialist leaders often sought to present their commitment to democracy as part of their wider struggle for a Socialist transformation of society. As the banner held over the stage at the conference of the Belgian Socialist Party in June 1945 declared: 'La Victoire de la Démocratie sera celle du Socialisme'. Writing shortly before the collapse of the Fourth Republic, the French Socialist leader, Guy Mollet, adopted a very similar tone, declaring that the members of the SFIO were committed to what he termed a 'démocratie socialiste', in which the political liberties of the existing regime would be supplemented by a real material equality of conditions.[23] West Germany's Socialists of the SPD argued pretty much along the same lines. In 1946, Richard Löwenthal, a Social Democrat exiled in London during the Third Reich, published his book *Jenseits des Kapitalismus* (Beyond Capitalism), in which he developed the vision of a 'demokratischer Sozialismus' that combined the teachings of

Karl Marx, Rudolf Hilferding and John Maynard Keynes.[24] Three years later, Willy Brandt argued at the annual convention of the SPD that the party's agenda of 'democratic socialism' was founded on a shared commitment to 'humanism, the rule of law, and social justice'.[25]

As such statements demonstrate, it would be wrong to exaggerate the degree of common ground among non-Communist political forces. Statements of faith in democracy on the part of many political leaders tended to be coupled with phrases whereby each political tradition sought to claim the mantle of being the 'true' defenders of democracy, of 'une vraie et saine démocratie'.[26] This competition for 'ownership' of democracy was perhaps most evident in France, where De Gaulle's decision to set himself up against the ethos and practice of the Fourth Republic obliged him to present himself and the party which he inspired, the RPF, as the advocates of a presidential (or, as de Gaulle preferred to term it, 'true') definition of democracy by which the will of 'la Nation dans ses profondeurs' would find its direct expression rather than being corrupted through the distorting prism of parliamentary politics.[27] Such tensions were, however, also present elsewhere, most notably in Germany, where two new states competed to be regarded as the 'true' embodiment of democracy, as well as in the Netherlands and Belgium, where the concept of the monarch as the personal embodiment of the will of the nation co-existed somewhat uncomfortably alongside the more impersonal language of parliamentary government. This tension between monarchical and parliamentary rule was most acute in Belgium where the attempts by Leopold III to return to Belgium as monarch between 1945 and 1950 in effect became a conflict between competing definitions of democracy. On the one hand, the principal non-Catholic political parties based their opposition to the king's attempts to resume his constitutional powers on the fact that there was no majority in the Parliament for him to do so. On the other hand, Leopold and his supporters spoke a more monarchical and at times sentimental language of the personal bond between the monarch and his people and denounced (with some justification) the refusal of the parliamentary politicians to test the will of the people by holding a referendum.[28]

Undoubtedly the most durable fault line was, however, that between Catholic and secular definitions of democracy. The rapid emergence after the war of powerful Christian Democratic parties in many of the states of Western Europe in effect brought forms of Catholic thought more to the fore in European political culture than had been the case at any point since at least the end of the nineteenth century. Consciously reinforced by the statements of the papacy during the pontificate of Pius XII, this distinctive Catholic approach to democracy was one that placed emphasis on the 'natural' communities of family and region, as well as on the need to construct a social order that respected Christian values of charity and solidarity. 'A true and healthy democracy', as Pius XII termed it, was one in which the power of the modern state was confined by respect for the dignity of the individual, and for the teachings of God.[29] This was also a definition of democracy which, by heritage and instinct, was distrustful of the individualist and liberal tradition that derived from the Enlightenment and the French Revolution of 1789 and which had led remorselessly to the capitalist materialism of the modern world, two world wars and, through the secular cult of the nation-state, ultimately to fascism.[30] Christian democracy did not, therefore, imply so much a Catholic acceptance of secular democracy, as a continuation of the efforts made by progressive Catholic activists since the end of the nineteenth century to make democracy Christian.[31] As the German Catholic intellectual Romano Giardini declared in 1946, in a phrase which was expressive of the militant mood of the moment, 'I am a proponent of democracy – but [I must] immediately add, [I am] a Catholic proponent who acknowledges absolute values and objective authorities as givens'.[32]

Such statements did not fundamentally undermine Catholic participation in the democratic political system. Claims of a distinctive Catholic definition of democracy tended to be more rhetorical than substantive; and, more so than within Europe's other political traditions, the events of the Second World War had brought about a fundamental realignment of Catholic political attitudes away from the inter-war infatuation with authoritarian and corporatist political models in favour of the acceptance of democracy. Almost perhaps because of the extent of this change, Christian Democrat leaders felt concerned to emphasize the distinctly Catholic inspiration that underlay their actions: their actions would be the means by which Christian values of civilization would finally permeate modern society or indeed, in a more maximalist formulation, of bringing about a Christian revolution.[33] This attitude was rooted too in a distinctly Catholic attitude to the concept of Europe. Behind Konrad Adenauer's oft-cited concept of a European *Abendland* lay a much broader sense of a Christian European civilization which, in contrast to the liberal primacy of the nation-state, would bring about a new era of European cooperation. To cite Romano Guardini once again: 'Either Europe becomes Christian or Europe will no longer exist'.[34]

Notwithstanding these differences of ideological definition, one of the central changes that emerged after the war was undoubtedly the sense that the 'building of democracy' was a shared task. Reinforced by the logic of Cold War polarization, the non-Communist political forces of Western Europe believed in the need to collaborate in order to bring about a stable democratic order. This disabused and rather pragmatic approach to the construction of a 'true democracy' took a number of largely inter-related forms. Above all, it was based on a vision of channelling the will of the people through a number of intermediate institutions, which – rather in the manner of a series of dykes constructed to break the force of a sudden flood – were primarily intended to blunt the impact of majoritarian will.

Majorities had a poor reputation in post-war Europe, which reflected a wider distrust of forms of mass mobilization. The better, and more mature, approach was therefore to construct a democracy where crowds would (or could) not emerge. In Germany, intellectuals such as Theodor Steltzer, Eugen Kogon, Jürgen von Kempski and Karl Jaspers warned against a 'centralized democracy of the masses' in the immediate aftermath of the catastrophe of the Second World War. They were sceptical of political parties, regarded national elections as plebiscatory, and embraced indirect forms of delegating power and authority to ensure the rule of democratic elites.[35] In contrast to them, Konrad Adenauer, Kurt Schumacher, Thomas Dehler and other West German party politicians were all for channelling democratic energies into political parties; but even they were doubtful as to whether the German people would cast their votes 'correctly'. In the autumn of 1949, Adenauer told the Allied High Commissioners for Germany that 'the political thinking of the Germans was still extremely disorderly'.[36]

The danger posed by what J.L. Talmon in his influential polemic *The Origins of Totalitarian Democracy* (published in 1952) termed 'the seemingly ultra-democratic ideal of unlimited popular sovereignty' led European politicians to perceive the making of a stable democracy as one in which an 'ordered' political liberty prevailed.[37] In electoral terms, this was to be achieved through well-organized elections, which would be contested by modern and disciplined political parties that accepted the laws of parliamentary democracy. The central institution of what Jean-Pierre Rioux rightly terms (with regard to the French Fourth Republic) this *gouvernement d'assemblée* was incontestably national parliaments.[38] It was in the privileged space of parliament that deputies would debate issues of national interest; as the elected representatives of the people, but also at a necessary distance from the people. This new parliamentary culture, memorably satirized by Wolfgang Koeppen in his 1953 novel *Das Treibhaus*,[39] was based on the widespread belief that the pace of modern social and economic change had rendered obsolete the amateur parliamentarism of the nineteenth century. The preparation of legislation was a complex and technical task, to which parliamentary deputies brought their particular forms of expertise and acted in collaboration with a wider range of 'experts', including civil servants, professional specialists and representatives of socio-economic groups such as trade unions, farmers' associations and employers' organizations. This somewhat opaque decision-making process operated at the national level, but also increasingly at the level of the international and European structures of decision-making, such as the North Atlantic Treaty Organization and the European Coal and Steel Community, as well as from the end of the 1950s the European Economic Community. Indeed, it was in those West European structures of decision-making that the new ethos of democratic decision-making reached its fullest expression in the construction of complex legislation, devised in the interests of the people but not by the people.

The privileging of this new technocratic democratic culture contributed to the widespread sense, increasingly voiced during the 1950s, of 'an end of ideology'.[40] The practice of democracy appeared to have moved beyond the clash of ideas, which had been displaced to the higher level of the struggle against Soviet Russia and, from the end of the 1950s onwards, an increasing awareness of the struggles for national liberation within the non-European world.[41] Within Europe, however, politics had become a more technical and inclusive process that was reflected in the more positive perception that developed of coalition government: it was by members of responsible political parties working together that the right solutions to contemporary problems would be developed. Conversely, this 'true democracy' eschewed personalized or direct forms of decision-making. Presidents were, as in the new French, Italian and German republics, to be elected by the deputies in parliament, rather than directly by the people, and their roles were deliberately intended to be non-partisan and consensual.

Similarly, referenda were distrusted as crude and unpredictable tools, which should largely be avoided. De Gaulle was, of course, an emphatic and influential defender of the tool of the referendum, which he used very deliberately as a means of challenging the much more widely accepted concept of parliamentary democracy. Indeed, in an almost unconscious reflection of the assumptions of the time, Jean Touchard, the author of a perceptive study of Gaullist ideology, commented that De Gaulle's advocacy of referenda placed him beyond the bounds of what was conventionally regarded as a democrat.[42] The 1950 referendum in Belgium on the future status of King Leopold III was held in response to pressure from the king and his supporters; but even among Leopold's supporters there was a recognition that its role could only be consultative and could not replace the sovereign will of parliament.[43] Similarly, in Sweden during the 1950s, two referenda were held, in 1955 on switching from driving on the left to driving on the right, and in 1957 on pension reform. The former resulted in a large majority in favour of maintaining driving on the left, which was overruled by parliament a few years later; while the latter was a highly complex proposal, involving three possible options, and had only a limited impact on the legislation subsequently enacted by parliament. As the long-serving Swedish social-democrat Prime Minister Tage Erlander commented, 'it is obvious that referendums are a strongly conservative force. It becomes much harder to pursue an effective reform policy if reactionaries are offered the opportunity to appeal to people's natural conservatism and natural resistance to change.'[44]

## The presence of the past

The muted terms in which many post-war politicians couched their espousal of democracy reflected the sense that democracy was less of a conscious choice than the consequence of the exhaustion or, in the case of Communism, the unacceptability of the alternatives. As Albert Camus, writing in *Combat* in 1947, commented, 'There may be no good political regime, but democracy is surely the least bad of the alternatives'.[45] This sense of 'two cheers for democracy' reflected the disabused nature of the mood in much of Europe in the post-war years.[46] Not merely in the defeated states but also among the victor states, there was a pervasive sense that the bitter conflicts and personal suffering of the preceding decades were too proximate for it to be possible to celebrate the making of a new democratic era.

Against this backdrop, the concept of 'true democracy' was therefore also used to contrast the present and the expected future with the immediate past of the 1920s and 1930s. During these decades, the experiences of democracy had been far from universally positive in Western and Central Europe. The Weimar Republic had collapsed under the onslaught of National Socialism and the Great Depression between 1930 and 1933. In 1938, the Austrians had all too willingly accepted the destructive integration of their First Republic into the Third Reich. Finally, the short-lived Spanish Second Republic had ended in a bloody civil war between anti-democratic nationalists and Popular Front republicans, which saw General Franco establish his military dictatorship supported by conservative forces. Moreover, the authoritarian regimes that had emerged in Europe during the inter-war years were perceived to have not been so much a negation of democracy as the corruption of democracy to serve radically different ends. In Italy, Mussolini and his Fascist colleagues had established a plebiscatory and charismatic democracy; in Germany, the National Socialists and their *Führer* Adolf Hitler had claimed to express the will of the *Volksgemeinschaft*; while in France Vichy's *Etat Français* had embarked on an experiment in authoritarian wartime democracy intended to establish a system of corporate representation which claimed to be more democratic than the corrupt parliamentarism of the Third Republic.

This highly problematic past allowed Western European discourses of 'true democracy' to unfold to a very large extent as a critique of the prior mistakes made by twentieth-century democracies in Europe. Governmental instability and executive weakness, class-based politics emerging from the unsolved social antagonisms that had divided European societies in the 1920s and 1930s, the abandonment of rational argumentation and the resort to passion, populist demagogy and the rule by extremes, violence and civil war – all these aspects of past experiences were discussed by Western European political leaders as problems and dangers inherent to a democratic form of government. Inseparably connected to this critique of the immediate past was therefore a willingness to learn from its mistakes.

Criticisms of the imperfect democratic past were widely voiced throughout post-war Europe. In France, for example, the electoral success of the Christian Democrat MRP in the immediate post-war years rested strongly on its espousal of a new democracy that would break with the failings of the pre-war Third Republic.[47] Unsurprisingly, however, it was in central Europe, and more especially in Germany, that such critiques were voiced most strongly. Not merely had democracy failed in Germany but by giving rise to the NSDAP it had led to the antithesis of the values upon which European civilization had been constructed. The writings of German intellectuals and political figures in the post-war decades were dominated by analysis of the causes of this catastrophe. For a figure such as Marie Baum (1874–1964), a social reformer, lecturer at the University of Heidelberg and a short-time member of the liberal *Deutsche Demokratische Partei* in the 1920s, the development of the Weimar Republic marked the destruction of European core values such as individual liberty, freedom of thought, Christian compassion and civic responsibility. This 'incurable apostasy from all old ideals' provided the explanation as to why the younger generations of Germans 'went off on peculiarly wrong tracks' during the 1920s leading ultimately to the destruction of democracy.[48]

In West Germany, political elites carefully distinguished between Germany's first democracy and its second, which was established after 1945. The slogan 'Bonn ist nicht Weimar' accompanied the history of the Federal Republic of Germany from the start, and political elites in West Germany were determined that 'Bonn' should not become 'Weimar' ever again. Two themes figured prominently in the debates on the Weimar Republic's fate: the lack of democrats among the German population and the class-based politics of the political parties which had given allegiance to class a higher priority than loyalty to the democratic order. Adenauer was convinced that the NSDAP had managed to acquire a mass following only because 'the political interest and sense of responsibility' had been very weak in large parts of Germany's society. In his memoirs, he explicitly denied that the National Socialists' rise to power was the result of the machinations of a small circle of business and military elites. Rather, he argued that a vast majority of Germans from the most diverse backgrounds did not have the 'right attitude of mind' with respect to democracy and liberalism.[49] This underlying cultural problem was, according to Adenauer and many other German intellectuals and political figures of the post-war years, exacerbated by the way in which political parties of the 1920s had failed to overcome their sectional perspectives. In their self-understanding these parties had been the representatives and agents of a particular social milieu (the working class, the bourgeoisie, the Catholics, etc.), and they understood their task to be to pursue the particular interests of their constituency even at the price of the common good. Thus, they had used the democratic state to push their narrow agenda but they had not been sufficiently concerned to act as the guardians of democracy.[50]

These critical and self-critical discussions about the immediate past were rooted in the very particular German context of a coming to terms with the

Nazi catastrophe. But they also reflected a wider post-war nervousness about Europe's democratic heritage. The French Revolution of 1789 had formed a central element of the means by which opponents of the Vichy Regime and of wartime German rule had legitimized their resistance actions in France.[51] But, once the war had ended, it was the relative absence of references to the events of 1789 and indeed the subsequent revolutions of 1848 and 1871 that, at least outside of Communist ranks, was the more remarkable in France. This was evident too in the highly contrasting approaches to the centenary of 1848 in Germany. While political and intellectual elites of the German Democratic Republic heralded '1848' as the birth of the Communist Manifesto and the historical awakening of the working class, the Federal Republic of Germany could only refer to 1848 as a first failed attempt to create a German nation-state on the basis of democratic and liberal principles.[52] Rather than such awkward modern history, there was unsurprisingly a tendency throughout post-war Europe to seek usable precedents in local democratic traditions or in the invocation of a largely imaginary democratic medieval past.

## The future of democracy

The legacy of past experience emphasized that democracy was not something that could simply be decreed, but a form of government, and more broadly a form of political culture, that had to be nurtured, protected and built in an incremental manner. Notions of the 'building' of democracy were widespread in Western Europe after the Second World War, mirroring the way in which so much of the material landscape of Europe had to be rebuilt after the destruction of the war years. This task of construction was inseparably tied to a determination to establish a more managed structure of democracy. Western European debates about 'true democracy' revolved to a very large extent around the problem of how democracy's potential for self-destruction could be minimized if not entirely eliminated. The question of how liberty and self-determination could be 'ordered' to perpetuate the democratic system, and how in practical terms Europeans could be educated to become democrats capable of governing themselves after all their political failures in the twentieth century, lay at the heart of much of the Western European discourse on democracy during the post-war decade. 'True democracy', therefore, was not a current reality, but a term of expectation that was structurally linked to both the self-critical assessment of the errors of the past *and* the diagnosis that the present did not yet live up to the ideal. There was no complacency about the challenge of rebuilding democracy after 1945; 'true democracy' would only materialize in the future.

Central to understanding the debates about the future of democracy is the fact that a majority of political elites, especially but not exclusively in those states such as Germany, which had succumbed to authoritarian rule over the preceding decades, were inclined to perceive the present in post-1945 Europe in terms of a deep crisis.[53] The latter seemed to be essentially driven by three factors, namely the decline of Europe's standing in the international system, the Soviet threat and the hegemony of the United States over Western Europe. Against the backdrop of this perception, the achievement of a stable form of democracy was thus seen as a means of mitigating if not entirely overcoming this sense of pervasive crisis.

This sense of crisis had its basis in the widespread perception that Europe had lost its position as the centre of the world during the period from 1914 to 1945.[54] European elites saw a weakened 'old world' dwarfed between two new superpowers that were systematically building global empires antagonistically opposed to each other. The urgent task for the leaders of the present generation was to protect the remaining influence that European states still had on world affairs and, if possible, to increase it in order to regain some of Europe's former status and power. In this context, the democratization of Europe and the projection of a European identity based on its liberal values appeared as a means of reasserting Europe's political pre-eminence.

Most immediately, the sense of European weakness had its origins in the threat posed by Communism and the expansionist policies of the Soviet Union.[55] In the eyes of many Western European politicians one half of Europe was already under Soviet domination, and they feared that the Soviet Union was preparing to bring the whole of Europe under its control in the near future. In this context, the realization of 'true democracy' was seen as a means of containing if not rolling back Communism. By binding their people to the model of a democratic society, Western European leaders would not only counter the appeal of Communism but would also prevent Europe from being subjugated to an essentially 'non-European' culture. The perception that the Soviet Union, and with it Communism, was a fundamentally alien and Asiatic force was widely held among post-war West European elites. As early as March 1946 Adenauer referred to 'Asia' beginning at the Elbe River in a letter written to the Social Democrat Wilhelm Sollmann, and in a conversation with de Gaulle in 1958, he similarly declared that the Soviet Union was an 'Asian dictatorship'.[56]

However, European discourses about 'true democracy' was not exclusively focused on the Soviet Union as the sole 'significant other' that generated notions of a Western European identity centring on democratic values. In many respects, the USA also served a similar function, as many European elites believed that they not only had to prevent Europe from being 'Sovietized' but also from being 'Americanized'.[57] European attitudes towards the 'friend in the West' were highly ambivalent. On the one hand, Western European elites accepted US-American hegemony, and even invited American intervention to reconstruct Europe, to spread democracy and prosperity, and to protect her from Communism.[58] At the same time, however, many European elites continued to feel culturally superior to the USA, which is why they strenuously looked for genuinely European traditions of democracy. They were fully aware that the USA was the dominant power in Western Europe and that the USA would not allow them to opt for any regime other than liberal democracy. Within this broader framework of liberal democracy, however, there were many options and there was a considerable range of choice and diversity. This helps to explain why throughout Western Europe, politicians were so concerned to strive to realize models of democracy that were in keeping with the respective national democratic traditions. There was no general and unqualified admiration of American democracy – and to a considerable extent European discourses on 'true democracy' were about realizing democracies that were 'true' because they differed from the American model.

All in all, the task of constructing a stable European form of democracy was therefore one to be accomplished by Europeans, working together across nation-state frontiers. In doing so, European political leaders built on the contacts that many had developed during their war years in exile, notably in London, but also on pre-existing networks such as those between Catholic political figures, which had been established during the inter-war years.[59] But they were also aided by the establishment of what one might term democratic-front organizations, such as the Congress for Cultural Freedom which, whatever the fact of their American funding and patronage, emerged as forums in which European intellectuals from a variety of national and ideological backgrounds came together to defend, though not uncritically, Western values of democracy and freedom.[60] In addition, the early assemblies of the European integration process (the Europarat, Montanunion, the WEU, and other ad hoc assemblies dealing with specific issues) served as sites of debate about the traditions and meanings of democracy in the European context.[61]

A similar rationale underlay European projects of colonial development in the non-European world. Although the efforts of the European imperial powers to assert their authority in territories such as Indochina, Malaya, and Palestine implicated them in highly authoritarian actions of repression, these same actions were often legitimized by the need to defend European values of democracy. This was most strikingly the case in Algeria, where the war that developed during the 1950s was for many French politicians one to defend Republican and European notions of legality and order against the agents of terrorist violence.[62] More generally, too, the justification of continued European colonial rule in areas such as sub-Saharan Africa, rested not only on the material benefits of 'development' but on how the colonial rulers were inculcating an understanding of European values of justice and democracy, in the subject populations. To grant them independence 'prematurely' would merely cause a repetition in Africa of the past failures of democracy in Europe.[63]

Democracy therefore, both in Europe and beyond, was to be built gradually over the course of a couple of generations by educating its citizens, and integrating democratic values into the fabric of society. 'True democracy' needed 'true democrats', and it was necessary to root the public rituals of democracy – elections, parliamentary debates, the passing of legislation – and its wider framework of legal institutions in a pervasive democratic culture. When Ralf Dahrendorf critically scrutinized the state of West Germany's democracy in his landmark book *Gesellschaft und Demokratie* in the 1960s, he found the rule of law as well as a liberal economic order to be firmly established in West Germany but he heavily criticized the persistence of an illiberal, even authoritarian, mentality in large parts of Germany's population, and demanded that the democratization of the minds of the Germans be pushed further.[64] The task of building 'true democracy', therefore, was an ongoing process and a continuous task, and in their self-understanding Europe's democratic elites were responsible for initiating and guiding this process of putting the democratic reconstruction of Western Europe on a sound footing.

This emphasis on the social and civic underpinnings of democracy was a strong element of political rhetoric in the decade following the Second World War, and it reflected the influence that notions of planning and of social welfare had on European political culture in this period. Building democracy in the eyes of many Western European political elites was a collaborative act that required the cooperation of all social forces and classes. This meant that after 1945, in contrast to what was perceived to have occurred in the inter-war decades, all social groups were partners in a political process, the wider purpose of which was to stabilize democracy. This understanding of a common responsibility in upholding the democratic form of government blurred ideological and partisan antipathies and overcame a class-based perception of political action. At the same time, it also placed obligations on citizens to perform their duties within the democratic system. Democracy was a serious process, which required its citizens to reject demagogic options, to take an interest in political affairs and to place the general interest above their individual interests.[65]

This sense of the duties of democratic citizens helps to explain the preoccupation in post-war political rhetoric with the 'health' of democracy, which needed to be measured in terms of the effectiveness of its operation and, most especially, the engagement of citizens with the democratic process. This was of course especially so in the post-fascist states of Italy and Germany, where the processes of Allied-imposed and internally generated re-education that occurred after the war were intended to purge the societies of the forms of behaviour and thinking that had rendered them vulnerable to the demagogic manipulation and seduction that had underpinned fascist rule.[66] However, the 'strengthening' of the republican body's health was important not only with respect to the lessons of the past, it was also crucial in the current competition with the Communist bloc. When Adenauer stated that for him Asia began at the Elbe River, he continued to explain that only an 'economically and spiritually healthy Western Europe led by Great Britain and France' would be able to block the further advance of Asia.[67] Adenauer left no doubt that for him a 'healthy Western Europe' was one based on 'true democracy', and that the realization of 'true democracy' was a way of perpetuating Western Europe's 'health'.

But this quasi-medical preoccupation with the health of democracy was not confined to the post-fascist states; it was evident in many other West European states, reflecting not only historical lessons about the vulnerability of democracy but also more present-minded concerns about how processes of social modernization were leading to more isolated and privatized lives.[68] The consequent distance, and mutual suspicion, that existed between the individual and the state was the central burden of the critique voiced during the 1950s by Pierre Mendès-France of the failings of the Fourth Republic. There was, in his words, an urgent need to re-engage citizens with the political process: 'Aujourd'hui, le citoyen et l'Etat sont devenus étrangers l'un à l'autre'.[69]

The 'health' of democracy rested not only on the solidarity between the state and its citizens, but also on material well-being. A strong democracy could only exist in a 'strong society', in which the state acted to protect its citizens from the dangers of unemployment, destitution and slum housing, and in which in return the citizens would act to protect democracy from authoritarian and totalitarian threats. This is why debates about 'true democracy' were inseparably tied to concepts of social welfare.[70] The seemingly logical consequence of the focus on the citizens' duties and obligations vis-à-vis the state was the state's obligation to promote and protect the prosperity of its citizens by keeping capitalism in check. This provided the basis of the emphasis on social democracy as the 'true democracy', since social democracy promised to tame free-market capitalism, to spread prosperity more widely, and to justify democracy through prosperity – the antithesis of for example the experience of the Weimar Republic.[71] The reformed free-market capitalism of a social democracy also seemed to be the best way to counter the Communist notion of prosperity for all. Building democracy, therefore, meant creating the right material conditions for the prosperity of the many, an idea which was well personified in Germany by Ludwig Erhard and his idea of a 'Soziale Marktwirtschaft' producing 'Wohlstand für alle', or by Tage Erlander and his notion of 'A Strong Society' in 1950s Sweden.[72] Many other post-war politicians, especially those on the European socialist or social-democratic left, articulated similar concepts. This was a future-oriented concept: it focused minds on how things were getting better, and would continue to get better in the future, thereby distracting Europeans from the divisive legacies of the past.

## Conclusion: Democratization and Europeanization

By emphasizing the ways in which similar attitudes to democracy were voiced by non-Communist political figures in Western Europe during the 15 years following the Second World War, this chapter has in some respects presented a distinctly one-sided account of politics in this period. It is emphatically not our intention to suggest that the themes highlighted here were universally accepted among political elites, and still less among the populations of post-war Europe. The sense of disillusionment that was widespread in much of Europe after the war reflected the way in which the new or re-established political regimes failed, often in some rather intangible way, to reflect the aspirations of their populations for a more responsive political system.[73] The democracy that the people experienced was not so much the one that they chose, as the one that was constructed for them; and the consequent distance between the governments and the governed was a durable feature of the politics of post-war Europe. 'They', the rulers, who did not understand 'us', the real people, rapidly established itself as a prominent theme not merely of oppositional movements such as *Uomo Qualunque* in Italy or subsequently Poujadism in France, but also more generally of popular attitudes to the political process.[74] Moreover, what one might describe as the only case of 'regime breakdown' in this period, the collapse of the Fourth Republic in France in 1958 and its replacement by the Gaullist Fifth Republic (emphatically endorsed by a referendum), demonstrated the durable tension within French post-war political culture between democracy as rule by an assembly and the more personalized democracy of a strong president, directly elected by the people and responsible to them without the intermediary role of political parties.[75]

Moreover, as the case of France well demonstrates, the convergence of the formerly somewhat diverse definitions of democracy around what became almost a 'standard' model in post-war Western Europe did not efface national ways of thinking about democracy. These had in many respects been reinforced, especially at an emotional level, by the events of the Second World War. In the Scandinavian states and the Low Countries, patriotic celebration of liberation from German rule encouraged the development of national narratives of democracy, whereby the struggle against German rule was perceived as only the latest stage in the centuries-long struggle of these states for self-determination and resistance to foreign rule.[76] Nor did the revivification of these national democratic traditions supplant more local and long-standing forms of democratic identity. Traditions of community self-government, of municipal freedoms and of regional identities had also been reinforced by the events of the Second

World War. In the absence of legitimate national government, the populations of occupied Europe had turned instead to alternative, and somewhat suppressed, traditions of local self-government. Similarly, in Germany after 1945, concepts of *Heimat* once again re-emerged as an alternative location for a democratic tradition. The local democratic movements of the nineteenth century were celebrated in western and southern Germany as proof that these territories were, in the words of one writer in the Pfalz, 'the land of origin of German democracy'.[77]

The inter-connectedness of democracy and Europe that emerged after 1945 did not therefore take place at the expense of the nation. As Alan Milward famously argued, the institutions of European cooperation that emerged in the post-war period often worked to reinforce the power of the nation-state.[78] Much the same, it could be argued, occurred at the level of political rhetoric. The tendency of European political leaders to conceive of democracy in broadly similar terms encouraged the development of an association between democracy and Europe which buttressed national discourses of democracy. This was evident in the way in which Europe itself became an identity, and a cause, that was conceived of in emphatically democratic terms. The cause of 'Europeanism' largely shed after 1945 the idealistic and occasionally somewhat reactionary political connotations it had acquired in the inter-war years.[79] Instead, the language of post-war European unification became a centrist and inclusive form of political rhetoric which passed, almost obligatorily, through a celebration of Europe's democratic traditions. That this highly selective account of Europe's modern history required a conscious politics of forgetting about more recent events has of course been well demonstrated by historians.[80] But what mattered more to the political leaders of post-war Europe was less the need to come to terms with the horrors of the immediate past than the construction of the democratic Europe of the present and the future.[81]

In these various ways, therefore, democracy and Europe became more closely associated in the immediate post-war period. Democracy was the symbol of West European identity in the face of the Soviet Union, especially after the blatant repression of the will of the Hungarian people in 1956 and the building of the Berlin Wall in 1961, but so too was Europe the historic 'home' of democracy, which is why the orientation of Western European elites towards the United States remained somewhat uneasy throughout the 1950s. This inter-relationship of democracy and Europe did not, however, prove to be unchanging. The social and cultural changes that occurred in the 1960s generated radical critiques of the limits of democracy, and more especially of the way in which the construction of democratic regimes after 1945 had failed to address the sources of inequality in society.[82] Added to that was a growing disappointment about the state and the pace of European integration, which from the perspective of the later 1960s did not appear to have lived up to the expectations of the late

1940s and early 1950s. Looking back on the dreams of the immediate post-war period in his memoirs written in 1968, the Rhineland Christian Democrat politician Herman Pünder could not help articulating his sense of deep disappointment. Very little of the great visions formulated in the immediate post-war era had been realized; only 'revolutionary times', he concluded, gave birth to 'great deeds, (...) and revolutionary times are what the free European states are apparently no longer experiencing today.'[83]

The transformations of the 1960s also gave a new momentum to alternative democratic traditions, including ones that derived their inspiration from revolutions (such as those in China, Latin America and Africa) located outside the borders of Europe. As a consequence the association of democracy and Europe became much more problematic. What had appeared to be a common European democratic culture was replaced by a much more contested political environment, in which different and conflicting definitions of democracy were advanced by a wide range of new social and political movements of the left and the right, by women's organizations, by separatist regional movements and indeed by some of those within the Catholic and Socialist movements which had formerly participated in the construction of the post-1945 political order.[84]

Placed in this longer perspective, the inter-relationship of democracy and Europe that occurred in the immediate post-war era appears less as a remorseless process related to long-term processes of modernization, than as a historically contingent phenomenon defined by the radical changes in the international environment brought about by the war and by the structures of social and political power that emerged in post-war Western Europe. This also perhaps points to a larger conclusion about the historical nature of Europeanization. As this volume seeks to demonstrate, Europeanization needs to be approached, not as a homogeneous or long-term process, but as an evolving and contingent phenomenon, which has taken different forms in different periods. Seen in this way, this chapter provides one example or 'site' of a process of Europeanization, characterized not merely by the emergence of a common political discourse among European political figures but also by the way in which that discourse became associated with the identity of Europe. Located in the material circumstances of the immediate post-war years, and the attitudes shared by many of the European political figures who came to the fore at this time, this instance of Europeanization flourished, but also ultimately came to an end.

## Notes

1. This is argued with reference to France in R. Vinen, *Bourgeois Politics in France, 1945–1951* (Cambridge and New York, 1995), pp. 1–7.
2. R. Aron, 'Les institutions politiques et l'occident dans le monde au xxe siècle' in R. Aron et al. *La démocratie à l'épreuve du xxe siècle* (Paris, 1960), pp. 11–15.

3. A. Trunk, *Europa, ein Ausweg? Politische Eliten und europäische Identität in den 1950er Jahren* (Munich, 2007), pp. 75 and 132.
4. See, for example, the essays in 'The Politics of Democracy in Twentieth-Century Europe', *European History Quarterly* XXXII (2002).
5. M. Conway, 'Democracy in Postwar Western Europe. The Triumph of a Political Model', *European History Quarterly,* XXXII (2002), 59–84. M. Conway, 'The Rise and Fall of Western Europe's Democratic Age 1945–73', *Contemporary European History,* XIII (2004), 67–88. V. Depkat, *Lebenswenden und Zeitenwenden. Deutsche Politiker und die Erfahrungen des 20. Jahrhunderts* (Munich, 2007).
6. For an exemplary study of the nuances of Communist rhetoric regarding democracy, see J. Gotovitch, *Du rouge au tricolore. Les Communistes belges de 1939 à 1944* (Brussels, 1992).
7. S. Berman, *The Social Democratic Moment. Ideas and Politics in the Making of Interwar Europe* (Cambridge Mass. and London, 1998). M. Conway, 'The Age of Christian Democracy. The Frontiers of Success and Failure' in T. Kselman and J. Buttigieg (eds), *Christian Democracy. Historical Legacies and Comparative Perspectives* (Notre Dame Ind, 2003), pp. 436–7.
8. D. Luyten and P. Magnette, 'L'idée du parlementarisme en Belgique', in *Histoire de la Chambre des Représentants de Belgique* (Brussels, 2003), pp. 19–46.
9. M. Conway and P. Romijn (eds), *The War for Legitimacy in Politics and Culture 1936–1946* (Oxford and New York, 2008). P. Romijn, *Burgemeesters in oorlogstijd. Besturen onder Duitse bezetting* (Amsterdam, 2006), pp. 601–32.
10. M. Koreman, *The Expectation of Justice. France 1944–1946* (Durham NC and London, 1999), pp. 1–188.
11. This was very typical of the rather ritualistic references to democracy made by de Gaulle in his wartime speeches in London and Algiers: J. Touchard, *Le gaullisme 1940–1969* (Paris, 1978), pp. 63–4.
12. R. Boehling, *A Question of Priorities. Democratic Reform and Economic Recovery in Postwar Germany* (Oxford and New York, 1996), pp. 207–10. P. Ginsborg, *A History of Contemporary Italy. Society and Politics 1943–1988* (London, 1990), pp. 100–1.
13. M. Conway 'The Rise and Fall of Western Europe's Democratic Age', 73–4.
14. *Les Dossiers de l'Action Sociale Catholique* July–August 1945, 293–5, 'Prélude à une semaine sociale', and September 1945, 368–80, 'Christianisme et Démocratie'.
15. K. Adenauer, *Erinnerungen, 1945–1953* (Stuttgart, 1965), p. 46.
16. E.g. J. Touchard, *Le gaullisme*, pp. 63–4 and 87.
17. SFIO Déclaration des principes, 24 February 1946, reprinted in G. Mollet, *Bilan et perspectives socialistes* (Paris, 1958), p. 109.
18. A. Steinhouse, *Workers' Participation in post-Liberation France* (Lanham MD and Oxford, 2001); T. Behan, *The Long-Awaited Moment. The Working Class and the Italian Communist Party in Milan, 1943–1948* (New York, 1997); D. Luyten, *Sociaal-economisch overleg in België sedert 1918* (Brussels, 1995), pp. 123–42; M. Fichter, 'Aufbau und Neuordnung. Betriebsräte zwischen Klassensolidarität und Betriebsloyalität' in M. Broszat, K.-D. Henke and H. Woller (eds), *Von Stalingrad zur Währungsreform. Zur Sozialgeschichte des Umbruchs in Deutschland* (Munich, 1988), pp. 469–549.
19. P. Ginsborg, *A History of Contemporary Italy*, p. 98; J.-P. Rioux, *The Fourth Republic 1944–1958* (Cambridge, 1987), pp. 97–111; T. Eschenburg, *Jahre der Besatzung, 1945–1949. Mit einem einleitenden Essay von Eberhard Jäckel* (Stuttgart and Wiesbaden, 1983), pp. 124–6.

20. S. Foley, *Women in France since 1789* (Basingstoke and New York, 2004), pp. 237–42; S. Chaperon, '"Feminism is dead. Long live Feminism!" The Women's Movement in France at the Liberation, 1944–1946', in C. Duchen and I. Bandhauer-Schöffmann (eds), *When the War was Over. Women, War and Peace in Europe, 1940–1956* (London and New York, 2000), pp. 146–60; A. Rossi-Doria, 'Italian Women enter Politics' in ibid., pp. 89–102.

21. G. Mollet, *Bilan et perspectives socialistes*, pp. 101–3.

22. *Le Peuple*, 8 October 1945, p. 3, 'Le Congrès du Parti Socialiste Belge'; S. Kramer, 'Belgian Socialism at the Liberation. 1944–1950', *Res Publica*, xx (1978), 131; C. Kesteloot, 'Le maintien de la Charte de Quaregnon. Débats et controverses (1942–1945)', *Socialisme* No. 243, 151–8.

23. *1885/1985. Cent ans de socialisme* (Brussels, 1985), p. 218; G. Mollet, *Bilan et perspectives socialistes*, pp. 98–9.

24. P. Sering (i.e. R. Löwenthal), *Jenseits des Kapitalismus* (Lauf near Nuremberg, 1946).

25. W. Brandt, 'Programmatische Grundlagen des demokratischen Sozialismus', May 1949, in K. Klotzbach, *Der Weg zur Staatspartei. Programmatik, praktische Politik und Organisation der deutschen Sozialdemokratie 1945–1965* (Berlin, 1982), p. 187.

26. *Vers l'Avenir* 20 December 1945, p. 2, 'Une conférence de M. du Bus de Warnaffe'.

27. J. Touchard *Le gaullisme*, pp. 259–60.

28. J. Gotovitch and J. Gérard-Libois, *Léopold III. De l'an 40 à l'effacement* (Brussels, 1991). L. van Ypersele, La question royale ou la guerre des images' in M. Dumoulin, M. Van den Wijngaert and V. Dujardin (eds), *Léopold III* (Brussels, 2001), pp. 303–22. See also more generally A. Schwarzenbach, 'Royal Photographs. Emotions for the People', *Contemporary European History*, xiii (2004), 255–80.

29. R. Pollock (ed.), *The Mind of Pius XII* (New York, 1955), pp. 62–9. M. Conway, 'The Age of Christian Democracy', pp. 51–3.

30. M. Mitchell, 'Materialism and Secularism. CDU Politicians and National Socialism, 1945–1949', *Journal of Modern History*, lxvii (1995), 278–308.

31. P. Misner, 'The Roman Catholic Hierarchy and the Christian Labor Movement. Autonomy and Pluralism', in L. Heerma Van Voss, P. Pasture and J. De Mayer (eds), *Between Cross and Class. Comparative Histories of Christian Labor in Europe, 1840–2000* (Bern, 2005), p. 111.

32. R. Krieg, *Catholic Theologians in Nazi Germany* (New York, 2004), pp. 127–8.

33. P. Letamendia, *Le Mouvement Républicain Populaire. Histoire d'un grand parti français* (Paris, 1995), pp. 47–52. See also G.-R. Horn and E. Gerard (eds.), *Left Catholicism 1943–1955. Catholics in Western Europe at the Point of Liberation* (Leuven, 2001).

34. P. Chenaux, *Une Europe vaticane? Entre le Plan Marshall et les Traités de Rome* (Brussels, 1990); R. Krieg, *Catholic Theologians in Nazi Germany*, p. 121; M. Mitchell, 'Materialism and Secularism', 297–9.

35. H. Mommsen, 'Von Weimar nach Bonn. Zum Demokratieverständnis der Deutschen', in A. Schildt and A. Sywottek (eds), *Modernisierung im Wiederaufbau. Die westdeutsche Gesellschaft der 50er Jahre* (Bonn, 1993), pp. 745–58, especially 753.

36. K. Adenauer, *Erinnerungen, 1945–1953*, p. 281.

37. J.L. Talmon, *The Origins of Totalitarian Democracy* (London, 1952), p. 251.

38. J.-P. Rioux, *The Fourth Republic*, p. 109.

39. W. Koeppen, *Das Treibhaus* (Stuttgart, 1953).

40. The notion of an end to ideological conflicts was increasingly debated in Europe during the later 1950s, notably at the colloquia organized by the Congress for Cultural Freedom: P. Grémion, *Intelligence de l'anticommunisme. Le Congrès pour la liberté de la culture à Paris 1950–1975* (Paris, 1995), pp. 317–77. R. Aron, *Mémoires* Vol. II (Paris, 1983), pp. 577–9. See also R. Aron et al., *La démocratie à l'épreuve du xxe siècle*. In Germany, the sociologist Helmut Schelsky coined the formula of the 'sceptical generation' which he argued had become thoroughly disillusioned after the experience of having been exploited by National Socialism for its totalitarian purposes: H. Schelsky, *Die skeptische Generation. Eine Soziologie der deutschen Jugend* (Dusseldorf and Cologne, 1957). Cf. also A. Schildt, 'Ende der Ideologien? Politisch-ideologische Strömungen in den 50er Jahren', in A. Schildt and A. Sywottek (eds), *Modernisierung im Wiederaufbau*, pp. 627–35.

41. J.-P. Sartre, 'Preface' to F. Fanon, *The Wretched of the Earth* (republished London, 2001), pp. 7–26.

42. 'Il semble difficile de soutenir que le général de Gaulle est un démocrate, au sens habituel du terme': J. Touchard, *Le gaullisme*, pp. 309–10.

43. P. Theunissen, *1950, le dénouement de la question royale* (Brussels, 1986), pp. 29–31. J. Duvieusart, *La question royale, crise et dénouement. juin, juillet, août 1950* (Brussels, 1975).

44. L. Lewin, *Ideology and Strategy. A Century of Swedish Politics* (Cambridge, 1988), pp. 218–37.

45. A. Camus, 'Democracy and Modesty', in J. Lévi-Valensi (ed.), *Camus at Combat. Writing 1944–1947* (Princeton, 2006), p. 287.

46. G. Orwell, 'Toward European Unity', republished in G. Orwell (ed. P. Davison), *Orwell and Politics* (London, 2001), pp. 473–9.

47. I. Woloch, 'Left, Right and Centre. The MRP and the Post-War Moment', *French History*, xxi (2007), 86–7.

48. M. Baum, *Rückblick auf mein Leben* (Heidelberg, 1950), pp. 293–4. Similar views were expressed by Arnold Brecht. See A. Brecht, *Aus nächster Nähe. Lebenserinnerungen, 1884–1927* (Stuttgart, 1966), p. 125; A. Brecht, *Mit der Kraft des Geistes. Lebenserinnerungen. Zweite Hälfte 1927–1967* (Stuttgart, 1967), pp. 126 and 142–3.

49. K. Adenauer, *Erinnerungen, 1945–1953*, p. 502.

50. K. Adenauer, *Erinnerungen, 1945–1953*, pp. 48–9, 51 and 53. H. Pünder, *Von Preußen nach Europa. Lebenserinnerungen* (Stuttgart, 1968), pp. 201–2; F. Friedensburg, *Es ging um Deutschlands Einheit. Rückschau eines Berliners auf die Jahre nach 1945* (Berlin, 1971), p. 46; W. Keil, *Erlebnisse eines Sozialdemokraten* (Stuttgart, 1948) Vol. II, pp. 212, 332–3, 336, 340, 458–9, 679 and 684.

51. H.R. Kedward, *Resistance in Vichy France. A Study of Ideas and Motivation in the Southern Zone 1940–1942* (Oxford, 1978), pp. 153–9.

52. E. Wolfrum, *Geschichspolitik in der Bundesrepublik Deutschland. Der Weg zur bundesrepublikanischen Erinnerung, 1948–1990* (Darmstadt, 1999), pp. 394–9.

53. H. Kaelble, *Europäer über Europa. Die Entstehung des europäischen Selbstverständnisses im 19. und 20. Jahrhundert* (Frankfurt am Main, 2001), pp. 128–38.

54. For the following cf. A. Trunk, *Europa, ein Ausweg*, pp. 154–71; H. Kaelble *Europäer über Europa*, pp. 136–8 and 157–63; V. Depkat, *Lebenswenden und Zeitenwenden*, pp. 221–6.

55. A. Trunk, *Europa, ein Ausweg*, pp. 171–95; V. Depkat, *Lebenswenden und Zeitenwenden*, pp. 226–8.

56. K. Adenauer 'To Wilhelm Sollmann' 16 Mar. 1946, in K. Adenauer (ed. H.P. Mensing), *Briefe 1945–1947*, (Paderborn et al., 1983), p. 191; K. Adenauer *Erinnerungen, 1945–1953*, p. 375.

57. Trunk, *Europa, ein Ausweg*, pp. 195–207; H. Kaelble, *Europäer über Europa*, pp. 138–57, 163–83.

58. J.L. Gaddis, *We Now Know. Rethinking Cold War History* (Oxford, 1997), pp. 26–53.

59. M. Conway, 'Legacies of Exile. The Exile Governments in London during the Second World War and the Politics of Post-War Europe', in M. Conway and J. Gotovitch (eds), *Europe in Exile. European Exile Communities in Britain 1940–45* (New York and Oxford, 2001), pp. 255–74; W. Kaiser, *Christian Democracy and the Origins of the European Union* (Cambridge, 2007).

60. P. Grémion, *Intelligence de l'anticommunisme*.

61. Trunk's study is based on the material handed down from these institutions. Cf. A. Trunk, *Europa ein Ausweg*.

62. R. Branche, *La guerre d'Algérie. Une histoire apaisée?* (Paris, 2005), pp. 349–59.

63. G. Morrell, 'A Higher Stage of Imperialism? The Big Three, the Trusteeship Council and the Early Cold War', in R.M. Douglas, M.D. Callahan and E. Bishop (eds), *Imperialism on Trial. International Oversight of Colonial Rule in Historical Perspective* (Lanham MD, etc., 2006), pp. 125–7.

64. R. Dahrendorf, *Gesellschaft und Demokratie in Deutschland* (Munich, 1965). For Dahrendorf's book in the context of West Germany's debate about democratization cf. M. Scheibe, 'Auf der Suche nach der demokratischen Gesellschaft', in U. Herbert (ed.), *Wandlungsprozesse in Westdeutschland. Belastung, Integration, Liberalisierung 1945–1980* (Göttingen, 2002), pp. 245–77.

65. V. Depkat, *Lebenswenden und Zeitenwenden*, pp. 213–15 and 383–4; P. Mendès-France 'La crise de la démocratie', in P. Mendès-France, *Oeuvres complètes* (Paris, 1987), Vol. IV, pp. 98–101.

66. L. Niethammer, *Entnazifizierung in Bayern* (Frankfurt am Main, 1973); R. Grohnert, *Die Entnazifizierung in Baden 1945–1949* (Stuttgart, 1991).

67. Adenauer, 'To Wilhelm Sollmann', p. 191.

68. e.g. M. Young and P. Wilmott, *Family and Kinship in East London* (London, 1957).

69. P. Mendès-France, 'La crise de la démocratie', p. 82.

70. H. Kaelble, *Sozialgeschichte Europas, 1945 bis zur Gegenwart* (Munich, 2007), pp. 332–60; H. Kaelble, *Europäer über Europa*, pp. 218–45.

71. See, for example, G. Eley, *Forging Democracy. The History of the Left in Europe, 1850–2000* (Oxford and New York, 2002), pp. 311–20.

72. L. Erhard, *Wohlstand für alle* (Dusseldorf, 1957); O. Ruin, *Tage Erlander. Serving the Welfare State, 1946–1969* (Pittsburgh, 1990), pp. 214–21.

73. M. Koreman, *The Expectation of Justice*, pp. 258–63.

74. L. Wylie, *Village in the Vaucluse*, 3rd ed. (Cambridge Mass. and London, 1974), pp. 206–11.

75. R. Rémond, *1958. Le retour de de Gaulle* (Brussels, 1983), pp. 119–39.

76. *Le Peuple*, 20 April 1945, p. 1, 'Le sentiment public sous l'occupation'; *De Nieuwe Standaard* 22–23 April 1945, p. 1, 'Waarom zouden wij voor elkander vreezen?'.

77. C. Applegate, *A Nation of Provincials. The German Idea of Heimat* (Berkeley, etc., 1999), pp. 242–3.

78. A. Milward, *The European Rescue of the Nation-State* (London, 1992).

79. See the contribution of Wardhaugh et al. in this volume.

80. H. Rousso, *Le syndrome de Vichy* (Paris, 1987). P. Lagrou, *The Legacy of Nazi Occupation. Patriotic Memory and National Recovery in Western Europe, 1945–1965* (Cambridge and New York, 2000).
81. A characteristic example of the genre is P.-H. Spaak, *Combats inachevés* 2 vols. (Paris, 1969).
82. K. Jarausch, *After Hitler. Recivilizing Germans, 1945–1995* (Oxford, 2006), pp. 99–184.
83. H. Pünder, *Von Preußen nach Europa*, p. 443.
84. G. Eley, *Forging Democracy*, pp. 341–83.

# 7
# Human Rights, the Memory of War and the Making of a 'European' Identity, 1945–75

*Tom Buchanan*

> Whatever the theory, [Western conceptions of human rights in practice] often applied only to Europeans, and sometimes to only some among the Europeans. (Humayun Kabir, 1947)[1]

One of the most novel and striking features of the immediate post-war world was the emphasis placed on the concept of universal human rights as the basis for a new and more secure world order. The highest embodiment of this principle was the signing of the Universal Declaration of Human Rights (UDHR) by 48 states[2] on 10 December 1948. However, the UDHR represented a last gasp of international agreement and its impact was swiftly stifled by the onset of the Cold War. Harold Laski, the British socialist and political scientist, had warned quite properly in 1947 that the Declaration may become another Kellogg–Briand Pact, 'introduced with an enthusiasm only surpassed by the contempt with which it was ignored by its signatories'.[3] Indeed, a combination of *Realpolitik* and the apparently irreconcilable conceptions of human rights across the Cold War divide ensured that no further progress could be made internationally towards creating a regime to safeguard such rights until the mid-1960s. Instead, the most immediate practical steps in this regard were taken at the 'European' level through the Convention for the Protection of Human Rights and Fundamental Freedoms (ECHR) signed in November 1950, and subsequently through its associated commission and court. Although somewhat neglected at the time and slow to develop in efficacy, the Convention has become a landmark in the emergence of Europe as a realm of legally enforceable human rights.[4]

This chapter is concerned with a period – bounded by the negotiation of the ECHR at one end and by the Helsinki Final Acts of 1975 at the other – in which questions of human rights and of European identity became inextricably interwoven. This was unprecedented, and the desire to avoid the mistakes of the immediate past, amid the shambles of post-war Europe and the perceived threat of Communism, was clearly of central importance.

Pierre-Henri Teitgen, presenting the first draft of the European Convention in September 1949, movingly recalled that his father had encountered a sign at Buchenwald concentration camp that read: 'Just or unjust, the Fatherland'. Henceforth, Teitgen concluded, there would only be *'just* Fatherlands' in Europe.[5] But how was this 'Europe' to be defined, both geographically and politically? And how did the Convention's relatively restricted conception of human rights relate to the more universalist vision associated with the human-rights campaigns that emerged in Europe from the late 1950s onwards? This chapter will explore how far the movement for the protection of human rights – at both governmental and non-governmental levels – can also be seen as a 'Europeanizing' movement, both within Europe itself and in terms of Europe's relations with the wider world.

It was by no means clear that such weight would be placed on the concept of human rights at the end of the war. Although significant statements of intent such as President Roosevelt's 'Four Freedoms' speech and the Atlantic Charter had appeared as early as 1941, in fact these were merely opening shots in a debate about how very different conceptions of 'rights' might be reconciled after the war.[6] None of the great powers could claim the moral high ground in this respect in 1945. The Western powers quite legitimately placed themselves within a tradition of personal and civil liberties (at least during peacetime) but also had to reckon with the colonialism of the European empires and the racial inequalities in the United States. The Soviet Union, meanwhile, emphasized social and economic rights over political freedoms, even if lip service had been paid to the latter in the 1936 'Stalin' Constitution. Hence, for all of the major powers any commitment to an agreed list of human rights that went beyond the merely rhetorical would require radical changes in their own political systems. Moreover, in the immediate aftermath of the war the advent of welfare states and nationalized industrial sectors in countries such as Britain and France added further complexity. Stafford Cripps, Chancellor of the Exchequer in Britain's post-war Labour government, objected (mistakenly) to the European Convention as a potential obstacle to the planned economy.[7] The Belgian academic Jean Hasaerts noted that the French Constitution of 1946 was essentially that of 1789 with many new rights (such as the right to strike and to nationalize property) 'frenziedly added' in a way that would leave lawyers and economists 'aghast'.[8]

It should also be noted that there was no great public campaign in Europe for a charter of human rights at this time. Indeed, human rights in the abstract are arguably never a 'popular' cause, and only become so when attached to specific abuses or located within a broader moral or religious framework. The anti-Communism of the early Cold War certainly gained much political mileage out of abuses of human rights – such as the imprisonment of leading Catholic clerics in Eastern Europe – but prominent anti-Communist movements, such as de Gaulle's *Rassemblement du Peuple Français*, were also distinctly authoritarian. Winston Churchill's call in 1948 to 'set the people free' was a protest against the British Labour government's restrictions on economic, rather than political, freedoms. The French *Mouvement Républicain Populaire* (MRP), the party of Pierre-Henri Teitgen and Robert Schuman, was perhaps the closest to a west European party of 'human rights' by the later 1940s, as well as being the most 'European' in its orientation. However, its outlook was coloured by a distinctively Catholic emphasis on the family and the devolution of power away from the state. (Hence Schuman's reference to the ECHR as forming the basis for the 'defence of human personality' against totalitarianism).[9]

Human rights have typically been promoted most forcefully by non-governmental organizations rather than by political parties. However, there was also a lack of leadership from this quarter. The French League of the Rights of Man was in steep decline in the immediate post-war years, arguably because it was too closely identified with the legal elites of the failed Third Republic and had not been strongly associated with the Resistance. Conversely, the International Association of Democratic Lawyers, which did emerge from the Resistance, was tainted by its close connections with the Communist Party.[10] In Britain the National Council for Civil Liberties also languished in this period, for similar reasons. It had gained a reputation for *illiberality* during the war and was briefly challenged by the more anarchistic Freedom Defence Committee in the immediate post-war years.[11] The German League for Human Rights was re-established in the British and US zones of occupation after 1945, but was easily infiltrated by those with a nationalistic or anti-Communist purpose and remained wracked by internal disagreements well into the 1950s.[12] In West Germany concerns about human rights were inevitably dominated by the plight of the Germans under Communist rule in the East, as well as by the fate of German prisoners of war in the Soviet Union.

The movement towards a European Convention, therefore, was primarily one driven by intellectual and political elites, rather than popular pressures.[13] Indeed, the British Conservative politician David Maxwell-Fyfe conceded that his own countrymen were 'completely uninterested in human rights' because they had never 'seen them go'.[14] The leading protagonists were lawyer-politicians of the centre-right such as Teitgen and Maxwell-Fyfe (later Lord Kilmuir), as well as lawyers and legal academics such as René Cassin (one of the architects of the UDHR). These men were impelled by personal experience to see the Convention as a necessary step away from the dictatorships of the recent past and towards a more united and peaceable Europe. Teitgen (like Cassin) was a former law professor who had been a leading non-Communist within the Resistance and was a prominent supporter of European integration. Cassin was a French First World War veteran whose commitment to human rights was closely linked to his pacifism.[15] Maxwell-Fyfe had been a part of the British prosecution team at the Nuremberg trials, many of whom went on to become leading advocates of human rights in the 1950s and 1960s.

The negotiations that led to the Universal Declaration in 1948 had been dominated by the clash between liberal and communist conceptions of human rights, and, to a lesser extent, by debates over whether human rights could truly be a universal concept. These tensions were resolved in two ways. First, the UDHR was only a declaration, and lacked legal force. As the writer Alex Comfort commented at the time, 'no single government of those who voted for it has implemented, or shows the slightest sign of implementing, all its provisions'.[16] Indeed, Covenants regarding its implementation were not signed until the mid-1960s. Secondly, the declaration was a compendious document, listing both political and socio-economic rights. The European Convention took a more pragmatic route. It listed only those 'fundamental [political] freedoms' of Western democracy which could be effectively guaranteed. As Teitgen argued, 'it is necessary to begin at the beginning and to guarantee political democracy in the European Union' prior to any further economic and social coordination.[17] The Convention's relatively brief list of rights concentrated on protecting personal liberties (such as freedom from torture, slavery and the right to free expression). In addition, a strong emphasis on protecting the domestic sphere from an intrusive state (hence, the right to marry and the right to respect for the home and family life) gave the Convention a somewhat conservative and Catholic flavour. Even the right to free elections was not included until a First Protocol was added in 1952, and the complementary European Social Charter was not signed until 1961. Moreover, the ECHR contained a panoply of reservations designed to calm the suspicions of signatory states. For instance, a 'colonial clause' stated that the Convention need not apply to overseas territories, and, under Article 15, states were allowed to suspend the Convention temporarily in times of war and emergency. (This was promptly invoked by the British government during its conflict with the 'Mau Mau' rebels in Kenya.)[18] There was no right of individual petition without the express consent of member states. In spite of all of these concessions, however, France did not ratify the Convention until as late as 1974.

The question remains as to why such progress was possible within Europe – at least within the 'Europe' envisioned by the Convention? The short answer is that the ECHR was the first substantive achievement of the Council of Europe: indeed, it was arguably the only achievement that was possible given the wildly conflicting interpretations of the Council's role. The Council of Europe had been founded under the March 1948 Brussels defence treaty of west European states. Both the Brussels Treaty and the Council's own Statute (5 May 1949) affirmed a commitment to 'individual freedom, political liberty and the rule of law'[19] as a basis for membership.

These democratic principles formed, under Article 3 of the Statute, a 'ticket of entry' to the Council, and states that failed to uphold them could, potentially, be expelled. The British foreign secretary Ernest Bevin famously regarded the Council of Europe with great suspicion. He was intent on developing a common political identity for the states of Western Europe as the basis for their defence against Communism, but was strongly opposed to any attempt to use the Council as a vehicle for European integration. Conversely, many of the politicians involved in the Council of Europe's Consultative Assembly were also involved in the European Movement. They were emboldened by the success of the May 1948 Hague Congress, an unofficial political gathering to promote European unity, and had already drafted a convention on human rights. Pierre-Henri Teitgen certainly saw the ECHR as a tangible step towards a European Union, and argued that the creation of a European court of human rights would send a clear message that 'Europe is born'.[20] However, the Council failed to fulfil these lofty ambitions. The anti-integrationist views of the British – and other – governments prevailed, and the movement for European integration proceeded down other routes. Therefore, the ECHR, which contained no integrationist dynamic (there was no intention, for instance to unify the legal systems of signatory states) came into existence almost apologetically, as the least objectionable and intrusive development of the Council's remit.

Where, then, was 'Europe' in the ECHR? The preamble to the Convention defined the signatories as 'the Governments of European countries which are likeminded and have a common heritage of political traditions, ideals, freedoms and the rule of law'. However, a number of qualifications needed to be made. First, this was a 'Europe' firmly situated within the geo-politics of the early 1950s. Mikael Rask Madsen has accurately described the signatories of the Convention as a Western, Cold War 'club', which saw the threat to human rights as primarily an external one, emanating from Soviet Communism.[21] However, the Convention was not NATO, and unlike the Atlantic alliance had no room for dictatorships such as Portugal. The initial signatories were all countries with a strong democratic tradition or were in the process of restoring democratic institutions after authoritarian rule or occupation.[22] Even so, Greece and Turkey, while both were functioning democracies in the 1950s, presented certain problems in this regard.[23] These caveats aside, the 'Europe' of the Convention was both inclusive and exclusive. While there was a clear prospect that other states might join from both Eastern and Southern Europe, this would only be on condition of their accepting the democratic values set out in the ECHR. As *The Times* commented, the Convention was a 'beacon to the peoples behind the Iron Curtain, and a passport for their return to the midst of the free countries'.[24] Secondly, the 'colonial clause' left it to individual states to decide whether the Convention should be extended to overseas territories. Britain chose to do so, with 'outstanding generosity'[25], in 1953; however, the ease with which states could suspend the Convention meant that, in practice, the colonial world was treated separately from Europe. Finally, there was no mention in the ECHR of the rights of ethnic or cultural minorities, or of immigrants. This was a marked change from the inter-war years, and showed that the approach associated with the failure of the League of Nations had been rejected. The implicit assumption that these were homogeneous societies reinforced the essentially 'Western' identity of the Convention.

In hindsight, the negotiation of the ECHR can be portrayed as a pioneering regional initiative – giving a lead to other regions such as Latin America – when progress at the international level was blocked. However, this is to underestimate the unique importance of the Convention, at least in the minds of its sponsors. After all, Europe was not simply one 'region' among many. It had been the centre of catastrophic political disturbances in the first half of the twentieth century, and therefore this first step *had* to be taken here, both because of what had happened in the previous half century and what might happen in the context of the Cold War. Teitgen argued that there must be a mechanism to prevent an undemocratic minority from seizing the levers of power. A 'conscience must exist somewhere which will sound the alarm to the minds of a nation menaced by this progressive corruption [*gangrène*]. To (...) show that they are progressing down a long road which leads far, sometimes even to Buchenwald or Dachau'.[26] In this sense the ECHR preamble – which presented the Convention as a logical and organic stage in the growth of democracy – was whistling in the dark. In reality these were vulnerable societies, and advocates of the Convention were deeply concerned that the excesses of the recent past could be repeated under a future 'totalitarian' Communist regime. As Andrew Moravscik has argued, the ECHR was largely driven by the concerns of states that had recently emerged from dictatorship, and cannot be seen as the result of democratic proselytizing by France and Britain (which typically, and complacently, saw themselves as the 'home' of human rights).[27]

A final point concerns the universality of the human rights conceived in the immediate post-war years, which was, in practice, somewhat illusory. During the negotiations for the UDHR, UNESCO explored this point by commissioning an international survey of distinguished intellectuals, marshalled by Jacques Maritain. The responses were subsequently published, along with the UNESCO experts' agreed list of 15 fundamental rights. This document now looks like an innovative attempt to reconcile 'Western' ideas of human rights with other non-Western traditions. However, the separate chapters on Muslim, Chinese and Hindu concepts are buried towards the back of the published collection, while the very prominent contribution from Mahatma Gandhi is brief and emphasizes duties over rights. In fact, the bulk of the original UNESCO memorandum and the responses to it were concerned with how to reconcile the Western liberal tradition with the Socialist/Marxist alternative, and the whole enterprise was primarily still a debate within European thought and politics. Perspectives from beyond Europe and North America were not seen as having anything to contribute to the current debate – hence the comment that 'the ferment of thought now apparent in the peoples of black and brown and yellow skin-colour, from Africa to the Far East, is destined to result in still other formulations [of human rights]'.[28]

After the signing of the ECHR, progress towards implementation was slow, suggesting no great urgency on the part of the signatories. Admittedly, a First Protocol was agreed even before the Convention had been signed. This added three important extra rights that were deemed either too overtly political or too controversial for inclusion in the original document: to own property, for parents to determine the education of their children in line with their own beliefs, and for free elections. However, the European Commission of Human Rights was not established until 1955, and the Court was only inaugurated four years after that. This slow pace coincided with a low ebb in concern for human rights at every level in Western Europe. A commitment to human rights was built into the ill-fated European Political Community (1953), but not mentioned in the Treaty of Rome (1957) that established the European Economic Community (EEC). Colonial governments frequently ignored human-rights concerns in their struggle against nationalist insurgencies. The British tactics in Kenya (the large-scale use of resettlement camps and the hanging of more than 1000 rebels) and the French use of torture in Algeria led outraged minorities in both countries to make comparisons with the genocidal violence of the Second World War.[29] More generally, campaigning for human rights either took place within a national context or was conditioned by the Cold War. Hence, the Left tended to campaign on behalf of political prisoners in right-wing dictatorships such as Spain and Portugal, or in the colonial world, while the Right and Catholics protested at persecution in the Soviet bloc and Yugoslavia. Peter Benenson, the founder of Amnesty International, later commented on the 'self-defeating character of like's concern with like' in the 1950s.[30] The narrowed horizons of the period were exemplified by the international competition held in 1953 to create a sculpture to commemorate the 'Unknown Political Prisoner'. The competition, which was secretly financed by the CIA, had a clear anti-Soviet orientation. Although the modernist winning design by the British sculptor Reg Butler was never realized, the intention was for it to be constructed on a gigantic scale in West Berlin.[31] Therefore, the somewhat complacent view that with the defeat of fascism the main threat to European freedoms came from an externally sponsored totalitarianism was reinforced in the cultural sphere.

This view was to be challenged from the late 1950s onwards with the emergence of a vibrant transnational movement for human rights, the first and most significant manifestation of which was the formation of Amnesty International. Amnesty was, in effect, launched by the publication of an article entitled 'The Forgotten Prisoners' in the *Observer* newspaper on 28 May 1961. The author was the British barrister Peter Benenson, a Catholic convert and former Labour Party parliamentary candidate who had campaigned throughout the 1950s on behalf of political prisoners in Franco's Spain.[32] There was a stark contrast between Benenson's article and the 1953 competition. Instead of merely commemorating 'unknown' political prisoners, the article in question named individuals imprisoned for their (non-violent) beliefs across the Communist, non-Communist and colonial worlds, and called for their release. Benenson was well aware that even repressive regimes were vulnerable to the power of publicity. He had, for instance, studied the success of the 'Tibor Dery Committees', organized throughout Western Europe to campaign for the release of the imprisoned Hungarian intellectual in 1957. Benenson's *Observer* article was carried or reported in newspapers world-wide, such as *Die Welt*, *Le Monde* and the *New York Herald Tribune*, and aroused a wave of interest. What had originally been intended as a year-long protest, akin to the 1960 UN World Refugee Year, swiftly evolved into a permanent campaigning organization with a volunteer membership in Britain and numerous other European countries.

At first sight it is tempting to locate the birth of Amnesty within a wholly universalist and Cold War, rather than a 'European', context. From the outset Amnesty's remit was wholly international. When Benenson published a book later that year, entitled *Persecution 1961*, only four of the nine case studies of political imprisonment were of Europeans.[33] Likewise, there was no doubting the formative influence of the international Cold War. Benenson's article argued that political imprisonment was essentially a consequence of the Cold War, because the conflict sustained dictatorships in countries such as the Soviet Union, China, Spain and Portugal. Indeed, he believed that a campaign for release of prisoners internationally would not simply palliate the symptoms of the Cold War but could actually begin the process of dissolving the East–West divide. However, while Amnesty's greatest weapon has always been its claim to political impartiality, during its early years Benenson was often forced to rely on Cold War institutions as the source of information and contacts for the fledgling organization. For instance, as early as 5 June 1961 Benenson wrote to the British Foreign Secretary seeking informal and regular contacts with the Information Research Department of the Foreign Office, a department specifically set up in 1948 to counter Communist propaganda.[34] It is also noteworthy that the first Amnesty activist to visit Berlin in 1961 met journalists at a meeting sponsored by the Congress for Cultural Freedom, the quintessential institution of the cultural Cold War and now known to have been CIA-funded.[35] Amnesty later found out to its cost that to seek to challenge the Cold War while making use of Cold War institutions was to play a highly dangerous game.

Even so, there are good reasons to emphasize the 'European' dimension to Amnesty. First, while Benenson's initiative in May 1961 had many different political and intellectual sources,[36] one very significant factor was his concern that there remained a real threat to human rights *within* what he called the 'democratic commonwealths'[37] of Western Europe. During 1961 he made repeated reference to the shortcomings of the ECHR – notably the lack of a right of individual petition in a number of countries and the absence of any automatic review when a state suspended the Convention. Benenson's concerns owed much to his own experiences campaigning in the years prior to 1961. Although Franco's Spain had been the focus of his most sustained interest during the 1950s, he had also been drawn increasingly into the bitter colonial struggles of the period. In particular, he had spent time on Cyprus – where he first arrived at the start of the Suez crisis in October 1956 – and protested against abuses by British forces in their struggle with the EOKA guerrillas. He became identified by the British government with a 'clique' of 'well-meaning people' who were 'diligent collators and investigators of Greek-Cypriot allegations against the security forces'.[38] Moreover, in 1959 he published a book which combined translated texts claiming torture by French forces in Algeria with documents related to alleged British human rights abuses in the struggle against the Kenyan Mau Mau. The book took its name, *Gangrene*, from the French text which had recently been banned and sequestered in France. In both cases Benenson detected a process whereby democratic governments used propaganda to demonize their colonial enemies in order to justify the use of unrestrained violence against civilian opponents. The link between this and the formation of Amnesty was embodied in the person of Maurice Audin. The 'disappearance' of this young French Algerian Communist in 1957 after torture in military custody formed a central theme of Benenson's *Gangrene*. A chapter of *Persecution 1961* was also devoted to his case, even though many believed Audin to be long dead.

Secondly, during the initial phase of Amnesty's existence, culminating in the award of the Nobel Peace Prize in 1977, the organization's strongest support was clearly in Western Europe and Scandinavia. This only began to change in the 1980s with the rapid growth of US membership. Following the publication of Benenson's article branches began to develop on an ad hoc basis, often on the basis of groups of sympathetic lawyers, journalists or religious congregations, or, indeed, of Benenson's personal contacts. The results were undeniably patchy – for instance, a meeting of French lawyers in June 1961 represented something of a false start for the French Amnesty section. Conversely, support was particularly strong in Scandinavia and Germany. A first meeting of the embryonic national sections was held in Luxembourg in the autumn of 1961, laying the basis for a permanent international organization. Five years later the great majority of Amnesty's local groups lay in six countries: Britain, Ireland, Germany, Denmark, Norway and Sweden. At the Copenhagen assembly in 1966 it was not surprising that three-quarters of some 230 delegates came from Scandinavia: more surprisingly, there were only two non-Europeans, from Canada and Australia.[39] More research is needed to investigate why Benenson's ideas flourished in some national environments and not in others. In Germany Amnesty clearly offered a way out of the powerful but distorting focus on the East German question, while in Sweden it accorded well with the country's sense of internationalist 'mission'. Benenson offered the following explanation in a 1976 speech in Berlin: 'That the idea of "Amnesty" should have received the greatest support in those countries which border the North and Baltic Seas is no accident. Nor is it that the German Section should become the largest. "Amnesty" seeks to re-state in contemporary terms what Martin Luther chose for his motto 450 years ago: "Gedanken sind zollvrei" [i.e. zollfrei]; ideas shall circulate freely'.[40] His theme that Amnesty was a latter-day Lutheran 'Community of Conscience' coincided with his own often-stated belief in a 'world conscience', and also echoed Teitgen's words in 1949.

Therefore, while Amnesty unquestionably possessed a universalist orientation from the outset, its organizational 'centre of gravity' in Benenson's phrase 'settled in [the] northern latitudes' of Europe, while the principal focus of its initial energies was on the threat to human rights within Europe and its colonies. This focus was maintained during the 1960s owing to the persistence of repressive regimes in Spain and Portugal and the 1967 *coup d'état* in Greece, as well as the continuing Cold War tensions within Europe.[41] Some of Amnesty's early successes included the release of the Czech Archbishop Beran and the German trade unionist Heinz Brandt, in both cases following high-profile missions of inquiry. Likewise, Amnesty's greatest crisis was triggered by its bruising involvement in the British colonial conflicts in Aden and Rhodesia. In the first case Amnesty came into conflict with the British Labour government when it alleged British use of torture; in the second, Amnesty acted as a secret conduit for British government funds to assist imprisoned opponents of Ian Smith's illegal settler regime.[42] This context changed dramatically from the late 1960s onwards, with the collective impact of decolonization, East–West détente, and the mid-1970s transitions to democracy in southern Europe. Moreover, in 1966 the British government finally allowed the right of individual petition under the ECHR. Human rights now seemed on a much more secure footing in Western Europe (although Benenson, having stood down as president in 1967, was later critical of Amnesty's failure to challenge British interrogation methods in Northern Ireland).[43] During the 1970s Amnesty was increasingly defined by its extra-European campaigns, notably in Latin America, and by its new emphasis on state-sanctioned torture.

By the 1960s a concern for human rights was being taken as an essential ingredient of an emerging 'European' identity. The eruption of human-rights activism made governments more sensitive to these issues, and the EEC (partly due to the development of the European Parliament) was increasingly willing to define itself in political as well as economic terms. For instance, the Spanish application for membership of the EEC in 1962 was never likely to succeed given the Franco regime's poor human-rights record, although Spain was granted preferential trading terms in 1970. A particularly striking example was the case of the Greek Colonels' dictatorship of 1967–74. The junta's decision to suspend the ECHR under Article 15 was challenged by a number of signatory states, and their complaint was upheld by the ECHR Commission. In December 1969 Greece withdrew from the Council of Europe ahead of a decision by the Committee of Ministers to expel it. The ECHR investigation into Greece's actions coincided with an Amnesty mission led by Anthony Marreco (another former Nuremberg prosecutor) and the American James Becket, which made startling and influential allegations of torture.[44] Although these pressures alone could not bring down the regime – this required the 1974 fiasco in Cyprus – it was clear that states could no longer behave in this manner while expecting to remain within the European 'club'. When the EEC Commission recommended opening negotiations for Greece's accession in January 1976, the 'consolidation of Greece's democracy' was cited as a powerful argument in favour.[45]

The ever greater salience of human rights was confirmed by the protracted negotiations that resulted in the signing of the Helsinki Final Accords by 35 states on 1 August 1975. The participants had very different expectations. The Soviet Union's goal was greater security: it desired (and received) recognition of the European borders redrawn by the Second World War. The West European states had no intention of challenging Soviet territorial control, but saw the opportunity to promote a common identity based on commitment to human rights. Hence, the seventh of ten fundamental principles agreed at Helsinki was 'Respect for human rights and fundamental freedoms, including the freedom of thought, conscience, religion and belief'. (However, it should be noted that this was balanced by a principle of non-intervention in other states' affairs.) Meanwhile, the US administration was concerned that the talks might be derailed by undue emphasis on human-rights issues and adopted a more pragmatic policy. The outcome was widely seen as a victory for the Soviet Union, which achieved concrete goals in return for an apparently unenforceable commitment to human rights. However, the principle of human rights had been introduced into international agreements for the first time: as one senior US diplomat commented, the most important feature of this component in Helsinki was that 'it was included at all'.[46] Moreover, 'Basket Three' of the Accords identified specific humanitarian measures related to questions such as reunification of divided families and freedom to travel for professional purposes. Helsinki emboldened 'dissidents' across the Soviet bloc (above all in Czechoslovakia, with the formation of Charter 77) and gave them a clear standard against which to judge the performance of their own governments. It also triggered a new wave of human-rights activism in the West, notably the emergence of Human Rights Watch.[47] Therefore the – often unintended – consequences of Helsinki proved to be highly significant.

Helsinki (properly titled the Conference on Security and Cooperation in Europe) played an important role within the evolution of the Cold War, but also contributed to the growth of a European identity. Many delegates were enthused by the sense that they were engaged in what Daniel Thomas has called a 'common European endeavour'. Indeed, an urbane and Francophile Romanian diplomat was heard to exclaim: 'Europe is here in this Conference: this is Europe!'[48] However, the Czech dissidents put a different interpretation on this point when they commented that: 'Helsinki represents a recognition of what is common to Europe (...) It is contrary to the script and spirit of the Helsinki conference if certain European nations and states keep alive practices conflicting with the European civilisation and cultural background'.[49] 'Europe', therefore, was increasingly being equated with a regime of human rights, and when East European opponents of Communist rule spoke of a 'return to Europe' they were alluding – among other aspirations – to an extension of this regime into their own countries. If the European Convention had put a very thin veneer on Teitgen's 'just Fatherlands' in 1950, by 1975 a more confident Western Europe was able to offer a far more attractive vision – underpinned, of course, by economic prosperity – of a common culture resting on guaranteed fundamental freedoms.

Fascism and war offered a complete negation of human rights that went far beyond the eclipse of a somewhat discredited inter-war democracy. It was experienced across Europe at the most profound level: the removal of the legal framework that had previously offered some protection for human security and dignity, and, just as alarmingly, the undermining of authority within the family. As Teitgen commented in 1951, the nightmare that his generation had faced was one of the 'nationalisation, absorption, monopolization, requisitioning of young people by the state', and the raising of children to 'worship force, violence, racialism and hatred'.[50] It is understandable, therefore, that in the immediate post-war era a fragile Western Europe should seek to define a benchmark of 'fundamental freedoms' and the mechanism to guarantee them, both as a means of political protection and of social restoration. There was no great public clamour for this step, and the range of rights was strictly limited to allow states to sign the ECHR while still building welfare states and controlling their colonial populations. In many respects, 'Europeanization' was implicit in this modest step, and only became explicit in hindsight. Even the abbreviated title by which the Convention is now commonly known, the '*European* Convention on Human Rights', is a latter-day arrogation which goes beyond the claims of the signatories.

Despite such slender beginnings, the Convention did not represent an evolutionary dead-end. Instead, the concept of human rights began to flourish in the 1960s and 1970s, as campaigning organizations such as Amnesty International successfully mobilized opinion – however patchily – within Western Europe. At the same time West European politicians – especially those on the centre-left – became increasingly comfortable with a language of human rights. Strikingly, Harold Wilson told the Labour Party conference in 1968 that: 'We are the party of human rights (...) this has been the central theme of this Government's actions from the day we took office [in October 1964]'.[51] This higher political profile coincided with three highly significant developments to capture the attention of diplomats and politicians. First, the ECHR machinery was reaching a stage of institutional maturity and developing a case law in areas such as access to justice. Secondly, the concept of human rights helped to fill the space for a political identity created by the great steps towards European economic integration after 1957. Human rights may not have been central to the early stages of European integration, but increasingly helped to define the project and gave it a certain nobility. Thirdly, the new politics of the later 1960s had rights – of gender, sexuality and ethnicity – at their very core: suddenly Europe was not only a realm in which certain fundamental freedoms were guaranteed but one in which new rights were being defined and, indeed, contested. By the mid-1970s, therefore, a concept of fundamental freedoms not only offered the basis for a common identity in Europe's external relations, but also an anchor for European governments in their dealings with their own populations.

## Notes

1. UNESCO, *Human Rights: Comments and Interpretations* (London & New York, 1949), pp. 191–2.
2. Eight states, principally the Soviet Union and its allies, abstained.
3. UNESCO, *Human Rights*, pp. 85–6. The Kellogg–Briand Pact of 1928 had called for the renunciation of war as an instrument of policy.
4. This has been evident in recent documents associated with the project of European integration. Hence the commitment to human rights and fundamental freedoms in article 6 of the Maastricht Treaty on European Union, 1992. Likewise, according to the EU's 'Europa' website (accessed 9/9/2008): 'Human rights, democracy and the rule of law are core values of the European Union (...) Respect for human rights is a prerequisite of countries seeking to join the Union'.
5. Cited in A.W. Brian Simpson, *Human Rights and the End of Empire: Britain and the Genesis of the European Convention* (Oxford, 2001), p. 673.
6. For the wartime context see Jan Herman Burgers, 'The road to San Francisco: The revival of the human rights idea in the twentieth century', *Human Rights Quarterly*, XIV, 4, November 1992, 447–77.
7. See Geoffrey Marston, 'The United Kingdom's part in the preparation of the European Convention on Human Rights, 1950', *International and Comparative Law Quarterly*, XLII 4, October 1993, 812–13.
8. UNESCO, *Human Rights*, p. 99.
9. Cited in A.H. Robertson, *Human Rights in Europe* (Manchester, 1963), p. 4.

10. See Mikael Rask Madsen, 'France, the UK and the "Boomerang" of the internation-alisation of human rights', in Simon Halliday and Patrick Schmidt (eds), *Human Rights Brought Home* (Oxford and Portland, Oregon, 2004), pp. 65–8.

11. See Tom Buchanan, 'Human rights campaigns in modern Britain', in Nick Crowson, Matthew Hilton and James McKay (eds), *NGOs in Contemporary Britain: Non-state Actors in Society and Politics in Britain since 1945* (Basingstoke, 2009).

12. See the paper by Lora Wildenthal, 'The origins of the West German human rights movement, 1945–1961', University of Connecticut, Human Rights Institute Research Papers, 2004, consulted online 15 November 2009.

13. One can contrast the high-profile – if often somewhat exaggerated – role of the non-governmental organizations in the negotiations leading to the Universal Declaration of Human Rights: see Kirsten Sellars, *The Rise and Rise of Human Rights* (Stroud, 2002), chap. 1.

14. A. W. Simpson, *End of Empire*, p. 741.

15. Obituary of Teitgen by Douglas Johnson in the *Independent*, 10 April 1997, consulted online 15 November 2009; paper given by Jay Winter on Cassin, The Hague, 25 April 2008.

16. *Tribune*, 18 November 1949.

17. Council of Europe, *Collected Edition of the Travaux Préparatoires* (hence *CETP*), vol. 1, (The Hague, 1975), p. 266.

18. See Caroline Elkins, *Britain's Gulag: The Brutal End of Empire in Kenya* (London, 2005), p. 96.

19. A.G. Harryvan and J. van der Harst (eds), *Documents on European Union*, (Basingstoke, 1997) p. 57.

20. *CETP*, vol. II, p. 180.

21. Mikael Rask Madsen, 'From Cold War instrument to supreme European court: The European Court of Human Rights at the crossroads of international and national law and politics', *Law & Social Inquiry*, XXXII, 1, 137–59, Winter 2007.

22. The Convention was signed on 4 November 1950 by Belgium, Denmark, France, West Germany, Iceland, Ireland, Italy, Luxembourg, the Netherlands, Norway, Turkey and the UK. Sweden and Greece signed on 28 November 1950.

23. On Turkey see Peter Benenson, 'How to fudge an election', *Spectator*, 15 November 1957, pp. 636–7.

24. *The Times*, 26 August 1950, cited in The Earl of Kilmuir, *Political Adventure* (London, 1964), p. 183.

25. Maxwell-Fyfe's phrase, written with evident sincerity in, Kilmuir, *Political Adventure*, p. 184.

26. *CETP* volume I, p. 292.

27. Andrew Moravcsik, 'The origins of human rights regimes: Democratic delegation in postwar Europe', *International Organization*, LIV 2, Spring 2000, 217–52.

28. UNESCO, *Human Rights*, Appendix 1, p. 255.

29. See Martin Evans, *The Memory of Resistance: French Opposition to the Algerian War (1954–1962)*, (Oxford, 1997), for instance, pp. 87 and 106; Peter Benenson (ed.), *Gangrene* (London, 1959), p. 31.

30. Peter Benenson papers, Amnesty International archive, London (AI), undated, handwritten lecture note.

31. See Robert Burstow, 'The limits of Modernist Art as a "Weapon of the Cold War": Reassessing the unknown patron of the Monument to the Unknown Political Prisoner', *Oxford Art Journal*, XX, 1, 1997, 68–80.

32. See Tom Buchanan, 'Peter Benenson', in *Oxford Dictionary of National Biography* (online edition consulted on 15 November 2009).

33. These were Maurice Audin (French Algeria), Antonio Amat (Spain), Constantin Noica (Romania) and Olga Ivinskaya (USSR). The remaining cases were from China, USA, the Philippines, South Africa and the Portuguese colony of Angola.

34. Peter Benenson papers, AI, Benenson to the Earl of Home, 5 June 1961.

35. L. Wildenthal, 'West German human rights movement', p. 20.

36. See Tom Buchanan, '"The truth will set you free": The making of Amnesty International', *Journal of Contemporary History*, xxxvii, 4, (2002), 575–97.

37. P. Benenson, *Gangrene*, p. 9.

38. Cited in Susan L. Carruthers, *Winning Hearts and Minds: British Governments, the Media and Colonial Counter-insurgency, 1944–1960* (Leicester, 1995), pp. 207 and 237.

39. In September 1966 there were 440 groups in all: they were mainly located as follows: Britain 190, Sweden 52, Denmark 40, Norway 38, Australia 28, and Ireland 19.

40. Peter Benenson papers, AI, typescript entitled 'Community of Conscience', presented on 5 June 1976, p. 9.

41. It was also extremely difficult for Amnesty to investigate cases in many parts of the world – for instance, at the International Executive Committee on 12/13 March 1966 it was reported that it was almost 'impossible' to obtain information from China and Vietnam (minutes, pp. 2 and 3).

42. See Tom Buchanan, 'Amnesty International in crisis, 1966–1967', *Twentieth Century British History*, xv, 3, (2004), 267–89.

43. Peter Benenson papers, AI, Benenson's letter to Mark Benenson, 12 March 1979.

44. See A.H. Robertson and J.G. Morrills, *Human Rights in the World*, (4th ed., Manchester, 1996), pp. 136–8; Egon Larsen, *A Flame in Barbed Wire: The Story of Amnesty International* (London, 1978), pp. 43–6.

45. A.G. Harryvan and J. van der Harst, *Documents*, p. 195.

46. John J. Maresca, *To Helsinki: The Conference on Security and Cooperation in Europe, 1973–1975*, (Durham NC, 1985), p. 154.

47. For an excellent account of Helsinki and its consequences see Daniel C. Thomas, *The Helsinki Effect: International Norms, Human Rights, and the Demise of Communism* (Princeton and Oxford, 2001).

48. D. Thomas, *Helsinki Effect*, p. 266; J. Maresca, *To Helsinki*, pp. 136–7.

49. Jiří Hájek and Zdeněk Mlynář, cited in D. Thomas, *Helsinki Effect*, p. 91.

50. *CETP*, vol. VIII (1985), pp. 154–6.

51. *Labour Party Annual Report*, 1968, p. 170. However, Wilson was making a party-political point as he sought to present the Conservatives as infected with the racist 'virus of Powellism'.

# 8
# Europeanization in the Monetary Sector, 1968–92

*Guido Thiemeyer*

## I  Introduction

Today, the common monetary policy is one of the most important aspects of the European Union. It is one of the policy fields in which Community institutions act like sovereign states. In particular, the European Commission and the Central Bank miss no opportunity to stress the significance and great success of the European Monetary Union, which came into being in 1999. Most existing accounts seem to suggest that there was a straightforward and even logical evolution from the beginnings of the supranational Common Market to the Monetary Union in the framework of the EU.[1] From an historical perspective, however, this understanding of European integration is problematic for several reasons:

- First, it maintains that the transition, since the 1950s, from Common Market to monetary union was inevitable. The European Union, therefore, is posited as the logical culmination of European history after the Second World War. Historical alternatives to the structure, geography, and economic aims of transnational and international relations in Europe since 1945 are completely neglected.
- Secondly, it underestimates the complexity of the integration process in the monetary sector. The European Monetary Union was only one possible result of international economic development since 1945, and it is up to historians to ask why it was realized as it was. What were the alternatives, and why did they not come into being?
- Thirdly, the following question arises: What did 'Europe' mean in this context? What concepts of 'Europeanization' existed in the monetary sector? In order to answer these questions, it is necessary to examine the motives behind European integration in the monetary sector, in order to show the driving forces which led to European monetary integration.

This chapter will examine the parameters of Europeanization in the monetary sector. The first section will focus on the key driving forces – the 'forces profondes' – of European monetary integration between 1958 and 1999. Next, three dimensions of Europeanization will be considered: was European integration in the monetary sector intentional? Was it an end in itself for certain actors? Or was European monetary integration merely an unintended consequence of economic and social structures? The subsequent section will then deal with the discourses of Europe in the monetary sector, that is, what exactly did 'Europe' mean in this particular field of the economy? The final section will explore whether monetary integration in Europe occurred in parallel with processes of disintegration in other areas. What, for example, was the relationship between the dissolution of the Bretton Woods international monetary system and the attempt, starting with the 'Werner Plan' in 1969, to realize a European Monetary Union?

## II  'Forces profondes' of European monetary integration

There were at least four major driving forces of European monetary integration in the 1960s. The first important step toward European monetary integration in the 1960s and 1970s was supported by the European Commission and the 'Comité d'action pour les Etats Unis d'Europe', with Jean Monnet as its primary representative. In October 1962, the European Commission presented its initial plan for European monetary integration, called 'Action Programme for the Second Stage'. Its main argument was that the economic union established with the Common Market required the fixity of exchange rates among the currencies of the member countries: 'Die Wirtschaftsunion setzt nämlich spätestens nach Abschluss der Übergangszeit (...) feste Wechselkurse zwischen den Währungen der Mitgliedstaaten voraus.'[2] This implied that a monetary union among EEC countries was not only politically desirable, but also an economic necessity emerging from the operation of the Common Market. The Commission's paper therefore argued that the governments of the member states should not only establish a monetary union but also reach an agreement about a common reserve pool for loans in case of inequalities in balances of payments. As to the third step of the Common Market, the Commission's proposal went even further:

> Die Errichtung der Währungsunion könnte das Ziel der dritten Stufe des Gemeinsamen Marktes warden. Die im Rat vereinigten Finanz- oder Wirtschaftsminister der EWG würden unter den zu gegebener Zeit festzulegenden Begingungen das Gesamtvolumen der einzelstaatli- chen Haushaltspläne und des Haushaltsplanes der Gemeinschaft sowie über die allgemeinen Bedingungen ihrer Finanzierung beschließen.

Der Rat der Notenbankpräsidenten würde zum Zentralorgan eines Zentralbanksystems von föderalistischem Zuschnitt.[3]

Indeed, the idea of European federalism was a characteristic feature of the European Commission in the 1960s, due in large part to the strong influence of its first president, Walter Hallstein. Even after he left office, however, at the end of the 1960s, the Commission did not abandon the idea of a monetary union: not only did the Commission of the EEC argue in favour of monetary unification, but the European Parliament also issued a major statement advocating the same – the so-called van Campen Report – and passed a resolution for a common monetary policy.[4]

Nonetheless, European monetary union on a federal basis proved to be unrealistic in the 1960s for several reasons. First (and most importantly), France would never have accepted further supranational European integration along these lines. Secondly, the accession of the United Kingdom failed due to a French veto. In light of the world-wide monetary crisis at the end of the decade, both the Commission and Monnet readopted their proposals. However, things had changed significantly: both Hallstein and de Gaulle had left office, and their successors proved to be much more pragmatic with respect to monetary questions. As a result, the 'Barre Plan' for European monetary cooperation, published by the Commission in February 1969, contained no reference to federalism. Instead, it pleaded for a common mechanism for monetary cooperation within the Community with a view to reaching a convergence of national policies in the medium-term. Compared to the first Hallstein proposals, this was a rather cautious approach; it had the advantage, however, of being acceptable to the French government. As such, the Barre report represented one of the bases of the famous Werner Plan for European monetary integration.[5]

Even after the failure of the Werner Plan, the Commission continued to press for a European Monetary Union. In his speech in Florence on 27 October 1977, the President of the European Commission, Roy Jenkins, again called for a European monetary organization, which seemed necessary after the breakdown of the Bretton Woods system and the oil price crisis.[6] His appeal was taken up by French President Valéry Giscard d'Estaing and German Chancellor Helmut Schmidt when they initiated the European Monetary System (EMS) in 1979.[7] A similar situation occurred a decade later when, in 1989, the report of the Delors Commission counselled economic and monetary union in three stages. This recommendation was subsequently taken up by François Mitterrand and Helmut Kohl with their initiation of the Maastricht treaty.

In general, the Commission was one of the most important protagonists for European monetary integration. In this context, monetary integration was by no means simply an end in itself, but rather represented a way to strengthen the EEC both economically and politically. The strengthening of the EEC in turn meant increased power for one of its core institutions, the European Commission. Thus, the deepening of European integration always entailed an extension of the power of the European Commission. Understanding this relationship is key to appreciating the dynamics of European monetary integration: the Rome Treaty had established a new actor in the field of international economic integration, and one which acted independently of national governments.

Another important driving force behind European monetary integration was the European desire for economic and monetary independence from the United States. After the Second World War, monetary stability in Europe was bolstered by the United States in the context of the Bretton Woods monetary system, which set the US dollar as the pivotal international currency. During the 1950s and the early 1960s this system operated smoothly, guaranteeing monetary stability within the transatlantic framework. By the mid-1960s, however, the Bretton Woods system had run into trouble as a result of the growing deficit in the United States in external trade and the budget deficit caused by its engagement in Vietnam. As the US dollar lost value, inflation was exported to Europe through the institutions of the Bretton Woods international monetary system of fixed exchange rates. The monetary system of the post-war world had been stable owing to the stability of the US dollar; when faced with economic and political problems, the United States government no longer cared about European interests in monetary stability. As the US Minister of Finance John Connally sarcastically summarized, 'It is our currency, but your problem.'

The inflation of the US dollar in the mid-1960s, and the concomitant neglect of European interests by the US government sparked European efforts for monetary integration. The proposal made by the French President Charles de Gaulle for the establishment of a new European monetary system based on an international gold standard is well known;[8] it is important to note, however, that he was not seeking the re-establishment of the international gold standard of the nineteenth century, but rather an international monetary system that was no longer dominated by the USA. As he made clear to his economic adviser, Alain Prate, in 1968, 'J'ai proposé l'or mais j'aurais pu accepter tout autre étalon, à condition qu'il soit indépendent des monnaies anglo-saxonnes.'[9] The aim was an international monetary system based on a neutral currency. Indeed, the efforts of the European Commission to endorse European monetary integration, described above, must be seen in this context. The various attempts at European monetary integration in the 1960s that led to the Werner Plan for a Monetary Union within the framework of the EEC were based not only on the efforts of the European Commission to extend its responsibilities, but were also the result of the neglect of European monetary interests by the United States.

The same pattern was replicated in the 1970s, when the German Chancellor Helmut Schmidt and the French President Giscard d'Estaing launched their proposals for the European Monetary System. Schmidt, in particular, was deeply disappointed at US unwillingness to respect European interests in monetary questions. After a conversation with Schmidt, Roy Jenkins noted in his diary the former's 'deep hostility towards Carter, whose behaviour over the Dollar was intolerable.'[10] Owing to the United States' lack of interest in European economic stability, Schmidt sought a framework for monetary stability in Europe that focused on the EEC rather than on a transatlantic relationship with the USA. Both the Werner Plan and the European Monetary System, which came into being in 1979, resulted from this emancipation of Western Europe from the United States in monetary policy. This consideration was also central in the debate over the Maastricht Treaty in the early 1990s: a common European currency, ultimately called the euro, was established to match the hegemony of the American dollar in international financial markets. This was an important factor for the French government and President François Mitterrand, who wanted to construct a European zone of monetary stability and to develop a distinct European 'monetary personality' that could negotiate on a basis of equality with the United States.[11]

Pascaline Winand once suggested that the United States acted as an external federator of Europe in the 1950s by supporting European integration within the framework of the European Coal and Steel Community and the European Defence Community.[12] It is argued here that in the 1960s and 1970s, the USA again acted as an external federator, but this time indirectly and unintentionally by neglecting European interests instead of – as in the 1950s – as an integral part of their foreign policy. To a certain extent, therefore, European monetary integration in the 1960s and 1970s was an unintended consequence of US monetary policy: because of their own economic problems, the United States was unable to provide monetary stability for Western European countries, thereby forcing Europe to organize its own monetary system.

A third and final important factor of European monetary integration was the role of the German economy and, consequently, German currency. Since the mid-1960s, Germany had grown to be the largest economy in Western Europe. As a consequence, the German currency – the Deutschmark – increased in value, particularly in relation to the US dollar, the French franc and the British pound. By the 1970s, the Deutschmark had become the leading currency in Western Europe, and policies set by the German central bank – the Deutsche Bundesbank – exerted considerable influence over the monetary policy of all European states. While German governments had not sought political hegemony in Europe, because economic power is closely related to political power, the economic and monetary strength of Germany had significant political implications. Smaller states, notably the Benelux countries and Austria, bound their currency in a fixed relation to the Deutschmark, leading to a *de facto* monetary union between these countries. Germany and the Deutsche Bundesbank consequently became the centre of European monetary policy. This was the main reason why the French government, in particular, tried to establish a European monetary union with a common central bank, where German and French central bankers would meet on equal terms. In 1988, the French Minister of Finance Edouard Balladur called for a reform of the European Monetary System in order 'to prevent one country from determining the objectives of economic and monetary policy for the group as a whole'.[13] European monetary integration became the paramount instrument for France to control and reduce German power in the monetary sector.[14] This motive had been a key factor in the French initiative for the Coal and Steel Community, and appeared again in the context of monetary issues when Germany became too powerful in this aspect of the economy. In this respect, 'Europe' and European integration were seen as a means to achieve a balance of political and economic power following the recovery of the German economy.

One final major structure paved the way for European monetary unification in the 1960s and 1970s: the operation of the Common Market led to an intensification of commerce among the EEC countries. Economic theory argues that open markets are an inexorable force leading to monetary unification. According to the theory of optimal currency areas developed by Kevin Dowed and Peter Greenaway, all participants in a common market try to reduce their transaction costs.[15] For this reason, within open markets there is always a trend toward the monopolization of currencies. The success of a currency depends on the number of transactions for which it is used; and, as the German economy was by far the largest in the 1960s and 1970s, the Deutschmark became the key currency in Western Europe. Seen from this perspective, European monetary integration was first and foremost driven by dynamic market forces, the anonymous actions of millions of people trying to reduce their transaction costs in growing intra-European trade. European monetary unification, therefore, was precipitated by the operation of the Common Market.[16]

Moreover, the operation of the Common Agricultural Policy (CAP), the first sector for which the EEC was responsible, required a common monetary policy. The Monetary Committee established by the European Commission argued on 8 May 1964 that the CAP would lead automatically to a regime of fixed exchange rates: 'The assumption became popular that the account unit for the CAP (the "green dollar") had created a quasi single currency in the EU.'[17] From this point of view, there seemed to be a neofunctionalist 'spill over' which would lead by a certain path-dependency to European monetary unification as a result of the operation of the Common Market and the CAP.

## III    Three narratives of European monetary integration

In recent years, historiography has developed rather different approaches to the explanation and description of European integration since the Second World War. Some describe this history as a re-emergence of the old world after its total destruction in two major wars.[18] Others focus on the extraordinary economic development of Western Europe since 1945, which, since the 1990s, has also included the eastern part of the continent.[19] Others again describe European history in a more negative way: the decline of Europe from the leading continent of the nineteenth century to a heterogeneous group of middle-range powers by the end of the twentieth.[20] I seek to explain European monetary integration from a different perspective, through exploring the following key questions: first, was monetary union a deliberate goal of European politics, or was it an incidental consequence of other decisions and developments? Secondly, what exactly did 'Europe' mean in the context of international monetary policy? Was it merely a (rather imprecise) geographical description, or did it actually correlate with particular political values and economic ideologies? Finally, I will examine how monetary integration in certain areas was always accompanied by disintegration in others; that is, European integration in the monetary sector always involved the exclusion of other countries.

### a)   Intentional and unintentional monetary integration

The process of Europeanization in the monetary sector was both intentional and unintentional. Since at least 1958 there had been a strong desire among certain actors to establish a monetary union on a supranational level. One of these was Jean Monnet and his 'Comité d'action', for whom 'Europe' was an end in itself and monetary unification an important instrument in establishing European unity: 'L'objectif serait la création d'un marché financier européen, avec une banque et un fond de réserve européen, l'utilisation en commun d'une partie des réserves nationales, la convertibilité des monnaies européennes, le libre movement des capitaux entre les pays de la communauté, enfin l'établissement d'une politique financière commune.'[21] This approach was part of the 'Monnet method', which sought the gradual integration of different sectors of the economy with a view to an ultimate goal of the 'unification' of Europe.

The same intention is evident in the European Commission's efforts to establish a European monetary union. In particular, the Hallstein Commission of the 1960s was a strong supporter of a European federal state following the example of the USA. According to Hallstein, the European Commission was the nucleus of a European federal government; a European Monetary Union under the direction of a European Central Bank was, therefore, a key goal for the Commission at that time.[22]

European monetary integration was also, however, an unintended consequence of other developments in the international monetary system. This was true, for example, in the case of American monetary policy of the 1960s and 1970s: faced with serious economic problems since 1965, the US government was no longer willing to provide monetary stability for Western Europe. This development unfolded against the backdrop of the exploding costs for the American military intervention in Vietnam. The US dollar declined in value, and the inflation rate in the USA rose to 7.5 per cent in 1969. As a result, the Bretton Woods international monetary system was dissolved and in 1970 the EEC countries made their initial attempt to establish a monetary union with the Werner Plan. Viewed through this lens, the beginnings of European monetary integration represented an unintentional consequence of American policy. This factor also played a decisive role in the creation of the European Monetary System in 1978–79, when Helmut Schmidt and Valéry Giscard d'Estaing criticized American unwillingness and inability to lead the Western world economically.

Another facet of unintentional European monetary integration is described by monetary theory. Monetary markets, as with markets in general, tend towards monopolization. As the West German economy had been by far the biggest in Western Europe since the 1960s, the Deutschmark gained ever greater importance. Despite being obstructed for political reasons by France and, to a certain extent, the UK, there was nonetheless a tendency toward unification of the European monetary markets that centred on the Deutschmark. In economic theory, a monetary union is a natural complement of the single market, reducing the uncertainty caused by fluctuating exchange rates: A monetary union emerges organically from the operation of free markets for goods and services.[23] There is no deliberate political intent behind this development; rather, integration is the unintended consequence of the operation of decentralized markets. This argument is very similar to the neo-functional approach of integration theory. Monetary integration is subject to an expansive logic of integration, often called 'spill over'.

### b) Discursive constructions of European monetary integration

What did Europe and Europeanization mean, respectively, in terms of monetary integration? As we shall see, these notions had varying connotations in the realm of monetary policy between 1969 and 1999. From the Commission's perspective, 'Europe' was primarily an area defined by common law and governed by the institutions of the EEC. As such, 'Europeanization' meant the extension of the authority of the European Commission. The power of the Commission had its origin in European law, stipulated since 1958 in a number of treaties. Considered in light of the theory of realism in international relations, the Commission, as the centre of power, was eager to extend its potency and gain additional control over the monetary sector. The notion of 'Europe' was thus ascribed to the European Community.

Another important driving force behind European monetary integration came from the European nation-states, particularly France and Germany. The combination of the breakdown of the Bretton Woods system since the mid-1960s, and American indifference to the need for monetary stability in Europe forced them to organize European monetary stability on their own. From this perspective, Europeanization was not an end in itself, but a means of attaining two goals that European nation-states could not reach alone: monetary stability in Europe and a currency strong enough to compete with the US dollar on a global scale. In this context, 'Europe' was constructed in opposition to US hegemony and as a barrier to global 'Americanization'. French Minister for Foreign Affairs Hubert Védrine summed this up by saying, 'Living in a US-dominated world is more a threat to our ideas than to our interests.'[24] In this context, 'Europe' was constructed as an anti-America, associated with opposition to unrestricted and uncontrolled competition in markets without any social protection. 'Europe' was defined as a third way between the socialist systems in the Eastern bloc and the perceived liberal capitalism of the USA. Most European nation-states articulated their own notions of this economic system; be it French 'planification' or German 'Soziale Marktwirtschaft', in each case they refer to an economic synthesis of liberal capitalism and centralized socialism. Moreover, they all played an important role in the development of a European identity by delimiting themselves from American (and other) political and economic systems.

Finally, a third important meaning of Europe in monetary aspects was related to the perception of inequality of economic power within the EEC. Since the 1960s the Deutschmark had become the leading currency in Europe. European monetary integration was meant to break German hegemony and secure French influence over European monetary policy. The notion of 'Europe', therefore, stood also for a balance of economic power within the EEC.

It could be asked how these rather different motives for monetary integration all relate to the notion of 'Europe'. Researchers in cultural history have repeatedly shown how images of and social discourses concerning the notion of 'Europe' have consistently played a major role in the search for a common identity.[25] 'Europe' has been – and will be – constructed in different and sometimes contradictory ways, and this applies equally to the connotation of 'Europe' in the monetary sector. There are at least two reasons for the discursive construction of Europe in the monetary sector. First, political pragmatism played an important role. Monetary unification in general needs a clear and strong institutional framework that can provide economic and political stability as well as cultural identity. Although the treaty of the European Economic Community of 1957 did not explicitly state the aim of monetary union, it nonetheless provided a stable political, economic and cultural framework and was therefore closely connected to the notion of Europe. These were good reasons to create a close relationship between the already existing EEC institutions and monetary integration. Secondly, the motives and driving forces behind European monetary integration were divergent and comprised both economic and political arguments. Tying them to the general topic of European integration simplified the process for a general public unfamiliar with the complex economic problems of monetary union. 'Europe', and the integration of Europe, was supported by a permissive consensus in most European societies until the 1990s. Particularly after the Second World War, the notion of Europe gained support because people expected it to overcome the problems posed by nation-states. While the image of Europe was rather blurred, it was exactly this vagueness that was a key advantage in communicating the complex concepts of a monetary union. Consequently, European monetary integration was both an end in itself and a means of achieving other political and economic goals.

### c) Integration and disintegration in the monetary sector

It is important to note that European monetary integration only ever pertained to a limited area of the European continent, and always excluded others. This has been true since the beginnings of monetary integration in the middle of the nineteenth century. The first international monetary union – the so-called Latin Monetary Union (LMU) – was founded in 1865 and comprised Belgium, France, Switzerland, and Italy.[26] Although the French government tried to incorporate the German states – namely Prussia and Austria – as well as Scandinavia, they only succeeded in integrating Greece in 1868. The LMU was based on a bimetallic standard, meaning that coins made of gold and silver served as currencies in a fixed ratio of 1:15.5. The *de facto* dissolution of the union occurred in August 1914 with the start of the First World War, and formally ended in 1926. For the French the LMU was a means of fostering diplomatic dominance in continental Europe, despite the fact that all attempts to integrate the German states and the UK failed.[27] A second important monetary union was the Scandinavian Monetary Union, founded in 1872. It, too, was destroyed by the outbreak of war in 1914, and formally dissolved in 1927. Yet another key monetary arrangement of the late nineteenth century was the International Gold Standard. Although the origin of this first international monetary system was in Europe (i.e., the UK and Germany), it became the first global system by integrating both the United States and Japan. It is important to note that each of these international monetary arrangements integrated certain areas while excluding others. In 1872, the International Gold Standard covered the newly founded German Reich, the UK, the Netherlands and the Scandinavian Monetary Union. From a German perspective (i.e., Bismarck's), the gold standard was a way to isolate France after the war of 1870–71, not only in the diplomatic but also in the economic sector. As with all international monetary arrangements, the International Gold Standard collapsed in 1914, and all of the British attempts to revive it in the 1920s failed utterly. After the monetary anarchy of the inter-war period, the Bretton Woods international monetary system succeeded in providing monetary stability in the transatlantic framework until the early 1970s. Again, the integration of Western Europe was coterminous with the disintegration of the eastern part of the continent. Bretton Woods was an instrument to exclude the Soviet-dominated world, a monetary arrangement that could be interpreted as the monetary branch of containment policy. Even the European Monetary System (EMS) of 1979 integrated the members of the EEC, leaving aside others (for instance, Switzerland) that had been part of the Bretton Woods system. Moreover, the exclusion of Eastern Europe that had started with Bretton Woods continued. The same can be said of the European Monetary Union established with the Maastricht Treaty in 1992. It was meant to integrate the whole Community, leaving aside the United Kingdom, Denmark and Sweden (who decided on free terms not to join the Monetary Union), but also Switzerland (that had been part of the Bretton Woods system) and, again, Eastern Europe. As such, integration of certain areas in the monetary sector always went along with disintegration of others.

## IV   Conclusions

European monetary integration between 1969 and 1999 was propelled by four major driving forces. For the European Commission, monetary unification within the EEC was an end in itself because it led to an extension of competencies and powers of the Commission and the EEC in general. The European Commission, therefore, was an important driving force behind monetary integration. There was, however, a certain evolution in the Commission's position towards a common currency. The first Hallstein Commission saw monetary integration as a cornerstone of a European federal state. After the confrontation with Gaullism in the 1960s, however, the European Commission became much more pragmatic. Roy Jenkins pleaded only for an intensification of European monetary cooperation as an alternative to the Bretton Woods system. Another driving force was the United States and its quest for hegemony in international financial markets. Until the middle of the 1960s, the Bretton Woods monetary system – with the US dollar as the pivotal currency – provided monetary stability in Europe and the Western world. But, owing to economic and financial problems, the United States was no longer willing to respect European interests in monetary questions; this was the key reason for Western European cooperation in the monetary sector. What had previously been a relationship of mutual protection between the USA and Western Europe had turned into a competitive one. The result of this development was the European Monetary Union of 1999. Another driving force behind European monetary integration was the presence of millions of actors in international European markets trying to reduce their transaction costs: the dynamics of a liberal market economy meant that the Deutschmark would have monopolized the currency had markets worked without political intervention. Because having the Deutschmark as the dominant European currency was unacceptable to other nations for political reasons, the euro became the supranational money. It is impossible to single out any one of these driving forces or ideas of 'Europeanization' as the most important in the monetary sector; each was significant, but at different times and to different extents. The process of Europeanization in the monetary sector can only be understood as a combination and interplay of these different driving forces and motives.

Europeanization in the monetary sector is a story of profound complexity. On the one hand, there was obviously a strong desire for monetary union: the European Commission and the European Parliament had political reasons, and interest groups in emerging transnational markets had economic ones. Consequently, European monetary integration was, to a large extent, brought about intentionally. On the other hand, this chapter has shown that European monetary integration was also the result of American unwillingness to consider European interests in monetary questions. Seen from this perspective, European monetary integration was the unintended consequence of American policy.

What did 'Europe', and 'Europeanization', mean in the monetary sector? Again, the answer to this question is complex: from both the European Commission's and Parliament's perspective, they stood for the intensification and enlargement of the EEC: 'Europe' was identified with the EEC. For the French, 'Europe' was closely identified with a specific economic solidarity. This meant that in monetary questions, the dominance of the Deutschmark and the Deutsche Bundesbank had to be controlled by integration. The goal was that monetary decisions for Europe would not be taken by one national institution, but rather in a collective fashion, with all those concerned providing input. 'Europe' therefore was construed as a means of achieving French 'republican solidarity'. This was closely connected to another notion of 'Europe': an economic order that stood in contrast to the perceived liberal 'free competition' of the USA, and the socialist model of the former Soviet bloc. 'Europe' in this context was perceived as a third way between unrestricted liberalism and authoritarian socialism. Finally, the idea of 'Europe' was used for pragmatic reasons during monetary integration: it provided a way to communicate the highly complex questions of monetary integration to a broader public.

A final characteristic of 'Europeanization' in the monetary sector is that the integration of certain areas always went along with the disintegration of others. This was the case with the first monetary unions in

Europe in the second half of the nineteenth century, and it was likewise typical of monetary integration in the twentieth century. From a German perspective, the International Gold Standard that came into being in the 1870s was a means of excluding and isolating France in international relations. The Bretton Woods system in the 1950s and 1960s was meant to exclude Soviet influence in Western Europe. European monetary integration in the 1970s and 1990s was a way of challenging the hegemony of the US dollar. Finally, the establishment of the EMS in 1979 fostered monetary integration in Western Europe while destroying transatlantic integration.

## Notes

1. See for instance: Kenneth Dyson and Kevin Featherstone, *The Road to Maastricht. Negotiating Economic and Monetary Union* (New York, 1999); Mark Baimbridge and Philip Whyman, *Economic and Monetary Union in Europe. Theory, Evidence and Practice* (Cheltenham, 2003).
2. ['The economic union requires after the end of the transition period at the latest, fixed exchange rates between the currencies of the member countries.'] Europäische Wirtschaftsgemeinschaft, Kommission COM (64) 400, 30.9.1964, in: Europa Archiv, Folge 22 (1964), D572–D580, here D 579.
3. Ibid. ['The establishment of the monetary union could be the main objective for the third phase of the Common Market. The Ministers of Finance and Economy in the Council of the EEC would – at a later date – decide on the budget of the Community and the general conditions for financing. The Council of presidents of the national central banks would become the central institution of a federal central bank system.']
4. Dieter Gehrmann and Sabine Harmsen (eds), *Monetäre Integration in der EWG. Dokumente und Bibliographie* (Hamburg, 1972), pp. 24–33.
5. Andreas Wilkens, 'Der Werner-Plan. Währung, Politik und Europa 1968–1971', in Franz Knipping and Matthias Schönwald (eds), *Aufbruch zum Europa der zweiten Generation. Die europäische Einigung 1969–1984* (Trier, 2004), pp. 217–44; Hubert Zimmermann, *Money and Security. Troops and Monetary Policy in Germany's Relations to the United Kingdom and the U.S., 1950–1971* (Cambridge, 2002).
6. Europas Herausforderung und Chance. Rede des Präsidenten der Kommission der Europäischen Gemeinschaften, Roy Jenkins, in Florenz am 27 Oktober 1977, in: Europa-Archiv Vol. 33 (1978), D 1–11.
7. Peter Ludlow, *The Making of the European Monetary System* (London, 1982); Guido Thiemeyer, 'Helmut Schmidt und die Gründung des Europäischen Währungssystems 1973–1979', in Franz Knipping and Matthias Schönwald (eds), *Aufbruch zum Europa der zweiten Generation. Die Europäische Einigung 1969–1984* (Trier, 2004), pp. 245–68.
8. K. Dyson and K. Featherstone, *The Road to Maastricht*, p. 83.
9. [I suggested gold but I would have accepted any other means, provided it was independent of Anglo-Saxon currencies.] Alain Prate, 'Le général de Gaulle et les institutions de Bretton Woods', in *La France et les institutions de Bretton Woods 1944–1994. Colloque tenu à Bercy les 30 juin et 1er juillet 1994* (Paris, 1995), p. 85.
10. Roy Jenkins, *European Diary* (London, 1989), p. 225.
11. K. Dyson and K. Featherstone, *Road to Maastricht*, p. 84.

12. Pascaline Winand, *Eisenhower, Kennedy and the United States of Europe* (Basingstoke and London, 1993), pp. 1–64.
13. Patrick McCarthy, 'France looks at Germany or how to become German (and European) while remaining French', in *France–Germany, 1983–1993: The Struggle to Cooperate* ed. by Patrick McCarthy (New York, 1993), p. 58.
14. Matthias Kaelberer, *Money and Power in Europe. The Political Economy of European Monetary Cooperation* (New York, 2001), pp. 169–200.
15. Kevin Dowed and David Greenaway, 'Currency Competition, Network Externalities and Switching Costs. Towards an Alternative View of Optimum Currency Areas', in: *Economic Journal* CIII (1993), 1180–9.
16. Carsten Hefeker, 'Die Europäische Währungsintegration nach dem Zweiten Weltkrieg: Politik, Ideologie oder Interessen?', in Christian Henrich-Franke, Cornelius Neutsch and Guido Thiemeyer (eds), *Internationalismus und Europäische Integration im Vergleich. Fallstudien zu Währungen, Landwirtschaft, Verkehrs- und Nachrichtenwesen* (Baden-Baden, 2007), pp. 57–82; eidem *Interest Groups and Monetary Integration. The Political Economy of Exchange Regime Choice* (Boulder, 1997); Barry Eichengreen, *A More Perfect Union? The Logic of Economic Integration. Essays in International Finance* (Princeton, 1996).
17. M. Kaelberer, *Money and Power in Europe*, p. 88.
18. Walter Laqueur, *Europe since Hitler* (London, 1970).
19. Tony Judt, *Postwar. A History of Europe since 1945* (London and New York, 2005).
20. Eric Hobsbawm, *Age of Extremes. The Short 20th Century* (London, 1994).
21. [The objective would be to create a European financial market, with a bank and a European reserve fund, a common use of part of the national reserves, the convertibility of European currencies, and the free movement of capital between the countries of the community, finally establishing a common fiscal policy.] Jean Monnet, *Mémoirs* (Paris, 1976), p. 502; Eric Roussel, *Jean Monnet* (Paris, 1996).
22. Wilfried Loth and Wolfgang Wessels (eds), *Walter Hallstein. The Forgotten European?* (Basingstoke, 1998).
23. Francesco Giordano and Sharda Persaud, *The Political Economy of Monetary Union. Towards the Euro* (London and New York, 1998), pp. 184–90.
24. Quoted in Harm Schröter, *Americanisation of the European Economy. A Compact Survey of American Economic Influence in Europe since the 1880s* (Dortrecht, 2005), p. 1.
25. This is the main agument in the work of Wolfgang Schmale. See for instance: Wolfgang Schmale, *Geschichte Europas* (Vienna, 2001).
26. Guido Thiemeyer, *Internationalismus und Politik. Währungspolitische Kooperation im europäischen Staatensystem 1865–1900* (Munich, 2008).
27. Luca Einaudi, *Money and Politics. European Monetary Unification and the International Gold Standard, 1865–1873* (Oxford, 2001).

# Part Three
# Europe Emergent

# 9
# Europeanization through Violence? War Experiences and the Making of Modern Europe

*Robert Gerwarth and Stephan Malinowski*

> 'Les universités européennes ont été le berceau de la civilisation.
> Mais il y a aussi une autre éducation européenne,
> celle que nous recevons en ce moment:
> les pelotons d'exécution, l'esclavage, la torture, le viol –
> la destruction de tout ce qui rend la vie belle.
> C'est l'heure des ténèbres.'
> Romain Gary, *Éducation européenne* (1945)

## I

Unlike the more ambivalent transnational concepts of 'Americanization' and 'Globalization', the increasingly popular term 'Europeanization' is generally used to describe unambiguously positive processes of political, socio-economic and cultural integration within the institutional framework of the European Union.[1] Peaceful forms of cross-cultural encounters, shared values, free trade, transnational exchanges of ideas, a culture of compromise, and increasing inter-state cooperation are, or so it seems, at the heart of what we commonly perceive as 'Europeanization'; a transnational process that culminated in the EU, a realm of peace and prosperity in which the demons of a nationalist past have become history.[2]

It is commonplace today to contrast this process with the violent upheavals and nationalist confrontations that characterized the late nineteenth and the first half of the twentieth century – from colonial rivalries to wars within Europe – and to view 'Europeanization' as a lesson that Europeans learnt from their violent and ultimately self-destructive pasts. Influential works by Tony Judt and James Sheehan, for example, have juxtaposed the divisive nature of nationalisms, wars, and destruction of Europe's early twentieth century on the one hand and European internationalization with its emphasis on transnational discourses, peaceful conflict resolution, and cultural convergence on the other.[3]

There is, of course, nothing inherently wrong with a historical interpretation in which the astonishingly swift reconstruction of post-war (Western) Europe and the indisputable successes of European integration are emphasized as remarkable achievements. On the other hand, however, a binary model of European conflict and 'Europeanization' can easily result in a somewhat unsatisfactory 'happy history' of European integration, a history which contrasts sharply with the shared European experiences of violence that shaped the lives of millions of Europeans. Indeed, wars and conflicts were by definition the result of difference and division and not, in the main, self-referentially European. States (mainly nation-states) were the agents in these military conflicts, which is why their histories have usually been written within national frameworks of analysis. Yet, as Ute Frevert has rightly pointed out, the two world wars *also* constituted genuinely transnational conflicts in which millions of people gathered intense experiences of (voluntary and involuntary) mobility and cross-border contacts.[4] Between 1914 and 1945, and, in some parts of Europe until much more recently, ethnic conflicts, wars and civil wars, were indeed the most defining transnational experiences of border-crossing and intercultural exchange and they, too, contributed to a vast array of (intended or unintended) contacts and transfers of ideas and personnel across real or imagined borders as well as to the reordering of 'mental maps'.[5]

In assessing the unintended effects of these (often involuntary) contacts and border crossings on the process of Europeanization – understood here as a convergence of life experiences within Europe – we do not wish to dispute the primarily *divisive* nature of violence, and recognize the importance of maintaining the sense of proportion frequently demanded by critics of transnational history.[6] Europeans obviously did not become 'European' as a result of violence. Yet if, as the authors of the introduction to this volume emphasize, 'Europeanization' is not to be understood as a one-dimensional, teleological process that began in the ruins of war-torn Europe in 1945 and ended with the creation of the supra-national EU, we should at least consider the possibility of viewing violence as a quintessential part of what René Girault and Hartmut Kaelble have emphasized as an important dimension of 'Europeanization', namely *l'Europe vécue:* the Europe of shared experiences.[7] Although it would go beyond the scope of this essay to offer a comprehensive analysis of the myriad ways in which violent experiences contributed to the process of 'Europeanization', we hope to make suggestions for future empirical studies on the matter.

Indeed, the idea that peaceful European integration, democracy and violence are not mutually exclusive has been posited before. Immediately after the end of the Second World War, Theodor Adorno and Max Horkheimer pointed to the dialectic of progress, while a number of historians in recent decades have convincingly demonstrated the compatibility of and historical connections between European democracy and mass violence.[8] As John

Horne and others have pointed out, the cultural and political currents generally identified as pillars of European civilization – Christianity, the Enlightenment, science, and democracy – have also contributed to war and revolution, often decisively.[9] Furthermore, as Daniel Schönpflug and Martin Aust have recently argued, some of the most enduring transnational learning processes in twentieth-century Europe were prompted by mutual hostility, conflict, and war.[10] Recent publications on Nazism have furthermore demanded a 'Europeanized perspective' on the history of the Third Reich, not in order to play down German responsibility for the Second World War or the Holocaust, but to address transnational connections brought about by intra-European fascist collaboration, expulsion and the redrawing of geographical and mental maps that are insufficiently explained from a nation-centric perspective.[11] A recent example of the fruitfulness of such an approach is Mark Mazower's *Hitler's Empire*, which investigates the ill-fated and ultra-violent attempts at Nazi empire-building from a genuinely transnational and 'Europeanized' perspective.[12]

Our essay will build on this relatively recent body of scholarship and our own research interests in order to formulate some tentative hypotheses about the connections between violence and (de-)Europeanization. By discussing the 'Europeanizing' effects of two violent projects of epic dimensions, namely European colonialism and the two world wars, we engage with what one may call the 'dark side' of transnational history in order to promote an ambivalent concept of 'Europeanization' that weaves together histories of extremely violent encounters and border-crossings and those of economic success, democratic reorientation, and collective recovery. In other words: our purpose is not to replace the meta-narrative of peace and prosperity at the heart of Europeanization with a dysfunctional version of the European civilization thesis in which violence becomes the kit of European identity. Instead, we want to emphasize multiple dynamics and to complicate the 'happy' image of Europeanization that still dominates in scholarly and political debates. At the same time, we aim to test the usefulness of 'Europeanization' as a transnational conceptual approach for the investigation of aspects of European history that are often perceived as the direct opposite of 'Europeanization'.

We are aware that it could be argued that the dynamics described in this chapter are ultimately not distinctively European, but rather increasingly manifest in different forms across the globe. This is only partly true, however, since their origin was distinctly European even if they were subsequently globalized. Furthermore, we believe that Europe should not be treated as a sealed-off entity, but as a constellation of states whose peculiar and often violent interaction with each other (and the rest of the world) gave it its distinct character in the late nineteenth and early twentieth centuries. 'European' identity was generally most strongly developed when it was threatened by real or imagined 'others', be they rebellious

African tribes, immigrants, or 'Asian' Bolshevism. In this chapter we will distinguish between aspects of extra-European 'Europeanization' (that is, imperial projects aimed at wielding power over non-European territories and populations), and projects that contributed to the largely unplanned violent 'Europeanization' of Europe between 1914 and 1945.

## II

The 'golden age' of colonialism in the late nineteenth and early twentieth centuries is generally viewed as a period when intra-European tensions and rivalries were decisively exacerbated, contributing to the 'clash of the titans' in 1914.[13] It is often suggested that only the process of *decoloni-zation* after the Second World War helped to defuse nationalist rivalries on the colonial periphery, while at the same time providing important impulses for European economic integration.[14] However, without denying that colonialism was clearly also a factor in *de*-Europeanization, it simultaneously constituted a shared European experience characterized by transnational learning processes, particularly with respect to the (generally violent) treatment of non-European native peoples and the construction of colonial identities of white supremacy. In this context, four aspects of colonial history seem particularly relevant to the subject of 'Europeanization' and deserve closer attention here: colonialism's character as a transnational European project; the convergence of colonial experiences of dominance and violence; the repercussions of these experiences on Europe itself; and, finally, the evolving patterns of mutual observation and transnational knowledge transfers.

From Christopher Columbus, an Italian trained in Portugal in the fifteenth century and financed by Spain to 'discover' the New World, to the trans-nationally coordinated wars of European decolonization in the 1950s and 1960s, colonialism was an experience that many European states shared. To a large extent, the similarities in the modes of colonial rule and oppression chosen by states such as Britain, France, Germany, the Netherlands and Portugal – from economic pressure to systematic mass murder – were a result of mutual observation and transnational emulation.[15] Thus, unsurprisingly, violent conquest, the maintenance of colonial rule, and, in the twentieth century, the 'modernizing mission', followed similar pan-European patterns that led not only to the familiar European rivalries but also to shared learning experiences.[16]

When entering the colonial realm, Europeans often left their specific national contexts behind and formed new groups with other Europeans rather than with their respective colonial subjects. The crew of the Congo steamer on which Joseph Conrad's protagonist Marlow penetrated the *Heart of Darkness*, for example, was just as 'European' in composition as the non-fictional crew which brought the Polish-British anthropologist,

Bronislaw Malinowski, to New Guinea a few years later.[17] Like so many other scholars working in colonial settings, Malinowski's expedition relied heavily on European infrastructures and European cooperation.[18] The German explorer Hermann Wissmann had already referred to these pan-European structures in the early 1890s, when he dedicated his memoirs to King Leopold II of the Belgians for whom he felt 'deepest gratitude' for supporting his expeditions.[19]

One of the most striking aspects of the ways in which these explorers described their colonial experiences was the distinction between 'savages' and 'Europeans'. In the 1920s, Malinowski, for example, referred to the relationship between the colonial actors and the natives in terms of 'European culture' and 'non-European culture'. Even during the Second World War, at the height of divisive intra-European violence, Malinowski continued to refer to the unity of European culture and identity which appeared just as self-evident from his 'African perspective' as it had been 25 years earlier in the Pacific Islands.[20] Fifteen years later, the ethnologist and heroine of the French resistance, Germaine Tillion, who sought to strengthen the bonds between Algerians and France through a new educational system, used a similar terminology, speaking of 'European' culture and education that had to be spread across Northern Africa.[21]

The convergence of European experiences obviously did not automatically lead to 'Europeanization'. In the long term, European settler communities demonstrated how colonial migration led the settlers away from Europe and towards new structures that were neither 'colonial' nor 'European', of which the development of distinct national identities in the United States, Canada, South Africa, New Zealand, and Australia represents the clearest example. In terms of formative, collective European experiences, it is nevertheless debatable whether these emigrant groups were actually 'lost' to Europe in the late nineteenth century, as various Europeans discussed with growing concern.[22] Even in the United States, citizens claiming 'European origin' still represent around 74 per cent of the overall population. In all of the former white settler colonies, powerful links to Europe endure. Even today, from South America to Australia and the United States, these population groups of European origin cultivate distinct identities which set them apart from groups with non-European backgrounds.[23]

If we consider shared experiences as a key aspect of 'Europeanization', then the settler colonies are of particular relevance. The worlds in which the settlers lived can be described as mixed European 'zones of experiences'.[24] Three inter-related aspects of this settler culture seem particularly relevant for the subject of 'Europeanization': first, there is the transnational, mostly pan-European composition of the settler colonies. In Africa, Asia and the white dominions, settler communities more often than not were heterogeneous in national composition. This transnational composition, combined with a frontier situation in which 'white' settlements felt threatened by the native population, created a situation in which 'race' became more important than nationality. In these contexts – and this is the second aspect relevant to the process of 'Europeanization' – the settlers systematically distinguished themselves from the 'natives'. Overseas, the internal European boundaries, which were so clearly delineated on the continent, tended to fade in importance. What was regarded as 'European', and what was not, appeared to be far more evident from the perspective of the settlers abroad than in the European capitals. A third characteristic of European settlements in colonial contexts is the 'frontier situation' in which settlers were bound together by fear of real or imagined 'enemy natives'. The 'thin white line' of European settlers, so they feared, could always potentially be crushed in a colonial uprising.[25] In these fragile 'Islands of White', the boundary between 'us' and 'them' was defined along the colour bar, not necessarily along 'national' lines.[26] The new 'us' was composed of Europeans who transcended national differences. They came to define their shared identity against that of the indigenous population, and invented legal codes and conventions designed to perpetuate separation between the groups. In one recorded case in the 1890s, Indians living in African colonies were explicitly required to salute 'Europeans' whenever they encountered them.[27] Colonial uprisings were widely interpreted as attacks on the 'European civilization' represented by the white settlers.[28] The metaphor of the trek and the laager, with which the nationally heterogeneous settlers conquered and subdued new territories and joined forces in violent attacks on the 'savages', accurately describes the process of transnational 'European' identity-building in the colonies.

One of the largest European settler communities in Africa, the 'pieds-noirs' in Algeria, consisted of shopkeepers, craftsmen and merchants from France, Spain, Italy, Malta, Switzerland and Germany.[29] In most contemporary sources (both French and Arab), these settlers were commonly referred to as 'Europeans' and not as Frenchmen. Their living quarters in Algerian towns and cities were known as the 'European quarters'.[30] The Algerian independence movement, the FLN, targeted 'European' facilities as part of its urban terror campaigns. As it stated in the summer of 1956: 'Descendez n'importe quel Européen, de dix-huit à cinquante-quatre ans. Pas de femmes, pas d'enfants, pas de vieux.'[31] In its tracts, the threat that 'représailles terribles s'abattront sur la population civile européenne' pointed to a conflict in which 'Europeans' could become legitimate targets.[32] The dichotomy between Algerians and 'Europeans', which blurred the internal national differences between Europeans, was also used in many decolonization manifestos within Europe. Jean-Paul Sartre's famous preface to Frantz Fanon's *Wretched of the Earth*, for example, was addressed not to his fellow Frenchmen, but rather explicitly to 'the Europeans'.[33]

Frontier and laager mentalities produced solidarity towards fellow Europeans and aggressive exclusion of, and violence towards, the 'native other'. The parallel, sometimes joint European penetration of the non-European world led to a continually expanding European 'settler archive' where experiences of colonial rule were stored and accessed.[34] This was reflected in transnational distinctions between Europeans and natives evolving in the fields of criminal law and voting rights as well as in the construction of a new ethnic category: 'Europeanness'.[35] The introduction of such a category was sanctioned by 'scientific findings' which offered 'proof' of racial differences. The German anatomist, Frederick Tiedemann, for example, was very much in line with colleagues throughout Europe when he emphasized in a lecture at the Royal Society in London that the brain of the 'negro' was more similar to that of an orangutan than to the brain of a European, and that any legal equality for native African populations was therefore out of the question.[36] Biological justification for the creation of new colonial legal norms was aimed at permanently separating Europeans and natives from each other, a process that was aided by strict marriage and workplace regulations, as well as colonial urban planning.[37]

Although 'counter-acculturation' – the cultural and physical 'blending' of European settlers and indigenous populations – certainly occurred in the colonial sphere, it remained the exception. *Demarcation* from the 'natives', on the other hand, became the rule in all colonial contexts in which Europeans formed substantial minorities.[38] This tendency greatly increased during the nineteenth century for a number of reasons, of which the rise of 'scientific' racism and increased immigration of European women (along with the greater sexual autarchy this entailed) were of particular importance.

These patterns of exclusion and inclusion have not altogether disappeared. In the political rhetoric of conservative and nationalist politicians today, Europe's borders have to be 'defended' against illegal immigrants from former African colonies. Although this kind of rhetoric is employed in many European states, it appears to be particularly pronounced among members of the radical intellectual right in France. Extra-parliamentary groups that once sought to maintain control over French-dominated Algeria through violence have now formed organizations such as the *Groupement de Recherche et d'Etudes pour la Civilisation Européenne*. This intellectual circle, widely known by its acronym, GRECE, calls for the expulsion of all Arabs and Africans from France, and the concomitant eradication of their cultural influence. In so doing, GRECE is stepping outside of the traditional boundaries and concepts of French nationalism. It is no longer the integrity of France that is at stake but rather the 'defence' of European civilization against the influence of the former colonies.[39] The members of GRECE do not base their argument on the concept of the nation, but rather on a broadly defined notion of European culture: Europe is a place where Africans and other 'people of colour' do not fit.[40] The metaphor of the colonial laager, once used to describe European settlements in Africa, is now being used to describe the 'beleaguered' old world. The frontier of the laager has shifted to Europe itself and the alleged threat from the colonial 'other' provides a rallying cry for a common European identity in defence of common values.

Although the direct impact of colonialism and decolonization on Europe itself is sometimes exaggerated, there is plenty of evidence that the constructed dichotomy between Europeans and 'natives' in the colonies was imported back into Europe. This applies not only to the thousands of European settlers who returned to Europe after decolonization and who cultivated their own cultures of remembrance;[41] it also applies to those former colonial officials, who were frequently 'recycled' as experts for foreign policy or development aid.[42] The continuities between colonial and post-colonial projects, from European economic policy to foreign policy, were indeed considerable. Alongside megalomaniac plans such as Hermann Sörgel's *Atlantropa* project (which proposed to close the Straits of Gibraltar, to evaporate the Mediterranean and join Africa to Europe),[43] EEC development aid projects provided a way of continuing European cooperation in the colonial sphere. At the time of its founding, the EEC consisted predominantly of sovereign colonial powers (some still embroiled in wars of decolonization), which had explicitly included the 'development' of their overseas territories in the EEC's founding statutes.[44] In a rapidly changing international context, Europeans now sought to present themselves as 'developers' of other continents in general, and Africa in particular.[45]

Systematic mutual observation, international European collaboration, and transnational learning processes were, however, in no way limited to peaceful development policy. They were equally prominent in the contexts of colonial conquest and the repression of colonial revolts.[46] The violence unleashed by Europeans in the colonial sphere tended to follow highly similar patterns which included the deployment of indigenous auxiliary forces, the division of native populations into 'hostile' and 'friendly tribes', the construction of concentration camps, and the regular use of forms of warfare outlawed in Europe. From routine torture to the use of poison gas and aerial bombing campaigns (employed by the Spanish in Morocco a few years before Mussolini's air force did the same in Ethiopia), Europeans tended to use highly similar forms of colonial subjugation which they would have considered as 'inappropriate' within Europe.[47] Mutual observation and transnational learning processes are also well documented for the wars of decolonization in Malaya, Indochina, Kenya, and Algeria, where Britain and France drew on each other's experiences in 'counter-insurgency' warfare.[48]

Despite the well-known tensions between European colonial powers in the late nineteenth and early twentieth centuries, they also cooperated in staking colonial claims. This usually entailed a coordination of exploitation and a mutual toleration of violence, even in places where this violence assumed genocidal proportions. At the Berlin Africa Conference of 1884–85, for example, the assembled diplomats not only divided Africa into spheres of interest and agreed on the joint economic exploitation of the Congo, but also signed an agreement that in the event of a European war, the combatants would not deploy any 'coloured' troops.[49] This form of segregation also dovetailed with the spatially limited validity of The Hague Land War Convention or the Kellogg–Briand Pact, whose rules for civilized warfare and the proscription of war were conceived for Europe and not for the colonies.[50] When these conventions were perceived to have been violated, for example in the case of Germany's ill-fated attempts to instigate a jihad in the Near East against French and British colonial troops in late 1914,[51] Swiss missionaries protested vigorously against this breach of European conventions not to employ 'savages' against white soldiers.[52] The German response to the Allies' use of colonial troops in the Great War and, more importantly, to France's and Belgium's decision to deploy more than 20 000 black troops during the occupation of the Rhineland was similarly met with horror (across all political and religious divides) at this 'violation' of European norms of warfare.[53]

On other occasions, however, Europeans cooperated militarily in various colonial 'trouble spots'. The brutal crushing of the Boxer Rebellion by the Eight Nations Alliance illustrates the fact that, despite prevailing tensions in the colonial sphere, Western powers were willing to cooperate when they felt that their common interests were threatened. Despite the arguably global alliance which intervened militarily in China and which saw the German General Alfred von Waldersee entering Beijing alongside the Bengalese cavalry of the British colonial army, European collaboration remained at the heart of the Boxer expedition and demonstrated that intra-European rivalries and conflicts could be transcended when common European interests seemed to be under threat in the colonial realm.[54]

## III

The Great War and its immediate aftermath had a seemingly paradoxical effect on Europe: on the one hand, it obviously reinforced the fragmentation of the continent and increased national tensions to an unprecedented extent. The first age of economic globalization came to an abrupt end at the same time that close cultural and dynastic ties that had existed between the combatants right up until 1914 ceased to exist and were replaced by mutual hostility, suspicion and heavily fortified borders.[55] In this respect, the Great War certainly served as one of the key factors underpinning *de*-Europeanization in the first half of the twentieth century. On the other hand, however, the Great War also prompted international debate about European identity and Europe's future place in the world on a historically unprecedented scale. Alongside the birth of ultra-nationalist movements across Europe, intellectuals all over the continent embarked on an intensified search for ideas of intra-European collaboration and, in some cases, even European unity.[56] The League of Nations, originally designed as a global institution, turned out to be distinctively European in its outlook and the distribution of power within its key agencies after the US Senate refused to ratify the Versailles Treaty. Most of the issues dealt with by the League – from refugees, to minority questions, to European reconstruction – had been precipitated by the Great War and demanded a Europeanized response articulated and implemented by a genuinely Europeanized civil service, the Secretariat.[57] The League also provided the stage on which some of the most daring plans for European reconciliation and integration – those articulated by Stresemann and Briand – were first presented. It is true that the initiatives for closer European collaboration presented by Stresemann and Briand came to nothing; young Europeanist movements of the 1920s that grew out of the circles around Romain Rolland, Richard Coudenhove-Kalergi, Tomas Masaryk, Ortega y Gasset and others could not dispel dominant nationalist sentiments. Nevertheless, their ideas about a new European order, triggered by the destruction of what Stefan Zweig called *The World of Yesterday*,[58] lived on even in the second post-war period of the twentieth century.[59]

More immediately, and on the level of pan-European *experiences*, the Great War and its immediate aftermath created spaces for intensified transnational personal encounters and exchanges, not only between anti-war Dadaists in Zurich's *Cabaret Voltaire*, but also between soldiers of different national backgrounds who fought on the same side. The war itself significantly intensified transnational mobility and created pan-European networks that survived beyond the end of hostilities in November 1918. The wartime alliance of Germany, Austria, and Hungary, for example, lived on in the paramilitary networks of the extreme right as well as clandestine attempts to establish, in the mid-1920s and again in the 1930s, a 'White International' which was to be based in neutral Switzerland and to include representatives of both the defeated and the victorious states of Europe bound together in anti-Communist beliefs. In this context, the 'future of Europe' was a prime concern, as Waldemar Pabst, responsible for the murder of Rosa Luxemburg, long-serving military organizer of the Austrian *Heimwehr* and author of the White International's manifesto, phrased it. What exactly this 'future Europe' of ultra-nationalists was to look like was a divisive question consciously avoided by Pabst who confined himself to stating that the ultimate European mission of the White International was 'the replacement of the old trinity of the French Revolution [*liberté, égalité, fraternité*], (...) with a new trinity: authority, order, and justice'.[60] The Russian and Hungarian Bolshevik revolutions had simultaneously created sizeable refugee communities in cities such as Vienna, Prague, Berlin and London, where tens of thousands of disgruntled and displaced counter-revolutionaries from Russia and Hungary had to adapt to new lives while seeking support from like-minded Europeans for their various plots to bring about the downfall of international Communism.[61]

The Great War and its violent aftershocks between 1917 and 1923 also produced a large number of European adventurers who travelled the battlefields of post-war Europe from Anatolia to Upper Silesia, civil-war torn Russia and the Baltic States in search of violent action, material gain or ideological fulfilment. For the British Black and Tans, whose violent journey led from the trenches of Flanders to post-war Ireland and Palestine, or those ex-officers of the former Central Powers who joined forces with Russia's White Armies, fought with (and against) Baltic nationalists in Lithuania before assuming 'advisory' roles in Ataturk's ethnic cleansing campaigns in Anatolia, *l'Europe vécue* was a Europe of violence.[62] Adoration of violence, newly radicalized and genuinely pan-European forms of anti-Semitism, as well as war-induced notions of masculinity, served as transnational touchstones for these movements and formed the basis of unlikely alliances and even friendships. After the temporary stabilization in European politics in the 1920s, this social type resurfaced in the 1930s. During the Spanish Civil War, both sides of the conflict were backed by considerable numbers of international volunteers: with up to 75 000 Italians, 19 000 Germans and around 700 of Eoin O'Duffy's Irish Blueshirts fighting on Franco's side, and up to 30 000 foreign nationals (the vast majority of them Europeans) joining the Republican International Brigades,[63] the civil war provided a pan-European stage for violent encounters and transnational solidarity, so vividly described in countless memoirs and the literary accounts of André Malraux, Arthur Koestler and George Orwell.[64] All of these accounts emphasize the peculiar experiences of transnational cooperation on both sides of the Spanish Civil War, experiences and encounters prompted by conflict. Although the Spanish Civil War was undoubtedly a highly divisive event, divisions did *not* follow national lines.

The Europeanization of conflict and the (generally involuntary) 'transnationalization' of violent experience were taken to their extremes during the Nazi war of conquest after 1939. Under the auspices of radical racial and social inequality, Nazi policies triggered an unprecedented wave of incidental transnational experiences that were shared by millions of soldiers, civilians, refugees, and POWs.[65] During the Second World War, for example, between 8 and 10 million forced labourers worked in Germany. By 1944, one out of three workers in the German armaments industry and one quarter of the workforce in the machine-building and chemical industries were foreigners.[66] It is not suggested that these traumatic experiences turned Poles and Czechs into 'Europeans'; for many of them, however, the change of place reconfigured the perception of nationhood and nationality, either by radicalizing earlier notions or destabilizing and modifying them. This is particularly true for the pan-European phenomena of resistance and collaboration. An example is the acclaimed novel, *Éducation européenne*, published in 1945, wherein Lithuanian refugee Romain Gary tells the story of the 14-year-old Polish boy Janek Twardovski, who joins an underground resistance movement near Wilno after his parents have been murdered by the Germans. The group is a motley crew that includes Russians, Ukrainians, Belorussians, and Jewish Poles. Despite being surrounded by the most extreme violence, the disparate members of the resistance group manage to abandon their national prejudices and develop a transnational identity. In a key scene, one of the protagonists points out: 'Le patriotisme, c'est l'amour des siens. Le nationalisme, c'est la haine des autres. (...) Il y a une grande fraternité qui se prépare dans le monde, les allemands nous auront valu au moins ça'.[67] Gary's interpretation of transnational encounters as an unintended result of German force was partly informed by his own war-induced life experiences: born in (then Russian) Lithuania and educated in France, Gary served as a fighter pilot for the Free French during the Second World War before becoming a high-ranking diplomat. However, the notion of 'Europeanization through violence' can likewise be found in the memoirs of many other members of the European resistance.[68]

The war indeed created new European communities of émigrés in North and South America, Australia and Britain, which became home to various European governments-in-exile. These governments in turn provided support to Belgian, Czech, Slovak, French, Luxembourger, Greek, Norwegian, Dutch, Polish and Yugoslav exile communities, as well as to Jewish refugees from Germany and other occupied territories.[69] While the shared experiences of European exile could reinforce extreme nationalism, it also prompted different ways of thinking about European identity. War and destruction thus stimulated new forms of interaction between various European resistance groups and radicalized earlier plans for European integration.[70] In 1942, for example, the committed anti-fascist Austrian refugee and former League of Nations official, Egon Ranshofen-Wertheimer, suggested that the destructiveness of Hitler's New Order had made Europeans more conscious of their interconnectedness. Without intending to, Hitler had destroyed the 'myth of sovereignty' and taught Europeans to think beyond their national borders.[71] Although not everyone would have agreed with such sentiments in 1942, there is certainly some truth in Mark Mazower's argument that 'Nazi conquest linked together the peoples of Europe more tightly than they had ever been connected before' and that in turn, 'those fighting the Germans also found it necessary to plan in European terms'.[72] Both Nazi and Allied propaganda invoked images of transnational European solidarity to bolster their war effort; as the Italian historian Federico Chabod observed in his book *Storia dell'idea Europa*, which he started to work on during the war, 'in these last years there has been and still is much talk of Europe and European civilization and so on. Appeals, articles in newspapers and magazines, discussions and polemics: in all, the word "Europe" has been tossed around with unusual frequency, for good reasons and bad.'[73]

If Nazism appeared to the vast majority of contemporaries to be the very opposite of 'European civilization', Hitler's crusade against Bolshevism also appealed to many conservative and fascist Europeans who rallied to the anti-Soviet cause. At the beginning of Operation Barbarossa, in June 1941, some 600 000 non-Germans fought alongside Nazi Germany against the Soviet Union. At the height of the Second World War, in 1943, every third soldier defending the German lines was in fact of non-German origin. In the spring of 1945, half of the roughly one million members of the SS were non-Germans from 15 different European nations. Romanians, Finns, Lithuanians, Latvians, Ukrainians, Hungarians, Spaniards, Belgians, Swedes, and Norwegians made Hitler's army very 'European' indeed.[74] Nazi efforts to 'Europeanize' the German armed forces were intensified immediately after the defeat at Stalingrad. Nazi propaganda labelled Operation Barbarossa a 'crusade for Europe' in order to mobilize non-German 'volunteers' to fight the perceived 'Asian' threat of Bolshevism on the one hand, and American materialism and imperialism on the other. A new 'Song for Europe' was broadcast, stamps with the slogan 'European United Front against Bolshevism' were issued, and Nazi propaganda maintained that 'born out of discord, struggle and misery the United States of Europe has at last become a reality'.[75]

The Europeanization of evil found its most internationally recognizable form in the pan-European figure of the collaborator, the Vidkun Quislings, Léon Degrelles, Pierre Lavals, Anton Musserts, Andrey Vlasovs, Emanuel Moravecs, Eoin O'Duffys, and William Joyces of Europe.[76] Certainly, their aspirations for 'Europe' often diverged substantially from the place in Hitler's New Order which the German authorities were willing to grant them. They had to experience first hand that the Nazis' 'Europe' was a German Europe and that nationalism provided a major obstacle to the realization of a political union of European fascists. Some of the activists, however, continued to emphasize their war-induced experiences as a source of personal 'Europeanization'. The memoirs of British fascist leader Sir Oswald Mosley, for example, describe his transformation from a nationalist to a 'European' as a result of the Second World War: 'I now feel equally at home in England, France and Germany; in a sense all Europe is my home. In seventeen years of living in Europe, following a lifetime of visits, in the rigours of war (...), I have become fully and completely a European.'[77]

For the victims of Nazi violence, too, absolute destruction could go hand in hand with very intense forms of transnational encounter, which fundamentally reshaped the lives of millions of Europeans. This applied not only to the horrors of the Nazi concentration camps, which are discussed elsewhere in this volume,[78] but also to another example: the case of Berlin in the spring and summer of 1945 illustrates how a city devastated by war became a stage for European encounters triggered and characterized by violence, a stage on which hundreds of thousands of civilians, soldiers, refugees, POWs, and forced labourers from almost every European country engaged with each other in various ways amid an epic nightmare of violence and destruction.[79]

Any analysis of the paradoxical relationship between violence and Europeanization would also have to discuss how transnational experiences of war, expulsion and destruction were remembered and transformed into 'lessons' for European integration. Whereas war commemoration and hero cults after the Great War primarily served as a source for nationalist mobilization (even where the forms – notably the cult of the Unknown Soldier and medievalist forms of monuments – followed transnational patterns), the same cannot be said about the post-1945 period.[80] Commemoration of the Second World War soon focused on European reconciliation as the only possible lesson to be learnt from the war. Increasingly, the suffering caused by war and conflict was emphasized as a shared European experience. It was this perspective which made certain transnational forms of commemoration possible, from the erection of the Cross of Coventry on top of the reconstructed Dresden *Frauenkirche* to the repeated meetings between François Mitterrand and Ernst Jünger, or Helmut Kohl's attendance at the commemoration ceremonies on the beaches of Normandy.

Certainly, neither the civilian populations of Coventry and Dresden nor the German and French soldiers at Verdun had any intention or desire to die for Europeanization. It was in retrospect, prompted by the need to explain what appeared to survivors to have been a senseless conflict and to heal the wounds of fundamentally divisive events, that these events developed a distinctively Europeanizing effect.[81] Moreover, it is a trend that continues to the present day: in the recent Brussels-based exhibition, '50 Years of the European Adventure', for example, the Museum of Europe presented a girl's dress made of Allied flags, the illustrated memoirs of a young Hungarian in Budapest in 1956, a British soldier's diary kept during the Suez crisis and Stasi memorabilia as objects 'which tell us in a moving way what Europeans have experienced over the last 50 years'.[82] The focus on civilians' suffering allowed for a commemorative perspective in which subjection to violence, expulsion, and bombing terror could retrospectively be interpreted as a basis for Europeanization through the convergence of experiences.[83]

## IV

For obvious reasons, the term 'Europeanization' is most frequently used to describe processes of positive change, integration and peaceful convergence within the historical realm that has become today's European Union. It is impossible to dispute that the legacies of the Enlightenment and Christianity, or the integrating effects of European trade and cultural exchange constituted the crucial factors in the process of Europeanization. What has been argued in this chapter, however, is that analyses of 'Europeanization' are incomplete if they ignore the processes of unintended convergence of experience of millions of Europeans brought about by war and conflict. War and the destruction of entire cities, of national certainties, and of traditional forms of identity were common experiences for most Europeans. It may not be an accident that the construction of a distinctly European identity occurred in direct response to some of the most violent aspects of European history. Pan-Europeanism tended to remain on the political margins until the era of the two world wars, and ideas of European integration were only implemented after periods of extreme, self-destructive violence.[84]

If large-scale violence in Europe and Europe's colonial possessions did produce convergent life experiences, transnational learning processes, and forms of emulation, the construction of a collective war memory in recent decades has also helped to turn originally divisive events into a shared legacy, in which human suffering, irrespective of national context, is emphasized more strongly than immediately after 1945. In this meta-narrative of European identity, colonialism and the two world wars have become constant reminders that the Europe of the future has learnt the lessons of the past.[85] For all these reasons, war and conflict should not be understood as the opposite of convergence, unification and compromise, but as an integral part of the complicated dynamics of Europeanization.[86]

## Notes

1. See, for example: R. Harmsen and T. Wilson, 'Introduction: Approaches to Europeanization', *Yearbook of European Studies*, XIV (2004), 13–26; T. Börzel and T. Risse, 'Europeanization: The Domestic Impact of European Union Politics' in K.E. Jorgensen et al. (eds), *Handbook of European Union Politics* (London, 2006), pp. 483–504. See also D. Dinan, *Europe Recast: A History of the European Union* (Basingstoke, 2004).
2. See, for example: P. Valéry, *Variété I* (Paris, 1924) and K. Jaspers, 'Vom Europäischen Geist' in: idem, *Rechenschaft und Ausblick: Reden und Aufsätze* (Munich, 1951), pp. 275–311; O. Asbach, 'Die Erfindung des modernen Europa in der französischen Aufklärung', *Francia*, XXXI (2004), 55–94; A. Pagden (ed.), *The Idea of Europe: From Antiquity to the European Union* (Cambridge and New York, 2002).
3. T. Judt, *Postwar: A History of Europe Since 1945* (New York and London, 2005); J. Sheehan, *Where Have All the Soldiers Gone? The Transformation of Modern Europe* (New York, 2008).
4. U. Frevert, 'Europeanizing German History', *Bulletin of the German Historical Institute*, XXXVI (2005), 9–31, particularly 13–15.
5. See the thematic issue on 'mental maps' edited by C. Conrad, *Geschichte und Gesellschaft*, XXVIII (2002), pp. 340–514.
6. H.-U. Wehler, 'Transnationale Geschichte – der neue Königsweg historischer Forschung?' in G. Budde, O. Janz and S. Conrad (eds), *Transnationale Geschichte: Themen, Tendenzen und Theorien* (Göttingen, 2006), pp. 161–74, here p. 168; A. Thompson, *The Empire Strikes Back? The Impact of Imperialism on Britain from the Mid-Nineteenth Century* (Harlow and New York, 2005), pp. 3f; C. Hall and S. Rose (eds), *At Home with the Empire: Metropolitan Culture and the Imperial World* (Cambridge and New York, 2006).
7. H. Kaelble, 'Europäisierung' in M. Middell (ed.), *Dimensionen der Kultur- und Gesellschaftsgeschichte* (Leipzig, 2007), pp. 73–89, here pp. 77–8; idem, 'Europabewußtsein, Gesellschaft und Geschichte: Forschungsstand und Forschungschancen' in

R. Hudemann and K. Schwabe (eds), *Europa im Blick der Historiker* (Munich, 1995), pp. 1–30.

8. M. Horkheimer and T.W. Adorno, *Dialectic of Enlightenment* (New York, 1972); M. Mazower, *Dark Continent: Europe's Twentieth Century* (London, 1998); M. Mann, *The Dark Side of Democracy: Explaining Ethnic Cleansing* (New York and Cambridge, 2005).

9. J. Horne, 'War and Conflict in Contemporary European History, 1914–2004' in K.H. Jarausch and T. Lindenberger (eds), *Conflicted Memories: Europeanizing Contemporary Histories* (New York and Oxford, 2007), pp. 81–95, here p. 83.

10. M. Aust and D. Schönpflug (eds), *Vom Gegner lernen: Feindschaften und Kulturtransfers im Europa des 19. und 20. Jahrhunderts* (Frankfurt am Main and New York, 2007). For a similar model of transnational learning processes, see: W. Schivelbusch, *The Culture of Defeat: On National Trauma, Mourning, and Recovery* (London, 2003).

11. See: K.K. Patel, 'In Search of a Transnational Historicization: National Socialism and its Place in History' in K. Jarausch and T. Lindenberger (eds), *Conflicted Memories*, pp. 96–116; A. Bauerkämper, 'The Ambiguities of Transnationalism: Fascism in Europe between Pan-Europeanism and Ultra-Nationalism, 1919–1939', *Bulletin of the German Historical Institute London*, IXXX (2007), 43–67.

12. M. Mazower, *Hitler's Empire: Nazi Rule in Occupied Europe* (London and New York, 2008).

13. P.M. Kennedy, *The Rise of the Anglo-German Antagonism, 1860–1914* (London, 1982); E.J. Hobsbawm, *The Age of Empire, 1875–1914* (London, 1987).

14. H. Kaelble, 'Europeanization', p. 85. The European economic reorientation away from the colonies and towards the European market can be observed for a number of countries. See, for example, for France: D. Lefeuvre, *Chère Algérie: La France et sa Colonie, 1930–1962* (Paris, 2005).

15. T. Todorov, *The Conquest of America: The Question of the Other* (New York, 1984).

16. This also applies to the most violent chapters of colonial expansion: genocide. See: A.D. Moses (ed.), *Empire, Colony, Genocide: Conquest, Occupation and Subaltern Resistance in World History* (Oxford and New York, 2008); idem, 'The Holocaust and Colonialism' in Peter Hayes and John Roth (eds), *The Oxford Handbook of Holocaust Studies* (Oxford, 2009).

17. On the context, see: R.B. Edgerton, *The Troubled Heart of Africa: A History of the Congo* (New York, 2002), pp. 48 and 57.

18. G.W. Stocking Jr. and K. Maclay, 'Malinowski: Archetypes from the Dreamtime of Anthropology' in: eidem (ed.), *Colonial Situations: Essays on the Contextualization of Ethnographic Knowledge* (Madison, 1991), pp. 9–74. On the anthropological contrast between Europe and 'the others', see: T. Asad (ed.), *Anthropology and the Colonial Encounter* (New York, 1973).

19. H. Wissmann, *Im Innern Afrikas: Die Erforschung des Kassai während der Jahre 1883, 1884 und 1885* (Leipzig, 1891).

20. B. Malinowski, 'The Pan-African Problem of Culture Contact', *American Journal of Sociology*, XLXIII (1943), 649–65, quotation on p. 660.

21. G. Tillion, *L'Afrique bascule vers l'avenir* (Paris, 1999).

22. S. Conrad, *Globalisierung und Nation im Deutschen Kaiserreich* (Munich, 2006), pp. 229–78.

23. S.P. Huntington, *Who Are We? The Challenges to America's National Identity* (New York and London, 2004); S.P. Huntington and L.E. Harrison, *Culture Matters: How Values Shape Human Progress* (New York, 2000).

24. D. van Laak, 'Kolonien als "Laboratorien der Moderne"?' in S. Conrad and J. Osterhammel (eds), *Das Kaiserreich transnational: Deutschland in der Welt*

*1871–1914* (Göttingen, 2004), pp. 257–79, here pp. 266–7. D. Cannadine, *Ornamentalism: How the British Saw Their Empire* (London, 2002).

25. A.H.M. Kirk-Greene, 'The Thin White Line', *African Affairs*, LXXIX (1980), 25–44.
26. D. Kennedy, *Islands of White, Settler Society and Culture in Kenya and Southern Rhodesia, 1890–1939* (Durham, 1987), pp. 11–31, 128–46; C. Elkins and S. Pedersen, *Settler Colonialism in the Twentieth Century: Projects, Practices, Legacies* (New York and London, 2005).
27. T. von Prince, *Gegen Araber und Wahehe: Erinnerungen aus meiner ostafrikanischen Leutnantszeit 1890–1895* (Berlin, 1914), p. 3.
28. C. Elkins and S. Pedersen, 'Introduction: Settler Colonialism: A Concept and Its Uses' in eadem (eds) *Settler Colonialism*, pp. 1–20. For Britain: S. Constantine, 'Migrants and Settlers' in W.R. Louis (ed.), *The Oxford History of the British Empire* (Oxford and New York, 1999), pp. 163–87.
29. D. Lefeuvre, 'Les pieds-noirs' in M. Harbi and B. Stora, *La Guerre d'Algérie 1954–2004: La fin de l'amnésie* (Paris, 2004), pp. 267–86.
30. G. Pervillé, 'Pour en finir avec les "Pieds-Noirs"', Bordeaux, January 2004: http://guy.perville.free.fr/spip/article.php3?id_article=34, consulted on 15 November 2009; P. Mannoni, *Les français d'Algérie: Vie, mœurs, mentalité: de la conquête des Territoires du Sud à l'indépendance* (Paris, 1993).
31. [Take any European from eighteen to fifty-four years old. No women, no children, no elderly] as quoted in: G. Pervillé, 'Le terrorisme urbain dans la guerre d'Algérie (1954–1962)' in J.-C. Jauffret and M. Vaisse (eds), *Militaires et guérilla dans la guerre d'Algérie* (Brussels, 2001), pp. 447–67, quotation on p. 455.
32. [terrible retribution will fall upon the civilian population in Europe.]Ibid., p. 453.
33. See Jean-Paul Sartre's preface to F. Fanon, *The Wretched of the Earth* (New York, 1965).
34. A term used by L. Veracini, 'Colonialism and Genocides: Towards an Analysis of the Settler Archive of the European Imagination' in D. Moses (ed.), *Colony, Empire, Genocide,* pp. 148–61.
35. B. Gammerl, *Untertanen, Staatsbürger und andere. Der Umgang mit ethnischer Heterogenität im Britischen Weltreich und im Habsburgerreich, 1867–1918*, PhD thesis, FU Berlin, pp. 103–52 and 184–213.
36. F. Tiedemann, 'On the Brain of the Negro, Compared with That of the European and the Orang-Outang', *Philosophical Transactions of the Royal Society of London* XXVI (1936), 497–527. On the context, see the short survey provided by D. Claussen, *Was heisst Rassismus?* (Darmstadt and Munich, 1994/2007).
37. J.S. Furnivall, *Netherlands India: A Study of a Plural Economy* (Cambridge, 1944); M.G. Smith, *The Plural Society in the British West Indies* (Berkeley, 1965); A.D. King, *Colonial Urban Development. Culture, Social Power and Environment* (London and Boston, 1976); Z. Çelik, *Empire, Architecture, and the City: French-Ottoman Encounters, 1830–1914* (Seattle, 2008); idem, *Urban Forms and Colonial Confrontations: Algiers under French Rule* (Berkeley, 1997).
38. J. Osterhammel, *Kolonialismus: Geschichte, Formen, Folgen* (Munich, 1995), p. 92.
39. A.-M. Duranton-Crabo, 'Du combat pour l'Algérie française au combat pour la culture européenne. Les origines du Groupement de Recherche et d'Etudes pour la Civilisation Européenne (GRECE)' in J.-P. Rioux and J.-F. Sirinelli (eds.), *La guerre d'Algérie et les intellectuels français* (Paris, 1991), pp. 59–78.
40. 'Définitions pour l'Europe', *Cahiers universitaires*, 21 January 1965, pp. 25–7; B. Stora, *Le Transfert d'une mémoire – De l'Algérie française au racisme anti-arabe* (Paris, 1999).

41. E. Buettner, *Empire Families: Britons and Late Imperial India* (Oxford, 2004); J.-J. Jordi, *L'Arrivée des Pieds-Noirs* (Paris, 2002); B. Stora, 'La solitude des incomprises. La guerre d'Algérie dans les écrits de femmes européennes (1960–2000)' in J.C. Jauffret (ed.), *Des hommes et des femmes en guerre d'Algérie* (Paris, 2003), pp. 124–50.

42. Detailed statistics on the British case can be found in: PRO, CO 1017/666. See, too J.M. Hodge, 'British Colonial Expertise, Post-Colonial Careering and the Early History of International Development' in Corinna Unger and Stephan Malinowski (eds), *Modernizing Mission: Approaches to 'Developing' the Non-Western World after 1945 (Journal of Modern European History,* 2009); V. Dimier, 'L'institutionalisation de la Commission européenne (DG Développement) du rôle des leaders dans la construction d'une administration multinationale 1958–1975', *Revue Études internationales,* XXXIV (2003), 401–27.

43. H. Sörgel, *Atlantropa* (Zurich, 1932). See also: D. van Laak, *Weiße Elefanten: Anspruch und Scheitern technischer Großprojekte im 20. Jahrhundert* (Stuttgart, 1999).

44. D. van Laak, *Imperiale Infrastruktur: deutsche Planungen für eine Erschliessung Afrikas 1880 bis 1960* (Paderborn, 2004), pp. 342–63.

45. E. Deschamps, 'Quelle Afrique pour une Europe unie? L'idée d'Eurafrique à l'aube des années trente' in M. Dumoulin (ed.) *Penser l'Europe à l'aube des années trente* (Louvain-la-Neuve, 1995), pp. 95–150; T. Moser, *Europäische Integration, Dekolonisation, Eurafrika: Eine historische Analyse über die Entstehungsbedingungen der Eurafrikanischen Gemeinschaft von der Weltwirtschaftskrise bis zum Jaunde-Vertrag 1929–1963* (Baden-Baden, 2000).

46. A recent collection of essays on this topic reveals striking similarities in European concepts of the self and the enemy 'other', and also concepts of colonial warfare. T. Klein and F. Schumacher (eds), *Kolonialkriege: militärische Gewalt im Zeichen des Imperialismus* (Hamburg, 2006).

47. U. Mücke, 'Agonie einer Kolonialmacht: Spaniens Krieg in Marokko (1921–1927)' in Klein and Schumacher (eds), *Kolonialkriege,* pp. 248–71; A. Mattioli, *Experimentierfeld der Gewalt. Der Abessinienkrieg und seine internationale Bedeutung 1935–1941* (Zurich, 2005); G.B. Künzi, *Italien und der Abessinienkrieg 1935/36. Kolonialkrieg oder Totaler Krieg* (Paderborn, 2005).

48. See the British Foreign Office reports on Algeria, for example in: TNA, FO 371/131682, FO 371/131689, FO 371/131654, FO 371/125913. On knowledge transfers between Britain and France during the wars, see: G. Pervillé, 'Décolonisation "à l'algérienne" et "à la rhodésienne" en Afrique du Nord et en Afrique australe' in C.-R. Angeron and M. Michel (eds), *L'ère des décolonisations, Actes du Colloque d'Aix-en-Provence* (Paris, 1995), pp. 26–37; F. Klose, 'Menschenrechte und koloniale Gewalt: Eine komparative Studie der Dekolonisierungskriege in Kenia und Algerien', PhD theses, LMU Munich (2007); and M. Thomas, *The French North African Crisis: Colonial Breakdown and Anglo-French Relations, 1945–62* (Houndmills, 2000); R. Trinquier, *Guerre, Subversion, Révolution* (Paris, 1968), p. 245; idem, *La Guerre Moderne* (Paris, 1961). See also: J.A. Nagel, *Learning to Eat Soup with a Knife: Counterinsurgency Lessons from Malaya and Vietnam* (Chicago and London, 2005). Recent debates on colonial massacres have raised the question of whether a special type of European 'colonial warrior' developed in the nineteenth and twentieth centuries, but this has yet to be systematically examined. See the ongoing PhD project by Christoph Jens Kamissek (EUI Florence), 'Kolonialkrieger: Eine transnationale Kulturgeschichte imperialer Gewalt im späten 19. und im frühen 20. Jahrhundert'.

49. S. Förster, W.J. Mommsen, R.E. Robinson, *Bismarck, Europe, and Africa: The Berlin Africa Conference 1884–1885 and the Onset of Partition* (Oxford and New York, 1988); D. van Laak, *Über alles in der Welt, Deutscher Imperialismus im 19. und 20. Jahrhundert* (Munich, 2005), p. 68.

50. Dieter Fleck (ed.), *Handbuch des humanitären Völkerrechts in bewaffneten Konflikten* (Munich, 1994).

51. A similar, equally unsuccessful attempt was made by Nazi Germany in 1941. See: K.-M. Mallmann and M. Cüppers, *Halbmond und Hakenkreuz: Das Dritte Reich, die Araber und Palästina* (Darmstadt, 2006).

52. M. Pesek, 'Für Kaiser und Allah: Ostafrikas Muslime im Grossen Krieg für die Zivilisation, 1914–1919', *Bulletin der Schweizerischen Gesellschaften Mittlerer Osten und Islamische Kulturen*, ixx (2005), 9–18.

53. See: C. Koller, *'Von Wilden aller Rassen niedergemetzelt': Die Diskussion um die Verwendung von Kolonialtruppen in Europa zwischen Rassismus, Kolonial- und Militärpolitik (1914–1930)* (Stuttgart, 2001); S. Maß, *Weiße Helden, schwarze Krieger. Zur Geschichte kolonialer Männlichkeit in Deutschland, 1918–1964* (Cologne, 2006); Iris Wigger, *Die 'Schwarze Schmach am Rhein': Rassistische Diskriminierung zwischen Geschlecht, Klasse, Nation und Rasse* (Münster, 2006).

54. S. Dabringhaus, 'Die Boxer: Motivation, Unterstützung und Mobilisierung' in M. Leutner and K. Mühlhahn (eds), *Kolonialkrieg in China: Die Niederschlagung der Boxerbewegung, 1900–1901* (Berlin, 2007), pp. 60–8; T. Klein, 'Straffeldzug zur Verteidigung der Zivilisation: Der "Boxerkrieg" in China (1900–1901)' in Klein and Schumacher (eds), *Kolonialkriege*, pp. 145–81; M. Elvin, *Another History: Essays on China from a European Perspective* (Broadway, 1996).

55. On cultural proximity and exchanges between Britain and Germany before 1914, see: D. Geppert and R. Gerwarth (eds), *Wilhelmine Germany and Edwardian Britain: Essays on Cultural Affinity* (Oxford and New York, 2008).

56. Z. Steiner, *The Lights That Failed* (Oxford and New York, 2005).

57. P. Clavin, 'Europe and the League of Nations' in R. Gerwarth (ed.), *Twisted Paths: Europe 1914–1945* (Oxford and New York, 2007), pp. 325–54.

58. S. Zweig, *Die Welt von Gestern: Erinnerungen eines Europäers*, (Stockholm, 1944).

59. P.M. Lützeler, *Die Schriftsteller und Europa: Von der Romantik bis zur Gegenwart* (Baden-Baden, 1992).

60. Waldemar Pabst Papers, BA Berlin, NY 4035/6, pp. 37–9. On the context of war-induced transnational encounters after 1918, see: R. Gerwarth, 'The Central European Counterrevolution: Paramilitary Violence in Germany, Austria and Hungary after the Great War', *Past & Present*, CC (2008), 175–209.

61. On Russian communities in Prague, see: C. Andreyev and I. Savický, *Russia Abroad: Prague and the Russian Diaspora, 1918–1938* (New Haven and London, 2004).

62. On these themes, see: R. Gerwarth and J. Horne (eds), *Paramilitary Violence after the Great War* (Cambridge, 2010 forthcoming).

63. A. Beevor, *Battle for Spain: The Spanish Civil War 1936–1939* (London, 2006); H. Thomas, *The Spanish Civil War* (London, 1990).

64. G. Orwell, *Homage to Catalonia* (London, 1999); A. Koestler, *Spanish Testament* (London, 1937); André Malraux, *L'Espoir* (Paris, 1937).

65. P. Ahonen et al., *People on the Move: Forced Population Movements in Europe in the Second World War and its Aftermath* (Oxford and New York, 2008).

66. U. Herbert, *A History of Foreign Labour in Germany, 1880–1980* (Ann Arbor, 1990); idem, *Geschichte der Ausländerpolitik in Deutschland: Saisonarbeiter, Zwangsarbeiter, Gastarbeiter, Flüchtlinge* (Munich, 2001); idem, *Fremdarbeiter: Politik und Praxis des 'Ausländer-Einsatzes' in der Kriegswirtschaft des Dritten Reiches* (Berlin, 1985).

67. [Patriotism is the love of one's own. Nationalism is the hatred of others. There is a great fraternity brewing in the world, at least the Germans have given us that] R. Gary, *Education européenne* (Paris, 1945), p. 246.

68. See, for example, P. Parin (2003) 'Lebensroman eines Truthahnjägers' in idem *Die Leidenschaft des Jägers* (Hamburg, 2003).

69. M. Conway and J. Gotovitch (eds), *Europe in Exile: European Exile Communities in Britain, 1940–1945* (Oxford and New York, 2001).

70. The visions for Europe articulated by the German Kreisau circle are particularly well investigated. See: U. Karpen (ed.), *Europas Zukunft: Vorstellungen des Kreisauer Kreises um Helmuth James Graf von Moltke* (Heidelberg, 2005); G. Brakelmann, *Helmuth James von Moltke: 1907–1945: Eine Biographie* (Munich, 2007). On Altiero Spinelli's and Ernesto Rossi's 'Manifesto for a free and united Europe' of 1941, see: the source collection 'The Resistance and the European Idea' on http://www.ena.lu/, consulted on 15 November 2009.

71. E. Ranshofen-Wertheimer, *Victory is Not Enough: The Strategy for a Lasting Peace* (New York, 1942), pp. 167–202.

72. M. Mazower, *Hitler's Empire*, p. 569.

73. F. Chabod, *Storia dell'idea Europa* (Bari, 1961), p. 8.

74. R.-D. Müller, *An der Seite der Wehrmacht: Hitlers ausländische Helfer beim 'Kreuzzug gegen den Bolschewismus' 1941–1945* (Berlin, 2007). See, too: P. Davies, *Dangerous Liaisons: Collaboration and World War II* (Harlow and New York, 2004) and G. Paul, *Die Täter der Shoah: Fanatische Nationalsozialisten oder ganz normale Deutsche* (Göttingen, 2002).

75. Quoted in C. Child, 'The concept of the New Order' in: A. and V. Toynbee (eds), *Survey of International Affairs, 1939–1946: Hitler's Europe* (London, 1954).

76. C. Dieckmann, B. Quinkert and T. Tönsmeyer (eds), *Kooperation und Verbrechen: Formen der 'Kollaboration' im östlichen Europa 1939–1945* (Göttingen, 2003).

77. Oswald Mosley, *My Life* (London, 1968), p. 431.

78. See the chapter contribution by Henning Grunwald in this volume. See, too: C. Kleiser, 'Wer spricht für wen? Repräsentations- und sprachkritische Bemerkungen zur Rede vom "europäischen Gedächtnis", ausgehend von der politischen Essayistik Jorge Semprúns', in *Zeitgeschichte*, xxxv (2008), 123–37.

79. On Berlin after April 1945 as a site of transnational encounter, see the forthcoming book by S.-L. Hoffmann, *Berlin unter Alliierter Besatzung: Lokale Begegnung und globale Politik*.

80. R. Koselleck and M. Jeismann, *Der Politische Totenkult: Kriegerdenkmäler in der Moderne* (Munich, 1994); J.M. Winter, *Remembering War: The Great War between Memory and History in the Twentieth Century* (New Haven and London, 2006); idem, *Sites of Memory, Sites of Mourning: The Great War in European Cultural History* (Cambridge, 1995); O. Janz, *Das symbolische Kapital der Trauer: Nation, Religion und Familie im italienischen Gefallenenkult des Ersten Weltkriegs* (Tübingen, 2008); S. Goebel, *The Great War and Medieval Memory. War, Remembrance and Medievalism in Britain and Germany, 1914–1940* (Cambridge, 2007); M. Cornwall (ed.), *War Commemoration in East-Central Europe after 1918* (Cambridge, 2009).

81. T. Lessing, *Geschichte als Sinngebung des Sinnlosen* (Munich, 1919).

82. http://www.expo-europe.be/

83. E. Barnavi, 'Un musée de l'Europe pour les Européens' in A. Marès (ed.), *La culture et l'Europe: Du rêve européen aux réalités* (Paris, 2006), pp. 53–64.

84. From a German perspective: V. Conze, *Das Europa Der Deutschen: Ideen von Europa in Deutschland zwischen Reichstradition und Westorientierung (1920–1970)* (Munich, 2005).

85. On colonialism and the Holocaust in European memory, see also: D. Diner, *Gegenläufige Gedächtnisse: Über Geltung und Wirkung des Holocaust* (Göttingen, 2007).

86. D. Gosewinkel '"Anti-Europa" in der europäischen Zeitgeschichte?', unpublished manuscript, July 2008. We are grateful to the author for providing us with a copy of the text prior to publication.

# 10

# Modernism, Modernization and Europeanization in West African Architecture, 1944–94

*William Whyte**

In 1944 the architect and author Edwin Maxwell Fry sailed to West Africa where he had been appointed town-planning adviser to the British Governor. A few months later his wife and partner, Jane Drew, joined him. Over the next decade they were to design a series of high-profile and highly important projects. They planned new towns and villages, built the University of Ibadan and the National Museum of Ghana, reshaped the nature of Nigerian and Ghanaian architecture, and wrote a series of influential essays and books on tropical building.[1] Arriving in West Africa, Fry claimed to have found no building industry; 'Nor was there any architecture worthy of the name, nor any background of architecture'.[2] The situation, Fry and Drew concluded, resembled 'that of architecture in the dark ages in Europe'.[3] 'Traditional African building', they argued, was 'unsuitable for the development of a modern civilization'.[4] What was needed was a 'European importation' – and, more specifically, the adoption of European modernist architecture, albeit moderated by the demands of the local climate and customs. This was far from unique; in fact, it was just one part of a wider movement of modernism which found its expression in many other projects.[5] Nonetheless, it is a particularly striking example of an attempt at the self-conscious Europeanization of architecture: the deliberate imposition of 'European' ideas and aesthetics on an African colony.[6]

More strikingly still, however, this ostensibly Europeanized architecture – and the argument that justified it – survived decolonization. Indeed, it can be argued that Nigeria and Ghana, in particular, turned with an ever-increasing enthusiasm to modernist architecture after independence; ironically ensuring that the removal of European political power was memorialized by European architecture.[7] As the architectural historian Henry-Russell Hitchcock put it in 1977: 'while the west was more and more losing political control of Africa and Asia, its cultural influence on those continents did not necessarily decline, indeed as regards architecture it probably increased.'[8] Although Fry and Drew's work became outmoded, the assumptions that had driven their architecture were never superseded. In other words, here was political de-Europeanization accompanied by the intensification of apparently Europeanized architecture.

For many at the time this appeared to be an unintentional – even unconscious – development, growing solely out of the material realities of modernist architecture. And, indeed, that argument could be made. In the years after independence, West Africa lacked the infrastructure, the training, and the industrial base to build the skyscrapers, factories and other modern buildings that modern life appeared to demand. It looked to European-trained architects and European-based construction companies to design and build the new nations. In some respects, that remained the case throughout this period – and even afterwards. As Nnamdi Elleh put it in 1997, 'The only way the nations of Africa can maintain modern architecture is by depending on western countries for the supply of both prefabricated industrial materials and skilled labour.'[9] But it would nonetheless be a mistake to conclude that this absorption of Western methods, materials, and even personnel was unthinking – or that it amounted to a simple Europeanization of practice, although it was attacked as such by critics. Rather more important for our purposes is the motivation for this process, and the terms of the debate that surrounded it.

From the 1940s onwards, modernist architecture was defended – and attacked – in an argument that conflated three key concepts: modernism, modernization and Europeanization. Those who favoured the idioms brought by Maxwell Fry saw in them the incarnation of modernity. Those who opposed them believed them to be the embodiment of colonial, European ideals. Arguably, both attitudes reveal a certain amount of conceptual confusion: after all, modernism does not mean one thing; its meanings are more multiple and ambivalent than either of these arguments allowed. Modernism was not exclusively European, nor was Europe exclusively modernist – or even, it might have been said, wholly modernized.[10] But this fusing of terms is important. In the first place, it reflects a fundamental Europeanization of discourse. Drawing on centuries-old European ideas about architecture, the language and analytical tools with which modern architecture was debated in West Africa were themselves derived from European debates. In that sense – however paradoxical or perverse it may seem – even those who rejected modernism in West Africa as European were nonetheless participating in what can be seen as a European discourse and using ideas about architecture, identity, authenticity and nationalism derived from European thought. In the second place, the widely shared assumption that modern architecture was European is highly revealing: exposing attitudes both to Europe and to Europeanization and suggesting some ways in which the idea of Europe continued to be an influence in West Africa even after direct European control had ceased.

## Architecture and imperialism

This West African example is, of course, just one episode in a much longer-running dispute about the role of architecture in modern societies. Whether imperial architecture, in particular, should reflect the styles of the colonized or the colonizer has always been a vexed question. In 1873, for example, the English architect T. Roger Smith argued that the buildings of the British Raj should make no concessions to Indian idioms. 'As our administration exhibits European justice, order, law, energy, and honour – and that in no hesitating or feeble way', he wrote,

> so our buildings ought to hold up a high standard of European art. They ought to be European both as a rallying point for ourselves, and as raising a distinctive symbol of our presence to be beheld with respect and even with admiration by the natives of the country.[11]

Even at the time he was, of course, opposed by other writers; and in the early years of the twentieth century, when the British began to build New Delhi, a suitably imperial style had still not been created. While the viceroy, Lord Hardinge, wanted 'buildings of a bold and plain character with oriental adaptation', the architect, Edwin Lutyens, was determined to follow European precedent. His collaborator, Herbert Baker, sought something in between. 'It must not be Indian, nor English, nor Roman, but it must be Imperial', he cried – adding, with a flourish, 'Hurrah for despotism!'[12] The result was a fusion of different details: some Buddhist, some Roman, some British, some Hindu, and all extremely idiosyncratic; a hybrid style that was entirely *sui generis*. Nor was this debate about an authentic imperial architecture confined to the British Empire. As Gwendolyn Wright has shown, the French were equally uncertain about what constituted an appropriate colonial style.[13] Likewise, as Brian McLaren has highlighted, Italian imperialism was synonymous with an 'ambivalent modernism', unclear about its relationship with indigenous architecture.[14]

As this suggests, the debate about colonial architecture was never reducible to a simple battle between European and indigenous styles. After all, even apparently 'traditional' architecture was itself a construct – and arguably a European construct at that.[15] Moreover, the argument about architectural style was further complicated by the fact that – from the first – indigenous populations chose to adopt elements of colonial architecture themselves. Elites in particular embraced foreign architecture as a symbol of their own success: proof of their capacity to purchase rare and costly products; a sort of conspicuous construction, as it were. In the mid-eighteenth century, for example, the ruler of Lagos, Oba Akinsemoyin, employed European slave traders to rebuild his palace with bricks and Portuguese-inspired ornamentation.[16] Likewise, in the 1920s and 1930s, high-status families in British-ruled Nigeria embraced

European styles and architectural effects. Concrete, especially, was seen as emblematic of wealth, and cement was sometimes used to plaster mud houses in imitation of European concrete construction.[17]

The advent of modernism added still further complications. This was a style that claimed to be universal. The modern world, modernists argued, was characterized by mass culture, mass production and the machine. New materials and new ways of life called for a new architecture, the architecture of the International Style.[18] Yet, although modernism was intended to be a simple reflection of modernity – not a new style but a new architecture – it was in fact something rather different. It was an architecture that quickly and deliberately developed national and ethnic inflections.[19] In a colonial context, this meant that modernism had a double-edged meaning. Thus, the Italian architect Giovanni Pellegrini, in his 1936 *Manifesto of Colonial Architecture,* advocated modernism because it would overcome 'the undisciplined mental laziness of the [native] inhabitants'.[20] Here modernism was nationalism. By contrast, the Office of Public Instruction in French-ruled Morocco embraced modern architecture because it was, as they wrote, 'a new architecture born in Europe, which accords better with Morocco than with the skies of Paris or Germany'.[21] Here modernism was internationalism. The tensions between these two conceptions of the modern movement in architecture can be found throughout the world.

But, if the nature of architecture in general – and modernism in particular – was contested in the colonial period, then this was nothing compared with the battles that followed decolonization.[22] Was there, asked architects, any room for a European architecture in a de-Europeanized world? Was the International Style sufficiently cosmopolitan to ensure that it could be used by Africans and Asians without fear of deracination? Or, was Europeanization a simple, inescapable fact? Certainly, some have believed this to be the case, with the Bangladeshi-American architect Kazi Khaleed Ashraf asking in 1998, 'is the Europeanization of the planet the true telos of mankind?'[23] The paradoxes of modernism – and the importance of this question – were made plain in the building of Chandigarh, the new capital of the Punjab, erected after Indian independence and partition. This was the first great expression of the newly self-governing nation; designed, as Nehru put it, to be 'symbolic of the freedom of India, unfettered by the traditions of the past (...) an expression of the nation's faith in the future'.[24] Previous styles – both colonial and indigenous – were consequently rejected in favour of an assertive modernism, master-planned by the prophet of the New Architecture, Le Corbusier, and his collaborators, Maxwell Fry and Jane Drew. Corbusier's self-proclaimed ambition of creating a way of building that was 'neither English, nor French, nor American, but Indian' sat uneasily with his apparent belief that Indian art and architecture was hopelessly anachronistic. 'What is the significance of Indian style in the world today', he asked, 'if you accept machines, trousers and democracy?'[25]

Sure enough, the result was what even his disciples recognized to be 'a complex of buildings, which are culturally European'.[26] Yet Nehru himself was pleased, arguing that Chandigarh was a powerful embodiment of the new and modern India: its concrete and its sophisticated planning serving to symbolize the nation's entry into the technocratic world.

## Modernizing West Africa

All these themes – and all these apparent contradictions – were played out in British West Africa in the years after 1944. In Maxwell Fry and Jane Drew, the British rulers of West Africa had chosen two convinced modernists: convinced, that is, that the modern world called for a new and modern architecture. 'There is now an approach to architecture that is common in all countries', declared Fry in 1959.[27] It was that approach which he and Drew were attempting to import into Africa. Nor were individual buildings enough. The architects of the modern movement hoped to solve the wider problems of town planning, and Fry – who had been involved in a radical attempt to replan London in the 1940s – was committed to a programme of urban redevelopment.[28] The assumptions which shaped Fry's work in England were, he claimed, also relevant in Africa. 'The difference between African towns and European is marginal', he argued; 'both are heading in the same direction'.[29] The direction they were pointing was towards a modern – and a modernist – future. Modern architecture and town planning, Fry and Drew believed, would modernize West Africa.[30] 'The west african [*sic*] coast has lain for centuries outside the main currents of world development', Fry proclaimed.[31] Modern architecture would bring it back into line.

As this suggests, the advent of modernism in West Africa was underwritten by an interesting blurring of terms. Fry and Drew's work was, they claimed, 'an instrument of introduction to European life and thought'. But it was also (and this only a couple of sentences later) 'a matter, more precisely, of planning (...) for modern life in the fullest sense of the term'.[32] In these few phrases, the conflation of modernism, modernization and Europeanization is made manifest. Nor does the matter end there. At times, Fry and Drew also conflated modernization with Westernization. But, although the 'West' was sometimes distinguished from 'Europe', this was not usually the case; indeed, the 'West' was often subsumed within 'Europe'.[33] This is a noteworthy concatenation of themes, and one that is frequently repeated by other writers and other architects both then and now.[34] Modernism, Fry seemed to be arguing, is an embodiment of modernity, a cause and consequence of modernization.[35] Europe, he seems to have assumed, is the apotheosis of modernity. Modernization will thus make Africa more like Europe, which is to say, more like the modern world.

Fry and Drew were at times conscious of the problems inherent in this analysis. They often talked of the need to produce an authentically

African modernism and sought to use indigenous motifs and climatically appropriate designs to create a regional variant of the International Style.[36] They also acknowledged more intangible influences too. As Jane Drew put it: 'The west can only really bring western concepts, but the western man designing in Africa, and for Africa, is bound to be affected not only by climatic but psychological factors.'[37] Nonetheless, underlying all this was a unifying – but also potentially destabilizing – set of assumptions. Their fusing of modernism, modernization and Europeanization is, more than anything else, their legacy in West Africa.

This conflation of concepts can be found throughout Fry and Drew's work. Their *Village Housing in the Tropics* (1947), for example, notes the 'wide range of dwelling types' in West Africa: 'from grass and mud huts to elaborate houses in the European style.' Criticizing indigenous planning and vernacular houses alike, they attributed their failings to – among other things – 'poverty' and 'primitive methods of construction'.[38] The solution, as their illustrations showed, was rational replanning and the adoption of modern materials and ways of building. When possible, they hoped to make still more striking statements, as at their high-modernist University College Ibadan. Here, concrete and plate-glass, modern ideas of community and modern means of construction all came together. Jane Drew argued that 'our task as architects was to design this University in Africa and as part of its culture so that Africans would recognize it as theirs'.[39] Yet, she never really specified how this was to be done, and so – aside from some rather stylized references to local art and a series of cleverly designed screens, intended to shield the buildings from the sun – it is hard to see quite how this campus expressed itself as African, let alone as Nigerian. Fry himself had acknowledged the difficulties of reconciling African architecture and 'the technological patterns of the west'.[40] Ibadan perhaps marks a moment in which he found the gap too great to bridge.[41]

The college at Ibadan, declared the Colonial Secretary, Oliver Lyttelton, was to be 'a symbol of enlightenment and a beacon for the future'.[42] Strikingly, this appears to be exactly how it was understood by many. When Ibadan was opened, its buildings were admired by locals not because they were believed to be an alien importation, but because they 'were modern and very impressive'.[43] Indeed, in Wole Soyinka's *roman à clef, Ibadan*, the new buildings are presented as a symbol of the new Nigeria. 'I still prefer the old site', complains one character. 'Your soul is simply conservative, full stop', replies another; to which his friend responds, 'It's like this Independence (...) they're tearing up everything, and wait till you see the replacements.'[44] In this context, modernism is an aspect of modernization and not a part of Europeanization.[45] Or, as one commentator put it in 1960, 'most Nigerians probably prefer the modern, twentieth-century look of Maxwell Fry's buildings. For (...) the young Nigerian cares little about the foreignness of this architecture. On the contrary, when he sees a building in the middle of Ibadan that could equally well be seen in Chicago or Frankfurt, he feels he is catching up with the rest of the world, that Nigeria is no longer an unimportant backwater.'[46] Fry and Drew were in fact surprised to find that their efforts to employ local materials were rejected. Drew recalled that an attempt to construct houses from packed earth misfired: 'we got a backlash. It was political, if concrete was right for Europeans it must be right for them!'[47]

Although Drew was probably unaware of it, concrete had been used in Nigerian architecture long before she tried to wean the public off it. Elites in Ibadan had, of course, been applying it to their houses for a generation.[48] Yet, nonetheless, the concrete she was using was foreign. Modernism was foreign. University College Ibadan – to choose an example – was foreign; indeed, it was European. That was, in a sense, the point.[49] The college itself, complained one American visitor, 'out-oxfords Oxford';[50] while 'the highlight of university life', recalled a discontented member of staff, 'was an annual performance of a Gilbert and Sullivan opera'.[51] The architecture was rather more avant-garde – but it was nonetheless instantly recognizable. As the writer Elspeth Huxley put it:

> These scholastic buildings are arresting because they are original and try to lead into an African architecture that will be permanent and notable. But why is one irresistibly reminded of an international fair, why does one look round for the Palace of Industry, for the statue of a giant and giantess striding to work with a baby and a blunt, unserviceable tool?[52]

Little wonder then, that some European writers greeted Ibadan and the other modernist works with some suspicion. 'Modern architecture is the symbol of the rigidity of mechanized, materialistic, Western culture', wrote the Ibadan academic Ulli Beier.[53] What Africa, what Nigeria, and what Ibadan needed, they argued, was a more authentic, indigenous approach.

These views were also shared by a number of African critics too. At a pragmatic level, the buildings and plans offered by Drew and Fry were often regarded as unserviceable, irrelevant, or simply inappropriate.[54] Ideologically, too, foreign art and architecture was increasingly seen as problematic – hence the establishment in 1959 of the self-consciously nationalistic Zaria School, which sought to evolve an authentic Nigerian art.[55] In the political sphere, there were some rumblings too. The Action Group, a pro-independence movement in West Nigeria, rejected Fry and Drew's work in Ibadan. 'When we come to rule our own country ourselves', they wrote,

> we shall ruthlessly undo everything not to our liking done by the imperialists – we shall even go to the point of turning the whole buildings of University College Ibadan (as it now exists in our minds) into

a leper colony or a lunatic asylum or levelling them to the ground (...)
Every trace of imperialist cultural penetration will be wiped out.[56]

Although this attack does not distinguish between form and function, it
does nonetheless suggest that not everyone was happy. For a significant few,
at least, the Europeanized architecture of Ibadan and elsewhere was simply
wrong.

## Architecture and independence

Independence did not, however, bring with it a rejection of modernism in
architecture. Indeed, quite the reverse was true. Far from seeing modernism as European and therefore inappropriate, postcolonial Ghanaians and
Nigerians appear to have seen modernism as an entirely apposite style to
adopt. The centrepiece for the celebrations of Ghanaian independence
was the National Museum of Ghana: designed by a British architect in the
International Style, and topped off with an aluminium dome which was
made in England and shipped out just in time for the party.[57] It joined
other, expressly modernist buildings – symbols, it was hoped, of the new
and newly independent state. As the *Ashanti Times* put it in 1957: 'One of
the most striking aspects of progress in Ghana in recent years has been the
amount of physical development (...) Everywhere fine modern buildings are
springing up signifying the changing face of the new nation.'[58] In Nigeria,
too, independence was expressed through concrete, steel and plate glass.
The United Africa Company celebrated the birth of a nation in 1960 with a
series of advertisements which symbolized change in Africa with modernist
buildings.[59] Even critics, like the Nigerian writer E.M.W. Bruce, visualized a
future in which the country would be filled with skyscrapers,[60] while 'Femi
Coker celebrated the concrete towers of Ibadan as the 'relics of our age'.[61]

It would obviously be wrong to suggest that newly independent
Nigerians and Ghanaians were mistaken about modernism. This adoption
of a modernist architecture should not be seen as unthinking or unwitting
or as a sort of self-enslavement of the kind attacked by critics like Frantz
Fanon: an attempt to imitate the mores and material culture of the colonizer.[62] Modernism was, after all, more than capable of being reinterpreted
and re-appropriated.[63] That, in many ways, was its great attraction. Kwame
Nkrumah's decision to employ modernism as an expression of Ghana's
independence, for example, did not just reflect a cultural inferiority complex. It was also, as Nnamdi Elleh puts it, 'a deliberate and subversive act':
using the colonists' own architecture to demonstrate Ghana's freedom from
colonialism.[64] Modernism likewise possessed the clear virtue of belonging
to no one ethnic group within either country. It could be seen as a suitably neutral style for the new nation, rather as English was adopted as a
*lingua franca* by many multi-ethnic, multi-lingual, post-colonial nations.[65]

Modernist architecture was thus not adopted ignorantly or foolishly.[66] This was a conscious – and an informed – choice of architectural idiom.

Two forces above all propelled people towards the architecture imported by Fry and Drew. In the first place, even after independence, the association between modernism and modernization remained unchallenged. The Lagos *Daily Times* illustrated 'PROGRESS IN GHANA TODAY' with a series of pictures of modernist buildings.[67] Theophilus Adelodun Okin, in his *The Urbanized Nigerian* (1968) likewise observed that Africa was 'a continent in which the magic word *progress* is encountered everywhere – spoken or represented in terms of physical environment.' This meant a turn towards the International Style. Indeed, the book he recommended for further reading on this topic was Fry and Drew's text on tropical housing. 'Since it is not very dignifying to build in the traditional way, with cheap traditional materials,' Okin concluded, 'many of the elite group are reluctant to build "outdated" houses.'[68]

This association with the elite is likewise worth noting. Indeed, it was the second force pushing the newly independent states of West Africa towards modernism. Not only, as Hess has suggested, did the use of modernist architecture emphasize the importance of the state.[69] This Europeanized way of building was also strongly associated with the governing elite. Just as a colonial elite had built modernist buildings for themselves, so a post-colonial elite – often educated in Europe or by Europeans – chose to inhabit equally modern structures. Naturally, this was not what Fry and Drew had intended. For them, modernism was simply modern. It was certainly not elitist – indeed, it was meant to be egalitarian and progressive.[70] But, as Toyin Falola observes, in Nigeria at least:

> Many buildings became prominent parts of the landscape due to their architectural uniqueness, isolated location, or the significance of their functions. As most of the new buildings were either offices or occupied by Europeans or senior Nigerian bureaucrats, they quickly became symbols of power, with a positive meaning to Nigerians aspiring to power or influence, who began to hope for an opportunity to occupy such buildings and enjoy the luxury and power associated with them.[71]

Independence brought just such an opportunity – and it was one that the New Nigerian Elite seized on with alacrity. The result was, in Hugh and Mabel Smythe's words, that 'an increasing number of residences or other buildings follow European, rather than indigenous architecture'.[72]

The modernist embrace did not, of course, appeal to everyone. The disjunction of a newly independent African nation which continued to reveal its cultural dependence on Europe was too much for some. Although he welcomed Fry and Drew's work as a brave attempt to create an authentic African approach to building, Udo Kulturmann was shocked by much of the other contemporary architecture on the continent. 'The valid tradition of the African must be fundamentally differentiated from European culture and revived as such', he wrote.[73] More specifically, writing in 1964, Percy Mark condemned post-independence Nigerian architecture. 'All the towns I have seen in this part of the world are the most terrible (...) heart-breaking and depressing, jumble of European architectural clichés gone wild.'[74] Likewise, despite his utopian vision of a skyscraper-filled Nigeria, E.M.W. Bruce condemned foreign architects and foreign buildings as 'a threat to our own indigenous architecture which they have now almost completely replaced.' He called for 'houses of the people, for the people, by the people.' 'We (...) in Nigeria', he went on, 'can train our own architects to use what local materials and building methods are available and bring back our tradition and culture which are fast fading into the limbs of "Western Civilization"'.[75] As late as 1969 – nine years after independence – commentators were still complaining that 'Nigerian architects have no roots in the soil', that 'they speak and design in a foreign language'.[76] It was a debate that was set to continue.

## Building the nation: The case of Abuja

The search for a uniquely Nigerian architecture was the consequence of the all-consuming search for a broader, deeper, more authentically Nigerian identity.[77] As Toyin Falola and Matthew Heaton put it: 'The underlying cause of all the problems that Nigeria has experienced in the 1960s and has experienced since then is (...) "the national question." What is Nigeria? Who are Nigerians? How does a country go about developing a meaningful national identity?'[78] Civil war in the 1960s, corruption in the 1970s, and political instability in the 1980s only added further salience to this search.[79] Within that context, the decision to found a new federal capital in the geographical centre of the country represented an opportunity to create a true heart for the new nation – a symbol of unity and Nigerian identity. Nevertheless, this new capital could not escape older assumptions about the relationship between architecture and the proper path to modern life. As such, the foundation of Abuja in 1981 is an important test case of the ways in which modernism, modernization, and Europeanization continued to influence West African architecture.

The building of Abuja was intended to help create a self-consciously Nigerian architecture.[80] And, indeed, the official rhetoric which surrounded this project suggested that just such an effort had been made.[81] This was, declared the architect John Eke Abandy, 'our symbol of what a perfect Nigerian city would look like'.[82] The reality was, however, that a foreign architect, working within a recognizably modernist idiom, produced a plan which owed very little to indigenous traditions.[83] True enough, the architect was not European – he was Japanese. It was true too that Nigerian modernism had changed and developed and was no longer as beholden to strictly

European models.[84] It was also true that Abuja owed as much to Washington DC and Tokyo as it did to any European city.[85] In that sense, at least, this was not simple Europeanization. Nevertheless, what is striking is the extent to which this process was conceived of as a battle between Nigerian and European ideals. The creation of Abuja thus involves many of the same issues as the construction of Ibadan University, the National Museum of Ghana, and the housing developments which were criticized in the 1960s. As a result, it reflects precisely the same dilemmas that were experienced a generation before.

In the first place, it is clear that the use of foreign architects and foreign designs produced buildings which were widely regarded as European in inspiration.[86] As an anonymous – presumably British – architect complained in 1985:

A British new town authority provided plans and housetypes for use in Abuja, and undertook detailed road and house layouts. And here in the middle of the African landscape are built British new town row housing and four and five-storey tenement blocks. Seemingly no attempt has been made to suit the housing to African needs and the Nigerian climate.[87]

In the second place, the building of Abuja reveals the ways in which older associations between modern architecture, the elite, and the state were perpetuated in the 1980s. As Roland Depret complained in 1983, all across Africa the 'European model remains alive, despite efforts on behalf of cultural decolonization, and a rise on the social ladder is most often reflected by construction of an upper floor (apartments), or by giving up the courtyard house for a villa.'[88] Nigeria witnessed this process in microcosm. As the administrator of Abuja, Major A.A.U. Kana, put it in 1986, the result was that across the country and even in the capital, foreign architecture predominated in great public projects. In Lagos, he wrote, 'Two of our monumental buildings, the National Theatre and the Murtala Muhammed Airport are exact replicas of buildings in Europe. A look round Abuja should reveal more.'[89] Thirdly – and still more importantly – Abuja expresses the way in which modernism and modernization continued to be confused. Modernism, argued the president of the Nigerian Institute of Architects in 1985, was inevitable. 'We cannot design buildings in the traditional form of mud huts', he argued, 'since functions performed within our physical environment today are far removed from those performed by our ancestors in their mud-huts and thatched roofs.'[90] High-rise, high-tech, concrete tower-blocks were, he argued, the modern way forward.

So it was that the conflation of modernism, modernization, and Europeanization continued. This was true for those who praised the city – and for those who saw it as another example of Nigeria's failure to develop its own unique way of building. Abuja's supporters saw it as modern, and equated modernity with modernism. Its opponents saw it as modernist and equated that with Europe. More precisely, they traced in this adopted architecture evidence of inauthenticity, of an abandonment of Nigerian and African ideals. Complaining about the cultural life of Nigeria, Wole Soyinka observed, 'in a country into which even snow-tires are imported, what can one expect? Our architectural program is easily the area of our greatest failure in terms of cultural enracination.'[91] Fortune Ebie, in a review of recent building in 1982, was still more precise: 'many designs strike me as alien copies of what is available in Europe,' he wrote; 'I would like to see a design bearing the print of a truly Nigerian architecture.'[92] These general criticisms – and there were many – could also be specifically applied to Abuja. As Major Kama put it, drawing on his experience of the capital: 'Granted that the education of our Architects is western, our way of life and activities are fashioned after Western Models, it is still unpardonable that we have imbibed European building practice hook, line and sinker.'[93] The continuity of this critique – which manages to subsume 'the West' within 'Europe' and which stretches from before independence and into the 1990s – is surely significant.

## Conclusion

So what was going on? Was this continuing dependence on foreign architects and foreign architectural models a product of West Africa's cultural or material poverty? Was it the result of a cultural inferiority complex? Was it neo-colonial? Certainly, some writers have assumed so. They have seen modernism as a form of 'cultural colonialism',[94] or even as 'brainwashing'.[95] 'In the adoption of modernism,' writes Michele Lamprakos, 'the image of the colonizer has become the self-image of the colonized.'[96] Nigerians in the 1980s and 1990s shared these doubts. 'Nigerian Society', wrote V.O. Bolarin in 1986, 'has for some decades believed that anything foreign was better than whatever was available in Nigeria.'[97] 'All of us, including myself,' wrote Chief J.G.O. Adegbite in 1991, 'are western trained, we are therefore so western-ized in our ideas and ways of life to the detriment of our good cultural and sociological background, heritage, beliefs and practices.'[98] 'Our architects', declared Isidore C. Ezema, three years later, 'should make more attempts at drawing from our heritage rather than aping what others have worked hard to establish.'[99]

No doubt there is something in this. After all, the new nations of West Africa were forced to rely on imported expertise and on locals who had had a foreign education.[100] They had to use imported materials and equipment too – and this clearly had an impact. As Bolarin put it, to produce a true Nigerian architecture one would need 'a Nigerian Crane, Excavator, tractor, Crawler tractors with direct drive, wheel tractors, Bulldozers, Scrapers, Truck and Wagons, pumping equipment, Crushers concrete mixers etc.'[101]

The problem of identifying an authentically 'Nigerian', 'Ghanaian', or 'African' architecture should also not be ignored; after all, this was a continent wracked with religious, regional and ethnic divisions. These were countries ruled by small elites who adopted the architecture of their previous colonial rulers and consequently perpetuated colonial attitudes and colonial architectures. The continuing economic power and cultural importance of Europe – the place which educated so many of the elite, including its architects – should not be dismissed.

Yet there is also more to it than that. For one thing, it is evident that the meanings of modernism did in fact change. What had been imperial architecture was taken up as a truly national style. What had been imposed by colonial rulers was willingly adopted by newly-freed nations. Across British West Africa, modernism was not always understood as European or seen as explicitly foreign. Rather, it could be interpreted as an expression of modernity; as both a cause and a consequence of modernization. Explicitly under the empire, and implicitly thereafter, Europe was the embodiment of modernity, the benchmark against which West Africa's modernization could be judged. The result was a Europeanized, hybridized architecture. In the 1950s, Elspeth Huxley saw in the new and modern Nigerian Parliament a combination of the 'Festival of Britain crossed with a Beau Geste Fort'.[102] This was apparently how the nation hoped to express its modern identity. Thirty years later, Abuja was founded to 'create a new cultural identity which would be truly Nigerian in character', and was celebrated by its admirers for what one called 'its beauty and modernism'.[103] Truly Nigerian, truly modern, truly beautiful: what to some was a sell-out was to others entirely appropriate.

This discourse drew on ideas of progress and of modernity which had their origin in Europe; it was in that sense the aesthetic equivalent of the universal acceptance of modernization theory that James Ferguson found in his ethnographic study of the Zambian Copperbelt. There, the notion of 'modernization' had become normative: 'Listening to the difference between "the village" and "the town", or "African" tradition versus "European" modernity', he wrote, 'I often had the unsettling sense that I was listening to an out-of-date sociology textbook.'[104] The same might be said of architectural debate in Nigeria or Ghana from the 1950s onwards. Still more significantly, the counter-discourse, which sought to substitute an 'authentic', 'indigenous' architecture for an 'inauthentic', 'European' modernism, also drew on similar assumptions. In the years after independence, critics of modernism argued that a new indigenous architecture must emerge from traditional buildings; that it must be an authentic regional style; that it must merge 'the newly activated African tradition (...) and the latest technical and construction methods from abroad'.[105] In the 1980s and 1990s a similar cry went up. Ironically, of course, this was exactly what Fry and Drew had argued that they were doing: using modern architecture to create 'a dialect of internationalism'.[106]

As this suggests, such a search was not confined to Nigeria and Ghana. For, as Gwendolyn Wright has shown, the rulers of Francophone Africa before and after independence were also similarly preoccupied.[107] In fact, it was a quest that had preoccupied European architects for more than two hundred years. It underwrote the Gothic Revival of the nineteenth century, and sustained the modern movement of the twentieth.[108] The Romantic nationalism of the late-nineteenth century was, perhaps, its greatest monument.[109] The assumption that each age would produce its own architecture, and that each nation would develop its own particular approach, drove architectural debates and architectural development alike.[110] As the hugely influential historian and advocate of the modern movement, Nikolaus Pevsner put it: 'There is the spirit of the age, and there is national character. The existence of neither can be denied, however averse one may be to be generalizations.'[111] Thus the debate in West Africa was just a continuation of a much longer argument – and an argument that had its origins in Europe.

Nor was this debate about culture and authenticity restricted to architecture. The parallels with Kwame Anthony Appiah's exploration of African literature, for example, are self-evident.[112] The search for authenticity inspired debates about books and paintings as well as buildings and plans. Arguments about the architecture of Nigeria and Ghana do, however, offer a particularly helpful context for conceptualizing the problem of Europeanization. They reveal European and African architects, intellectuals, and politicians engaged in a debate about the nature of Africa and African nationalism, which was also a debate about Europe – and the conclusions they reached are striking. They suggest, for example, that 'Europe' and the 'West' were seen as synonymous. Despite the Cold War, there are absolutely no references in these texts to the USSR or Eastern Europe, or to any alternative, Soviet path to modernity or modern architecture. Despite the importance of America – in architectural, economic, and political terms – Europe continued to be seen as the benchmark of modernity and the source of modern architecture. Above all, despite 50 years of debate, the fundamental confusion of modernism, modernization, and Europeanization was never overcome.

In that sense, the important thing about the advent and development of modern architecture in West Africa is not that it represents the Europeanization of indigenous building practices and styles. It did not in any meaningful sense. Rather, it is the fact that the discourse about architecture rested upon a particular image of Europe and drew on European concepts and European discourses to articulate it. For some, modernism was appropriate because it embodied modernity, a modernity which was itself exemplified in European culture. For others, modernism was highly problematic because modernism equated with Europeanization. Modernism's proponents included those who wished to Europeanize

Africa and those who sought simply to modernize Africa. Modernism's opponents included those who wished to modernize Africa but sought to de-Europeanize it. What they shared was a common frame of reference: a common conflation of modernism, modernization, and Europeanization; and a common desire to construct an authentically African, Ghanaian, or Nigerian architecture. For more than 50 years, then, West Africans were engaged in a debate about Europeanization. This was a Europeanization of discourse which was at once far more powerful and more pervasive than the architecture that was ostensibly its subject.

## Notes

\* I am deeply grateful to participants in a series of workshops for their comments on previous versions of this essay. Zoë Waxman likewise kindly offered improvements, while Rhodri Windsor Liscombe generously shared his research with me. I must also acknowledge the History Faculty of the University of Oxford which paid for a research trip to West Africa.

1. Rhodri Windsor Liscombe, 'Modernism in Late-Imperial British West Africa: The work of Maxwell Fry and Jane Drew, 1946–1956', *Journal of the Society of Architectural Historians* LXV (2006), 188–215.

2. Maxwell Fry, 'European Importation', *Progressive Architecture*, December 1962, pp. 83–6, p. 84.

3. Maxwell Fry and Jane Drew, *Tropical Architecture in the Humid Zone* (London, 1956), p. 20.

4. Fry, 'European Importation', pp. 80–2. Although see also, Maxwell Fry, *Art in a Machine Age: A Critique of Contemporary Life through the Medium of Architecture* (London, 1969), pp. 141–2; Maxwell Fry and Jane Drew, 'Colonial Housing and Planning', *AA Journal*, November 1946, pp. 53–61, 57.

5. See, for example, Nobuyuki Ogura, 'Ernst May and Modern Architecture in East Africa', in ArchiAfrika, *Modern Architecture in East Africa around Independence* (Dar-Es-Salaam, 2005), pp. 81–8; *Architect and Building News* 224 (1963), pp. 953–8.

6. Hannah Le Roux, 'Modern Architecture in Post-Colonial Ghana and Nigeria', *Architectural History* XLVII (2004), 361–92.

7. Janet Berry Hess, 'Imagining Architecture: the structure of nationalism in Accra, Ghana', *Africa Today* XLVII (2000), 35–8.

8. H.-R. Hitchcock, *Architecture: Nineteenth and Twentieth Centuries* (4th ed.; Harmondsworth, 1977), p. 2.

9. Nnamdi Elleh, *African Architecture: Evolution and Transformation* (New York, 1997), p. 244.

10. Gwendolyn Wright, 'The Ambiguous Modernisms of African Cities', in Okwui Enwezor (ed.), *The Short Century: Independence and Liberation Movements in Africa, 1945–1994* (Munich, 2001), pp. 225–33. More generally, see Sarah Williams Goldhagen, 'Something to Talk About: Modernism, discourse, style', *Journal of the Society of Architectural Historians* LXV (2005), 144–67.

11. Quoted in Thomas R. Metcalfe, *An Imperial Vision: Indian Architecture and Britain's Raj* (London and Boston, 1989), p. 1.

12. Christopher Hussey, *The Life of Sir Edwin Lutyens* (1950; Woodbridge, 1989), pp. 247, 265–6, 277.

13. Gwendolyn Wright, *The Politics of Design in French Colonial Urbanism* (Chicago and London, 1991).
14. Brian McLaren, *Architecture and Tourism in Italian Colonial Libya: An Ambivalent Modernism* (Seattle and London, 2006).
15. See, for example, Jon Lang, Madhavi Desai and Miki Desai, *Architecture and Independence: The Search for Identity – India 1880–1980* (New Delhi, 1997). More particularly, see Gani Odutokun, 'Art in Nigeria since Independence', in Peter P. Ekeh and Garba Ashiwaju (eds), *Nigeria Since Independence: The First 25 Years, Vol. vii: Culture* (Ibadan, 1989), pp. 139–51, pp. 142–3.
16. B.A. Agiri, 'Architecture as a Source of Lagos History', in Ade Defuye, Babatunde Agiri and Jide Osuntokun (eds), *History of the Peoples of Lagos* (Lagos, 1987), pp. 341–50, p. 345.
17. Olufunke Adeboye, 'Elite Lifestyle and Consumption in Colonial Ibadan', in Adeboyo Oyebade (ed.), *The Foundations of Nigeria: Essays in Honour of Toyin Falola* (Trenton, NJ, and Asmara, 2003), pp. 281–303, pp. 286–7.
18. Le Corbusier, *Vers une Architecture* (Paris, 1923); Henry-Russell Hitchcock and Philip Johnson, *The International Style* (1932; London and New York, 1995).
19. See, for example, Elizabeth Darling, *Re-Forming Britain: Narratives of Modernity before Reconstruction* (London, 2007) and Alan Powers, *Britain: Modern Architectures in History* (London, 2007). See also Alona Nitzan-Shiftan, 'Contested Zionism–Alternative Modernism: Erich Mendelsohn and the Tel Aviv Chug in Mandate Palestine', *Architectural History* xxxix (1996), 147–80.
20. Krystyne von Henneberg, 'Imperial Uncertainties: Architectural syncretism and improvisation in Fascist Colonial Libya', *Journal of Contemporary History* xxxi (1996), 373–95, 373.
21. Wright, *Politics of Design*, p. 129.
22. Generally, see Lawrence J. Vale, *Architecture, Power, and National Identity* (New Haven and London, 1992).
23. Kazi Khaleed Ashraf, 'Reincarnations and Independence: The modern architecture of South Asia', in Kazi Khaleed Ashraf and James Balluardo (eds), *An Architecture of Independence: The Making of Modern South Asia* (New York, 1998), pp. 23–9, p. 23.
24. Quoted in Ravi Kalia, *Chandigarh: The Making of an Indian city* (1987; New Delhi, 1999); p. 21.
25. Ibid., pp. 163 and 105.
26. Alison and Peter Smithson, 'The Function of Architecture in Cultures-in-Change', *Architectural Design* xxx (1960), 149–50.
27. London, Royal Institute of British Architects (RIBA) Archives, Uncat. Fry Texts, 'Chandigarh Architecture' (18 August 1959).
28. William Whyte, 'MARS group (*act.* 1933–1957)', *Oxford Dictionary of National Biography* (accessed 11 December 2009).
29. RIBA, Uncat. Fry Texts, untitled talk (n.d., 1960s?), pp. 1, 2–3.
30. See also T.C. McCaskie, *Asante Identities: History and Modernity in an African Village, 1850–1950* (Edinburgh, 2000), pp. 205–7.
31. RIBA, F&D/1/2, Chandigarh articles and film scripts, Maxwell Fry, 'The Gold Coast School Building Programme' (n.d.), p. 1.
32. Maxwell Fry, 'West Africa', in J.M. Richards (ed.), *New Buildings in the Commonwealth* (London, 1961), pp. 103–28, p. 103.
33. For a rare exception, see Jane B. Drew, 'Introduction', *Architectural Design* xxv (1955), 137–9. It is worth noting that in this case, Drew self-consciously included

America within her understanding of the 'West', comparing the climate and society of West Africa to California rather than Europe.

34. See, for example, Hess, 'Imagining Architecture', p. 45, where modernity and modernism are similarly conflated.
35. Fry, 'European Importation', p. 84.
36. Fry, 'West Africa', p. 104.
37. Drew, 'Introduction', p. 139.
38. Jane Drew and Maxwell Fry, *Village Housing in the Tropics* (London, 1947), p. 23.
39. RIBA, F&D/4/5, Jane Drew's Notes on Hospital Design, undated lecture on university design.
40. Fry, *Art in a Machine Age*, p. 142.
41. See Liscombe, 'Modernism in Late-Imperial British West Africa', for a discussion of this theme.
42. [Lagos] *Daily Times*, 20 November 1952, p. 5.
43. Olumuyiwa Awe, 'Ibadan: recollections and reflections', in Tekena N. Tamuno (ed.), *Ibadan Voices: Ibadan University in Transition* (Ibadan, 1981), pp. 67–102, p. 78.
44. Wole Soyinka, *Ibadan: The Penkelemes Year – A Memoir, 1946–65* (London, 1994), p. 3.
45. Barnabus Nawangwe, 'Architectural Modernism in Post-Independence Uganda', in *Modern Architecture in East Africa*, pp. 149–58.
46. Ulli Beier, *Art in Nigeria, 1960* (Cambridge, 1960), p. 18.
47. RIBA, Jane Drew Autobiography, p. 74.
48. Adeboye, 'Elite Lifestyle and Consumption in Colonial Ibadan', pp. 286–7.
49. Lord Hailey, *An African Survey Revisited 1956* (London, 1957), p. 1223.
50. Clive S. Gray (ed.), *Inside Independent Nigeria: The Diaries of Wolfgang Stolper, 1960–62* (Aldershot, 2003), p. 8.
51. Ulli Beier, 'A Moment of Hope: Cultural developments in Nigeria before the First Military Coup', in Okwui Enwezor (ed.), *The Short Century: Independence and Liberation Movements in Africa, 1945–1994* (Munich, 2001), pp. 45–9, p. 46.
52. Elspeth Huxley, *Four Guineas: A Journey through West Africa* (London, 1954), p. 136.
53. Beier, *Art in Nigeria*, p. 19.
54. Generally, see: Toyin Falola, *Development Planning and Decolonization in Nigeria* (Gainesville, 1995), pp. 158–9.
55. Chike Dike, 'Nigerian Art past, present, and future', in John Sheerhan (ed.), *Celebrate! Nigerian Art for the Commonwealth* (Abuja, 2003), pp. 28–44, p. 36.
56. *Nigerian Tribune*, 13 October 1952, p. 4.
57. Mark Crinson, *Modern Architecture and the End of Empire* (Aldershot, 2003), pp. 149–53.
58. *Ashanti Times*, 6 March 1957, p. 1.
59. See, for example, *West Africa*, 9 April 1960, p. 419; 10 September 1960, p. 1039.
60. E.M.W. Bruce, 'Nineteen Sixty-Nine (1)', *Nigerian Tribune* 31 August 1959, p. 5.
61. 'Femi Coker, 'Towers of the West: Relics of our age', *Nigerian Tribune*, 1 September 1960, p. 10.
62. Fritz Fanon, *Black Skin, White Masks* (trans. Charles Lam Markmann; 1967: London, 1986).
63. William Whyte, 'How do Buildings Mean? Some issues of interpretation in the history of architecture', *History and Theory* XLV (2006), 153–77.
64. Nnamdi Elleh, 'Architecture and Modernism in Africa, 1945–1994', in Enwezor (ed.), *The Short Century*, pp. 234–45, p. 237.

65. Hess, 'Imagining Architecture', p. 45.
66. Though cf. Janet Berry Hess, *Art and Architecture in Post-colonial Africa* (Jefferson NC and London, 2006), p. 1.
67. *Daily Times*, 1 July 1960, pp. 8–9.
68. Theophilus Adelodun Okin, *The Urbanized Nigerian: An Examination of the African and His New Environment* (New York, 1968), pp. 17, 34.
69. Hess, 'Imagining Architecture', p. 45.
70. Fry, 'European Importation'.
71. Falola, *Development Planning*, p. 79.
72. Hugh H. Smythe and Mabel M. Smythe, *The New Nigerian Elite* (Stanford, 1960), p. 59.
73. Udo Kultermann, *New Directions in African Architecture* (trans. John Maas; London, 1969), p. 12. See also pp. 25–8.
74. Percy Mark, 'Thoughts on Building in Tropical Africa', *West African Builder and Architect* IV (May–June 1964), 52–3, 52.
75. E.M.W. Bruce, 'New Nigerian Architecture', [Ibadan] *Nigerian Tribune*, 7 August 1959, p. 2.
76. Mr Adeolu, quoted in *West African Builder and Architect* 7:2 (July–August 1967), p. 97.
77. See Abubakar Momoh and Said Adejumobi (eds), *The National Question in Nigeria: Comparative Perspectives* (Aldershot, 2002).
78. Toyin Falola and Matthew M. Heaton, *A History of Nigeria* (Cambridge, 2008), p. 158.
79. Adebayo Oyebade, 'Reluctant Democracy: The state, the opposition, and the crisis of political transition, 1985–1993', in Adebayo Oyebade (ed.), *The Transformation of Nigeria* (Trenton NJ and Asmara, 2002), pp. 137–66.
80. Louis C. Umeh, 'The Building of a New Capital City: The Abuja experience', in Robert W. Taylor (ed.), *Urban Development in Nigeria* (Aldershot, 1993), pp. 215–28. See also Margaret Peil, 'How Abuja Measures Up', *West Africa* 3483 (21 May 1984), pp. 1066–7.
81. Vale, *Architecture, Power, and National Identity*, pp. 134, 145.
82. John Eke Abandy, 'Between Cup and Lip', *N[igerian] I[nstitute of] A[rchitects] Journal* 1.1 (May 1981), p. 18.
83. Elleh, *African Architecture,* pp. 318–28.
84. These changes in Nigerian modernism are analysed – and attacked – in Ola Uduku, 'Modernist Architecture and "The Tropical" in West Africa: The tropical architecture movement in West Africa, 1948–1970', *Habitat International* XXX (2006), 396–411.
85. Elleh, 'Architecture and Modernism', p. 241.
86. Ted Stevens, 'Abuja: Nigeria's new capital gets under way', *RIBA Journal* LXXXIX (July 1982), 464–8.
87. 'An Architect', 'Capital Folly of Nigeria', *Architects' Journal* CLXXXII (20 November 1985), 69–78, 71.
88. Roland Depret, 'The Assimilation of Traditional Practices in Contemporary Architecture', in Brian Brace Taylor (ed.), *Reading the Contemporary African City* (Singapore, 1983), pp. 60–72, p. 65.
89. A.A.U. Kana, 'A Critque of Architectural Practice in Nigeria', *NIA Journal* 2.2 (April–June 1986), pp. 41–44, p. 41.
90. Olufemi Majekodunmi, 'The Architectural Profession in Nigeria Today', *NIA Journal* 2.1 (July–September 1985), pp. 39–40, p. 39.

91. Wole Soyinka, 'Twice Bitten: The fate of Africa's culture producers', in Olusegun Obasanjo and Hans d'Orville (eds), *Challenges of Leadership in African Development* (New York, 1990), pp. 153–69, p. 155.
92. Fortune Ebie, 'Non-Optimal Utilization of Indigenous Manpower in Architecture', *NIA Journal* I (March 1982), 7–9, 8.
93. Kama, 'A Critique of Architectural Practice in Nigeria', p. 42.
94. A.D. King, 'Exporting Planning: The colonial and neo-colonial experience', in Gordon E. Cherry (ed.), *Shaping an Urban World* (London, 1980), pp. 203–26.
95. William J.R. Curtis, *Modern Architecture since 1900* (London, 1996), p. 567.
96. Michele Lamprakos, 'Le Corbusier and Algiers: The *Plan Obus* as colonial urbanism', in Nezer AlSayyad (ed.), *Forms of Dominance: On the Architecture and Urbanism of the Colonial Enterprise* (Aldershot, 1992), pp. 183–210, p. 206.
97. V.O. Bolarin, 'Indigenous Architecture: The Nigerian experience', *NIA Journal* II (April–June 1986), 29–30, 29.
98. J.G.O. Adgebite, 'The Need for the Development of Indigenous Architecture in Nigeria', *NIA Journal* VI (April–June 1991), 27–32, 28.
99. Isidore C. Ezema, 'The Classical Revival in Architecture: Invigorating or debilitating in Nigeria?', *NIA Journal* VIII (January–June 1993), 4–12, 9.
100. On this in general, see Brian Brace Taylor, 'Demythologizing Colonial Architecture', *Mimar* XIII (1984), 16–25.
101. Bolarin, 'Indigenous Architecture: The Nigerian experience', p. 30.
102. Huxley, *Four Guineas*, p. 169.
103. Aminu Olusola, *Abuja: Nigeria's New Capital* (Abuja, 1993), p. 128.
104. James Ferguson, *Expectations of Modernity: Myths and Meanings of Urban Life on the Zambian Copperbelt* (Berkeley, 1999), p. 85.
105. Kultermann, *New Directions*, p. 12. See also, William J.R. Curtis, 'Towards an Authentic Regionalism', *Mimar* XIX (1986), 24–31.
106. Fry, 'West Africa', p. 104.
107. Wright, *Politics of Design* and 'Ambiguous Modernism'.
108. Georg Germann, *The Gothic Revival in Europe and Britain: Sources, Influences, and Ideas* (trans. Gerald Onn; London, 1972); Panayotis Tournikiotis, *The Historiography of Modern Architecture* (Cambridge, MA and London, 1999).
109. Rosalind P. Blakesley, *The Arts and Crafts Movement* (London, 2006) is a good introduction to this theme. See also Barbara Miller Lane, *National Romanticism and Modern Architecture in Germany and the Scandinavian Countries* (Cambridge, 2000).
110. William Whyte, 'The Englishness of English Architecture: Modernism and the making of a national International Style', *Journal of British Studies* (forthcoming).
111. Nikolaus Pevsner, *The Englishness of English Art* (London, 1956), p. 16.
112. Kwame Anthony Appiah, *In My Father's House: Africa in the Philosophy of Culture* (London, 1992), pp. 95–8.

# 11
## 'Die Briten kommen'. British Beat and the Conquest of Europe in the 1960s

*John Davis**

For centuries high culture has transcended national boundaries. During the twentieth century, and especially in the post-war period, popular culture has also become transnational. Comparative studies of popular culture remain, though, relatively rare, and much of what has been produced is concerned with cinema, as an element in the supposed Americanization of Western Europe. This emphasis is potentially misleading. Cinema is characterized by a particular structure dictated by the heavy capital requirements of the industry, which is consequently dominated by a handful of major companies operating from one world centre. Even independent films require finance at a level beyond the reach of amateurs; there is consequently no significant 'garage' sector in film, and cinema's influence is inevitably a 'top-down' one. Popular music is different. The development of the international record industry from the 1960s has been accompanied by the proliferation of amateur performers at every level of competence. The multinational producers who run the industry have always sought – and needed – to draw upon this pool of potential. As a result the music market has always been partly shaped by the artistic preference of performers and the waves of consumer fashion – forces which were in fact interlinked. This was particularly true at the time that the industry first became genuinely transnational in the 1960s. What follows is an attempt, drawing upon a large body of recent studies of the beat era in continental Europe, to examine the way in which these forces shaped the process of cultural transfer during the years of the beat revolution, when Europe for the first time acquired a shared pop music language. This chapter argues that the process of cultural Europeanization described here was one determined above all by the tastes of performers and consumers. It was driven by a spirit of emulation, strong enough to destroy national cultural and linguistic barriers. The result was that the continent's music scene was comprehensively conquered by the British pioneers, but the rest of Europe submitted willingly and deliberately: this was no 'Coca-colonization' or cultural imperialism.

European record industries had responded to first-wave American rock'n'roll by attempting to produce local substitutes. The British, French and German variants – Cliff Richard, Johnny Hallyday, Peter Kraus – remain relatively familiar, but there was also Pim Maas, 'RCA's official Dutch Elvis',[1] a Danish Elvis, Ib Jensen,[2] and at least two contenders for the Norwegian title – Per-Elvis Granberg and 'The Scandinavian King', Roald Stensby.[3] Figures such as Hallyday and Kraus made considerable reputations by bringing rock'n'roll standards to local audiences, translated into the local tongue. In France in particular the popular music industry was dominated in the early 1960s by the so-called *yé-yés*, who devoted themselves to bringing Anglo-Saxon music to France in translation.[4] The attempt succeeded to the extent that sales of classic rock – Elvis excepted – were limited in continental Europe,[5] but it was open to the criticism that what was produced in Europe was anodyne, inauthentic and commercially driven. As a result, the genuine article – original US rock'n'roll – gained a kind of samizdat status on the continent, sought out by aficionados who hunted down imported discs or trekked out to American bases to hear it.[6] Those who found the real thing and were galvanized by it became intensely critical of local imitations.

The British situation was different. The absence of a language barrier diminished the scope for any British *yé-yé* movement. The usual obstacles were produced by the conservative forces of the BBC and the record industry, but Chuck Berry, Eddie Cochran, Buddy Holly, Little Richard, Gene Vincent and Presley regularly made the British charts in the late-1950s.[7] Britain also saw the most extensive spread of the skiffle craze from the mid-1950s. Cast in an unambiguously American idiom, it produced a generation of amateur musicians, many of whom would graduate to professional careers.[8] Britain possessed a sizeable popular music 'sector' – including both amateur and professional performers – before the emergence of the Beatles. And, although British music charts contained a substantial share of saccharine, there was gold among the dross. The Shadows, and later the Beatles and the Rolling Stones, built on an existing base.

It was doubtless for this reason that British music was first taken up by continental amateurs. In the face of *yé-yé* and *Schlager*[9] ascendancy, and after the rapid collapse of first-wave US rock'n'roll, British musicians became the models for continental aficionados. British groups were fêted as representing musical authenticity and spurning the synthetic, commercial output of the *yé-yés* and their equivalents outside France. The French rock'n'roll purist Eddy Mitchell had anticipated having to devote his career to traditional chanson before the British invasion revived something that he could understand as rock.[10] 'L'Angleterre sauvait le rock', as his colleague Dick Rivers put it.[11]

To understand this it is necessary to start not with the Beatles and the Rolling Stones but with the Shadows, who were enormously influential in the development of continental music. Best known in Britain in these years as Cliff Richard's backing group, in Europe they enjoyed an independent reputation, resting not just on their instrumental virtuosity, but on the unfamiliar and entrancing sound of the Fender Stratocaster guitar played by Hank Marvin. Rivers and his first group, the Chats Sauvages, idolized 'this fabulous group'.[12] In Switzerland, experiencing 'a veritable Shadows-Boom' from 1962, 'where were you when you first heard "Apache"?' became a 'Kennedy question' for Swiss rockers.[13] One whole disc of a recent Norwegian pop-rock history compilation is devoted to the 'Shadows era'.[14] 'Shadowsbands' spread across the continent.[15]

But the Beatles' impact was immeasurably greater, and was compounded by the simultaneous emergence of the Rolling Stones and other British bands. British invasion groups dominated European charts for a couple of years after Beatlemania hit Europe in 1964: Paul Rutten's statistical analysis of the Dutch charts shows 45 per cent of chart points going to English groups.[16] By June 1964 seven out of the top ten songs in the *Bravo* Musicbox chart in West Germany were sung by Liverpool bands (including the Beatles' two German-language recordings). Six months earlier the only British singer in the top ten had been Cliff Richard, singing in German.[17] In Scandinavia the 'British invasion' was before all else a 'Beatles invasion'. The group's first overseas tour was to Sweden in October 1963, their success prompting Gerry and the Pacemakers, the Searchers, the Swinging Blue Jeans, the Rolling Stones, the Animals, the Who and seven other major British groups to follow.[18] Twenty-two Beatles songs made the Swedish charts between 1963 and 1966, 13 of them reaching number one; likewise, 22 Beatles songs entered the Norwegian charts between *From Me to You* in June 1963 and the end of 1966.[19] Even the backwardness of Salazar's Portugal was disturbed by a British invasion, the Beatles appearing in Lisbon in May 1964 and the Stones, the Searchers, the Dave Clark Five and Gerry and the Pacemakers subsequently hitting the country 'em força'.[20] Predictably, resistance was fiercest in France, mainly taking the *yé-yé* form of purloining the songs of others to convey them in French. Only two unrepresentative Beatles ballads, the inescapable *Yesterday* and McCartney's 'joke French tune'[21] *Michelle*, made number one in their original versions during the peak years of Beatlemania,[22] but several of the group's songs were covered by *yé-yé* singers, who customized them for performance by a solo vocalist.[23]

The first apparent French Beatles imitators were Les Lionceaux from Reims, who had played as a twist band and a Shadowsband before being adopted by Lee Halliday, uncle by marriage of Johnny Hallyday.[24] Convinced that the days of instrumental bands were numbered, Halliday persuaded his charges to sing. To reinforce this artistic decision, Halliday showed Les Lionceaux photographs of the Beatles and induced them to adopt Beatles-style suits on stage.[25] Similarly, the Spanish record company Zafira assembled a four-man group called Los Brincos, suitably attired, in the belief that 'if you could have a Beatlemania across the entire world, it should be possible to create a "Brincosis" in Spain'.[26] The British keyboard player Brian Auger shared a set in Mannheim with 'Gerd Jacob und seine Swing Kats', all men in their 40s with receding hairlines, who had grown their hair long at the back in order to comb it forward and produce a Beatles appearance. Although a swing band, they sang Beatles songs – 'Sie loffs you, ja, ja, ja'.[27] Carlos Mendes, of The Sheiks – 'the Portuguese Beatles' – sang in 'a nasal tone' in imitation of John Lennon.[28] In a still more literal tribute, the Danish band The Spitfires renamed themselves The Lennons, while a rhythm-and-blues band formed in Lidingö in Sweden in 1964 called itself The Jaggers.[29] Joël Rive, of the French band The Boots, explained that '[we adopted] the name The Boots on account of the boots I had bought in London, genuine Anella and Davide, like the ones the Beatles wore'.[30] In German-speaking Switzerland, the Pirates – the 'Basler Beatles'[31] – sported 'mop-top' haircuts, but it was Les Sauterelles, who had started as a Shadowsband in 1962, who turned themselves into 'Die Swiss Beatles' in 1964, with the mandatory collarless suits. They serenaded the real Beatles at Zurich airport when their role models stopped *en route* to Australia in 1964.[32] Imitation extended to other leading British groups. The Italian singer Caterina Caselli adopted a hairstyle modelled on that of the Rolling Stones' Brian Jones and dubbed 'the golden helmet'.[33] The French *chanteuse* Stone (née Annie Gautrat), among the first women to produce 'rock British-style', likewise copied Jones's hairstyle, as well as the Union Jack vest worn by the Who's John Entwistle.[34] The French band The Somethings modelled themselves on The Kinks.[35] Other groups simply latched onto the symbols of 'swinging London'. Norway's leading band, The Pussycats, who had evolved from a Shadowsband on hearing the Beatles in 1964, traveled in a red London double-decker bus.[36] Their compatriots the Mojo Blues wore Mod suits and even mini-skirts (though the group was all-male) in 1967.[37] John Stephen dressed the Swedish band The Caretakers in Carnaby Street suits.[38]

Imitation raised the language question. The Shadows were an instrumental group and mimicking them tested only instrumental skill. The emergence of British invasion bands from 1963, however, demanded more of European imitators. Some ducked the challenge: Les Fingers, a successful French Shadowsband, disbanded because 'Mersey Beat was sweeping all before it'.[39] Most, though, like Halliday's Lionceaux, taught themselves to sing. But in which language? Les Lionceaux sang in French, and national record industries still assumed that records would only sell in local markets if performed in the local language. Indeed, a low point in European pop music was reached when German producers recorded the Shadows' *Apache*, originally an instrumental release, with *ersatz* German lyrics.[40] Spain's exposure to rock'n'roll had led to the development of *spanglish*, 'the pseudo-idiom much used in Spanish rock' – 'Chi lof yu, ye ye ye.'[41] Some singers in the early 1960s had applied themselves to recording in unfamiliar languages: 'More than ever, music is criss-crossing Europe', commented *Salut les Copains* in March 1963, 'The Italians are familiar with Cliff Richard, the French love Celentano and Johnny Hallyday has recorded a disc in German.'[42] Briefly, pop's spoils went to the polyglot: Salvatore Adamo, Sicilian born, who made his reputation in France, spoke English, German, Italian and Dutch as well as French.[43] Françoise Hardy had by 1965 recorded 46 songs in her native French, 13 in Italian, six in German and four in English.[44] The Danish singer Gitte had several hits in Germany between 1963 and 1980.[45] The Greek-born singer Nana Mouskouri spoke six languages and enjoyed substantial success in France.[46] The German singer Ria Bartok lived in both London and Paris and was fluent in four languages.[47] The Dutch singer Suzie spoke perfect Swedish, Danish, English, French and German, as well as Dutch, and she did indeed have 18 Swedish releases between 1963 and 1971, six German-language songs in the West German charts in the mid-1960s and hits in Dutch and in English in the Netherlands in the same period.[48]

Even British singers contributed to this trend, hoping to increase sales or, more precisely, to prevent European producers buying the rights to a song and 'giv[ing] it to a Nana Mouskouri or a Caterina Valente'.[49] Petula Clark recorded *Downtown* in French, German and Spanish, while Sandie Shaw recorded in French, Italian, Spanish and German from 1965.[50] West Germany was the most promising market for British singers from at least the early 1960s. Cliff Richard repeatedly entered the West German charts with German-language recordings,[51] and even some of the 'British invasion' pioneers – the Searchers, Manfred Mann, the Swinging Blue Jeans – sang in German.[52] The Beatles themselves reluctantly re-recorded two early hits in German: *She Loves You* as *Sie liebt dich* and *I Wanna Hold Your Hand* as *Komm gib mir deine Hand*. Both made the charts, but only augmented the far greater success of the English versions;[53] the Beatles never released another foreign-language recording.[54] The American singer Gene Pitney, who had previously 'had to record my songs in Italian, German, French or Spanish' for the European market, remained grateful to the Beatles for making English-language songs acceptable everywhere: 'after 1964, the charts in most countries were about 50 per cent English-language records, and in some places you had to sing in English or you wouldn't chart at all.'[55] Thereafter, for a British group or singer to record in any European language was usually an admission of failure in the British market, and those who did so were generally on the way down. The most substantial exception was the German graduate Spencer Davis, who was allowed by his record company, Philips, to release a German-language recording in 1966 only after a reader campaign organized by *Bravo* – although the result, *Det War in Schöneberg*, flopped in West Germany.[56]

Most rock purists were alienated by *yé-yé/Schlager* practice, and resolved on principle to sing in the language of Elvis and the Beatles. Dick Rivers' 'boyhood dream' on separating from his original backing group, the Chats Sauvages, in 1962 had been to become an international rock star, singing his own compositions in English with top-notch musicians.[57] Many argued that European languages were inappropriate vehicles for Anglo-Saxon music.[58] Germans who sang in German were '*Schlager* apes', according to 'Lord Ulli', of the Berlin band, The Lords.[59] This was a matter of principle – 'my preference, partly out of snobbery but mainly out of a desire for authenticity, was to sing in English. I performed around 70 per cent of my club repertoire in English', explained the French anglophile Ronnie Bird.[60] When this artistic preference was reinforced by the enthusiasm for London and for all things British, it became routine to sing in English. In the Netherlands the proportion of Dutch-language songs fell from 20 per cent in 1963 to around 10 per cent between 1966 and 1970, though the number of Dutch singers grew in that period. After 1966, the proportion of Dutch-produced songs in English seldom fell below 50 per cent. English-language songs accounted for 84 per cent of the Dutch charts by 1966.[61] The title index to Hans Olofsson's survey of Swedish pop between 1954 and 1969 suggests that only around 20 per cent of songs recorded *by Swedish groups* were in any language other than English.[62]

Ian MacDonald argues that the Beatles' decision to sing only in English encouraged 'the promotion of the English language around the world', which was 'one of their most substantial, and least documented, achievements'.[63] So it was, eventually, but in the mid-1960s English was still a minority possession in Europe. Herbert Imholz, of the Hamburg group Mama Betty's Band, only discovered the meaning of the songs his group had sung after learning English when working in Hong Kong in the 1970s: 'Then I heard several of the old songs that we used to play, and I often thought: 'Blimey – so that's what that meant!'[64] For Swiss performers English 'was the obligatory language, although most singers had gained no great command of it'; Walty Anselmo, 'the Zurich Hank Marvin' in the Shadowsband 'The Limelight', was captivated by the Beatles on first hearing *Twist and Shout* in 1964. Anselmo was a guitarist, and could sing English only by 'copy[ing] out the text syllable by syllable, without really understanding its meaning'.[65] The German singer of the Spanish beatband Los Bravos, Michael Kögel (Mike Kennedy) likewise mastered the group's English repertoire by 'learning the lyrics phonetically'.[66] The French singer Sullivan (*né* Jacques Dantriche) spoke of adding *Twist and Shout* to his group's repertoire without knowing English, 'but we were not the only ones to sing in "yaourt" – 'yaourt' meaning 'pseudo-English sung phonetically'.[67] The lead singer of the Harburg beatband The Rascals, Peter Wurst, a.k.a. 'Tommy Star', sang 'wretched' English, 'but he sang very loud'.[68]

The problematic consequences emphasized the amateurism of European pop. One was the adoption of awkward English names. European beat groups – indeed, beat groups everywhere – overwhelmingly took English names, including the definite article. As Manfred Weißleder, owner of the Hamburg Star Club, complained in 1965, 'whether they're from Japan, Israel or Finland, they're called The Strangers, The Devils, The This, The That or The Other'. He celebrated the discovery of an English group with a German name, The Hummelflugs.[69] The cachet of an English name in West Germany led the Berlin group The Lords to consider suing a Hamburg band with the same title.[70] Klitsch's study of German beat nonetheless lists 13 'Beatniks', 13 'Strangers', 13 'Thunderbirds', 11 'Sharks', 10 'Jets' (and one 'Jet's'), 7 'Lightnings', 7 'Dukes', 7 'Gents', 7 'Phantoms', 6 'Red Devils' and 6 'Snobs'.[71] One Ruhrgebiet group called themselves 'Georgie and the Blue Flames' after seeing Georgie Fame and the Blue Flames in London in 1962, changing their name to The German Blue Flames when recording contracts beckoned.[72] Other names were more improbable – or simply more gauche: The Mushroams,[73] The Sheapes,[74] The London Fog,[75] The Four Renders,[76] The Dentals,[77] The Haddocks,[78] The Burpers,[79] The Fumigants,[80] The German Rackets,[81] Edgar and the Breathless,[82] Barry Window and the Movements,[83] Jack and the Rippers,[84] The Girlsboys,[85] I Corset Drop,[86] The Upper Parts,[87] etc. – or, like The Rattles,[88] plucked from English dictionaries.

On the rare occasions when bands sang their own compositions with English lyrics they invited embarrassment. The Berlin band The Lords were ridiculed for the primitive English in their single *Poor Boy* of 1965, with the repeated line 'and she learned me to say (...) life is very hard to stay'.[89] This risk could be minimized by using published English lyrics for the familiar songs that comprised most of the repertoire, but it remained where songs had been learned from the radio or from discs. In West Germany, where several British singers were available to provide transcriptions, locals risked becoming the victims of practical jokes which their limited English prevented them from spotting. 'Kingsize' Taylor claimed to have induced the Hamburg band the Four Renders briefly to change their name to the Four Skins by suggesting that 'skin' was a scouse term of endearment.[90] 'The German bands used to come and say: "Could you write out the words to that song?"' Ian Edwards, of Ian and the Zodiacs, reminisced in 2005, 'So we'd say: "Yes, we'll write the words out," and we used to put in very bad English words (...) I take this opportunity to apologise to the bands and hope they didn't make records with the same language.'[91] Some did. The Hamburg group The Bats notoriously sang the words 'some stupid cunt' on the 1964 Live at the Star Club LP,[92] and it is likely that similar improprieties occurred in unrecorded performances.

They were not reciting Schubert *Lieder*, and, arguably, if such embarrassments were avoided, beat lyrics were not so profound as to require the singer to understand his or her song. Achim Reichel, lead singer of the Hamburg group The Rattles, the leading German group of the beat years, recalled asking British bands the meaning of English lyrics and being told 'it doesn't really matter as long as the feeling comes across'.[93] Gradually, though,

Reichel came to doubt that uncomprehending 'feeling' was sufficient in a performer. Olgerd Wököck of the Phantom Brothers remembered a conversation in which Reichel advocated a German-language rock, but 'we completely rejected it. We were rock'n'rollers, and a rock'n'roller didn't sing in German'.[94] Such artistic wilfulness was only reinforced by pressure from record companies to sing in the local language.[95] This doubtless reflected their fear of the kind of linguistic disasters described above, but companies generally thought it commercially prudent, once the appeal of the British groups became evident, to produce local-language covers of British songs. Where the singers themselves still saw their primary task as that of proselytizing for Anglo-Saxon music in a hostile climate, this might prove acceptable. In Italy, most obviously, where the dominant form of popular music was still the Sanremo *canzone* tradition, most of the principal beat groups produced Italian covers of British and American songs and one, Dik Dik, concentrated largely upon that genre.[96] Elsewhere, though, musicians interpreted such pressure as an attempt to turn them into *yé-yés*. Following one confrontation, the five-man Berlin band The Lords, forced to record their first single in German, refused to be photographed for the sleeve, producing instead a cover picture of five *Melonen* (bowler hats, symbolizing Englishness).[97]

Songs delivered in a language which their performers could not understand were likely to be imitative and derivative. The Berlin rocker Drafi Deutscher had begun by singing in English, but decided that 'it is only possible to convey a real message in your own language',[98] and subsequently sang in German. The Danish band The Donkeys laid the foundations for future Danish pop by moving away from English-language covers, while the Hep Stars of Stockholm became the first major Swedish band to record in their native tongue with *I Natt Jag Drömde* ('Last Night I Dreamed') in 1966.[99] Their compatriots Tages aspired in their 1967 album *Studio* (recorded in London) to create 'a Swedish blue-yellow LP' by melding their compositions with Swedish folk songs.[100]

Nonetheless, the enthusiasm for Britain and things British during the years of Beatlemania created real obstacles to the development of an autonomous rock tradition anywhere in Europe – not just the need to sing in an unfamiliar language but also the difficulty of airing original repertoire. The *Hobbymusiker* who created the beat scene in the clubs of Europe enjoyed reproducing the standard British numbers which had first inspired them, and several bands specialized in the repertoire of particular British groups. Audiences were enthusiasts too, who saw the groups as 'living jukeboxes',[101] providing live versions of songs familiar from radio or disc. Klitsch reproduces an exhaustive list of songs performed by the Bremen band The Mushroams between March 1964 and May 1968.[102] The repertoire of three hundred songs performed in these five years shows how hard a successful club band had to work. It also demonstrates how extensive was the canon available by the mid-1960s. It is often claimed that the Beatles were forced to compose because the stock of covers could not fill the eight-hour shifts required in Hamburg.[103] Whether or not this is true, there was no such shortage by the mid-1960s, and the incentive to write new songs, unfamiliar to an audience who knew what they wanted to hear, diminished. The Mushrooms' three hundred songs (the majority British in origin) included only four by the group themselves. As Christian Evo, of the French band Pollux, put it: 'why bother composing when all that was needed was to reproduce the songs of others?'[104]

This effect was reinforced during the Beatlemania years when, in the words of Herbert Hildebrandt, of the Rattles, 'what was once a music for insiders became a cultural commodity for the young'.[105] A process developed by which enthusiasm for the Beatles' music mutated into Beatlemania, with Beatles memorabilia outselling records, and then into a fixation with Swinging London and all things British. The West German teen magazine *Bravo* (read by a third of the Federal Republic's teenagers[106]) shifted from its early Cold War enthusiasm for the USA to promote Britain's trend-setters, culminating in sponsorship of the Beatles' German *Blitztournee* in 1966.[107] In the summer of 1964 the French pop magazine *Salut les Copains* described the pleasures of a London which offered four hundred places to dance – 35 in Soho alone.[108] The British Consul in Bordeaux told the Paris embassy in 1966 that for French youth, Britain was 'the country of the Beatles, of liberty from parental control, of everything "with-it" – the teenagers' Dreamland'.[109] While European youth still drew its image of the USA from Hollywood or even the Wild West yarns of Karl May, it was easy for young tourists to see Britain at first hand. Many did. By 1970, when the British Tourist Authority first surveyed Britain's tourists by age, 34 per cent of all Western European non-business visitors to the UK were found to be aged between 16 and 24; the more detailed BTA survey of London visitors in 1975 found 45 per cent of visitors to the capital in that age group.[110] The *Star Club News*, journal of the organization which had brought so many British singers to Germany in the early 1960s, offered readers a trip to London, including a Beatles concert at Hammersmith, in December 1965.[111] 'To spend a few days in London', the pop journalist Jean-Pierre Frimbois suggested in 1965, 'is to live at the heart of the crucible in which the music of our time is being cast.'[112] London was magnetic. Stone's reward for becoming France's Miss Beatnik in 1966 was a London trip: 'That is my dream – I've never been there, and what really interests me, quite apart from winning Miss Beatnik, is to walk down Carnaby Street for real.'[113] Rock autobiographies describe the pilgrimage to Swinging London, whether Antoine, 'the first hippie of French song',[114] making repeated trips to seek London life and love in 1965–66,[115] or Michel Polnareff, begging the music producers of Denmark Street to record an English version of his French hit *La Poupée qui Fait 'Non'*.[116] London was more accessible than Greenwich Village and Laurel Canyon.

This cultural contact, however, produced little cultural exchange. Los Bravos' 1966 hit *Black is Black* deprived Britain's youth of the illusion that 'Spanish groups went around dressed in bullfighters' clothes and sang flamenco songs',[117] but it was an exception. Leading French singers increasingly came to London to record, but, with the fleeting exception of Françoise Hardy in 1964–65, had no British hits.[118] The Rattles played at Liverpool's Cavern Club and, less glamorously, the Plaza in St Helens.[119] They became the first German band to have a British fan club,[120] and were said by their record company to be mentioned by British fans in the same breath as the Searchers, the Rolling Stones, the Merseybeats and the Beatles,[121] but their only British hit was *The Witch* in 1970.[122] The European impact on the British music scene was infinitesimal. Hank Marvin was the only one of the four Shadows to have heard of Johnny Hallyday in 1962, two years after his first single;[123] asked by *Salut les Copains* to name the French singers familiar to him, Ringo Starr produced a stereotypically English list of *chansonniers* and *yé-yés*, including Johnny Hallyday, Brigitte Bardot, Charles Aznavour and Maurice Chevalier.[124]

Several performers who remained obscure in Britain forged a good career on the continent by trading on their Britishness. To German promoters 'either you were an Englishman or you were an arse',[125] as Klaus Dreymann, of the Team Beats Berlin, put it. 'At the time, Germany liked the idea of "foreign", that is British groups that gave them the comfort of being an "original" item', recalled Chris Warman, who prospered in Frankfurt as drummer of the little known Southampton group Gene Anthony and the Lonely Ones.[126] Britain's pop diaspora lived with local resentment and the awareness that they had left rock's mainstream – 'it's great', exclaimed Graham Bonney, a Londoner big in Germany, 'but not quite the same as being a hit in Britain'.[127] They understood, though, that the aura surrounding a British performer secured them recognition and rewards which might otherwise have eluded them. One of the early Liverpool exiles, Ted 'King Size' Taylor, with his group The Dominoes, made more than 500 appearances at the Hamburg Star Club without succeeding in Britain.[128] English groups like the Liverpool bands Ian and the Zodiacs[129] and Casey Jones and the Governors and singers such as Cliff Bennett, Lee Curtis and Bonney made their reputations almost exclusively in West Germany.[130] Vince Taylor, 'a marketing creation *avant l'heure*', in Dick Rivers' view, was conspicuously successful in France but unknown in Britain.[131] The Rokes became Italy's second most popular beat band when they moved to that country in 1963, following six uneventful years performing in Britain and Germany,[132] while the Deejays, formed in the late 1950s, found success only after moving in 1963 to Sweden, where they released more than 20 singles in five years.[133]

All this underlined the subordinate status of European artists in a milieu developed by British groups and reinforced by the fashionable nature of the British pop 'product'. This prompted the claims of Weißleder and others that

British predominance rested primarily on effective marketing: 'a hit owes 20 per cent to the band and eighty per cent to the promotion'.[134] Whatever the truth of this, it does appear that commercial pressures restricted continental groups to the emulation of British models. When they reached the recording studio, it made commercial sense to promote them as national versions of British pioneers. Les Somethings were described on their one 45 as 'France's first *franglais* group'.[135] Lee Halliday's puff for Les Lionceaux's second single proclaimed: 'You like the Beatles? Then you'll like Les Lionceaux.'[136] Following Weißleder's experiment of September 1962, when for a week only Liverpool bands played at the Star Club,[137] impresarios staged faux-English events. The Kaufleutensaal in Zurich, for instance, staged 'The Big Show of Liverpool' in 1964.[138] The Ruhr town of Recklinghausen turned its annual jazz festival into a beat festival and itself sought to emulate Liverpool – 'also a workers' town with a certain *poésie de tristesse*'.[139] The Recklinghausen event included a beat competition settled by jury decision, sometimes augmented by a public vote.[140] Such competitions proliferated in West Germany and elsewhere. United Artists marked the German release of the first Beatles film, *A Hard Day's Night* (entitled *Yeah Yeah Yeah* in West Germany) by promoting a series of contests – 'Wer spielt so wie die Beatles?' ('Who plays like the Beatles?') – in major West German cities, with a cash prize and a record contract at stake.[141] Similarly, Tages of Göteborg, the principal Swedish group before Abba, found fame by winning the 'Westcoast Beatles' competition in 1964.[142] In Denmark The Beethovens, though disciples of Chuck Berry, won a record contract from EMI through victory in a 1964 competition to find 'Denmark's Beatles'. Copenhagen hosted a 'Denmark's Rolling Stones' competition in 1963 to find the Danish Cliff Richard.[143] That competition between groups which European commentators considered a source of creativity in British bands merely stimulated the emulation of British models in Europe. Complex chord progressions and harmonies made 'playing like the Beatles' no easy business – the bass guitarist of the Hague band Q65 admitted in 1989 that his band had played Stones numbers by choice because the Beatles' chords were too difficult[144] – but the competitions transparently rewarded imitation rather than originality.[145] The prize of a record contract made them genuinely competitive, but they could only be guaranteed to produce competent tribute bands. There was no certainty that the winners could produce original material; generally the record companies wanted them to produce native-language versions of English-language hits for which the companies had secured the rights. Demand for this product was dwindling, though. An interview with several discerning French teenagers conducted by *Salut les Copains* in 1965 suggested that, although opinions varied on whether pop was better sung in French or English, nobody liked English-language songs copied into French: it was 'better to succeed with a new song than to latch on to an American or English hit which you more or less ruin. The copy can never match the original.'[146]

European performers faced a dilemma. Large numbers of young people were drawn to perform by enthusiasm for particular artists or genres. They played the songs that had enthused them in the style of the original performers, yet with the emergence of the singer-songwriter in the 1960s, groups were expected to display greater creativity than an orchestral player or a *Schlager* star. Once commercial pressure encouraged emulation of the stars, such creativity became less attainable, and when performers like Reichel eventually sought to break the Beatles/Stones mould, opportunities for independence were diminishing. Looking back on a thwarted pop career after 40 years, Michel Mathieu ('Bob'), drummer of Les Lionceaux, who 'aped the Beatles',[147] in Rivers' dismissive phrase, concluded that 'we should have written our own songs from the start. All we did was to perform the songs of others. We waited until the last moment before doing something of our own.'[148]

By the mid-1960s it was not difficult to buy British records in Europe, as it had earlier been hard to buy authentic American rock, and it was unclear why European teenagers should buy local imitators. Radio Bremen's Hans Kerncek considered most German beatbands mere 'followers of the anglo-saxon pioneers'.[149] His station was busy turning the TV show *Beat-Club Bremen* into a German equivalent of ITV's *Ready, Steady, Go* – a 'genuine English beat programme', identified by a variant of the London Transport logo.[150] It offered British bands 'free publicity for their latest releases in an increasingly attractive market'.[151] If *Beat-Club Bremen* did not host the Beatles or the Rolling Stones, it attracted middle-ranking British groups like Manfred Mann,[152] and had no need of lesser-known German bands.

The spread of discotheques from the mid-1960s further reduced the demand for live performers.[153] Sensing the change, Weißleder sold his interest in the Hamburg Star Club in 1967; aptly, the club closed on the last day of the 1960s.[154] Star Club veteran Ted 'King Size' Taylor thought German bands to be 'getting better and better' by the mid-1960s,[155] but with the balance between recorded and live music shifting towards the former in the mid-1960s, Britain's dominance became clear. Most conspicuously, London's superiority as a recording centre became more significant as the beatband yielded to the disco. German bands 'lived in a country where there was no infrastructure for touring beat musicians, and no professional management', Reichel recalled.[156] Manfred Gambler, of the Bildstock band The Ghost Riders, remembered the group's first single being recorded 'in a prehistoric studio', where 'the sound engineer was an old man who said straight away "forget stereo: it doesn't sound right (...) I know what I am doing. I used to work with Zarah Leander".'[157] Poor studio facilities, unsympathetic sound engineers and semi-detached session musicians had been the lot of the early British rockers recording in Denmark Street.[158] By the mid-1960s, though, London's studios were the envy of the continent. Françoise Hardy told *Mademoiselle Age Tendre* in 1966 that although she would buy mini-skirts and boots in the boutiques in the Kings Road, 'when I go to London, it is almost always for the same reason: to record a disc or a TV show'.[159] Considering French production standards 'absolutely terrible',[160] Hardy urged Dick Rivers to 'try out the state-of-the-art facilities of the London studios'.[161] Rivers enthused over the separate layered recording of vocals and instruments, unknown in France, and the virtuosity of his session musicians, including the young Jimmy Page. 'In France', he told *Salut les Copains* in 1965, 'session musicians have no feeling for the music they play. Try talking to them about the "Nashville style" and you might as well be speaking Hebrew. In London they get straight into it. Even the older ones have absorbed the spirit of the music.'[162] The Cliff Richard look-alike Rex Gildo, one of West Germany's most successful singers, travelled to London to record in 1966 because 'I am sick and tired of German recording studios and their antiquated recording equipment'; in London, moreover, 'the studio musicians are all of my age'.[163] Two of Sweden's leading bands, The Shanes and Tages, prided themselves on having recorded in 'the famous Abbey Road studios'.[164] 'Every artist of a certain calibre ended up going to London to record', Ronnie Bird recalled; returning to London's Olympic Studios in 1968, Rivers ran into Sacha Distel, Johnny Hallyday and Mireille Mathieu.[165] London was where Michel Polnareff went to acquire a Rickenbaker guitar in 1965, where Robert Fitoussi of The Boots went to buy a Vox AC30 amplifier and where Dick Rivers went to recruit a new backing group.[166] In consequence, when British invasion hysteria subsided, London remained the centre of the European pop industry.

Continental record companies implicitly accepted the market leadership of the British and of the resurgent American industry. From 1966 West German companies concentrated upon the competition for local rights to British songs which, they judged, would sell themselves.[167] The West German charts were dominated by Anglo-saxons and by native *Schlager* artists like Roy Black – 'archenemy' to beat lovers,[168] but still the most successful performer of the second half of the decade in the *Bravo* charts.[169] In the Netherlands 1966 saw the proportion of anglo-american music in the charts peak at 69 per cent (42 per cent British, 27 per cent American); it remained above 50 per cent for the remainder of the decade.[170] In France not only did the imitative beat groups disappear from the mid-1960s, but the *yé-yé* mission of translating Anglo-saxon classics for the French public became otiose. The more popular performers – Hallyday, Vartan, Claude François – survived on indigenous material but the *yé-yé* tradition was dead.[171]

In their musical manifesto of 1966, Italian critic Piero Vivarelli, lyricist Sergio Bardotti and singer Lucio Dalla asserted that 'in 1966 musical nationalism is a nonsense'.[172] In the pop world of the mid-1960s, boundaries had indeed been broken down within Europe. Various strategies adopted by local record industries – the manufacture of Elvis substitutes, the *yé-yé* practice of converting Anglo-Saxon classics into the local tongue, the promotion of polyglot singers to penetrate different continental markets – had all proved redundant in the face of the 'British invasion'. Rutten shows that in the Dutch charts 'continental European music', i.e. music produced in Europe outside the Netherlands, accounted for only 5 per cent of hits between 1960 and 1985. Between 1967 and 1970 the proportion fell almost to zero.[173] The concept of a multilateral European integration in pop music would survive only in the quirky form of the Eurovision Song Contest – though if that forum had a *lingua franca* it was English.[174] In fact the language barrier, normally the sturdiest obstacle to European cultural integration, had proved strikingly flimsy in the face of the combination of performer discretion and consumer sovereignty described here: in the beat years European performers wished to play, and the European audience wished to hear, British music.

This story of Anglo-Saxon cultural conquest has been sufficiently evocative of models of Americanization to encourage the assumption that it should be seen as a side-effect of the more obvious diplomatic and economic assimilation of Europe by the USA. This remains, though, an assumption, and one yet to be vigorously scrutinized. As Victoria de Grazia points out, the literature on cultural Americanization remains limited by comparison with the volume of studies on other aspects of the phenomenon;[175] if the USA did exercise a cultural hegemony over Europe in this period, we still know very little about how it was done. Attempts to force the 'British invasion' into a general model of Americanization can appear strained: a recent collection of essays on the concept, where the contributors were under instructions to assess the Americanization of high and low culture, includes the strange claims that some of the Beatles' German fans believed them to be American,[176] and that 'the Beatles themselves had survived the lean years before they broke into the US market by playing Hamburg'.[177] In a teenage market, the golden age of American rock was distinctly *passé* by the mid-1960s. As the 15-year-old 'Régis' told *Salut les Copains* in 1965, English rock was preferable to American because 'now that Presley sings to a backing of violins and the greats (Buddy Holly and Eddie Cochran) are dead, it's across the Channel that you find the real thing'.[178]

The first point to make about the 'British invasion' is the obvious one – that it was British. American influences on the Beatles and the Rolling Stones are obvious, but their music was not simply derivative: the Beatles did not conquer the USA in 1964 by copying American models. Contained within this simple truth, moreover, is a subtler point about the nature of cultural transfer. American influence in Europe is generally taken to have been conveyed as part of the USA's Cold War cultural mission on the continent or as a concomitant of American economic strength, but nobody ever depicted the Rolling Stones as tools of Cold War diplomacy and nobody could imagine that 1960s Britain possessed the economic muscle to force its cultural exports upon anybody. What is described here is a more democratic process than that, driven by the stylistic preference of performers and consumers in Europe – and by a degree of contact that derived from the proximity of Britain to the continent. The many British bands who learned their trade in Hamburg, Europe's role as an outlet for second-ranking British performers, the emergence of the Swinging City as a pilgrimage centre for European youth and the eagerness of successful European performers to record in London's studios all bear witness to a cultural contact that was transnational but not transatlantic. One must remember how broad the Atlantic was in the pre-jumbo age – and how narrow the Channel.

In fact what was happening was the dilution of earlier American dominance of popular music, as the industry became more pluralistic, acquiring more regional centres. What has been described here was the development of London as a regional centre for an embryonic European music industry. The contrasting stylistic evolution of the USA and continental Europe in the wake of the British invasion reinforces the point. The impact of British groups on American musicians in 1964–65 was enormous, but the original American influence upon the British sound, and the developed state of American pop music, meant that British beat did not stifle the US music industry. The emergence of folk-rock, following the somewhat theological, if bitter, dispute between the advocates and opponents of the electric guitar,[179] fused British innovations with an American vernacular, cementing the latter into mainstream pop and ending any prospect that American music would remain a derivative of British beat.[180] Europe, however, was characterized by folk genres completely removed from the sound world of the Beatles: in West Germany, as Klitsch puts it, 'beat was as far distant from Bavarian folk music as the north pole from the equator'.[181] In some places vernacular music simply remained resolutely uncommercial, as in the Netherlands, where an independent Dutch musical tradition survived outside the recording studio on the folk circuit.[182] Where it had already been commercialized, as with the *chanson/canzone* performers in France and Italy, established stars such as Georges Brassens (who could draw a crowd of 90 000 in Paris even at the height of Europe's beat boom in 1966[183]) could largely ignore the beat revolution. In neither case was there any stylistic fusion. As a result, continental beat remained stylistically subservient to British models, and the English language was adopted willingly, for artistic reasons, by performers who could not understand it. This was, though, less a harbinger of Anglo-Saxon cultural hegemony than a reflection of the weakness of the existing European industry. The British invasion, breaking down local barriers as it did, was a precondition for later development.

The unnatural British domination of Europe described in this chapter was inevitably transient. The technical quality of her recording studios and the cultural capital accumulated during the 1960s may have given London a lasting edge, but other elements of British modishness proved less durable. During the 1970s the belief that *echt* pop had to be sung in the language of the Beatles dwindled. Musicians became less inhibited about singing in their own tongues, though the change was always qualified by an awareness that English would open more doors in an international market. Local rock styles also emerged in the 1970s as the practice of mimicking British models palled, though they generally steered clear of vernacular folk, and clearer still of *chansonniers* like Brel or Brassens. 'Krautrock', which finally satisfied Achim Reichel's wish for an authentic German music,[184] grew out of progressive rock and the experimental classical music of Stockhausen. Rap, although obviously initially imported, was cultivated largely by Europe's ethnic minorities. In the 1990s the wheel came full circle with the development of 'Britpop', drawing nostalgically upon the 1960s British pioneers.[185] By 1991 Simon Frith could write of the development of a pan-European industry, in which 'British consumers already have more in common with their European neighbours than with the USA'.[186]

In his study of the impact of the Beatles, the Dutch musicologist Ger Tillekens invites his readers to imagine a 1960s pop revolution founded not on the electric guitar but on the accordion, and emanating not from Britain but from France or Belgium.[187] In fact it was always likely, given the greater circulation of first-wave rock'n'roll in the United Kingdom, that the next phase in the development of popular music would be launched from Britain, and, given the impact of the Stratocaster, that it would be guitar-driven, but the rhetorical question reminds us that the process described here was an artistic and a social one. It might appear to be an exercise in cultural imperialism, but it was not. It did not reflect the strength of an economic superpower or promote the objectives of a Cold War cultural mission, nor was it the product of any Eurovision-type effort at pan-continental integration. The British conquest of European popular music was a peaceful one, freely – enthusiastically – accepted by those affected. Indeed, that enthusiasm was a central feature of the story, explaining the sometimes demeaning exercises in emulation described here, prompting the development of a cultural and stylistic movement out of a purely musical one and overturning language barriers in the process. It produced what was, surely, the first genuinely pan-European movement in popular culture.

## Notes

* I am grateful to the helpful and friendly staff of the Archiv der Jugendkulturen in Berlin and to all those who have supplied me with information or helped me to masquerade as a polyglot: Katharina Boehmer, Sunniva Engh, Gerda Frank-Gemmill, Carolyne Larrington, Frieder Missfelder, Roger Pearson, Judy Quinn, Philippa Soeldenwagner, Nigel Townson and Cornelia Wilde.

1. www.rockabilly.nl/artists/pimmaas.htm, accessed 15 November 2009; F. Steensma (ed.), *Oor's Eerste Nederlandse Pop-Encyclopedie* (Amstrerdam, 13th edition, 2002), p. 242.
2. T. Bille, *Dansk Rock Leksikon* (Copenhagen, 2002), p. 241.
3. J. Eggum, B. Ose and S. Steen, *Norsk Pop & Rock Leksikon. Populaermusik I Hundre År* (Oslo, 2005), pp. 208, 496.
4. The term was coined by the French sociologist Edgar Morin, in '*SLC*', *Le Monde*, 6 July 1963, to suggest the repetition of the American 'yeah' in rock and roll music. The French rocker Dick Rivers surmised that Morin had published his 'pompous article' after hearing 'some of our 45s, and perhaps even doing the twist in private', D. Rivers, *Rock'n'Roll Récit* (Saint-Amand-Montrond, 2006), p. 117.
5. Eddie Cochran and Gene Vincent did not reach the French top 30 before 1963, Chuck Berry not until 1964, Little Richard and Buddy Holly not at all, D. Lesueur, *Hit Parades, 1950–1998, Alternatives et Parallèles* (Paris, 1999); Berry and Holly did not make the German charts until 1963, Cochran only with the re-release of *Summertime Blues* in 1968 and Vincent and Little Richard not at all: *Hit Bilanz. Deutsche Chart Singles, 1956–1980* (Norderstedt, 2000).
6. 'I discovered Elvis Presley through a mate in the merchant navy who had brought back his discs from the USA', Jean Sarrus of Les Problèmes; Ronnie Bird would listen to Radio Luxembourg late at night to hear American music, C. Eudeline, *Anti-Yé-Yé. Une Autre Histoire des Sixties* (Paris, 2006), pp. 171, 102; J.-P. Pasqualini, *Les Yé-Yés* (Baumes-les-Dames, 2005), p. 28. The Golf Drouot club was said to be the only place in Paris where American discs could be heard, Eudeline, *Anti-Yé-Yé*, p. 42.
   Rock'n'Roll was rarely played on German radio in the late 1950s, U. Krüger, 'Rock'n'Roll + Skiffle = Beat', in U. Krüger and O. Pelc (eds), *The Hamburg Sound. Beatles, Beat und Große Freiheit*, p. 76.
7. G. Betts, *Complete UK Hit Singles, 1952–2006* (London, 2006), pp.78, 169, 384, 488, 651–2, 884–5.
8. P. Frame, *The Restless Generation. How Rock Music Changed the Face of 1950s Britain* (London, 2007).
9. The term *Schlager* was applied in Germany and elsewhere in northern Europe to light and catchy pop melodies.
10. 'That explains plausibly Eddy's unlimited admiration for the Beatles, those original tunesmiths who have revived a repertoire which had, it must be admitted, become somewhat tired', *Salut les Copains* [*SLC*], 32, March 1965.
11. [England saved rock music] Rivers, *Rock'n'Roll*, p. 129.
12. Rivers, *Rock'n'Roll*, p. 78.
13. S. Mumenthaler, *Beat, Pop, Protest. Der Sound der Schweizer Sixties* (Lausanne, 2001), pp. 44, 45.
14. *Norsk Rocks Historie, vol 2, Shadowstida, 1960–1964* CD, Universal Music AS, Oslo, 2004, 982496 5.
15. Toni Vescoli, recalled that '[the Shadows'] guitar sound got under the skin', and formed Les Sauterelles in admiration, Mumenthaler, *Beat, Pop, Protest*, 39. The Danish band The Clifters, were a Richard/Shadows-inspired group, Bille, *Dansk Rock Leksikon*, p. 108. For the Berlin band The Twangy Gang, whose name reveals the influence of the Stratocaster, see H.-J. Klitsch, *Shakin' All Over* (Düsseldorf, 2000), p. 149.
16. P. Rutten, *Hitmuziek in Nederland, 1960–1985* (Amsterdam, 1991), p. 184.

17. *Bravo* 1964/25, 21–27 June 1964, ibid., 1963/52, 29 December 1963. See also K. Farin et al., *50 Jahre Bravo* (Berlin, 2005), p. 35.
18. L. Lilliestam, *Svensk Rock: Musik, Lyrik, Historik* (Göteborg, 1998), p. 85.
19. B. Lundberg and A. Bohm, *Yeah! Yeah! Yeah! The Beatles Erövrar Sverige* (Stockholm, 2003), p. 75. For Norway see the online VG chart: http://lista. vg.no/show_list.php (accessed 20 December 2007 and subsequently.)
20. L. Pinheiro de Almeida and T. Large, *Beatles em Portugal* (Lisbon, 2002), p. 27ff; A. Pires, *As Lendas do Quarteto 1111* (Lisbon, 2007), p. 34.
21. I. MacDonald, *Revolution in the Head. The Beatles' Records and the Sixties* (2nd ed., London, 1995), p. 140.
22. Lesueur, *Hit Parades*, pp. 48–63, 52.
23. Pasqualini lists eleven songs recorded by major French singers, including Hallyday, Claude François and Frank Alamo: J.-P. Pasqualini, *Les Yé-Yés*, pp. 26–7. Magic Records produced a five-volume CD compilation of French covers of Beatles songs, entitled *La France et les Beatles*, in 2007.
24. Lee Halliday, who was American, spelled his surname (itself a stage-name) with an 'i'. Johnny Hallyday, a French-born Belgian christened Jean-Philippe Smet, spelled his adopted surname with a 'y': D. Looseley, 'Fabricating Johnny', *French Cultural Studies*, XVI (2), 2005, 191–203.
25. 'Lee said to us "you're going to sing." He showed us photos of the Beatles and other Liverpool groups: "instrumental – that's finished; singing like Les Chaussettes Noires – that's finished"', Michel Mathieu ('Bob'), of Les Lionceaux, quoted by A. Dumont, *Ils Étaient une Fois Les Lionceaux* (Strasbourg, 2004), p. 70, and see photographs on p. 87.
26. A. Oro, *La Legión Extranjera. Foráneos en la España Musical de los Sesenta* (Lleida, 2001), p. 26.
27. B. Auger, 'Beat from Hamburg', in Krüger and Pelc (eds), *The Hamburg Sound*, p. 120.
28. P. Gonçalves, 'O Rock Portugal dos 60', 7 June 2007, on the Blitz site, http://blitz. aeiou.pt/gen.pl?p=stories (accessed 15 November 2009); M. Lopes, 'Sheiks, os Beatles do "deserto"', in 'Bandas Portuguesas Anos 60', link at http://rockfellas. tripod.com/english.htm (accessed 15 November 2009).
29. Bille, *Dansk Rock Leksikon*, pp. 285–6; *Stora Popboken. 729 Toppartister, Ord och Bild* (Stockholm, 1966), p. 44.
30. Eudeline, *Anti-Yé-Yé*, p. 273.
31. R. Matti, L. Müller and T. Riedo, *Als die Haare länger wurden. Die Sixties in Basel* (Basel, 2000), p. 73.
32. Mumenthaler, *Beat, Pop, Protest*, pp. 66, 58, 105–6.
33. T. Tarli, *Beat Italiano. Dai Capelloni a Bandiera Gialla* (Rome, 2005), p. 138.
34. Eudeline, *Anti-Yé-Yé*, pp. 138, 148.
35. Eudeline, *Anti-Yé-Yé*, p. 397.
36. Eggum, Ose Steen, *Norsk Pop & Rock Leksikon*, p. 426.
37. Ibid., p. 349.
38. See the cutting from the Stockholm paper *Expressen*, nd but? 1966 in the John Stephen papers, Victoria and Albert Museum, AAD/1998/5/16.
39. J. Chalvidant and H. Mouvet, *La Belle Histoire des Groupes de Rock Français des Années 60* (Paris, 2001), p. 98.
40. The same treatment was applied to the Tornadoes' *Telstar* and Johnny and the Hurricanes' *Red River Rock*: B. Matheja, *1000 Nadelstiche. Biographen, Discographen,*

*Cover & Fotos. Amerikaner & Briten singen deutsch, 1955–1975* (Hambergen, 2000), p. 15.

41. J. Ordovás, *Historia de la Musica Pop Española* (Madrid, 1987), p. 52; Oro, *La Legión Extranjera*, p. 31.
42. *SLC*, 8, March 1963.
43. *SLC*, 32, March 1965; for Adamo in Germany see *Bravo*, 1966//15, 4 April 1966.
44. *SLC*, 31, February 1965.
45. *Hit Bilanz. Deutsche Chart Singles, 1956–1980* (Norderstedt, 2000), p. 92.
46. G. Verlant, with J.-D. Brierre, D. Duforest, C. Eudeline and J. Vassal, *L'Odyssée de la Chanson Française* (Paris, 2006), p. 100.
47. 'Deutsches Mädchen aus Paris?', *Bravo*, 1964/42, 18 October 1964, and K. Tyler, liner notes for *La Belle Époque. EMI's French Girls, 1965–1968*, EMI CD, 0946 3 89899 2 9 (2007).
48. *Bravo*, 1964/49, 6 December 1964; *Hit Bilanz. Deutsche Chart Singles, 1956–1980* (Norderstedt, 2000), pp. 226–7; F. Bouwman, med medewerking van de Stichting Nederlandse Top 40, *Hit Dossier, 1939–1994* (Haarlem, 1994), p. 284; H. Olofsson, *Stora Popboken. Svensk Rock & Pop, 1954–1969* (Stockholm, 1995), p. 336.
49. L. Yaskiel, in M. Radcliffe, *Pop in Translation*, BBC Radio 4, 15 December 2007.
50. Radcliffe, *Pop in Translation*. Shaw's full discography can be found at her website: http://www.sandieshaw.com/catalogue.php (accessed 15 November 2009.) Kieron Tyler notes that 'any French record fair will file the Sandie Shaw records amongst the native performers', K. Tyler, liner notes for *La Belle Époque. EMI's French Girls, 1965–1968*, EMI CD, 0946 3 89899 2 9 (2007).
51. Cliff enjoyed 13 German-language hits in the German charts between 1961 and 1971, including two number ones – 'Rote Lippen soll man küssen' (1963) and 'Das ist die Frage aller Fragen' (1964): *Hit Bilanz. Deutsche Chart Singles, 1956–1980*, p. 191.
52. The Searchers re-recorded two songs, *Sugar and Spice* and *Needles and Pins*, as *Süß ist sie* and *Tausend Nadelstiche* in 1963 and 1964; Manfred Mann, whose singer Paul Jones had O-Level German, recorded *She* as *Sie* in 1964 while the Swinging Blue Jeans recorded two songs in German in 1964: Matheja, *1000 Nadelstiche*, pp. 184–5, 152, 202–3; Radcliffe, *Pop in Translation*.
53. George Martin in Radcliffe, *Pop in Translation*; 'She Loves You', released in Germany in January 1964, stayed in the charts for 21 weeks, 'Sie liebt dich', released in March, for only nine; 'I Wanna Hold Your Hand', released a week later, stayed in the charts for six months, giving the Beatles their first German number one, while 'Komm, gib mir deine Hand', released in April 1964, managed only 14 weeks and peaked at number five: *Hit Bilanz. Deutsche Chart Singles, 1956–1980*, p. 26.
54. I. MacDonald, *Revolution in the Head*, p. 81, fn.1.
55. S. Leigh, *Let's Go Down the Cavern. The Story of Liverpool's Merseybeat* (London, 1984), p. 122.
56. *Bravo*, 1966/25, 13 June 1966 and 1966/41, 3 October 1966; Matheja, *1000 Nadelstiche*, 91. The Scottish singer Lulu was another exception. If hardly at rock's cutting edge in the late 1960s, she enjoyed commercial success in Britain, but used German-language releases to keep a foothold in the West German market. She released four records in German between 1966 and 1971, Matheja, *1000 Nadelstiche*, pp. 149–50.
57. Rivers, *Rock'n'Roll Récit*, p. 88.

58. 'The French are incapable of singing rock properly. The language simply doesn't lend itself to the rhythm', Régis, age 15, in 'Rock Français ou Rock Anglo-Saxon?', *SLC*, 30, January 1965. Cf. Mike Warner, *né* Michael Werner, of Bielefeld, lead singer of Mike Warner and the Rebels, etc.: 'The German language and rock music: there's an unhappy marriage – and one that conflicts with my aesthetic sense', Klitsch, *Shakin'All Over*, p. 349.

59. H.D. Mannel and R. Oberling, *Beatgeschichte(n) im Revier* (Recklinghausen, 1993), p. 86.

60. Eudeline, *Anti-Yé-Yé*, p. 119.

61. Weighted by popularity: P. Rutten, *Hitmuziek in Nederland, 1960–1985* (Amsterdam, 1991), pp. 116–17, 121, 185.

62. Olofsson, *Stora Popboken*, pp. 420–39.

63. MacDonald, *Revolution in the Head*, p. 81, fn.1.

64. Klitsch, *Shakin' All Over*, p. 55.

65. Mumenthaler, *Beat, Pop, Protest*, pp. 93, 53.

66. Oro, *La Legión Extranjera*, p. 57, n.5.

67. Eudeline, *Anti-Yé-Yé*, p. 361.

68. K.-C. Schulze-Schlichtegroll, 'Zwischen Hädrich und Star Club – die drei intensiven Jahre der Harburger Twist- und Beatband "The Rascals"', in R. Busch (ed.), *Die Beatles in Harburg, 1961* (Hamburg, 1996), pp. 124–5.

69. 'Einmal Anders', *Star Club News*, 5, May 1965.

70. *Star Club News*, 4, April 1965.

71. Klitsch, *Shakin' All Over*, Index, pp. 450ff.

72. Klitsch, *Shakin' All Over*, pp. 317, 176.

73. Klitsch, *Shakin' All Over*, p. 366. The name was a combination of 'mushroom', inspired by the Pilzkopf haircut, and, for no obvious reason, 'roam'.

74. Matti, Müller and Riedo, *Als die Haare länger wurden*, p. 88. The name was a combination of 'shape' and 'sheep.'

75. Klitsch, *Shakin' All Over*, p. 189.

76. Klitsch, *Shakin' All Over*, pp. 391–2. The name was an adaptation of 'foreigners'.

77. Two of whose members were the sons of dentists, Klitsch, *Shakin' All Over*, p. 231.

78. A Basle rhythm-and-blues band, Mumenthaler, *Beat, Pop, Protest*, p. 137.

79. Competitors in the 1966 Recklinghausen Beatfestival, Mannel & Oberling, *Beatgeschichte(n) im Revier*, p. 125.

80. From Milan, Tarli, *Beat Italiano*, p. 171.

81. Klitsch, *Shakin' All Over*, p. 189.

82. Inspired by Jerry Lee Lewis's 1958 hit *Breathless*, Klitsch, *Shakin' All Over*, pp. 140–1.

83. Matti, Müller and Riedo, *Als die Haare länger wurden*, p. 94. The lead singer was Urs Fenster.

84. From Gävle in Sweden, Olofsson, *Stora Popboken*, pp. 173–4.

85. Olofsson, *Stora Popboken*, p. 145.

86. From Naples, Tarli, *Beat Italiano*, p. 179.

87. A Harburg beatband: L. Krüger, 'Beat in Harburg', in Busch (ed.), *Die Beatles in Harburg, 1961*, p. 157.

88. The lead singer, Achim Reichel, found the word in an English dictionary: 'Rattle, we read, meant to make a noise or a racket. That sounded good, so we promptly

agreed to be The Rattles', A. Reichel, 'With the Rattles', in Krüger and Pelc, *The Hamburg Sound*, p. 139.

89. Klitsch, *Shakin' All Over*, p. 83; 'Poor Boy' is included in Bear Family Records' compilation *The Lords, Singles, Hits und Raritäten*, BCD 16452 AR.

90. U. Krüger, 'We Could Not Believe the Sound: Interview with Ted "King Size" Taylor and John Frankland', in Krüger and Pelc (eds), *The Hamburg Sound*, p. 115.

91. Krüger, in Krüger and Pelc (eds) *The Hamburg Sound*, p. 131.

92. Klitsch, *Shakin' All Over*, p. 388.

93. Interview in S. Kloos (ed.), *POP 2000. 50 Jahre Popmusik und Jugendkultur in Deutschland* (Hamburg, 1999), p. 46.

94. Klitsch, *Shakin' All Over*, p. 385.

95. E.g. Christian Evo of Pollux, Eudeline, *Anti-Yé-Yé*, p. 133.

96. Testani, *Enciclopedia del Rock Italiano*, p. 137.

97. Mannel and Oberling, *Beatgeschichte(n) im Revier*, p. 86.

98. Klitsch, *Shakin' All Over*, p. 134.

99. Bille, *Dansk Rock Leksikon*, 147–8; Lilliestam, *Svensk Rock*, p. 88.

100. Lilliestam, *Svensk Rock*, p. 87.

101. Klitsch, *Shakin' All Over*, p. 127.

102. Klitsch, *Shakin' All Over*, pp. 71–4.

103. E.g. Brian Auger, in Krüger and Pelc, *The Hamburg Sound*, p. 120.

104. Eudeline, *Anti-Yé-Yé*, p. 128.

105. Klitsch, *Shakin' All Over*, p. 378.

106. Statistic from 1970, D. Siegfried, *Time is on My Side. Konsum und Politik in der Westdeutschen Jugendkultur der 60er Jahre* (Göttingen, 2006), p. 280.

107. Farin et. al, *50 Jahre Bravo*, pp. 38–47.

108. J.L.B., 'Avec les Teenagers Anglais. Les Folles Nuits de Londres', *SLC*, 23, June 1964.

109. Report from D. Mitchell, 17 May 1966, in file 'Britain Through French Eyes', The National Archives, FO 146/4630.

110. 1970 survey in G. Young, *Tourism: Blessing or Blight?* (London, 1973), p. 32; BTA, 'Survey among Visitors to London, Summer 1975', November 1975, London Metropolitan Archives, GLC/DG/PR/04/293.

111. *Star Club News*, 12, December 1965.

112. 'L'Île du Rock', *SLC*, 31, February 1965.

113. Eudeline, *Anti-Yé-Yé*, p. 151.

114. Pasqualini, *Les Yé-Yé*, p. 85, Eudeline, *Anti-Yé-Yé*, p. 205.

115. Antoine (Richard Bletsch), *Oh Yeah! Souvenirs, 1944–1974* (Paris, 2007), pp. 155ff. Eudeline, *Anti-Yé-Yé*, p. 208.

116. Recorded as *The Doll Who Said 'No'*, M. Polnareff, with Philippe Manœuvre, *Polnareff par Polnareff* (Paris, 2004), p. 35.

117. Ordovás, *Historia de la Musica Pop Española*, p. 84.

118. Hardy's highest British placing was sixteenth with 'All Over the World' in 1965. Johnny Hallyday, massively successful in France, never entered the British top 50, Betts, *U.K. Hit Singles*, p. 365.

119. *Mersey Beat*, 26 March–9 April 1964.

120. According to *Bravo*, 1964/6, 9 February 1964.

121. W. Walendowski, *Star Club Hamburg. Die Legende Lebt* (Marl, 2006), p. 12.

122. Betts, *U.K. Hit Singles*, p. 677.

123. R. Gaillac, 'Quatre Gentlemen se Penchent sur leur Passé (Récent)', *SLC*, 4, November 1962.
124. He also mentioned Sylvie Vartan, Richard Anthony, Charles Trenet, Gilbert Bécaud and Claude François. Brian Jones could manage only Hallyday, Hardy, Vartan and Anthony: 'Match: Beatles Contre Rolling Stones'. *SLC*, 29, December 1964.
125. Klitsch, *Shakin' All Over*, p. 164.
126. A. Clayson, *Hamburg. The Cradle of British Rock* (London, 1997), p. 50.
127. *East London Advertiser*, 20 January 1967.
128. Clayson, *Hamburg*, p. 226; U. Krüger, 'We Could not Believe the Sound: Interview with Ted "King Size" Taylor and John Frankland', in Krüger and Pelc (eds) *The Hamburg Sound*, pp. 112ff.
129. Clayson, *Hamburg*, p. 107; U. Krüger, 'I Went back to Hamburg: Interview with Ian Edwards', in Krüger and Pelc (eds), *The Hamburg Sound*, pp. 126ff.
130. Clayson, *Hamburg*, p. 226.
131. *Rock'n'Roll Récit*, 65; for Taylor, Chalvidant and Mouvet, *Groupes de Rock Français*, pp. 172–9; P. Saka (ed.), *Les Années Twist* (Paris, 1996), pp. 26–7.
132. They had previously been called the Shel Carson Combo and had been Gene Vincent's backing group for two years: G. Testani, *Enciclopedia del Rock Italiano* (Roma, 2006), p. 348; Tarli, *Rock Italiano*, pp. 163–4.
133. See http://koti.mbnet.fi/wdd/deejays.htm (accessed 15 November 2009); Olofsson, *Stora Popboken*, pp.105–7; Clayson, *Hamburg*, pp. 14fn.
134. Editorial, *Star Club News*, 2, February 1965.
135. Eudeline, *Anti-Yé-Yé*, p. 397.
136. Chalvidant and Mouvet, *Groupes de Rock Français*, p. 116; Dumont, *Lionceaux*, p. 78.
137. H.O. Gottfridsson, 'British Beat in Hamburg', in Krüger and Pelc (eds), *The Hamburg Sound*, p. 106.
138. Mumenthaler, *Beat, Pop, Protest*, p. 76.
139. D. Baacke, *Beat – die sprachlose Opposition* (Munich, 1972), p. 33.
140. Mannel and Oberling, *Beatgeschichte(n) im Revier*, pp. 90–1.
141. Baacke, *Beat*, p. 132; D. Siegfried, *Time is on My Side. Konsum und Politik in der Westdeutschen Jugendkultur der 60er Jahre* (Göttingen, 2006), p. 215. The Lords made their name by winning the West Berlin competition, Klitsch, *Shakin' All Over*, p. 142.
142. Olofsson, *Stora Popboken*, p. 343.
143. Bille, *Dansk Rock Leksikon*, pp. 71, 74, 242, 131.
144. G. Tillekens, *Het Geluid van de Beatles* (Amsterdam, 1998), p. 7.
145. In February 1966 The Guitarmen won the Saarland Beatles Show wearing 'shiny black polyester wigs like mother's mop', Klitsch, *Shakin' All Over*, p. 260.
146. Eva, aged 19, in 'Rock Français ou Rock Anglo-Saxon?', *SLC*, 30, January 1965.
147. Rivers, *Rock'n'Roll Récit*, p. 102.
148. Dumont, *Lionceaux*, p. 101.
149. Siegfried, *Time is on My Side*, p. 344.
150. Siegfried, *Time is on My Side*, pp. 342–3.
151. U. Nielsen, *40 Jahre Beat-Club* (Berlin, 2005), p. 20.
152. Mike and Lisa d'Abo to Uschi Nerke, in U. Nehrke, *40 Jahre mein Beat-Club. Meine persönlichen Erlebnisse und Erinnerungen* (Benitz, 2005), p. 56.
153. Klitsch, *Shakin' All Over*, pp. 128–9.
154. Walendowski, *Star Club Hamburg*, p. 204.

155. Clayson, *Hamburg*, p. 219.
156. Klitsch, *Shakin' All Over*, p. 376. Weißleder stressed that the Rattles 'had no promotion in the press, on the radio or on television', *Star Club News*, 2, February 1965.
157. Klitsch, *Shakin' All Over*, p. 268.
158. See, e.g., Frame, *Restless Generation*, pp. 284, 395.
159. 'Ils ont passé la Manche', *Mademoiselle Age Tendre*, 27, January 1967, p. 44.
160. Interview by M. Zagha, *Le Top des Pops*, BBC Radio 4, 16 August 2005.
161. Rivers, *Rock'n'Roll Récit*, p. 131.
162. *SLC*, 32, March 1965.
163. *Bravo*, 1966/45, 31 October 1966.
164. Lilliestam, *Svensk Rock*, pp. 93–4.
165. Eudeline, *Anti-Yé-Yé*, p. 116; Rivers, *Rock'n'Roll Récit*, p. 162.
166. Polnareff, *Polnareff*, p. 35; Eudeline, *Anti-Yé-Yé*, p. 272; Rivers, *Rock'n'Roll Récit*, p. 130.
167. Klitsch, *Shakin' All Over*, pp. 70, 82.
168. Michael Leckebusch of Beat-Club Bremen: Siegfried, *Time is on My Side*, p. 346.
169. C. Müller, *Das BRAVO Chart-Lexikon. Alle Interpreten und Hits der BRAVO-Charts, 1956–2005* (Niederkassel, 2006), p. 363, etc.
170. Rutten's calculation, weighted by popularity of songs, *Hitmuziek in Nederland*, p. 184.
171. Pasqualini, *Les Yé-Yé*, p. 95.
172. G. Borgna, *Storia Della Canzone Italiana* (Milan, 1996 ed.), p. 329.
173. Rutten, *Hitmuziek in Nederland*, pp. 110–11.
174. 26 nations in addition to Britain and Ireland have entered songs in English in the Contest's first 50 years, I. Raykoff, 'Camping on the Borders of Europe', in I. Raykoff and R.D. Tobin (eds), *A Song for Europe. Popular Music and Politics in the Eurovision Song Contest* (Aldershot, 2007), p. 1fn.
175. V. De Grazia, *Irresistible Empire. America's Advance Through Twentieth-Century Europe* (Cambridge, MA, 2005), pp. 553–4. In De Grazia's index 'Rock'n'Roll' occurs twice, 'Elvis Presley' once.
176. A. Stephan, 'Cold War Alliances and the Emergence of Transatlantic Competition: An Introduction', and 'A Special German Case of Cultural Americanization', in A. Stephan (ed.), *The Americanization of Europe. Culture, Diplomacy, and Anti-Americanism after 1945* (New York and Oxford, 2nd Edition, 2007), pp. 16, 81. The claim is made twice but not sourced. Since German Beatles fans knew all about their heroes' horoscopes ('Das Schicksal der Beatles!', *Bravo*, 1966/24, 6 June 1966), their teeth ('Zähne wie die Beatles', *Bravo*, 1966/9, 21 February 1966) and even, Weißleder suggested, 'which side Paul McCartney sleeps on, or what insoles Ringo wears' (*Star Club News*, 6, June 1965), there was little excuse for confusion about the group's origins.
177. From an otherwise perceptive essay by Hugh Wilford, 'Britain: In Between', in Stephan (ed.), *Americanization of Europe*, p. 33.
178. 'Rock Français ou Rock Anglo-Saxon?', *SLC*, 30, January 1965.
179. R. Unterberger, *Turn! Turn! Turn! The 60s Folk-Rock Revolution* (San Francisco, 2002), chs 1–4, etc.
180. M.B. Kelly, 'Doc Rock', *The Beatles Myth. The British Invasion of American Popular Music, 1956–1969* (Jefferson NC, 1991).
181. Klitsch, *Shakin' All Over*, p. 15.
182. According to Tillekens, *Geluid van de Beatles*, p. 56.

183. Verlant, et al., *L'Odyssée*, p. 118.
184. Reichel fronted the psychedelic group A.R. & Machines.
185. J. Harris, *The Last Party. Britpop, Blair and the Demise of English Rock* (London, 2003). Harris describes Oasis as 'a limp post-modern pantomime based loosely on the career of The Beatles', p. 339.
186. S. Frith, 'Anglo-America and its Discontents', *Cultural Studies*, v(3), 1991, 266.
187. Tillekens, *Geluid van de Beatles*, p. 25.

# 12
## 'Nothing more cosmopolitan than the camps?' Holocaust Remembrance and (de-)Europeanization

*Henning Grunwald*

> Europe, on the fast track to integration, seems more and more to be finding a common unifying memory in the events of World War II, and – what is increasingly emerging *a posteriori* as its core event – the Holocaust. Such a commonly shared European memory is not only assuming the salience of an arsenal of remembrance. No, it is also being transformed into a veritable foundational, a seminal event – quite comparable to a certain extent to the Reformation or the French Revolution, an event, to which historical memory, as it thickens into a catalog of narrations and values, seems to lead back.
>
> (Dan Diner)[1]

> Die verwandelnde Gegenständlichkeit ist der Preis, den das Lebendige zahlt, um überhaupt in der Welt bleiben zu können.
>
> (Hannah Arendt)[2]

Is there an obligation to remember the Holocaust? What is European about it, and does it make us more European to honour this obligation? In his essay on the 'Ethics of Memory', the philosopher Avishai Margalit describes memory as the essence of 'thick relations', linking individuals and groups to their immediate social vicinity: families, friends, tribes. Memory is a central *social* category, he argues, but only in special cases is it a *moral* one. Where 'gross crimes against humanity' are concerned, this 'morality' – as distinct from the 'ethics' – of memory entails an obligation to 'preserve memory': to speak a language, to build institutions, and to practise rituals of memorialization. The distinction begs the question of who exactly is bound by this obligation to remember, as Margalit himself emphasizes: 'humanity is no community of memory. (...) So who should carry the "moral memory" on behalf of humanity as a whole?'[3]

One possible answer (and this is where the topic becomes interesting for our research into Europeanization) is: the Europeans. Clearly, crimes such as the mass enslavement of forced labourers in the Second World War, the massive, forcible resettlement of millions of ethnically-defined undesirables in the course and wake of conflict, and the destruction of the European Jews were transnational in their conception, perpetration and certainly in their consequences. To what degree is this true also of their memorialization? And what, if anything, is the connection with Europeanization of the crimes and their memory, on the one hand, and the growing importance of European identities and frames of reference, on the other? Is Europe really on the verge of becoming a 'community of memory', as Aleida Assmann has recently argued? If so, how much does Europe owe (in both senses of the word) to the 'negative founding myth'[4] that Dan Diner sees in the Holocaust?

This chapter first surveys attempts to frame Europeanization in terms of collective memory and collective identity through the respective lenses of political science, law, sociology, and of our own discipline. Reservations about the inflation of the term 'memory' in historical studies – voiced for example by Alon Confino or Lutz Niethammer – notwithstanding, a number of scholars have asserted the centrality of the Holocaust in this context, both as the object of European collective memory and as the catalyst of its emergence. Having said that, important disagreements continue to exist. On a methodological level, these pertain to what exactly constitutes collective memory. Regarding issues of content, many question the mutual compatibility of national narratives about genocide during the Second World War, and whether European memory supplants, complements, or contradicts these. Nevertheless, the very fact that, since the turn of the millennium, attention is being paid to the collective memory of the Holocaust, and further that attempts are being made to relate them (more or less convincingly) to Europeanization are, in themselves, significant.

Proceeding broadly chronologically from 1945, this chapter focuses primarily on the two Germanies, Poland and France. It takes a necessarily unsystematic look at the forms of Holocaust memorialization that developed, especially on the sites of the camps, and asks in what sense the legacy of genocide was invested with national, European, or even universal and ideological meaning and thrust. Given the scope of this chapter and the chronological and geographical breadth, my examples – the transformation of camps into memorials, a brief look at East German television, the Bitburg controversy, the debates on Jedwabne and the Vélodrome d'Hiver, and finally the International Task Force on Holocaust Education, Remembrance and Research (ITF) – are necessarily limited and the merits of their selection therefore open to debate.

My argument is firstly that, despite attempts at political manipulation, the memory of genocide had a Europeanizing dimension. Even with the 'freezing of memory' during the Cold War,[5] its alignment with the ideological exigencies of the political status quo was neither complete nor unambiguous. The vociferous reactions to Ronald Reagan's travel plans in 1985 illustrate this: his visit to Bitburg military cemetery, and the remarks that seemed to equate the German soldiers buried there with the Jews killed in the SS camps (both termed 'victims') provoked an outcry, and as a consequence a visit to Bergen-Belsen concentration camp was hastily tacked on to the itinerary. There, however, protesters not only demonstrated against Reagan's visit, but also against the perceived marginalization of Holocaust memory in West German political culture. In deliberately leaving camp memorials out of the initial plans for Reagan's visit, no doubt the last thing Chancellor Kohl's aides envisaged were German policemen having to manhandle Hasidic protesters to clear the way for the presidential motorcade into Bergen-Belsen. Meanwhile, Youri Vorontsov, Soviet ambassador to France, laid a wreath at Oradour-sur-Glane, site of an infamous massacre committed by *Waffen-SS* troops in 1944, to honour the 'eternal memory of French patriots and Soviet patriots'. This move, poignantly affirming the European and historical friendship binding France and the Soviet Union, attracted not only the applause of the French Communist Party, but also the much more unlikely acclamation of Margaret Thatcher.[6]

Playing on themes of anti-Americanism, anti-German sentiment, and the evocation of anti-fascist coalitions in which Communists featured prominently, the Bitburg affair signalled one of the ways in which the manipulation or political cropping of wartime memories was limited and could even prove counter-productive. Contrary to Kohl's intentions, more, not less, attention was paid to the Nazi persecution of the Jews, and the a-historical and insensitive 'Americanization' of Holocaust memory contrasted unfavourably with the European affirmation of anti-fascist solidarity (though both owed much to the politics of Cold War history).

Secondly – and this, too, is illustrated by the Bitburg episode – I argue that the relationship between (collective) memory of genocide and a strengthening European identity is complex. As Robert Gerwarth and Stephan Malinowski state earlier in this volume, the idea is not so much to overturn as to complicate the received notion (or 'happy history') of smooth and unambiguous post-war progress towards an ever-closer European Union. Not only is Holocaust memory tied to factors transcending Europe, but it is likewise fraught with contradictions even insofar as it is a European phenomenon. Indeed, while memory can serve as a unifying force, it can also prove equally divisive, not only erecting barriers between communities but also creating fractures within them.[7] The notion of France as a country of resisters relegated stories about French complicity in the deportation of Jews to the margins of newspapers and national identity, from the first disputes over the restitution of Parisian apartments to their rightful Jewish owners returning in 1945, to the under-acknowledged demolition of the Vélodrome d'Hiver (over which official remorse was expressed only in the mid-1990s, when François Mitterrand commissioned a memorial and his successor Chirac acknowledged French guilt in the *Rafle*). Just as Polish self-categorization as the primary sufferers of Nazi occupation was cast in national and then political terms, thus leaving little room for the commemoration of Jewish victims as such, so the Austrian self-stylization as the Nazis' first victims obstructed acknowledgement of Austrian responsibility in the genocide and supported a general view that, 'All suffering of the Jews during this period was inflicted upon them by the Germans and not by the Austrians; Austria bears no guilt for all of these evil things, and where there is no guilt, there is no obligation for restitution.'[8] Holocaust memory was by no means the driver of a straightforward, unidirectional process of Europeanization.

## Collective memory and Europeanization

The study of memory politics or 'collective remembrance' of both the Holocaust and of Europeanization has burgeoned. But are these proliferations related? That there is a 'memory boom' (or a 'memory wave', or even a 'memory mania') in the humanities is not disputed, merely celebrated or bemoaned. Alon Confino, for example, asserts the centrality of memory in cultural history ('a leading term, recently perhaps the leading term') before highlighting the 'fragmentation' of this field of study which 'lacks critical reflections on methods and theory'.[9] Wulf Kansteiner echoes this criticism, and remarks that much of what passes for study of memory has been editorially 'relabelled' and actually pursues research agendas which previously sailed 'under separate colors'.[10] Certainly, surging interest in Holocaust memorialization is an important factor in the disciplinary ascendancy of memory studies. Jan-Werner Müller argues that the Holocaust, by virtue of passing from 'communicative memory' (i.e., living) into 'cultural memory' drives a preoccupation with memory, as 'a final battle over the content of a future cultural memory is being waged by witnesses and as the intellectual legacies to be passed on and the dominant representations of the past are being contested'.[11] Jeffrey Olick links to the Holocaust the increase in redress claims and the 'politics of victimization and regret' as strategies for political conflict in multicultural societies, while Aleida Assmann underscores this point in less stark terms when she argues that the Holocaust provides a language and a template for the perception and articulation of other traumatic experiences.[12] Whether or not one agrees with Pierre Nora's assertion that 'whoever says memory says Shoah', it is clear that one can plausibly argue for a link, a mutual reinforcement between Holocaust memorialization and memory studies.[13]

But what about Europeanization? For that, we must first take a look at the terms 'collective memory' and 'collective identity'. Collective memory can be defined as 'collectively shared representations of the past'. Despite most users tracing their understanding of the term to Maurice Halbwachs (a student of Durkheim), Wulf Kansteiner has pointed out that they are nonetheless often uncomfortable with Halbwachsian 'anti-individualism' – that is, his emphasis on the social determination of memory.[14] As a result, the uses of 'collective memory' sometimes diverge from the claimed intellectual ancestry of the term, as for example when they extrapolate all too readily from individual to collective memory (this is the sense in which Pieter Lagrou speaks of a 'metaphor laden with problems'). Other scholars have tried to shed the Durkheimian baggage by introducing new terms such as 'mass individual memory' (Müller), 'collective remembrance' (Winter and Sivan), 'personal history making' (Rosenzweig and Thelen), or by simply reverting to the time-honoured concept of 'myth'.

In most contexts, collective memory implies a constructed and somehow official, elevated version of the past – *Gedächtnis, Andenken* rather than *Erinnerung*. Official memory is often infused with a telos, most pertinently (just to dismiss the white elephant from the room) that of the nation. In the words of Jeffrey Olick, 'memory and the nation have a peculiar synergy. Even when other identities compete with or supplant the national in postmodernity, they draw on the expanded role for memory generated in the crucible of the nation-state'.[15] Despite their best intentions, even scholars interested in applications of the concept transcending the nation-state find it hard at times to escape the implications of this 'synergy'. Jan-Werner Müller, in the volume quoted above on memory and power in post-war Europe, for example, writes that 'at a basic conceptual level (...) the essays collected here distinguish between 'collective' or 'national' memory on the one hand, and mass individual memory on the other'. The terms 'collective' and 'national' are used interchangeably, in other words, as synonyms.[16]

What about Europe? European collective memory is emphasized by those arguing for an emerging European identity as well as by those contesting it. Klaus Eder and Willfried Spohn, for example, set out to investigate 'transnational interest networks, transnational institutions and transnational communications spheres as mechanisms of the evolution of a European civic identity and memory'. Does it smack of Treitschkean teleology, 'Europeanized', to want to analyse 'the development of a European identity due to the reconstruction of national identities in an emerging Europe public sphere, where collective memories are contrasted, debated and reorganized'?[17] Pieter Lagrou and Tony Judt (in 'Myth and Memory in post-war Europe'), on the other hand, emphasize the elaborate and conflict-laden construction of particular versions of the recent past, the contested nature of war memories and the difficulties in reconciling them (the latter predicts an equivalent of *Historikerstreit* for Eastern Europe in the near future).

Lutz Niethammer connects the very origins of the term 'collective identity' in the writings of Carl Schmitt, Georg Lukacs and Carl Gustav Jung to a sense of crisis. It was coined (or the notion of identity expanded from a usage that had almost exclusively individual implications as in personal, individual identity) precisely to ward off a perceived threat to (national) identity construction in the wake of the First World War, and included from the outset an implicit moment of demarcation and exclusion. Even if one does not share Niethammer's open scepticism about efforts at European identity construction (for example, his disdainful comparison between the Copenhagen 'Declaration of European Identity' and Aldous Huxley's super-state slogan 'community, identity, stability' appears a little far-fetched[18]), it is worth considering whether the current popularity of the term is not indicative of a sense of disorientation, a lack of a clear sense of purpose and direction for the European project.[19]

Arguments for a more ambiguous link between European memories and present-day European identity are also on offer. Thomas Risse adapted his and Maria Green Cowles' three-step model for the study of Europeanization (goodness of fit – institutional mediation – actor strategies) to the changes in 'nation-state identity' in the UK, Germany and France since 1945.[20] In the case of Germany, it is the a-historicity of the newly emerging, post-war nation-state identity that facilitates the incorporation of a European identity alongside and overlapping with the national one, whereas in France and the UK, historically-developed notions of national particularity at times posed as obstacles, and at others hurried Europeanization along.

Whereas in Risse's argument Holocaust memory plays only an implicit role, it is deliberately eschewed in Jay Winter's and Emmanuel Sivan's volume dedicated to the remembrance of war in the twentieth century. As well as the sheer bulk of existing research, the authors justify their decision by citing the contentiousness of the issue and the possibility of appearing to seek a 'historicizing' of the Holocaust. The mere 'risk' of making the Holocaust fit into a general 'history of warfare, akin to the American treatment of Indians or the rape of Nanking' prompts this omission. This in itself, however, can be construed as an indication of the increasing virulence of Holocaust memory as a subject of historical inquiry and of its role as a nucleus for debates over collective identity.[21]

In short, Europe is identified as a space of particularly dense and contested collective memory or memories.[22] This is often linked inextricably with Europe as the site of the Holocaust. As Dan Diner states, 'Europe – the realm of the old continent, where the Holocaust was after all perpetrated, and where its remembrance certainly has a real impact on political discourse and political reality to come.' This view is expanded upon by Aleida Assmann: 'In Europe, the historical site of the German genocide of the Jews, Holocaust memory has a different quality and resonance (...) In Europe this memory is anything but abstract and removed, but rather deeply engraved in local and national history.'[23] Such statements reveal the palpable move away from considering national contexts in isolation and towards a more trans-national perspective.[24] Scholars disagree, however, on whether there is an adaptation of national identities to accommodate another layer of identity

(Kohler-Koch's model), or whether we are beginning to witness a supplanting of separate and incompatible national memories with a European collective memory, or at least with a permanent substantial modification of national memories to allow for their partial merging into a 'shared collective memory', as Assmann and Müller appear to suggest.

## Holocaust memorialization in post-war Europe

Primo Levi's account of his arrival at Auschwitz powerfully evokes the multi-national composition of the camp populations. This is illustrated when he describes, for example, his lengthy search for his countrymen (or, at least, for Italian speakers) in order to help him understand the most basic rules of survival in the camp, or explains that a truly savvy inmate could identify a stranger's nationality by the numerical range into which his tattoo fell.[25] Although the very mention of Levi forbids any romanticizing of this forced community of victims, it is striking that the idea of commemorating dead comrades and of affirming international solidarity within the camp community played a prominent role in shaping inmates' ideas about memorializing their plight and defiance. A little more than a week after the liberation of Buchenwald, for example, on 19 April 1945, in a carefully choreographed ceremony, a temporary memorial was dedicated to the inmates of the camp (consisting of a wooden obelisk bearing the simple inscription 'KLB 51 000', for *Konzentrations-Lager* Buchenwald and the number of victims). Although most of the inmates and most of the members of the inmates' committee organizing the ceremony were German, it was a matter of course that the pledge of remembrance and anti-fascist defiance was read out in a number of languages. The highlight of the ceremony was an oath to continue the struggle – 'We will only cease our struggle when the last of the guilty ones has been sentenced in the court of all nations' – which in itself referred to an international community perceived to be the counterweight to Nazi oppression. Earlier, the inmates had marched in to the sound of their respective national anthems, with the exception, interestingly, of the camp resistance, which had entered the parade ground to the sound of the *Internationale*.[26]

Both the makeshift nature of the memorial and its location on the *Appell-platz* indicate that the actual memorial was to be the camp itself, the preservation of which most survivors assumed as a matter of course – both in Buchenwald and elsewhere. In fact, before the American authorities transferred control of Weimar and its surroundings to the Soviet forces, the camp was used as a kind of memorial-cum-educational facility. In the haste of their flight, the SS guards had left a pile of corpses next to the crematoria operating at the limits of their capacity, where they were discovered by the liberators on 11 April 1945. On 15 and 16 April this pile of corpses was reconstructed, using the bodies of inmates overcome by their debilitation *after* the liberation, in order to demonstrate the extent of the horror to the

1000 or so Weimar citizens who were escorted through the camp grounds on General Patton's orders.

In the following days, the pile was kept intact using the bodies of recently deceased ex-prisoners, while a second one was constructed on a trailer to illustrate the practice of carting excess corpses through the camp for burial or burning off-site. Former inmates volunteered for demonstrations of the atrocities committed against them using straw puppets dressed in prisoner's garb. The inmates' committee even proposed to commit the SS guards themselves to serve as a permanent, living memorial: dressed in the same clothes as their former charges, living in the same quarters, with the same rations, and spending their lives tending to the exact preservation of the camp sites, including pulling weeds out of the parade ground.[27] While this was never enacted, the effect of the demonstrations that did take place – now primarily for the benefit of US military visitors – was such that on 30 April the chief medical officer of the US Army in Germany recommended that they be continued. When their cessation was ordered on 9 May, almost four weeks after the liberation, it was not because this somewhat macabre practice of memorialization per se was rescinded, but rather because, after repair and cleaning, the now relatively appealing camp facilities precluded a realistic impression of the hardship of the inmates' lives.[28]

When the East German Socialist Unity Party (SED) took control of camp memorialization, the idea of maintaining the camps themselves as memorials was made impossible by their continued utilization as 'special' labour and internment camps.[29] What remained, however, was the desire to record the international dimension of both the suffering and the community it forged. Hermann Henselmann, the director of the Academy of Fine Arts at Dessau, was commissioned to design a memorial. He envisaged linking the name of Buchenwald, like that of Goethe, indelibly to Weimar, 'and I mean that in a positive sense: Through the suffering of the terror, inmates from 36 nations are forged into the solidarity of the new Europe'. Water, the 'symbol of life', was to spout from 36 individual outlets and fuse into one stream, while soil from each country was to be ceremonially buried at the site, in central Weimar.[30] As Volkhard Knigge observes, this projected memorial did 'not simply announce the arrival of an entirely new world but also seeks to convey how this world came to be. From the night of fascism (...) springs new life (...) through the martyrdom, death and solidarity of the KZ inmates. The concentration camp is not only the germ cell of the new Germany, but of a new Europe'.[31]

In the course of the 1950s and 1960s, the logic of Cold War separation asserted itself ever more strongly upon the contours of camp memorial sites. In their (winning) 1952 conception for the Buchenwald memorial on the Ettersberg, Bertolt Brecht, Reinhold Lingner and sculptor Fritz Cremer envisaged an ensemble that was both a stage (literally; it is a 13 000-spectator amphitheatre) for commemorative performance and an embodiment of

Cold War doctrine. A group of figures – inmates – 12 metres tall on a base measuring 15 metres, stares belligerently west, with clubs and rifles raised. The motto, 'Here freedom began – when will it embrace everyman?' (*'Hier fing die Freiheit an – Wann wird frei sein jedermann?'*) is chiselled into the base. 'The stony inmates (...) all look westwards with an expression of worried concern on their faces. Their posture and gestures, however, express their determination to fight for the definitive destruction (*endgültige Vernichtung*) of fascism in a united Germany', the artists explain. Indeed, the SED subsequently intervened to make the figures express this message with even greater clarity than Cremer's first models did.[32]

As the inmates were reduced to the archetypal Communist resister, the largest group of victims, the Jews, dropped from sight. This was unsurprising, perhaps, in a year when the East German Jewish Communist Paul Merker was implicated in the 'cosmopolitan' plot 'revealed' by the defendants in the Slansky trial in Prague. Among other charges, it was alleged that Merker's advocacy for restitution payments from East Germany to Nazi victims was designed to starve the GDR financially, thus making it more easily penetrable by 'international finance'; neither the absurdity of the charge nor the ancestry of the language in which it was couched require commentary. Merker's personal tragedy aside, it is striking how successfully *East* German implication in the genocide was marginalized. In the open-ended question 'what is significant in German history', 13 per cent of respondents in the West, but only 1 per cent of respondents in the East replied 'the Holocaust' (compared with 23 per cent and 36 per cent, respectively, for 'the Second World War').[33]

Neither this tightening of the reins in camp memorialization nor the stronger emphasis on the nation apparent in the language above was limited to East Germany, or, for that matter, to the East. At the official West German dedication of the Bergen-Belsen memorial in November 1952 (the same year that Brecht, Cremer, and Lingner submitted their proposal anticipating the defeat of fascism in a united Germany), Yugoslavia was the only Eastern bloc country to send a representative. The message of remorse and shame (*'Diese Scham nimmt uns niemand ab'*) that President Heuss delivered was typical of the elite remembrance that Heuss, Schumacher and, more ambiguously, Adenauer encouraged but that did not translate into stringent judicial persecution of the perpetrators in West German society. Nor did it stand in the way, as Jeffrey Herf has demonstrated, of suppressing memory of the causal link between the German assault on the Soviet Union and the latter's conquest of Eastern Europe and Eastern Germany.[34]

In Poland, where the camp sites *were* preserved, the opening of the Auschwitz memorial in April 1967 made explicit what the Buchenwald memorial stopped just short of proclaiming. Camp survivor and Polish Prime Minister Cyrankiewicz enjoined the Federal Republic to give up policies with 'National Socialist pedigree', to recognize Poland's western frontier, and to renounce its 'lusting after atomic weapons'. Soviet General Pietrenko, who had helped liberate the camp in 1945, called on the USA to stop the war in Vietnam. At the same time as the victims were stylized and honoured as resisters and martyrs, they were also marked as Polish patriots. Nothing encapsulates this more clearly than the ritual conferring of the highest order of the Polish People's Republic – the Grunwald Order – upon the victims/martyrs (a giant replica was prominently integrated into the memorial); but we might also cite the red triangle (marked with the letter P for Poland) which was used liberally in the memorial.[35] 'Catholic-Communist Martyrology left no space' for those not mandated by the official version of resistance and sacrifice by Poles and Communists: gypsies, homosexuals, prostitutes and so forth. While Jews were given their own pavilion among the nations, it proved short-lived; within a few short months, the onset of the Yom Kippur War had occasioned its closing for 'repairs'.[36]

In France, the nationalization of camp memory is even clearer. After initial use as an internment camp, Natzweiler-Struthof was declared the French 'national necropolis' for the victims of deportation (the category which Jews were invited to assume in France). Whereas other camps commemorated – at least initially – the multinational composition of their prisoner populations, in Struthof it was in some ways the reverse. A commemorative plaque for the international victims of deportation notwithstanding, the primary goal was to make Struthof – located in Alsace and thus in a region where patriotism was perennially in need of disambiguation – a national monument. To this end, ashes or soil from the burial grounds of other concentration camps were brought to Struthof, not (as in the case of Buchenwald) to give the remains of foreigners a piece of home in which to rest, but rather to bring home the remains of deported Frenchmen.[37]

From these (necessarily) limited observations, it appears that a number of qualifications may be made to the argument that the Cold War 'froze' and de-nationalized memory of the war. The Cold War did act as a catalyst for suppressing some and emphasizing other aspects of the wartime experience, as Judt, Diner, Lagrou and Assmann have argued; certainly, a waning of internationalism and the idea of a united Europe emerging from the camp experience is evident. But did the 'Cold War's chemistry' really act as 'the great neutralizer of the substrate of nationalism and the particularistic memories bound up with it' (Diner)? In the case of Poland, nationalist resurgence coincided with – indeed, was encouraged by – the assertion of Soviet control. In a situation where police, border guards and armed forces were effectively controlled from Moscow, it was tempting to fan the flames of Polish nationalism as a kind of *Ersatz* arena for staging fantasies of unity and homogeneity (violently, of course). More than 200 000 Ukrainians were forcibly 'repatriated' or, in a second, slightly less brutal but equally gruelling wave, resettled away from the Soviet border to north-western Poland (that is, into the recently incorporated former German territory).[38]

In fact, the experience of National Socialist occupation and persecution, while providing for homogeneous experiences of victims regardless of their nationality, did not feed directly into a unified European consciousness. On the contrary, the memory of these experiences was harnessed to bolster projects of national reconstruction, as well as being utilized by both East and West in the emerging Cold War confrontation. Pieter Lagrou argues that the exigencies of shoring up and reconstructing national consciousness in the aftermath of the triple humiliation of military defeat, National Socialist occupation, and liberation by foreign armies dictated a repression of the less heroic aspects of life during the Second World War in the memory regimes of post-war Belgium, France and the Netherlands:

> The dominating collective experience was not heroism: it was, rather, economic hardship, individual suffering, humiliation and arbitrary persecution. The liberated societies of Europe were traumatized, and their now fragile national self-consciousness was in urgent need of the kind of patriotic epic that only the resistance could deliver. In this context, persecution as a more fundamental experience was unacceptable, something not to be spoken of.

Underneath this overarching argument, Lagrou distinguishes between three groups: resistance veterans, forced labourers, and victims of persecution. While in each case wartime experience and its post-war reconfiguration was 'shaped by the straitjacket of post-war patriotism', each group was 'united less as citizens of different states and more by the shared experience of resistance, forced economic migration or Nazi persecution'.[39] Owing to efforts at reconciling wartime humiliation with the self-image and loyalty claims of the nation-state, occupation and persecution experiences – despite being 'closely identical' – were recast in national discourses of remembrance, so that 'the memories they engendered were quite divergent'.[40]

The 'straitjacket' of post-war reconstruction of national consciousness was, in other words, a roadblock on a path to potential (albeit limited) Europeanization through shared remembrance of wartime victimization. It is unfortunate from our perspective that Lagrou excludes an examination of the German case on 'a logical ground' as both the Federal Republic of Germany and the German Democratic Republic show parallels to the developments he describes and analyses.[41]

As a Europeanizing agent, much more important than the rather vague conception of a new Europe entertained by Henselmann and others was the anti-German feeling engendered by Nazi occupation. As Dutchman Ian Buruma puts it, it 'was comforting to know that a border separated us from the nation that embodied the evil. They were evil, so consequently we must have been good. The fact that we grew up in a country which had suffered under the German occupation meant, to us, that we were on the side of the angels.' Tony Judt speaks of a 'European consensus' regarding this question, and Peter Esterhazy expresses the idea even more radically: 'To conceal one's own guilt by referring to Germany's crimes is a European habit. Hatred for the Germans is the foundation of the post-war period.'[42] In that sense, the main Europeanizing function of camp memorialization may have been to sustain this habit and consensus, its Europeanizing effect thus quite independent of overt political utilization. This was, moreover, a paradoxical Europeanization, turning as it did on the memory of German guilt at the same time as Western Germany was rearmed and integrated into NATO, and as the country emerged as one of the central participants in the Europeanization of Western Europe. This paradox may in part explain the depth of sentiment and alarm during the Bitburg affair, alarm at what was perceived (probably rightly) as an attempt to rewrite the basic script of memory of German guilt and Europeanization. It may also explain why in today's Europe, with German historical guilt undisputed but now also remote, the search for a Europeanized and a Europeanizing Holocaust memory is definitely on.

## Holocaust memorialization post-1989

It should first of all be said that it is in this post-1989 period that the trend towards Holocaust memorialization has been most pronounced. Many of the features of the 'memorialization landscape' that we take for granted were contested and/or inaugurated only in the mid-1990s: the Berlin Holocaust memorial, for instance, or the introduction of a memorial day (27 January) honouring the victims of fascism are of such recent vintage. Whereas in 1959, the Vélodrome d'Hiver was unceremoniously bulldozed (Salvador Dali blew up a replica of the Eiffel Tower on stage during the farewell celebrations, while the memorial plaque to the *Rafle* was an embarrassment to the property developers and was moved to an unobtrusive corner), in 1995 President Chirac publicly apologized for the role of the French state in the deportations. At the same time, the challenges to the modes and even the centrality of Holocaust remembrance have also increased since 1989. Jan Gross's book on the Jedwabne pogrom, the apology by the Polish government for the crimes of Poles against their Jewish neighbours and the debate this precipitated is a case in point. Optimistically, we might see an instance of national narrative – the Polish national victim self-categorization – becoming more nuanced to reflect the ambiguities of the wartime experience and even, perhaps, the complicity in genocidal violence. In France, intellectuals have debated whether remembrance of the Nazi genocide has unduly eclipsed the engagement with Stalinism's crimes and victims, to which critics reply that memory is not a zero-sum game. In Eastern Europe generally, scholars diagnose a sense that the Holocaust paradigm is too narrow to allow for adequate expression of wartime and post-war experiences of Communist as well as Nazi oppression.[43]

Surveying the explanations offered for the recent surge in Holocaust memorialization and its contestation, an emphasis on the juridical stands out. Not only sociologists of law such as Mark Osiel, but also such historians as Dan Diner and Henry Rousso highlight the importance of the law in facilitating Holocaust memory in Europe. The emphasis is not so much on trials (as it was in the mid-1940s, early 1960s and mid-1980s), but on other legal processes and modes of thought: restitution, Nazi gold, and compensation and pensions for forced labourers. Trials tend to be conducted within national jurisdictions (with the exception of Nuremberg). A corollary of the move away from trials as the primary arena of judicial remembrance is therefore the facilitation of transnational contexts of assessing claims and reconciling narratives. The claims for the centrality of legal modes of discourse in promoting the ascendancy of the *'régime d'historicité'* of paradigmatic Holocaust memory are strong. In accounting for the Europeanization of Holocaust memory, Rousso (who also assesses its 'globalization', as discussed below) provides four reasons, of which three (reparations, ascendancy of law, and discourses of victimization) are directly tied to law (the fourth, the 'de-nationalization of history' is a methodological rather than a substantive factor). Dan Diner's claims are, if anything, even stronger:

> The growing awareness concerning the Holocaust we do observe in Europe since 1989 seems to be a phenomenon largely moored in a basic anthropological assumption – the obvious, indeed organic interconnection between restituted private property rights and the evocation of past memories, or vice versa: Restitution of property as the result of recovered memory. This intriguing anthropological conjunction between property and memory can help explain why World War II and the Holocaust may well enjoy a long future in an emergent common European memory.[44]

This (re)turn to law as a primary *explanans* in accounting for the 'memory wave' and for the memory of the Shoah as one of 'memory mania's' prime drivers is all the more remarkable for its recent gestation. As late as 1997, in a presentation at Boalt Hall, Vera Ranki came to a diametrically opposed conclusion about the function of law, diagnosing with some alarm its normalizing, abstracting and banalizing influence on the perception of the Holocaust. In her view, there was a direct link – via legal discourse – between the trials of Zundel, Barbie and Pavlyushenko, on the one hand, and the 'Holocaust on ice' (where a competitor at a figure-skating tournament dressed in grey attire with Hebrew lettering and danced to the soundtrack of *Schindler's List*) on the other.[45]

## Conclusion

Is there an obligation to remember the Holocaust? What is European about it, and does it make us more European to honour this obligation? The answer of the Stockholm conference and the International Task Force for Holocaust Education, Remembrance and Research (ITF) to the first part of the question is an emphatic yes. 'The magnitude of the Holocaust', it affirms, 'must be forever seared into our collective memory' (Par. 3). The founding document pledges concrete steps to further Holocaust remembrance, including the establishment of a day of commemoration (Par. 6). On the geographic extent of this obligation, the Stockholm Declaration – adoption of which is a precondition for membership of the ITF – is more ambivalent. Although the first paragraph speaks of an 'indelible scar across Europe', the third calls on the 'international community' to take responsibility for the ITF's mission. In the membership accession procedure, this international community is further defined as those states 'commonly seen as democracies'. Willing and commonly recognized democracies seeking entry to the ITF commit resources to Holocaust memorialization and research, and accept the scrutiny of the existing members during the admission process (which includes year-long mandatory waiting periods). Further, they send teachers on training programmes in established member countries and establish a memorial day ('27 January or another day').

A look at the current ITF membership implies an answer to the second part of the question: an overwhelming 21 out of 24 member states are European. Interestingly, nine of the 27 EU countries are missing, notably Romania, Bulgaria, Slovenia, Finland, Spain and Portugal (as well as Cyprus, Malta and Ireland). In contrast, Switzerland, Norway and Croatia are part of the ITF though not the EU. Argentina, Israel and the USA complete the membership. The formation of the ITF is an example of the kind of clustering and self-reinforcing *practice* in which our research on the 'Europeanization of Europe' is interested. Two-thirds of the EU member states are part of the ITF, along with three other countries whose European credentials are hardly in doubt. The Europeanizing of and through Holocaust memory has here taken on a concrete institutional form; the forerunners – both discursive and institutional (such as the inauguration of Holocaust memorial days in France and Germany in 1995 and 1996, respectively) – can be construed as part of a positive feedback loop accumulating or accreting towards this institution. Which is certainly European, but which is also intricately linked to the national and (through both the mission statement and the extra-European members) to the global level. This is not a teleological argument. Ranki's diagnosis of a gradual withering away of Holocaust significance in 1997, but also (for example) Henry Rousso's tale of the curiously muted response to the Bitburg affair in France make it clear that we are at a particular point in a trajectory whose overall intensity – as well as its 'Europeanness' – may wane as well as wax.[46]

The extra-European ITF members also help address the questions with which the authors of this volume have grappled regarding the relationship between globalization and Europeanization. Sznaider and Levy have argued for a 'globalization' of Holocaust memory, and the diaspora of Holocaust survivors and their families, the universal relevance of the Holocaust as a template and language for the articulation of trauma, as well as evident global interest and the existence of a community of scholars are all illustrations of the validity of their point.[47] On the other hand, as with the relative robustness of the European human-rights regime (which can be traced back to the Nazi genocide), we do observe a certain European centre of gravity: the founding of the ITF, its original and subsequent membership, and even the specific ties of the non-European ITF members to the European sites and the European peoples involved in the genocide.

Let me finish with two contrasting notes. This chapter argued at the outset that Holocaust memory has not been the driver of a simple, unidirectional process of Europeanization. *Coming to terms* with the divisive potential and the incompatibility of national narratives, the discourse in various national contexts and across national boundaries, however, may well be such a driver. Holocaust memory may be one of the subjects of the 'transnational public sphere' postulated rather grandly by Eder and Spohn. By fostering awareness of the historical self-image of European neighbours, it may allow us to negotiate the sticking points, to identify where and why national narratives clash and to reconcile them – or, at the very least, to agree to disagree. Jan-Werner Müller and Aleida Assmann, while aware of the dangers (Assmann ambiguously refers to a European 'self-hypnosis') of taking too naïve a position along those lines, argue this. Indeed, even sceptics have to admit that the thought of Turkey joining the ITF would be an encouraging step in the direction of 'Europeanizing' its relationship to its own past.[48] On the other hand, it should be recalled that Charles Maier's 'surfeit of memory' referred not to a token of confidence, but rather to a symptom of crisis, the 'retreat from transformative politics'. Could the same be true of the current formation of a European collective memory and identity around the Holocaust, as Europe, unsure on a number of levels about its identity and future direction, searches for clues?

## Notes

1. D. Diner, 'Restitution and Memory: The Holocaust in European Political Cultures', *New German Critique*, XC, Taboo, Trauma, Holocaust (Autumn, 2003), 36–44, 36.
2. H. Arendt, *Vita Activa* (Munich, 1960), p. 87f.
3. A. Margalit, *The Ethics of Memory* (Cambridge, MA, 2002), p. 8f.
4. A. Assmann, 'Europe: A Community of Memory?', *GHI Bulletin*, XL (Spring 2007) 12–25, D. Diner, 'Restitution and Memory: The Holocaust in European Political Cultures', 36–44.

5. T. Judt, 'The Past is Another Country: Myth and Memory Making in Postwar Europe,' in J.-W. Müller (ed.), *Memory and Power in Post-war Europe: Studies in the Presence of the Past* (Cambridge, 2002), p. 157; A. Assmann, 'Europe: A Community of Memory?', 12–25, 15.

6. H. Rousso, 'The Reactions in France: The Sounds of Silence', in G. Hartmann (ed.), *Bitburg in Moral and Political Perspective* (Bloomington, 1986), p. 55f.

7. 'The result of such efforts to cope with German catastrophes is an insecure memory culture, full of taboos and given to controversy. (…) This emphasis on particular suffering has prevented the realization of the interconnectedness of the historical sources of pain which might encourage greater compassion. The intensely partisan politics of memory have, therefore, failed to produce a coherent and generally accepted reading of the German past.' K. Jarausch, 'Living with Broken Memories: Some Narratological Comments', in C. Klessmann (ed.), *Divided Past: Rewriting Post-war German History* (Oxford, 2001), pp. 189–90.

8. H. Uhl, 'Vom Opfermythos zur Mitverantwortungsthese: NS-Herrschaft, Krieg und Holocaust im Oesterreichischen Gedaechtnis', in C. Gerbel, et al. (eds), *Transformationen gesellschaftlicher Erinnerung: Studien zur Gedaechtnisgeschichte der Zweiten Republik* (Vienna, 2005), p. 57.

9. A. Confino, *Germany as a Culture of Remembrance. Promises and Limits of Writing History* (Chapel Hill, 2006), p. 170f. For 'memory mania' see C. Lenz and H. Welzer, 'Opa in Europa. Erste Befunde einer vergleichenden Tradierungsforschung', in H. Welzer (ed.), *Der Krieg der Erinnerung. Holocaust und Widerstand im europaeischen Gedaechtnis* (Frankfurt am Main, 2007), p. 7.

10. W. Kansteiner, 'Finding Meaning in Memory: A Methodological Critique of Collective Memory Studies', *History and Theory*, XLI, No. 2 (May, 2002), 179–97, 182.

11. Müller offers other explanations for the memory boom, too, but both in the space allocated and in explanatory power they are eclipsed by the Holocaust discussion. They include the acceleration of technological innovation which has made objects, texts and images of memory accessible, while Müller's argument about structural changes in our relationship to time, a sort of 'fin de siècle consciousness' as a driver behind the renaissance of memory read more convincingly in 1998 than now, more than ten years later, while the disappearance of rural Europe to which he refers is more gradual a shift, Müller, *Memory and Power*, pp. 13–17, quotes p. 14.

12. For Olick see Müller, *Memory and Power*, p. 16 and fn. 65; Assmann, 'Community of Memory?', 14.

13. Quoted in U. Raulff, 'Der Augenblick Danach', FAZ 8.7.1998.

14. W. Kansteiner, 'Finding Meaning in Memory', 179–97, 181.

15. J. Olick, 'Introduction', in *Social Science History* XXII, No. 4, Special Issue Memory and the Nation (Winter, 1998), 379. Cf. G. Delanty and C. Rumford, *Rethinking Europe. Social Theory and the Implications of Europeanization* (London, 2005), p. 95f.

16. J.-W. Müller, *Memory and Power*, p. 3. See also p. 27.

17. W. Spohn, 'National Identities and Collective Memory in an Enlarged Europe', in K. Eder and W. Spohn (eds), *Collective Memory and European Identity. The Effects of Integration and Enlargement* (Aldershot, 2005), here p. 1f, with reference to the entire collection of essays. In general, this work is somewhat less helpful and enlightening than its title might suggest. Regarding the European flag (which has continually boasted a dozen stars, regardless of increases in EC/EU membership),

for example, we learn that '[t]his political act is then represented – again following the model of the nation-state – with a flag (for the moment with 15 [sic] stars), which again is supposed to provoke a sense of pride (as flags often do).' (p. 218). Many of the definitions and explanations seem to boil down to an affirmation that being European is either linked to being a citizen of an EU member country or another country that is hoping to join the EU (see e.g. p. 213, 'core identity'), while the talk of a 'society of monkeys' (p. 203) is puzzling.

18. Declaration on European Identity, *Bulletin of the European Communities*, 12 (December 1973), pp. 118–22.
19. Assmann, 'Community of Memory?', 12.
20. T. Risse, 'A European Identity?' in J. Caporaso, M. Green Cowles, and T. Risse (eds), *Transforming Europe: Europeanization and Domestic Change* (Ithaca, 2001). Risse himself writes that the goodness of fit model is better suited to other subject areas, where Europeanizing force and its object are more clearly defined. For criticism see S. Bulmer, 'Theorizing Europeanization', in P. Graziano and M. Vink (eds), *Europeanization. New Research Agendas* (Basingstoke, 2007), pp. 51–3.
21. E. Sivan and J. Winter, 'Introduction' in E. Sivan and J. Winter (eds), *War and Remembrance in the Twentieth Century* (Cambridge, 1999), p. 4f.
22. 'Collective memory (…) plays a much greater role in the political discourse of some societies than others. It plays considerably more of a role in Europe, it is often observed, than in our own [i.e. American] society.' (M.J. Osiel, 'Ever Again: Legal Remembrance of Administrative Massacre', *University of Pennsylvania Law Review*, XLIV, No. 2 (December, 1995), 463–704, 476f.) Often, the three notions of European collective memory and identity and the Holocaust are linked in less than clear ways: 'The emergence of a common political culture is more than the abstract acceptance of universal principles. It is also the adoption of a narrative which creates identity. [...] The never ending mutterings of the collective memory which accompany all our political decisions and impose loyalty on us, these mutterings of collective identity cannot be suppressed. On the contrary, they must become explicit in order not to be marginalized.' N. Dewandre and J. Lenoble (eds.), *Projekt Europa. Postnationale Identität: Grundlage für eine europäische Demokratie* (Berlin, 1994), p. 97.
23. Assmann, 'Community of Memory?', 14; Diner, 'Restitution and Memory', 36–44, 39.
24. We can trace this movement in the shifting focus of the publications of the Lund University research project associated with the ITF and directed by Karlsson and Zander. Its 2003 volume was entitled 'Echoes of the Holocaust. Historical Cultures in Contemporary Europe' and professed itself just that ('a book about the role of history in European societies'). By contrast, the 2006 volume, 'The Holocaust on Post-War Battlefields', opens with a reference to the many 'European battlefields' (a perhaps slightly unfortunate shorthand) on which conflicts about memory politics are contested in the public sphere. While 'some of them' were 'clearly (…) situated within national borders', more were 'better described as trans- and international in scope (…) Holocaust contexts more often than not transcend national barriers.' K.-G. Karlsson and U. Zander (eds), *Echoes of the Holocaust. Historical Cultures in Contemporary Europe* (Lund, 2003), p. 7.
25. P. Levi, *If This Is A Man/ The Truce* (London, 1979), p. 21f.
26. V. Knigge, 'Buchenwald', in D. Hoffmann (ed.), *Das Gedächtnis der Dinge: KZ-Relikte und KZ-Denkmäler 1945–1995* (Frankfurt, 1998), p. 94f.
27. Hoffmann, *Gedächtnis der Dinge*, p. 10f.

28. ibid., p. 97f.
29. Of the 28 000 inmates of Soviet Special Camp Nr.2, around a quarter died (ibid. p. 117).
30. Ibid. pp. 100–2. The date of the town council meeting where Henselmann presented his ideas is mis-stated as 16 January 1945, it was actually on that date in 1947.
31. Ibid., p. 102.
32. ibid., pp. 127–35.
33. M. Wolfgram, 'The Holocaust through the Prism of East German Television: Collective Memory and Audience Perceptions', *Holocaust and Genocide Studies*, XX, No. 1 (Spring 2006), pp. 57–79, p. 58f.
34. J. Herf, 'The emergence and legacy of divided memory: Germany and the Holocaust after 1945', in Müller, *Memory and Power*, pp. 190–2.
35. D. Hoffmann, 'Einleitung', in idem, *Gedaechtnis der Dinge*, pp. 25–30.
36. J. Young, *The Texture of Memory: Holocaust Memorials and Meaning* (New Haven, 1994).
37. http://www.struthof.fr/en/la-memoire-du-campbr-apres-guerre/remembrance-of-the-camp-after-the-war/, 4 September 2008.
38. Waldemar Lotnik, *Nine Lives: Ethnic Conflict in the Polish Ukrainian Borderlands* (London, 1999), see e.g. p. 59 for account of 'ruthlessness' of Polish partisans by a participant.
39. P. Lagrou, *The Legacy of Nazi Occupation. Patriotic Memory and National Recovery in Western Europe, 1945–1965* (Cambridge, 2000), pp. 2–6, 301.
40. Ibid., p. 11.
41. Ibid., p. 7.
42. I. Buruma, *Erbschaft der Schuld: Vergangenheitsbewältigung in Deutschland und Japan* (Munich, 1994), p. 11; P. Esterházy, 'Alle Hände sind unsere Hände', SZ (11 October 2004). I am much indebted to Aleida Assmann's article already quoted for these illustrations.
43. G. Delanty and C. Rumford, *Rethinking Europe. Social Theory and the Implications of Europeanization* (London, 2005), pp. 99f.
44. H. Rousso, 'Histories of Memory, Policies of the Past: What For?', in K. Jarausch and T. Lindenberger (eds.), *Conflicted Memories. Europeanizing Contemporary Histories* (New York, 2007), pp. 30–2; D. Diner, 'Restitution and Memory', p. 39f.
45. 'Bitburg, the trials of Barbie and Zundel, and the *Historikerstreit* all happened within a few years of each other. These events were simultaneously signposts and agents in the process in which the Holocaust became an abstract concept, theorized and generalized history, with both the tragedy and the evil diluted and normalized.' V. Ranki, 'Holocaust History and the Law: Recent Trials, Emerging Theories', *Cardozo Studies in Law and Literature*, IX, No. 1, (Spring–Summer, 1997), 15–44, 40.
46. H. Rousso, 'The Sounds of Silence'.
47. D. Levy, and N. Sznaider, *Holocaust and Memory in the Global Age* (Philadelphia, 2005).
48. Müller, *Memory and Power*, p. 33, Assmann, 'Community of Memory?', 22.

# Conclusion

*Martin Conway**

Europeanization is an obstinately elusive concept. As the Introduction to this volume sought to demonstrate, attempts to arrive at a definition of Europeanization have tended either to become stranded on rather empty statements of the obvious, or have become entangled in the inherently self-referential nature of the term. This volume has not sought to present a solution to this problem; indeed, what might be termed the anti-conclusion of our collective endeavours is that efforts to arrive at a satisfactory single definition of the term are likely to fail. This should not, however, imply that the concept is lacking in either meaning or value. On the contrary, we believe that the essays in this volume demonstrate the value of examining the history of twentieth-century Europe through the prism of Europeanization. In doing so, it is, however, essential to approach Europeanization not as a fixed phenomenon (against which the tides of history might be measured), but as an inherently plural concept, that was part of the historical process and evolved over time.

These twin emphases on plurality and on change over time constitute the principal themes of this collection. We have chosen to adopt a deliberately eclectic approach to the phenomenon, testing its applicability to the diverse fields of international, political, cultural, economic and social history. Given the diversity of the subject-matter, it is hardly surprising that our tentative findings should emphasize the plurality of forms of Europeanization. The ways, for example, in which intellectuals imagined Europe in the 1930s did not, unless one adopts a crudely teleological approach, have much in common with how political and economic decision-makers constructed West European monetary integration in the 1970s and 1980s. This rather obvious conclusion serves nevertheless to underline an important point: Europeanization was over the course of the twentieth century not a unitary phenomenon which rose or declined in response to different factors, but something which has emerged in various different forms. Indeed, were it not (at least in the English language) so linguistically ugly, it might seem more accurate to speak of a variety of 'Europeanizations' rather than Europeanization in the singular.

This disaggregated perception of Europeanization also emphasizes the importance of change over time. That a team of historians should choose to draw attention to the way in which Europeanization has taken on different meanings and different shapes across the European twentieth century might again not seem surprising. It is, however, a point that is all the more worth making as the political changes that have flowed from the events of 1989 have led to a contemporary trend to celebrate the 'reunification' of Europe. The suggestion implied by such statements of a fixed definition of Europe, and more especially of its frontiers, is, however, at variance with the historical experience of the twentieth century. That Europe looked rather different in, say, 1914, 1942 and 1989 might appear to be little more than a statement of the obvious; but it serves to underscore the radical discontinuities that have characterized the history of the continent over the last hundred years. Internal frontiers, both those defined by states and those less tangible ones of language, culture and mentality, have moved markedly; but so too have external ones. Contemporary debates about the 'Europeanness' of Russia and Turkey demonstrate this point, but so too do the other Europes that have disappeared (or become less visible) over the course of the century, such as those on the southern littoral of the Mediterranean or in more distant settler societies, as a consequence of the demise of structures of European empire. Whatever else the twentieth century was, it was not 'the European century'.

As Europe has changed over time, so necessarily has Europeanization. Any attempt to construct an overarching history of Europeanization must therefore risk not only the familiar historical problem of anachronism, by labelling certain processes as European that at the time were not seen as such, but also the more fundamental problem of striving to see something which did not exist. Unlike other concepts such as modernization or Americanization, Europeanization does not possess the (relative) internal coherence which comes from it being measurable against a range of external criteria. Instead, the term exists only with reference to a Europe which itself was always evolving in shape and content, and which consequently lacks any meaning separate from (or 'above') its historical context.

Locating Europeanization within its historical reality also reorientates attention away from narratives of continuity to the specific clusters of factors within which particular forms of Europeanization emerged at particular times. This specificity explains the empirical character of many of the contributions to this volume. Rather than contributing to a single history of Europeanization, the authors are predominantly concerned with analysing self-contained instances of Europeanization. Some of those instances were consciously willed – one thinks most especially of the common purpose to 'build Europe' that emerged among certain West European political elites during the 1950s and 1960s – but many others were unintentional or inadvert: they took shape in domains such as architecture or popular music not because anybody willed them, but because of the interplay of other forces. Europeanization, thus, is not a phenomenon which has made its own history but which has more generally occurred as the consequence of other factors. This is perhaps most evident with respect to the Second World War. As is well known, the Third Reich was obliged, often despite itself, in the final years of the war to present the European nature of its cause, portraying its armies and the assemblage of allied and conscripted forces – upon which it had increasingly come to rely – as the defenders of an embattled Europe against its internal and external enemies. This propaganda was not without consequences: it brought to the fore a rhetoric of Europeanness which proved to be a durable element of the political and social culture of post-1945 Europe. But the more profound legacies of the Second World War lay quite obviously not in the intended outcomes of Nazi actions but in the way in which the military campaigns of the war, the mass movements of populations and the changes wrought in ideological and social attitudes by the events of the war contributed to other and quite different forms of Europeanization.

The twin emphases on plurality and change over time, thus, suggest the need for a more nuanced and historically-aware approach to Europeanization, which considers the term not as an abstract category but as a phenomenon which can only be conceptualized 'in action' within history. History does not on the whole consist of neat categories of change. Thus, rather than seeking to measure Europeanization, the task of the historian is more often to uncover the way in which the label of Europeanization has become attached to certain phenomena and not to others. This somewhat common-sensical methodology, which one might regard as characteristic of the anti-theoretical tenor of much recent historical writing, has, we hope, enabled us to avoid in this volume some of the pitfalls that we associate with more theoretical (or ideologically-loaded) approaches that depend explicitly or implicitly on the prior definition of an 'ideal type' of Europeanization. In particular, we hope that by studying Europeanization not in terms of what it is, but in terms of what it has been, we have demonstrated the need to analyse it in relation to the historical context in which forms of Europeanization emerged, and in many cases subsequently disappeared. While a 'rise and fall' metaphor may be the best means of capturing the historical nature of some of these processes, for others a geological metaphor may be more appropriate: as particular forms of Europeanization have developed and then eroded, so a certain residue has remained which has influenced the character of subsequent forms of Europeanization.

Approached in this way, Europeanization is less a specific field of enquiry than a way of conceptualizing wider trends in European history of the twentieth century, but also of the preceding centuries. The cautionary warnings that have necessarily tended to take precedence in the Introduction and Conclusion of this volume should not therefore be allowed to overshadow the real benefits that we believe lie in a historical approach to Europeanization. By analysing the history of twentieth-century Europe through the prism of Europeanization, it is possible to identify processes that are all too easily occluded by historical agendas defined by national or chronological frontiers. In order to do so, it is, however, also necessary to delineate the study of Europeanization from other forms of transnational or 'European' history.

It has become something of a commonplace in recent years to deplore the extent to which national mentalities have had a durable and deleterious impact on the writing of twentieth-century history. National 'ways of thinking' about history have proved remarkably long lasting, with a consequent emphasis on the distinctiveness of national historical experiences (what one might term a Europe of *Sonderwege*). But so too have national ways of 'doing history', through the national contexts in which historians have been trained, their careers pursued, their works published, and their source materials conserved. In response, there have been a variety of calls for the need to 'Europeanize' the writing of, and thinking about, history. At one level, this has encouraged a wish to be attentive to the transnational phenomena that have occurred during the twentieth century, to the ways in which the lives of individuals, ideological movements and the institutions of civil society have transgressed national frontiers.[1] At another level, it has encouraged historians to locate national historical experiences within a European context.[2] Finally, too, it has led historians to advocate the need to make Europe itself the subject of history.[3] As Michael Geyer has forcefully argued, Europe existed as 'a common space even when commonality was denied outright. It took shape for most of its history as an involuntary and highly conflictual space', but one within which the movement of people, the communicability between forms of civil society and the socio-economic interdependence of localities made Europe a tangible (if often distinctly disunited) reality.[4]

The historical study of Europeanization shares with these different approaches a wish to re-direct attention away from internalized national histories. But it is also more specific in its object of study. By focusing on the ways in which interconnections developed between phenomena in different areas of Europe, it seeks to identify the contexts in which Europe itself became the defining framework within which these phenomena took shape. It is important to emphasize in this respect that similarity is not enough. It is all too easy for all such attempts at the writing of a European history to take the form of an historical stamp collecting, whereby instances of similarity are seized from their diverse contexts and re-categorized as exempla of wider European trends. As the articles in this collection are, however, at pains to emphasize, what matters more is the degree of interconnectedness between the events or trends, and the consequent way in which they can be seen to have been European in nature. Thus, for example, the process by which a concept of human rights became part of a common discourse of European intellectual elites after 1945 or, in a very different register, forms of state violence initially developed in colonial situations were subsequently refracted back into the occupation politics of the era of the Second World War, stand as instances when the 'Europeanness' of the phenomenon appears more marked than the undoubted importance of forms of national distinctiveness. This is of course a question of degree, and there will quite rightly always be historians who prefer to situate the origins and character of such phenomena within a particular national context.[5] There are therefore no sealed categories of events or processes, which can be identified as European or national in nature. More often than not, they both take place at the same time. Nevertheless, in all such cases, the framework of Europeanization enables historians not only to make linkages between otherwise diverse phenomena, but also to analyse why some such processes or events have come to be seen as constitutive of Europeanization.

That Europeanization must remain to some degree in the eye of the beholder (or, more precisely, the historian) raises inevitably the issue of selection. As a number of the contributors to this volume point out, there has been a tendency to associate Europeanization either implicitly or explicitly with events and processes that were peaceful and progressive in nature.[6] Thus, for example, from the vantage point of the early twenty-first century, democracy appears to have been 'more' European than fascism; yet, from a historical point of view, the validity of such a judgement would at least appear open to question. In conceiving this volume, the contributors were therefore concerned to avoid the danger of concentrating on what one might regard as a somewhat sanitized canon of instances of Europeanization. Historians cannot pick and choose; and each instance of Europeanization needs to be studied on its own terms, regardless of how well it might fit with a teleological account of the development of the unified Europe of the early twenty-first century.[7] Thus, for example, the state violence of the 1940s has at least as much claim to form part of Europeanization as does the Treaty of Rome.

Nevertheless, the way in which certain phenomena have come to be seen as constitutive of Europeanization while others have not also draws attention to a further, and final, complexity in the study of the phenomenon. Europeanization is, as we have sought to argue in this volume, a tool for analysing the past; but it is also a discourse about the past, and like all such discourses it has its own history. Therefore, the path by which the label of Europeanization has become 'stuck' to particular phenomena and not others is in itself part of a historical approach to the subject. This discourse was not, of course, fixed in advance, and its meaning evolved in response to other forces. Thus, through analysing why at the time and in retrospect certain processes or events came to be seen as manifestations of Europeanization, one can perceive both the material processes and intellectual attitudes within which Europeanization has been, and continues to be, constituted.

Discourses, however, are not only moulded by other forces; they also develop their own power. This would seem to be particularly so in the case of Europeanization, which has at different moments across the twentieth century become a means whereby various political, intellectual and economic figures have legitimized their actions. In doing so, they have often been both opportunist and sincere. The intellectuals who opposed Soviet control of Eastern Europe in the 1970s and 1980s 'in the name of Europe', for example, did so because it provided a convenient discourse by which to oppose Communist internationalism, but also because they believed in the ideal of a Europe that would be politically reunited and in which what they regarded as certain core European values of freedom and justice would prevail. Moreover, like many such discourses of legitimation, that of Europeanization was not solely under the control of those who used it.[8] It also began to exercise an influence over the ways in which, to use the same example, East European dissidents conceived of their actions. Europe became an ideal, which legitimized certain actions while simultaneously de-legitimizing others, notably a narrow nationalism that came to be seen as nostalgic or non-European. In this way the discourse of Europeanization influenced not only the actions of the dissidents, but indeed of a wide range of the political class who came to the fore in the first decade after the collapse of the Communist regimes in 1989.

Europeanization, in sum, is not without consequences. By framing the way in which political leaders and a wide variety of other figures including intellectuals, business figures and religious leaders have justified their actions to others and to themselves, the discourse of Europeanization has developed its own power. This adds to the complexity but also the benefits of a historical approach to the phenomenon. By studying its evolution across the twentieth century, we are not only uncovering the patterns of the past, but one of the ways by which the present was made.

## Notes

*   I am grateful to my co-editor Kiran Patel for his comments on a first draft of this Conclusion.
1.  Gerd-Rainer Horn and Padraic Kenney (eds), *Transnational Moments of Change: Europe 1945, 1968, 1989* (Lanham MD and Oxford, 2004); Kiran Klaus Patel, *Nach der Nationalfixiertheit: Perspektiven einer transnationalen Geschichte* (Berlin, 2004).
2.  Ute Frevert, 'Europeanizing Germany's Twentieth Century', in *History and Memory* XVII (2005), 87–116; Martin Conway, 'The Greek Civil War: Greek Exceptionalism or Mirror of a European Civil War?', in Philip Carabott and Thanasis Sfikas (eds), *The Greek Civil War. Essays on a Conflict of Exceptionalism and Silences* (Aldershot and Burlington VT, 2004), pp. 17–39.
3.  Luisa Passerini *Europe in Love, Love in Europe* (New York, 1999).
4.  Michael Geyer, 'The Subject(s) of Europe', in Konrad H. Jarausch and Thomas Lindenberger (eds), *Conflicted Memories. Europeanizing Contemporary Histories* (New York and Oxford, 2007), pp. 254–80.

5. This is of course particularly true in the long-standing debates about the uniquely German or wider European origins of German racial policies in the Second World War. See for example, Mark Levene *Genocide in the Age of the Nation State* (London, 2005). But much the same could also be said about interpretations of French policies before and during the Algerian War. See notably Raphaëlle Branche *La guerre d'Algérie: une histoire apaisée?* (Paris, 2005). Indeed, perhaps the tendency of recent 'revisionist' accounts of the crimes committed by European states within and beyond Europe might be seen to have contributed involuntarily to a 're-nationalization' of the frameworks within which such actions are analysed.
6. The same point is made by Michael Geyer in 'The Subject(s) of Europe', p. 274.
7. That such approaches owe at least a little to Mark Mazower's influential book *Dark Continent: Europe's Twentieth Century* (London, 1998) is of course undeniable.
8. Martin Conway and Peter Romijn (eds), *The War for Legitimacy in Politics and Culture 1936–1946* (Oxford and New York, 2008).

# Index

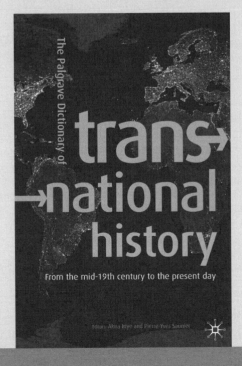